Contents

Acknowledgements	6
Waiting for Godot	7
Endgame	89
Happy Days	135
All That Fall	169
Act Without Words I	201
Act Without Words II	207
Krapp's Last Tape	213
Rough for Theatre I	225
Rough for Theatre II	235
Embers	251
Rough for Radio I	265
Rough for Radio II	273
Words and Music	285
Cascando	295
Play	305
Film	321
The Old Tune	335
Come and Go	351
Eh Joe	359
Breath	369
Not I	373
That Time	385
Footfalls	397
Ghost Trio	405
. . . but the clouds . . .	415
A Piece of Monologue	423
Rockaby	431
Ohio Impromptu	443
Quad	449
Catastrophe	455
Nacht und Träume	463
What Where	467

Acknowledgements

The publishers acknowledge with gratitude the permission of John Calder (Publishers) Ltd to include in this volume *The Old Tune*, an adaptation by Samuel Beckett of *La Manivelle* by Robert Pinget, first published by Editions de Minuit, Paris, and published by John Calder (Publishers) Ltd in 1963.

Samuel Beckett
The Complete Dramatic Works

by the same author

ELEUTHERIA
ENDGAME
HAPPY DAYS
KRAPP'S LAST TAPE and EMBERS
WAITING FOR GODOT: A TRAGICOMEDY IN TWO ACTS
COLLECTED SHORTER PLAYS OF SAMUEL BECKETT

THE THEATRICAL NOTEBOOKS OF SAMUEL BECKETT
General Editor: James Knowlson

Vol. I: Waiting for Godot
Edited by Dougald McMillan and James Knowlson

Vol II: Endgame
Edited by S. E. Gontarski

Vol III: Krapp's Last Tape
Edited by James Knowlson

Vol IV: the Shorter Plays
Edited by S. E. Gontarski

HAPPY DAYS: SAMUEL BECKETT'S PRODUCTION NOTEBOOK
Edited by James Knowlson

SAMUEL BECKETT

The Complete
Dramatic Works

———

faber and faber

This collection first published in 1986
by Faber and Faber Limited
3 Queen Square London WC1N 3AU
This paperback edition first published in 1990

Photoset by Wilmaset, Birkenhead, Wirral
Printed and bound in Great Britain by
Mackays of Chatham PLC, Chatham, Kent

Application for the performing rights of *The Old Tune* should be addressed to
Casarotto Company, National House, 60–66 Wardour Street, London W1V 3HP,
and of all other dramatic works included in this volume to Curtis Brown Ltd,
4th Floor, Haymarket House, 28/29 Haymarket, London SW1Y 4SP

A CIP record for this book is available from the British Library
ISBN 0-571-14486-1

Waiting for Godot

A tragi-comedy in two acts

Written in French in 1952. First performed in Paris in 1953. English version first performed in London in 1955, and published in 1956 by Faber and Faber.

CAST

ESTRAGON
VLADIMIR
LUCKY
POZZO
A BOY

ACT ONE

A country road. A tree. Evening.

ESTRAGON, *sitting on a low mound, is trying to take off his boot. He pulls at it with both hands, panting. He gives up, exhausted, rests, tries again. As before.*

Enter VLADIMIR.

ESTRAGON: [*Giving up again.*] Nothing to be done.

VLADIMIR: [*Advancing with short, stiff strides, legs wide apart.*] I'm beginning to come round to that opinion. All my life I've tried to put it from me, saying, Vladimir, be reasonable, you haven't yet tried everything. And I resumed the struggle. [*He broods, musing on the struggle. Turning to* ESTRAGON.] So there you are again.

ESTRAGON: Am I?

VLADIMIR: I'm glad to see you back. I thought you were gone for ever.

ESTRAGON: Me too.

VLADIMIR: Together again at last! We'll have to celebrate this. But how? [*He reflects.*] Get up till I embrace you.

ESTRAGON: [*Irritably.*] Not now, not now.

VLADIMIR: [*Hurt, coldly.*] May one inquire where His Highness spent the night?

ESTRAGON: In a ditch.

VLADIMIR: [*Admiringly.*] A ditch! Where?

ESTRAGON: [*Without gesture.*] Over there.

VLADIMIR: And they didn't beat you?

ESTRAGON: Beat me? Certainly they beat me.

VLADIMIR: The same lot as usual?

ESTRAGON: The same? I don't know.

VLADIMIR: When I think of it . . . all these years . . . but for me . . . where would you be . . .? [*Decisively.*] You'd be nothing more than a little heap of bones at the present minute, no doubt about it.

ESTRAGON: And what of it?

VLADIMIR: [*Gloomily.*] It's too much for one man. [*Pause.*

Cheerfully.] On the other hand what's the good of losing heart now, that's what I say. We should have thought of it a million years ago, in the nineties.

ESTRAGON: Ah stop blathering and help me off with this bloody thing.

VLADIMIR: Hand in hand from the top of the Eiffel Tower, among the first. We were presentable in those days. Now it's too late. They wouldn't even let us up. [ESTRAGON *tears at his boot.*] What are you doing?

ESTRAGON: Taking off my boot. Did that never happen to you?

VLADIMIR: Boots must be taken off every day, I'm tired telling you that. Why don't you listen to me?

ESTRAGON: [*Feebly.*] Help me!

VLADIMIR: It hurts?

ESTRAGON: Hurts! He wants to know if it hurts!

VLADIMIR: [*Angrily.*] No one ever suffers but you. I don't count. I'd like to hear what you'd say if you had what I have.

ESTRAGON: It hurts?

VLADIMIR: Hurts! He wants to know if it hurts!

ESTRAGON: [*Pointing.*] You might button it all the same.

VLADIMIR: [*Stooping.*] True. [*He buttons his fly.*] Never neglect the little things of life.

ESTRAGON: What do you expect, you always wait till the last moment.

VLADIMIR: [*Musingly.*] The last moment . . . [*He meditates.*] Hope deferred maketh the something sick, who said that?

ESTRAGON: Why don't you help me?

VLADIMIR: Sometimes I feel it coming all the same. Then I go all queer. [*He takes off his hat, peers inside it, feels about inside it, shakes it, puts in on again.*] How shall I say? Relieved and at the same time . . . [*He searches for the word.*] . . . appalled. [*With emphasis.*] AP-PALLED. [*He takes off his hat again, peers inside it.*] Funny. [*He knocks on the crown as though to dislodge a foreign body, peers into it again, puts it on again.*] Nothing to be done. [ESTRAGON *with a supreme effort succeeds in pulling off his boot. He looks inside it, feels about inside it, turns it upside down, shakes it, looks on the ground to see if anything has fallen out, finds nothing, feels inside it again, staring sightlessly before him.*] Well?

ESTRAGON: Nothing.

VLADIMIR: Show.

ESTRAGON: There's nothing to show.

VLADIMIR: Try and put it on again.

ESTRAGON: [*Examining his foot.*] I'll air it for a bit.

VLADIMIR: There's man all over for you, blaming on his boots the faults of his feet. [*He takes off his hat again, peers inside it, feels about inside it, knocks on the crown, blows into it, puts it on again.*] This is getting alarming. [*Silence.* VLADIMIR *deep in thought,* ESTRAGON *pulling at his toes.*] One of the thieves was saved. [*Pause.*] It's a reasonable percentage. [*Pause.*] Gogo.

ESTRAGON: What?

VLADIMIR: Suppose we repented.

ESTRAGON: Repented what?

VLADIMIR: Oh . . . [*He reflects.*] We wouldn't have to go into the details.

ESTRAGON: Our being born?

[VLADIMIR *breaks into a hearty laugh which he immediately stifles, his hand pressed to his pubis, his face contorted.*]

VLADIMIR: One daren't even laugh any more.

ESTRAGON: Dreadful privation.

VLADIMIR: Merely smile. (*He smiles suddenly from ear to ear, keeps smiling, ceases as suddenly.*] It's not the same thing. Nothing to be done. [*Pause.*] Gogo.

ESTRAGON: [*Irritably.*] What is it?

VLADIMIR: Did you ever read the Bible?

ESTRAGON: The Bible . . . [*He reflects.*] I must have taken a look at it.

VLADIMIR: Do you remember the Gospels?

ESTRAGON: I remember the maps of the Holy Land. Coloured they were. Very pretty. The Dead Sea was pale blue. The very look of it made me thirsty. That's where we'll go, I used to say, that's where we'll go for our honeymoon. We'll swim. We'll be happy.

VLADIMIR: You should have been a poet.

ESTRAGON: I was. [*Gesture towards his rags.*] Isn't that obvious.
[*Silence.*]

VLADIMIR: Where was I . . . How's your foot?

ESTRAGON: Swelling visibly.

VLADIMIR: Ah yes, the two thieves. Do you remember the story?

ESTRAGON: No.

VLADIMIR: Shall I tell it to you?

ESTRAGON: No.

VLADIMIR: It'll pass the time. [*Pause.*] Two thieves, crucified at the same time as our Saviour. One –

ESTRAGON: Our what?

VLADIMIR: Our Saviour. Two thieves. One is supposed to have been saved and the other . . . [*He searches for the contrary of saved*] . . . damned.

ESTRAGON: Saved from what?

VLADIMIR: Hell.

ESTRAGON: I'm going.
[*He does not move.*]

VLADIMIR: And yet . . . [*Pause.*] . . . how is it – this is not boring you I hope – how is it that of the four Evangelists only one speaks of a thief being saved. The four of them were there – or thereabouts – and only one speaks of a thief being saved. [*Pause.*] Come on, Gogo, return the ball, can't you, once in a way?

ESTRAGON: [*With exaggerated enthusiasm.*] I find this really most extraordinarily interesting.

VLADIMIR: One out of four. Of the other three two don't mention any thieves at all and the third says that both of them abused him.

ESTRAGON: Who?

VLADIMIR: What?

ESTRAGON: What's all this about? Abused who?

VLADIMIR: The Saviour.

ESTRAGON: Why?

VLADIMIR: Because he wouldn't save them.

ESTRAGON: From hell?

VLADIMIR: Imbecile! From death.

ESTRAGON: I thought you said hell.

VLADIMIR: From death, from death.

ESTRAGON: Well what of it?

VLADIMIR: Then the two of them must have been damned.

ESTRAGON: And why not?

VLADIMIR: But one of the four says that one of the two was saved.

ESTRAGON: Well? They don't agree, and that's all there is to it.

VLADIMIR: But all four were there. And only one speaks of a thief being saved. Why believe him rather than the others?

ESTRAGON: Who believes him?

VLADIMIR: Everybody. It's the only version they know.

ESTRAGON: People are bloody ignorant apes.

[*He rises painfully, goes limping to extreme left, halts, gazes into distance off with his hand screening his eyes, turns, goes to extreme right, gazes into distance.*

VLADIMIR *watches him, then goes and picks up the boot, peers into it, drops it hastily.*]

VLADIMIR: Pah!

[*He spits.* ESTRAGON *moves to centre, halts with his back to auditorium.*]

ESTRAGON: Charming spot. [*He turns, advances to front, halts facing auditorium.*] Inspiring prospects. [*He turns to* VLADIMIR.] Let's go.

VLADIMIR: We can't.

ESTRAGON: Why not?

VLADIMIR: We're waiting for Godot.

ESTRAGON: [*Despairingly.*] Ah! [*Pause.*] You're sure it was here?

VLADIMIR: What?

ESTRAGON: That we were to wait.

VLADIMIR: He said by the tree. [*They look at the tree.*] Do you see any others?

ESTRAGON: What is it?

VLADIMIR: I don't know. A willow.

ESTRAGON: Where are the leaves?

VLADIMIR: It must be dead.

ESTRAGON: No more weeping.

VLADIMIR: Or perhaps it's not the season.

ESTRAGON: Looks to me more like a bush.

VLADIMIR: A shrub.

ESTRAGON: A bush.

VLADIMIR: A — . What are you insinuating? That we've come to the wrong place?

ESTRAGON: He should be here.

VLADIMIR: He didn't say for sure he'd come.

ESTRAGON: And if he doesn't come?

VLADIMIR: We'll come back tomorrow.

ESTRAGON: And then the day after tomorrow.

VLADIMIR: Possibly.

ESTRAGON: And so on.

VLADIMIR: The point is —

ESTRAGON: Until he comes.

VLADIMIR: You're merciless.

ESTRAGON: We came here yesterday.

VLADIMIR: Ah no, there you're mistaken.

ESTRAGON: What did we do yesterday?

VLADIMIR: What did we do yesterday?

ESTRAGON: Yes.

VLADIMIR: Why . . . [*Angrily*.] Nothing is certain when you're about.

ESTRAGON: In my opinion we were here.

VLADIMIR: [*Looking round*.] You recognize the place?

ESTRAGON: I didn't say that.

VLADIMIR: Well?

ESTRAGON: That makes no difference.

VLADIMIR: All the same . . . that tree . . . [*Turning towards the auditorium*] . . . that bog.

ESTRAGON: You're sure it was this evening?

VLADIMIR: What?

ESTRAGON: That we were to wait.

VLADIMIR: He said Saturday. [*Pause*.] I think.

ESTRAGON: You think.

VLADIMIR: I must have made a note of it.

[*He fumbles in his pockets, bursting with miscellaneous rubbish*.]

ESTRAGON: [*Very insidious*.] But what Saturday? And is it

Saturday? Is it not rather Sunday? [*Pause.*] Or Monday? [*Pause.*] Or Friday?

VLADIMIR: [*Looking wildly about him, as though the date was inscribed in the landscape.*] It's not possible!

ESTRAGON: Or Thursday?

VLADIMIR: What'll we do?

ESTRAGON: If he came yesterday and we weren't here you may be sure he won't come again today.

VLADIMIR: But you say we were here yesterday.

ESTRAGON: I may be mistaken. [*Pause.*] Let's stop talking for a minute, do you mind?

VLADIMIR: [*Feebly.*] All right. [ESTRAGON *sits down on the mound.* VLADIMIR *paces agitatedly to and fro, halting from time to time to gaze into the distance off.* ESTRAGON *falls asleep.* VLADIMIR *halts before* ESTRAGON.] Gogo! . . . Gogo! . . . GOGO! [ESTRAGON *wakes with a start.*]

ESTRAGON: [*Restored to the horror of his situation.*] I was asleep! [*Despairingly.*] Why will you never let me sleep?

VLADIMIR: I felt lonely.

ESTRAGON: I had a dream.

VLADIMIR: Don't tell me!

ESTRAGON: I dreamt that –

VLADIMIR: DON'T TELL ME!

ESTRAGON: [*Gesture towards the universe.*] This one is enough for you? [*Silence.*] It's not nice of you, Didi. Who am I to tell my private nightmares to if I can't tell them to you?

VLADIMIR: Let them remain private. You know I can't bear that.

ESTRAGON: [*Coldly.*] There are times when I wonder if it wouldn't be better for us to part.

VLADIMIR: You wouldn't go far.

ESTRAGON: That would be too bad, really too bad. [*Pause.*] Wouldn't it, Didi, be really too bad? [*Pause.*] When you think of the beauty of the way. [*Pause.*] And the goodness of the wayfarers. [*Pause. Wheedling.*] Wouldn't it, Didi?

VLADIMIR: Calm yourself.

ESTRAGON: [*Voluptuously.*] Calm . . . calm . . . The English say cawm. [*Pause.*] You know the story of the Englishman in the brothel?

VLADIMIR: Yes.

ESTRAGON: Tell it to me.

VLADIMIR: Ah stop it!

ESTRAGON: An Englishman having drunk a little more than usual goes to a brothel. The bawd asks him if he wants a fair one, a dark one, or a red-haired one. Go on.

VLADIMIR: STOP IT!

[*Exit* VLADIMIR *hurriedly.* ESTRAGON *gets up and follows him as far as the limit of the stage. Gestures of* ESTRAGON *like those of a spectator encouraging a pugilist. Enter* VLADIMIR. *He brushes past* ESTRAGON, *crosses the stage with bowed head.* ESTRAGON *takes a step towards him, halts.*]

ESTRAGON: [*Gently.*] You wanted to speak to me? [*Silence.* ESTRAGON *takes a step forward.*] You had something to say to me? [*Silence. Another step forward.*] Didi . . .

VLADIMIR: [*Without turning.*] I've nothing to say to you.

ESTRAGON: [*Step forward.*] You're angry? [*Silence. Step forward.*] Forgive me. [*Silence. Step forward.* ESTRAGON *lays his hand on* VLADIMIR'*s shoulder.*] Come, Didi. [*Silence.*] Give me your hand. [VLADIMIR *half turns.*] Embrace me! [VLADIMIR *stiffens.*] Don't be stubborn! [VLADIMIR *softens. They embrace.* ESTRAGON *recoils.*] You stink of garlic!

VLADIMIR: It's for the kidneys. [*Silence.* ESTRAGON *looks attentively at the tree.*] What do we do now?

ESTRAGON: Wait.

VLADIMIR: Yes, but while waiting.

ESTRAGON: What about hanging ourselves?

VLADIMIR: Hmm. It'd give us an erection!

ESTRAGON: [*Highly excited.*] An erection!

VLADIMIR: With all that follows. Where it falls mandrakes grow. That's why they shriek when you pull them up. Did you not know that?

ESTRAGON: Let's hang ourselves immediately!

VLADIMIR: From a bough? [*They go towards the tree.*] I wouldn't trust it.

ESTRAGON: We can always try.

VLADIMIR: Go ahead.

ESTRAGON: After you.

VLADIMIR: No no, you first.

ESTRAGON: Why me?

VLADIMIR: You're lighter than I am.

ESTRAGON: Just so!

VLADIMIR: I don't understand.

ESTRAGON: Use your intelligence, can't you?

[VLADIMIR *uses his intelligence.*]

VLADIMIR: [*Finally.*] I remain in the dark.

ESTRAGON: This is how it is. [*He reflects.*] The bough . . . the bough . . . [*Angrily.*] Use your head, can't you?

VLADIMIR: You're my only hope.

ESTRAGON: [*With effort.*] Gogo light – bough not break – Gogo dead. Didi heavy – bough break – Didi alone. Whereas –

VLADIMIR: I hadn't thought of that.

ESTRAGON: If it hangs you it'll hang anything.

VLADIMIR: But am I heavier than you?

ESTRAGON: So you tell me. I don't know. There's an even chance. Or nearly.

VLADIMIR: Well? what do we do?

ESTRAGON: Don't let's do anything. It's safer.

VLADIMIR: Let's wait and see what he says.

ESTRAGON: Who?

VLADIMIR: Godot.

ESTRAGON: Good idea.

VLADIMIR: Let's wait till we know exactly how we stand.

ESTRAGON: On the other hand it might be better to strike the iron before it freezes.

VLADIMIR: I'm curious to hear what he has to offer. Then we'll take it or leave it.

ESTRAGON: What exactly did we ask him for?

VLADIMIR: Were you not there?

ESTRAGON: I can't have been listening.

VLADIMIR: Oh . . . nothing very definite.

ESTRAGON: A kind of prayer.

VLADIMIR: Precisely.

ESTRAGON: A vague supplication.

VLADIMIR: Exactly.

ESTRAGON: And what did he reply?

VLADIMIR: That he'd see.

ESTRAGON: That he couldn't promise anything.

VLADIMIR: That he'd have to think it over.

ESTRAGON: In the quiet of his home.

VLADIMIR: Consult his family.

ESTRAGON: His friends.

VLADIMIR: His agents.

ESTRAGON: His correspondents.

VLADIMIR: His books.

ESTRAGON: His bank account.

VLADIMIR: Before taking a decision.

ESTRAGON: It's the normal thing.

VLADIMIR: Is it not?

ESTRAGON: I think it is.

VLADIMIR: I think so too.

   [*Silence.*]

ESTRAGON: [*Anxious.*] And we?

VLADIMIR: I beg your pardon?

ESTRAGON: I said, And we?

VLADIMIR: I don't understand.

ESTRAGON: Where do we come in?

VLADIMIR: Come in?

ESTRAGON: Take your time.

VLADIMIR: Come in? On our hands and knees.

ESTRAGON: As bad as that?

VLADIMIR: Your Worship wishes to assert his prerogatives?

ESTRAGON: We've no rights any more?

   [*Laugh of* VLADIMIR, *stifled as before, less the smile.*]

VLADIMIR: You'd make me laugh, if it wasn't prohibited.

ESTRAGON: We've lost our rights?

VLADIMIR: [*Distinctly.*] We got rid of them.

   [*Silence. They remain motionless, arms dangling, heads
   sunk, sagging at the knees.*]

ESTRAGON: [*Feebly.*] We're not tied? [*Pause.*] We're not —

VLADIMIR: Listen!

   [*They listen, grotesquely rigid.*]

ESTRAGON: I hear nothing.

VLADIMIR: Hssst! [*They listen.* ESTRAGON *loses his balance, almost falls. He clutches the arm of* VLADIMIR, *who totters. They listen, huddled together.*] Nor I. [*Sighs of relief. They relax and separate.*]

ESTRAGON: You gave me a fright.

VLADIMIR: I thought it was he.

ESTRAGON: Who?

VLADIMIR: Godot.

ESTRAGON: Pah! The wind in the reeds.

VLADIMIR: I could have sworn I heard shouts.

ESTRAGON: And why would he shout?

VLADIMIR: At his horse.
  [*Silence.*]

ESTRAGON: [*Violently.*] I'm hungry.

VLADIMIR: Do you want a carrot?

ESTRAGON: Is that all there is?

VLADIMIR: I might have some turnips.

ESTRAGON: Give me a carrot. [VLADIMIR *rummages in his pockets, takes out a turnip and gives it to* ESTRAGON *who takes a bite out of it. Angrily.*] It's a turnip!

VLADIMIR: Oh pardon! I could have sworn it was a carrot. [*He rummages again in his pockets, finds nothing but turnips.*] All that's turnips. [*He rummages.*] You must have eaten the last. [*He rummages*]. Wait, I have it. [*He brings out a carrot and gives it to* ESTRAGON.] There, dear fellow. [ESTRAGON *wipes the carrot on his sleeve and begins to eat it.*] Give me the turnip. [ESTRAGON *gives back the turnip which* VLADIMIR *puts in his pocket.*] Make it last, that's the end of them.

ESTRAGON: [*Chewing.*] I asked you a question.

VLADIMIR: Ah.

ESTRAGON: Did you reply?

VLADIMIR: How's the carrot?

ESTRAGON: It's a carrot.

VLADIMIR: So much the better, so much the better. [*Pause.*] What was it you wanted to know?

ESTRAGON: I've forgotten. [*Chews.*] That's what annoys me. [*He looks at the carrot appreciatively, dangles it between finger and thumb.*] I'll never forget this carrot. [*He sucks the end of it meditatively.*] Ah yes, now I remember.

VLADIMIR: Well?

ESTRAGON: [*His mouth full, vacuously.*] We're not tied!

VLADIMIR: I don't hear a word you're saying.

ESTRAGON: [*Chews, swallows.*] I'm asking you if we're tied.

VLADIMIR: Tied?

ESTRAGON: Ti-ed.

VLADIMIR: How do you mean tied?

ESTRAGON: Down.

VLADIMIR: But to whom. By whom?

ESTRAGON: To your man.

VLADIMIR: To Godot? Tied to Godot? What an idea! No question of it. [*Pause.*] For the moment.

ESTRAGON: His name is Godot?

VLADIMIR: I think so.

ESTRAGON: Fancy that. [*He raises what remains of the carrot by the stub of leaf, twirls it before his eyes.*] Funny, the more you eat the worse it gets.

VLADIMIR: With me it's just the opposite.

ESTRAGON: In other words?

VLADIMIR: I get used to the muck as I go along.

ESTRAGON: [*After prolonged reflection.*] Is that the opposite?

VLADIMIR: Question of temperament.

ESTRAGON: Of character.

VLADIMIR: Nothing you can do about it.

ESTRAGON: No use struggling.

VLADIMIR: One is what one is.

ESTRAGON: No use wriggling.

VLADIMIR: The essential doesn't change.

ESTRAGON: Nothing to be done. [*He proffers the remains of the carrot to* VLADIMIR.] Like to finish it?

[*A terrible cry, close at hand. ESTRAGON drops the carrot. They remain motionless, then together make a sudden rush towards the wings. ESTRAGON stops half-way, runs back, picks up the carrot, stuffs it in his pocket, runs towards VLADIMIR who is waiting for him, stops again, runs back, picks up his boot, runs to rejoin VLADIMIR. Huddled together, shoulders hunched, cringing away from the menace, they wait.*

Enter POZZO and LUCKY. POZZO drives LUCKY by means

of a rope passed round his neck, so that LUCKY *is the first to appear, followed by the rope which is long enough to allow him to reach the middle of the stage before* POZZO *appears.* LUCKY *carries a heavy bag, a folding stool, a picnic basket and a greatcoat.* POZZO *a whip.*]

POZZO: [*Off.*] On! [*Crack of whip.* POZZO *appears. They cross the stage.* LUCKY *passes before* VLADIMIR *and* ESTRAGON *and exit.* POZZO *at the sight of* VLADIMIR *and* ESTRAGON *stops short. The rope tautens.* POZZO *jerks it violently.*] Back!

[*Noise of* LUCKY *falling with all his baggage.* VLADIMIR *and* ESTRAGON *turn towards him, half wishing half fearing to go to his assistance.* VLADIMIR *takes a step towards* LUCKY, ESTRAGON *holds him back by the sleeve.*]

VLADIMIR: Let me go!

ESTRAGON: Stay where you are!

POZZO: Be careful! He's wicked. [VLADIMIR *and* ESTRAGON *turn towards* POZZO.] With strangers.

ESTRAGON: [*Undertone.*] Is that him?

VLADIMIR: Who?

ESTRAGON: [*Trying to remember the name.*] Er . . .

VLADIMIR: Godot?

ESTRAGON: Yes.

POZZO: I present myself: Pozzo.

VLADIMIR: [*To* ESTRAGON.] Not at all!

ESTRAGON: He said Godot.

VLADIMIR: Not at all!

ESTRAGON: [*Timidly to* POZZO.] You're not Mr Godot, sir?

POZZO: [*Terrifying voice.*] I am Pozzo! [*Silence.*] Pozzo! [*Silence.*] Does that name mean nothing to you? [*Silence.*] I say does that name mean nothing to you?
[VLADIMIR *and* ESTRAGON *look at each other questioningly.*]

ESTRAGON: [*Pretending to search.*] Bozzo . . . Bozzo . . .

VLADIMIR: [*Ditto.*] Pozzo . . . Pozzo . . .

POZZO: PPPOZZZO!

ESTRAGON: Ah! Pozzo . . . let me see . . . Pozzo . . .

VLADIMIR: It is Pozzo or Bozzo?

ESTRAGON: Pozzo . . . no . . . I'm afraid I . . . no . . . I don't seem to . . .

[POZZO *advances threateningly*.]

VLADIMIR: [*Conciliating*.] I once knew a family called Gozzo. The mother had the clap.

ESTRAGON: [*Hastily*.] We're not from these parts, sir.

POZZO: [*Halting*.] You are human beings none the less. [*He puts on his glasses*.] As far as one can see. [*He takes off his glasses*.] Of the same species as myself. [*He bursts into an enormous laugh*.] Of the same species as Pozzo! Made in God's image!

VLADIMIR: Well you see —

POZZO: [*Peremptory*.] Who is Godot?

ESTRAGON: Godot?

POZZO: You took me for Godot.

ESTRAGON: Oh no, sir, not for an instant, sir.

POZZO: Who is he?

VLADIMIR: Oh, he's a . . . he's a kind of acquaintance.

ESTRAGON: Nothing of the kind, we hardly know him.

VLADIMIR: True . . . we don't know him very well . . . but all the same . . .

ESTRAGON: Personally I wouldn't even know him if I saw him.

POZZO: You took me for him.

ESTRAGON: [*Recoiling before* POZZO.] That's to say . . . you understand . . . the dusk . . . the strain . . . waiting . . . I confess . . . I imagined . . . for a second . . .

POZZO: Waiting? So you were waiting for him?

VLADIMIR: Well you see —

POZZO: Here? On my land?

VLADIMIR: We didn't intend any harm.

ESTRAGON: We meant well.

POZZO: The road is free to all.

VLADIMIR: That's how we looked at it.

POZZO: It's a disgrace. But there you are.

ESTRAGON: Nothing we can do about it.

POZZO: [*With magnanimous gesture*.] Let's say no more about it. [*He jerks the rope*.] Up pig! [*Pause*.] Every time he drops he falls asleep. [*Jerks the rope*.] Up hog! [*Noise of* LUCKY *getting up and picking up his baggage*. POZZO

jerks the rope.] Back! [*Enter* LUCKY *backwards.*] Stop!
[LUCKY *stops.*] Turn! [LUCKY *turns. To* VLADIMIR *and*
ESTRAGON, *affably.*] Gentlemen, I am happy to have met
you. [*Before their incredulous expression.*] Yes, yes,
sincerely happy. [*He jerks the rope.*] Closer! [LUCKY
advances.] Stop! [LUCKY *stops.*] Yes, the road seems long
when one journeys all alone for . . . [*He consults his
watch*] . . . yes . . . [*He calculates*] . . . yes, six hours,
that's right, six hours on end, and never a soul in sight.
[*To* LUCKY.] Coat! [LUCKY *puts down the bag, advances,
gives the coat, goes back to his place, takes up the bag.*]
Hold that! [POZZO *holds out the whip.* LUCKY *advances
and, both his hands being occupied, takes the whip in his
mouth, then goes back to his place.* POZZO *begins to put
on his coat, stops.*] Coat! [LUCKY *puts down bag, basket
and stool, advances, helps* POZZO *on with his coat, goes
back to his place and takes up bag, basket and stool.*]
Touch of autumn in the air this evening. [POZZO *finishes
buttoning his coat, stoops, inspects himself, straightens
up.*] Whip! [LUCKY *advances, stoops,* POZZO *snatches the
whip from his mouth,* LUCKY *goes back to his place.*] Yes,
gentlemen, I cannot go for long without the society of my
likes [*He puts on his glasses and looks at the two likes*]
even when the likeness is an imperfect one. [*He takes off
his glasses.*] Stool! [LUCKY *puts down bag and basket,
advances, opens stool, puts it down, goes back to his
place, takes up bag and basket.*] Closer! [LUCKY *puts
down bag and basket, advances, moves stool, goes back to
his place, takes up bag and basket.* POZZO *sits down,
places the butt of his whip against* LUCKY's *chest and
pushes.*] Back! [LUCKY *takes a step back.*] Further!
[LUCKY *takes another step back.*] Stop! [LUCKY *stops. To*
VLADIMIR *and* ESTRAGON.] That is why, with your
permission, I propose to dally with you a moment, before
I venture any further. Basket! [LUCKY *advances, gives the
basket, goes back to his place.*] The fresh air stimulates the
jaded appetite. [*He opens the basket, takes out a piece of
chicken and a bottle of wine.*] Basket! [LUCKY *advances,*

picks up the basket, goes back to his place.] Further!
[LUCKY *takes a step back.*] He stinks. Happy days!
[*He drinks from the bottle, puts it down and begins to eat.
Silence.* VLADIMIR *and* ESTRAGON *cautiously at first, then
more boldly, begin to circle about* LUCKY *inspecting him
up and down.* POZZO *eats his chicken voraciously,
throwing away the bones after having sucked them.*
LUCKY *sags slowly, until bag and basket touch the
ground, then straightens up with a start and begins to sag
again. Rhythm of one sleeping on his feet.*]

ESTRAGON: What ails him?

VLADIMIR: He looks tired.

ESTRAGON: Why doesn't he put down his bags?

VLADIMIR: How do I know? [*They close in on him.*] Careful!

ESTRAGON: Say something to him.

VLADIMIR: Look!

ESTRAGON: What?

VLADIMIR: [*Pointing.*] His neck!

ESTRAGON: [*Looking at his neck.*] I see nothing.

VLADIMIR: Here.

[ESTRAGON *goes over beside* VLADIMIR.]

ESTRAGON: Oh I say.

VLADIMIR: A running sore!

ESTRAGON: It's the rope.

VLADIMIR: It's the rubbing.

ESTRAGON: It's inevitable.

VLADIMIR: It's the knot.

ESTRAGON: It's the chafing.

[*They resume their inspection, dwell on the face.*]

VLADIMIR: [*Grudgingly.*] He's not bad looking.

ESTRAGON: [*Shrugging his shoulders, wry face.*] Would you
say so?

VLADIMIR: A trifle effeminate.

ESTRAGON: Look at the slobber.

VLADIMIR: It's inevitable.

ESTRAGON: Look at the slaver.

VLADIMIR: Perhaps he's a half-wit.

ESTRAGON: A cretin.

VLADIMIR: [*Looking closer.*] It looks like a goitre.

ESTRAGON: [*Ditto.*] It's not certain.

VLADIMIR: He's panting.

ESTRAGON: It's inevitable.

VLADIMIR: And his eyes!

ESTRAGON: What about them?

VLADIMIR: Goggling out of his head.

ESTRAGON: Looks at his last gasp to me.

VLADIMIR: It's not certain. [*Pause.*] Ask him a question.

ESTRAGON: Would that be a good thing?

VLADIMIR: What do we risk?

ESTRAGON: [*Timidly.*] Mister . . .

VLADIMIR: Louder.

ESTRAGON: Mister . . .

POZZO: Leave him in peace! [*They turn towards* POZZO, *who, having finished eating, wipes his mouth with the back of his hand.*] Can't you see he wants to rest? Basket! [*He strikes a match and begins to light his pipe.* ESTRAGON *sees the chicken bones on the ground and stares at them greedily. As* LUCKY *does not move* POZZO *throws the match angrily away and jerks the rope.*] Basket! [LUCKY *starts, almost falls, recovers his senses, advances, puts the bottle in the basket, returns to his place.* ESTRAGON *stares at the bones.* POZZO *strikes another match and lights his pipe.*] What can you expect, it's not his job. [*He pulls at his pipe, stretches out his legs.*] Ah! That's better.

ESTRAGON: [*Timidly.*] Please, sir . . .

POZZO: What is it, my good man?

ESTRAGON: Er . . . you've finished with the . . . er . . . you don't need the . . . er . . . bones, sir?

VLADIMIR: [*Scandalized.*] You couldn't have waited?

POZZO: No no, he does well to ask. Do I need the bones? [*He turns them over with the end of his whip.*] No, personally I do not need them any more. [ESTRAGON *takes a step towards the bones.*] But . . . [ESTRAGON *stops short*] . . . but in theory the bones go to the carrier. He is therefore the one to ask. [ESTRAGON *turns towards* LUCKY, *hesitates.*] Go on, go on, don't be afraid, ask him, he'll tell you. [ESTRAGON *goes towards* LUCKY, *stops before him.*]

ESTRAGON: Mister . . . excuse me, Mister . . .

POZZO: You're being spoken to, pig! Reply! [*To* ESTRAGON.]
Try him again.

ESTRAGON: Excuse me, Mister, the bones, you won't be
wanting the bones?

[LUCKY *looks long at* ESTRAGON.]

POZZO: [*In raptures.*] Mister! [LUCKY *bows his head.*] Reply!
Do you want them or don't you? [*Silence of* LUCKY. *To*
ESTRAGON.] They're yours. [ESTRAGON *makes a dart at
the bones, picks them up and begins to gnaw them.*] I
don't like it. I've never known him refuse a bone before.
[*He looks anxiously at* LUCKY.] Nice business it'd be if he
fell sick on me!

[*He puffs at his pipe.*]

VLADIMIR: [*Exploding.*] It's a scandal!

[*Silence. Flabbergasted,* ESTRAGON *stops gnawing, looks
at* POZZO *and* VLADIMIR *in turn.* POZZO *outwardly
calm.* VLADIMIR *embarrassed.*]

POZZO: [*To* VLADIMIR.] Are you alluding to anything in
particular?

VLADIMIR: [*Stutteringly resolute.*] To treat a man . . . [*Gesture
towards* LUCKY] . . . like that . . . I think that . . . no . . .
a human being . . . no . . . it's a scandal!

ESTRAGON: [*Not to be outdone.*] A disgrace!

[*He resumes his gnawing.*]

POZZO: You are severe. [*To* VLADIMIR.] What age are you, if
it's not a rude question. [*Silence.*] Sixty? Seventy? [*To*
ESTRAGON.] What age would you say he was?

ESTRAGON: Eleven.

POZZO: I am impertinent. [*He knocks out his pipe against the
whip, gets up.*] I must be getting on. Thank you for your
society. [*He reflects.*] Unless I smoke another pipe before I
go. What do you say? [*They say nothing.*] Oh I'm only a
small smoker, a very small smoker, I'm not in the habit of
smoking two pipes one on top of the other, it makes
[*Hand to heart, sighing*] my heart go pit-a-pat. [*Silence.*]
It's the nicotine, one absorbs it in spite of one's
precautions. [*Sighs.*] You know how it is. [*Silence.*] But
perhaps you don't smoke? Yes? No? It's of no importance.
[*Silence.*] But how am I to sit down now, without

affectation, now that I have risen? Without appearing to –
how shall I say – without appearing to falter. [*To*
VLADIMIR.] I beg your pardon? [*Silence.*] Perhaps you
didn't speak? [*Silence.*] It's of no importance. Let me see
. . . [*He reflects.*]

ESTRAGON: Ah! That's better.
[*He puts the bones in his pocket.*]

VLADIMIR: Let's go.

ESTRAGON: So soon?

POZZO: One moment. [*He jerks the rope.*] Stool! [*He points
with his whip.* LUCKY *moves the stool.*] More! There! [*He
sits down.* LUCKY *goes back to his place.*] Done it! [*He
fills his pipe.*]

VLADIMIR: [*Vehemently.*] Let's go!

POZZO: I hope I'm not driving you away. Wait a little longer,
you'll never regret it.

ESTRAGON: [*Scenting charity.*] We're in no hurry.

POZZO: [*Having lit his pipe.*] The second is never so sweet . . .
[*He takes the pipe out of his mouth, contemplates it*] . . .
as the first, I mean. [*He puts the pipe back in his mouth.*]
But it's sweet just the same.

VLADIMIR: I'm going.

POZZO: He can no longer endure my presence. I am perhaps
not particularly human, but who cares? [*To* VLADIMIR.]
Think twice before you do anything rash. Suppose you go
now, while it is still day, for there is no denying it is still
day. [*They all look up at the sky.*] Good. [*They stop
looking at the sky.*] What happens in that case – [*He takes
the pipe out of his mouth, examines it*] – I'm out – [*He
relights his pipe*] – in that case – [*Puff*] – in that case –
[*Puff*] – what happens in that case to your appointment
with this . . . Godet . . . Godot . . . Godin . . . anyhow
you see who I mean, who has your future in his hands . . .
[*Pause*] . . . at least your immediate future.

VLADIMIR: Who told you?

POZZO: He speaks to me again! If this goes on much longer
we'll soon be old friends.

ESTRAGON: Why doesn't he put down his bags?

POZZO: I too would be happy to meet him. The more people I

meet the happier I become. From the meanest creature one
departs wiser, richer, more conscious of one's blessings.
Even you . . . [*He looks at them ostentatiously in turn to
make it clear they are both meant*] . . . even you, who
knows, will have added to my store.

ESTRAGON: Why doesn't he put down his bags?

POZZO: But that would surprise me.

VLADIMIR: You're being asked a question.

POZZO: [*Delighted.*] A question! Who? What? A moment ago
you were calling me sir, in fear and trembling. Now you're
asking me questions. No good will come of this!

VLADIMIR: [*To* ESTRAGON.] I think he's listening.

ESTRAGON: [*Circling about* LUCKY.] What?

VLADIMIR: You can ask him now. He's on the alert.

ESTRAGON: Ask him what?

VLADIMIR: Why he doesn't put down his bags.

ESTRAGON: I wonder.

VLADIMIR: Ask him, can't you?

POZZO: [*Who has followed these exchanges with anxious
attention, fearing lest the question get lost.*] You want to
know why he doesn't put down his bags, as you call them?

VLADIMIR: That's it.

POZZO: [*To* ESTRAGON.] You are sure you agree with that?

ESTRAGON: He's puffing like a grampus.

POZZO: The answer is this. [*To* ESTRAGON.] But stay still, I
beg of you, you're making me nervous!

VLADIMIR: Here.

ESTRAGON: What is it?

VLADIMIR: He's about to speak.

[ESTRAGON *goes over beside* VLADIMIR. *Motionless, side
by side, they wait.*]

POZZO: Good. Is everybody ready? Is everybody looking at
me? [*He looks at* LUCKY, *jerks the rope.* LUCKY *raises his
head.*] Will you look at me, pig! [LUCKY *looks at him.*]
Good. [*He puts his pipe in his pocket, takes out a little
vaporizer and sprays his throat, puts back the vaporizer in
his pocket, clears his throat, spits, takes out the vaporizer
again, sprays his throat again, puts back the vaporizer in
his pocket.*] I am ready. Is everybody listening? Is

everybody ready? [*He looks at them all in turn, jerks the rope.*] Hog! [LUCKY *raises his head.*] I don't like talking in a vacuum. Good. Let me see.
[*He reflects.*]

ESTRAGON: I'm going.

POZZO: What was it exactly you wanted to know?

VLADIMIR: Why he —

POZZO: [*Angrily.*] Don't interrupt me! [*Pause. Calmer.*] If we all speak at once we'll never get anywhere. [*Pause.*] What was I saying? [*Pause. Louder.*] What was I saying?
[VLADIMIR *mimics one carrying a heavy burden.* POZZO *looks at him, puzzled.*]

ESTRAGON: [*Forcibly.*] Bags. [*He points at* LUCKY.] Why? Always hold. [*He sags, panting.*] Never put down. [*He opens his hands, straightens up with relief.*] Why?

POZZO: Ah! Why couldn't you say so before? Why he doesn't make himself comfortable? Let's try and get it clear. Has he not the right to? Certainly he has. It follows that he doesn't want to. There's reasoning for you. And why doesn't he want to? [*Pause.*] Gentlemen, the reason is this.

VLADIMIR: [*To* ESTRAGON.] Make a note of this.

POZZO: He wants to impress me, so that I'll keep him.

ESTRAGON: What?

POZZO: Perhaps I haven't got it quite right. He wants to mollify me, so that I'll give up the idea of parting with him. No, that's not exactly it either.

VLADIMIR: You want to get rid of him?

POZZO: He wants to cod me, but he won't.

VLADIMIR: You want to get rid of him?

POZZO: He imagines that when I see how well he carries I'll be tempted to keep him on in that capacity.

ESTRAGON: You've had enough of him?

POZZO: In reality he carries like a pig. It's not his job.

VLADIMIR: You want to get rid of him?

POZZO: He imagines that when I see him indefatigable I'll regret my decision. Such is his miserable scheme. As thought I were short of slaves! [*All three look at* LUCKY.] Atlas, son of Jupiter! [*Silence.*] Well, that's that I think. Anything else? [*Vaporizer.*]

VLADIMIR: You want to get rid of him?

POZZO: Remark that I might just as well have been in his
shoes and he in mine. If chance had not willed otherwise.
To each one his due.

VLADIMIR: You waagerrim?

POZZO: I beg your pardon?

VLADIMIR: You want to get rid of him?

POZZO: I do. But instead of driving him away as I might have
done, I mean instead of simply kicking him out on his
arse, in the goodness of my heart I am bringing him to the
fair, where I hope to get a good price for him. The truth is
you can't drive such creatures away. The best thing would
be to kill them.

[LUCKY *weeps*.]

ESTRAGON: He's crying.

POZZO: Old dogs have more dignity. [*He proffers his
handkerchief to* ESTRAGON.] Comfort him, since you pity
him. [ESTRAGON *hesitates*.] Come on. [ESTRAGON *takes
the handkerchief*.] Wipe away his tears, he'll feel less
forsaken.

[ESTRAGON *hesitates*.]

VLADIMIR: Here, give it to me, I'll do it.

[ESTRAGON *refuses to give the handkerchief. Childish
gestures*.]

POZZO: Make haste, before he stops. [ESTRAGON *approaches*
LUCKY *and makes to wipe his eyes*. LUCKY *kicks him
violently in the shins*. ESTRAGON *drops the handkerchief,
recoils, staggers about the stage howling with pain*.]
Hanky!

[LUCKY *puts down bag and basket, picks up handkerchief,
gives it to* POZZO, *goes back to his place, picks up bag
and basket*.]

ESTRAGON: Oh the swine! [*He pulls up the leg of his trousers*.]
He's crippled me!

POZZO: I told you he didn't like strangers.

VLADIMIR: [*To* ESTRAGON.] Show. [ESTRAGON *shows his leg.
To* POZZO, *angrily*.] He's bleeding!

POZZO: It's a good sign.

ESTRAGON: [*On one leg*.] I'll never walk again!

VLADIMIR: [*Tenderly.*] I'll carry you. [*Pause.*] If necessary.

POZZO: He's stopped crying. [*To* ESTRAGON.] You have replaced him as it were. [*Lyrically.*] The tears of the world are a constant quantity. For each one who begins to weep, somewhere else another stops. The same is true of the laugh. [*He laughs.*] Let us not then speak ill of our generation, it is not any unhappier than its predecessors. [*Pause.*] Let us not speak well of it either. [*Pause.*] Let us not speak of it at all. [*Pause. Judiciously.*] It is true the population has increased.

VLADIMIR: Try and walk.

[ESTRAGON *takes a few limping steps, stops before* LUCKY *and spits on him, then goes and sits down on the mound.*]

POZZO: Guess who taught me all these beautiful things. [*Pause. Pointing to* LUCKY.] My Lucky!

VLADIMIR: [*Looking at the sky.*] Will night never come?

POZZO: But for him all my thoughts, all my feelings, would have been of common things. [*Pause. With extraordinary vehemence.*] Professional worries! [*Calmer.*] Beauty, grace, truth of the first water, I knew they were all beyond me. So I took a knook.

VLADIMIR: [*Startled from his inspection of the sky.*] A knook?

POZZO: That was nearly sixty years ago . . . [*He consults his watch*] . . . yes, nearly sixty. [*Drawing himself up proudly.*] You wouldn't think it to look at me, would you? Compared to him I look like a young man, no? [*Pause.*] Hat! [LUCKY *puts down the basket and takes off his hat. His long white hair falls about his face. He puts his hat under his arm and picks up the basket.*] Now look. [POZZO *takes off his hat.*[1] *He is completely bald. He puts on his hat again.*] Did you see?

VLADIMIR: And now you turn him away? Such an old and faithful servant.

ESTRAGON: Swine!

[POZZO *more and more agitated.*]

VLADIMIR: After having sucked all the good out of him you chuck him away like a . . . like a banana skin. Really . . .

[1] All four wear bowlers.

POZZO: [*Groaning, clutching his head.*] I can't bear it . . . any longer . . . the way he goes on . . . you've no idea . . . it's terrible . . . he must go . . . [*He waves his arms*] . . . I'm going mad . . . [*He collapses, his head in his hands*] . . . I can't bear it . . . any longer . . .
[*Silence. All look at* POZZO.]

VLADIMIR: He can't bear it.

ESTRAGON: Any longer.

VLADIMIR: He's going mad.

ESTRAGON: It's terrible.

VLADIMIR: [*To* LUCKY.] How dare you! It's abominable! Such a good master! Crucify him like that! After so many years! Really!

POZZO: [*Sobbing.*] He used to be so kind . . . so helpful . . . and entertaining . . . my good angel . . . and now . . . he's killing me.

ESTRAGON: [*To* VLADIMIR.] Does he want to replace him?

VLADIMIR: What?

ESTRAGON: Does he want someone to take his place or not?

VLADIMIR: I don't think so.

ESTRAGON: What?

VLADIMIR: I don't know.

ESTRAGON: Ask him.

POZZO: [*Calmer.*] Gentlemen, I don't know what came over me. Forgive me. Forget all I said. [*More and more his old self.*] I don't remember exactly what it was, but you may be sure there wasn't a word of truth in it. [*Drawing himself up, striking his chest.*] Do I look like a man that can be made to suffer? Frankly? [*He rummages in his pockets.*] What have I done with my pipe?

VLADIMIR: Charming evening we're having.

ESTRAGON: Unforgettable.

VLADIMIR: And it's not over.

ESTRAGON: Apparently not.

VLADIMIR: It's only beginning.

ESTRAGON: It's awful.

VLADIMIR: Worse than the pantomime.

ESTRAGON: The circus.

VLADIMIR: The music-hall.

ESTRAGON: The circus.

POZZO: What can I have done with that briar?

ESTRAGON: He's a scream. He's lost his dudeen.
[*Laughs noisily.*]

VLADIMIR: I'll be back.
[*He hastens towards the wings.*]

ESTRAGON: End of the corridor, on the left.

VLADIMIR: Keep my seat.
[*Exit* VLADIMIR.]

POZZO: I've lost my Kapp and Peterson!

ESTRAGON: [*Convulsed with merriment.*] He'll be the death of
me!

POZZO: [*Looking up.*] You didn't by any chance see – [*He
misses* VLADIMIR.] Oh! He's gone! Without saying good-
bye! How could he! He might have waited!

ESTRAGON: He would have burst.

POZZO: Oh! [*Pause.*] Oh well then of course in that case . . .

ESTRAGON: Come here.

POZZO: What for?

ESTRAGON: You'll see.

POZZO: You want me to get up?

ESTRAGON: Quick! [POZZO *gets up and goes over beside*
ESTRAGON. ESTRAGON *points off.*] Look!

POZZO: [*Having put on his glasses.*] Oh I say!

ESTRAGON: It's all over.
[*Enter* VLADIMIR, *sombre. He shoulders* LUCKY *out of his
way, kicks over the stool, comes and goes agitatedly.*]

POZZO: He's not pleased.

ESTRAGON: [*To* VLADIMIR.] You missed a treat. Pity.
[VLADIMIR *halts, straightens the stool, comes and goes,
calmer.*]

POZZO: He subsides. [*Looking round.*] Indeed all subsides. A
great calm descends. [*Raising his hand.*] Listen! Pan sleeps.

VLADIMIR: Will night never come?
[*All three look at the sky.*]

POZZO: You don't feel like going until it does?

ESTRAGON: Well you see –

POZZO: Why it's very natural, very natural. I myself in your
situation, if I had an appointment with a Godin . . . Godet

. . . Godot . . . anyhow, you see who I mean, I'd wait till it was black night before I gave up. [*He looks at the stool.*] I'd like very much to sit down, but I don't quite know how to go about it.

ESTRAGON: Could I be of any help?

POZZO: If you asked me perhaps.

ESTRAGON: What?

POZZO: If you asked me to sit down.

ESTRAGON: Would that be a help?

POZZO: I fancy so.

ESTRAGON: Here we go. Be seated, sir, I beg of you.

POZZO: No, no, I wouldn't think of it! [*Pause. Aside.*] Ask me again.

ESTRAGON: Come come, take a seat, I beseech you, you'll get pneumonia.

POZZO: You really think so?

ESTRAGON: Why it's absolutely certain.

POZZO: No doubt you are right. [*He sits down.*] Done it again! [*Pause.*] Thank you, dear fellow. [*He consults his watch.*] But I must really be getting along, if I am to observe my schedule.

VLADIMIR: Time has stopped.

POZZO: [*Cuddling his watch to his ear.*] Don't you believe it, sir, don't you believe it. [*He puts his watch back in his pocket.*] Whatever you like, but not that.

ESTRAGON: [*To POZZO.*] Everything seems black to him today.

POZZO: Except the firmament! [*He laughs, pleased with this witticism.*] But I see what it is, you are not from these parts, you don't know what our twilights can do. Shall I tell you? [*Silence. ESTRAGON is fiddling with his boot again, VLADIMIR with his hat.*] I can't refuse you. [*Vaporizer.*] A little attention, if you please. [VLADIMIR *and* ESTRAGON *continue their fiddling,* LUCKY *is half asleep.* POZZO *cracks his whip feebly.*] What's the matter with this whip? [*He gets up and cracks it more vigorously, finally with success.* LUCKY *jumps.* VLADIMIR'*s hat,* ESTRAGON'*s boot,* LUCKY'*s hat, fall to the ground.* POZZO *throws down the whip.*] Worn out, this whip. [*He looks at* VLADIMIR *and* ESTRAGON.] What was I saying?

VLADIMIR: Let's go.

ESTRAGON: But take the weight off your feet, I implore you, you'll catch your death.

POZZO: True. [*He sits down. To* ESTRAGON.] What is your name?

ESTRAGON: Adam.

POZZO: [*Who hasn't listened.*] Ah, yes! The night. [*He raises his head.*] But be a little more attentive, for pity's sake, otherwise we'll never get anywhere. [*He looks at the sky.*] Look. [*All look at the sky except* LUCKY *who is dozing off again.* POZZO *jerks the rope.*] Will you look at the sky, pig! [LUCKY *looks at the sky.*] Good, that's enough. [*They stop looking at the sky.*] What is there so extraordinary about it? Qua sky. It is pale and luminous like any sky at this hour of the day. [*Pause.*] In these latitudes. [*Pause.*] When the weather is fine. [*Lyrical.*] An hour ago [*He looks at his watch, prosaic*] roughly [*Lyrical*] after having poured forth ever since [*He hesitates, prosaic*] say ten o'clock in the morning [*Lyrical*] tirelessly torrents of red and white light it begins to lose its effulgence, to grow pale [*Gesture of the two hands lapsing by stages*], pale, ever a little paler, a little paler until [*Dramatic pause, ample gesture of the two hands flung wide apart*] pppfff! finished! it comes to rest. But – [*Hand raised in admonition*] – but behind this veil of gentleness and peace night is charging [*Vibrantly*] and will burst upon us [*Snaps his fingers*] pop! like that! [*His inspiration leaves him*] just when we least expect it. [*Silence. Gloomily.*] That's how it is on this bitch of an earth.

[*Long silence.*]

ESTRAGON: So long as one knows.

VLADIMIR: One can bide one's time.

ESTRAGON: One knows what to expect.

VLADIMIR: No further need to worry.

ESTRAGON: Simply wait.

VLADIMIR: We're used to it.

[*He picks up his hat, looks inside it, shakes it, puts it on.*]

POZZO: How did you find me? [VLADIMIR *and* ESTRAGON

look at him blankly.] Good? Fair? Middling? Poor?
Positively bad?

VLADIMIR: [*First to understand.*] Oh very good, very very
good.

POZZO: [*To* ESTRAGON.] And you, sir?

ESTRAGON: Oh tray bong, tray tray tray bong.

POZZO: [*Fervently.*] Bless you, gentlemen, bless you! [*Pause.*] I
have such need of encouragement! [*Pause.*] I weakened a
little towards the end, you didn't notice?

VLADIMIR: Oh perhaps just a teeny weeny little bit.

ESTRAGON: I thought it was intentional.

POZZO: You see my memory is defective.
[*Silence.*]

ESTRAGON: In the meantime nothing happens.

POZZO: You find it tedious?

ESTRAGON: Somewhat.

POZZO: [*To* VLADIMIR.] And you, sir?

VLADIMIR: I've been better entertained.
[*Silence.* POZZO *struggles inwardly.*]

POZZO: Gentlemen, you have been . . . civil to me.

ESTRAGON: Not at all.

VLADIMIR: What an idea!

POZZO: Yes yes, you have been correct. So that I ask myself is
there anything I can do in my turn for these honest fellows
who are having such a dull, dull time.

ESTRAGON: Even ten francs would be welcome.

VLADIMIR: We are not beggars!

POZZO: Is there anything I can do, that's what I ask myself, to
cheer them up? I have given them bones, I have talked to
them about this and that, I have explained the twilight,
admittedly. But is it enough, that's what tortures me, is it
enough?

ESTRAGON: Even five.

VLADIMIR: [*To* ESTRAGON, *indignantly.*] That's enough!

ESTRAGON: I couldn't accept less.

POZZO: Is it enough? No doubt. But I am liberal. It's my
nature. This evening. So much the worse for me. [*He jerks
the rope.* LUCKY *looks at him.*] For I shall suffer, no doubt

about that. [*He picks up the whip.*] What do you prefer?
Shall we have him dance, or sing, or recite, or think, or –

ESTRAGON: Who?

POZZO: Who! You know how to think, you two?

VLADIMIR: He thinks?

POZZO: Certainly. Aloud. He even used to think very prettily
once, I could listen to him for hours. Now . . . [*He
shudders.*] So much the worse for me. Well, would you
like him to think something for us?

ESTRAGON: I'd rather he'd dance, it'd be more fun?

POZZO: Not necessarily.

ESTRAGON: Wouldn't it, Didi, be more fun?

VLADIMIR: I'd like well to hear him think.

ESTRAGON: Perhaps he could dance first and think afterwards,
if it isn't too much to ask him.

VLADIMIR: [*To* POZZO.] Would that be possible?

POZZO: By all means, nothing simpler. It's the natural order.
[*He laughs briefly.*]

VLADIMIR: Then let him dance.
[*Silence.*]

POZZO: Do you hear, hog?

ESTRAGON: He never refuses?

POZZO: He refused once. [*Silence.*] Dance, misery! [LUCKY
puts down the basket, advances towards front, turns to
POZZO. LUCKY *dances. He stops.*]

ESTRAGON: Is that all?

POZZO: Encore!
[LUCKY *executes the same movements, stops.*]

ESTRAGON: Pooh! I'd do as well myself. [*He imitates* LUCKY,
almost falls.] With a little practice.

POZZO: He used to dance the farandole, the fling, the brawl,
the jig, the fandango, and even the hornpipe. He capered.
For joy. Now that's the best he can do. Do you know
what he calls it?

ESTRAGON: The Scapegoat's Agony.

VLADIMIR: The Hard Stool.

POZZO: The Net. He thinks he's entangled in a net.

VLADIMIR: [*Squirming like an aesthete.*] There's something
about it . . .

[LUCKY *makes to return to his burdens.*]

POZZO: Woaa!

[LUCKY *stiffens.*]

ESTRAGON: Tell us about the time he refused.

POZZO: With pleasure, with pleasure. [*He fumbles in his pockets.*] Wait. [*He fumbles.*] What have I done with my spray? [*He fumbles.*] Well now isn't that . . . [*He looks up, consternation on his features. Faintly.*] I can't find my pulverizer!

ESTRAGON[*Faintly.*] My left lung is very weak! [*He coughs feebly. In ringing tones.*] But my right lung is as sound as a bell!

POZZO: [*Normal voice.*] No matter! What was I saying. [*He ponders.*] Wait. [*Ponders.*] Well now isn't that . . . [*He raises his head.*] Help me!

ESTRAGON: Wait!

VLADIMIR: Wait!

POZZO: Wait!

[*All three take off their hats simultaneously, press their hands to their foreheads, concentrate.*]

ESTRAGON: [*Triumphantly.*] Ah!

VLADIMIR: He has it.

POZZO: [*Impatient.*] Well?

ESTRAGON: Why doesn't he put down his bags?

VLADIMIR: Rubbish!

POZZO: Are you sure?

VLADIMIR: Damn it, haven't you already told us!

POZZO: I've already told you?

ESTRAGON: He's already told us?

VLADIMIR: Anyway he has put them down.

ESTRAGON: [*Glance at* LUCKY.] So he has. And what of it?

VLADIMIR: Since he has put down his bags it is impossible we should have asked why he does not do so.

POZZO: Stoutly reasoned!

ESTRAGON: And why has he put them down?

POZZO: Answer us that.

VLADIMIR: In order to dance.

ESTRAGON: True!

POZZO: True!

[*Silence. They put on their hats.*]

ESTRAGON: Nothing happens, nobody comes, nobody goes, it's awful!

VLADIMIR: [*To* POZZO.] Tell him to think.

POZZO: Give him his hat.

VLADIMIR: His hat?

POZZO: He can't think without his hat.

VLADIMIR: [*To* ESTRAGON.] Give him his hat.

ESTRAGON: Me! After what he did to me! Never!

VLADIMIR: I'll give it to him.

[*He does not move.*]

ESTRAGON: [*To* POZZO.] Tell him to go and fetch it.

POZZO: It's better to give it to him.

VLADIMIR: I'll give it to him.

[*He picks up the hat and tenders it at arm's length to* LUCKY, *who does not move.*]

POZZO: You must put it on his head.

ESTRAGON: [*To* POZZO.] Tell him to take it.

POZZO: It's better to put it on his head.

VLADIMIR: I'll put it on his head.

[*He goes round behind* LUCKY, *approaches him cautiously, puts the hat on his head and recoils smartly.* LUCKY *does not move. Silence.*]

ESTRAGON: What's he waiting for?

POZZO: Stand back! [VLADIMIR *and* ESTRAGON *move away from* LUCKY. POZZO *jerks the rope.* LUCKY *looks at* POZZO.] Think, pig! [*Pause.* LUCKY *begins to dance.*] Stop! [LUCKY *stops.*] Forward! [LUCKY *advances.*] Stop! [LUCKY *stops.*] Think!

[*Silence.*]

LUCKY: On the other hand with regard to —

POZZO: Stop! [LUCKY *stops.*] Back! [LUCKY *moves back.*] Stop! [LUCKY *stops.*] Turn! [LUCKY *turns towards auditorium.*] Think!

[*During* LUCKY's *tirade the others react as follows:* (1) VLADIMIR *and* ESTRAGON *all attention,* POZZO *dejected and disgusted.* (2) VLADIMIR *and* ESTRAGON *begin to protest,* POZZO's *sufferings increase.* (3) VLADIMIR *and* ESTRAGON *attentive again,* POZZO *more and more*

agitated and groaning. (4) VLADIMIR *and* ESTRAGON
protest violently. POZZO *jumps up, pulls on the rope.*
General outcry. LUCKY *pulls on the rope, staggers, shouts*
his text. All three throw themselves on LUCKY *who*
struggles and shouts his text.]

LUCKY: Given the existence as uttered forth in the public
works of Puncher and Wattmann of a personal God
quaquaquaqua with white beard quaquaquaqua outside
time without extension who from the heights of divine
apathia divine athambia divine aphasia loves us dearly
with some exceptions for reasons unknown but time will
tell and suffers like the divine Miranda with those who for
reasons unknown but time will tell are plunged in torment
plunged in fire whose fire flames if that continues and who
can doubt it will fire the firmament that is to say blast hell
to heaven so blue still and calm so calm with a calm which
even though intermittent is better than nothing but not so
fast and considering what is more that as a result of the
labours left unfinished crowned by the Acacacacademy of
Anthropopopometry of Essy-in-Possy of Testew and
Cunard it is established beyond all doubt all other doubt
than that which clings to the labours of men that as a
result of the labours unfinished of Testew and Cunard it is
established as hereinafter but not so fast for reasons
unknown that as a result of the public works of Puncher
and Wattmann it is established beyond all doubt that in
view of the labours of Fartov and Belcher left unfinished
for reasons unknown of Testew and Cunard left
unfinished it is established what many deny that man in
Possy of Testew and Cunard that man in Essy that man in
short that man in brief in spite of the strides of
alimentation and defecation is seen to waste and pine
waste and pine and concurrently simultaneously what is
more for reasons unknown in spite of the strides of
physical culture the practice of sports such as tennis
football running cycling swimming flying floating riding
gliding conating camogie skating tennis of all kinds dying
flying sports of all sorts autumn summer winter winter
tennis of all kinds hockey of all sorts penicillin and

succedanea in a word I resume and concurrently
simultaneously for reasons unknown to shrink and
dwindle in spite of the tennis I resume flying gliding golf
over nine and eighteen holes tennis of all sorts in a word
for reasons unknown in Feckham Peckham Fulham
Clapham namely concurrently simultaneously what is
more for reasons unknown but time will tell to shrink and
dwindle I resume Fulham Clapham in a word the dead
loss per caput since the death of Bishop Berkeley being to
the tune of one inch four ounce per caput approximately
by and large more or less to the nearest decimal good
measure round figures stark naked in the stockinged feet
in Connemara in a word for reasons unknown no matter
what matter the facts are there and considering what is
more much more grave that in the light of the labours lost
of Steinweg and Peterman it appears what is more much
more grave that in the light the light the light of the
labours lost of Steinweg and Peterman that in the plains in
the mountains by the seas by the rivers running water
running fire the air is the same and then the earth namely
the air and then the earth in the great cold the great dark
the air and the earth abode of stones in the great cold alas
alas in the year of their Lord six hundred and something
the air the earth the sea the earth abode of stones in the
great deeps the great cold on sea on land and in the air I
resume for reasons unknown in spite of the tennis the facts
are there but time will tell I resume alas alas on on in
short in fine on on abode of stones who can doubt it I
resume but not so fast I resume the skull to shrink and
waste and concurrently simultaneously what is more for
reasons unknown in spite of the tennis on on the beard the
flames the tears the stones so blue so calm alas alas on on
the skull the skull the skull the skull in Connemara in spite
of the tennis the labours abandoned left unfinished graver
still abode of stones in a word I resume alas alas
abandoned unfinished the skull the skull in Connemara in
spite of the tennis the skull alas the stones Cunard [*Mêlée,
final vociferations*] tennis . . . the stones . . . so calm . . .
Cunard . . . unfinished . . .

POZZO: His hat!

[VLADIMIR *seizes* LUCKY's *hat. Silence of* LUCKY. *He falls. Silence. Panting of the victors.*]

ESTRAGON: Avenged!

[VLADIMIR *examines the hat, peers inside it.*]

POZZO: Give me that! [*He snatches the hat from* VLADIMIR, *throws it on the ground, tramples on it.*] There's an end to his thinking!

VLADIMIR: But will he be able to walk?

POZZO: Walk or crawl! [*He kicks* LUCKY.] Up pig!

ESTRAGON: Perhaps he's dead.

VLADIMIR: You'll kill him.

POZZO: Up scum! [*He jerks the rope.*] Help me!

VLADIMIR: How?

POZZO: Raise him up!

[VLADIMIR *and* ESTRAGON *hoist* LUCKY *to his feet, support him an instant, then let him go. He falls.*]

ESTRAGON: He's doing it on purpose!

POZZO: You must hold him. [*Pause.*] Come on, come on, raise him up!

ESTRAGON: To hell with him!

VLADIMIR: Come on, once more.

ESTRAGON: What does he take us for?

[*They raise* LUCKY, *hold him up.*]

POZZO: Don't let him go! [VLADIMIR *and* ESTRAGON *totter.*] Don't move! [POZZO *fetches bag and basket and brings them towards* LUCKY.] Hold him tight! [*He puts the bag in* LUCKY's *hand.* LUCKY *drops it immediately.*] Don't let him go! [*He puts back the bag in* LUCKY's *hand. Gradually, at the feel of the bag,* LUCKY *recovers his senses and his fingers close round the handle.*] Hold him tight! [*As before with basket.*] Now! You can let him go. [VLADIMIR *and* ESTRAGON *move away from* LUCKY, *who totters, reels, sags, but succeeds in remaining on his feet, bag and basket in his hands.* POZZO *steps back, cracks his whip.*] Forward! [LUCKY *totters forward.*] Back! [LUCKY *totters back.*] Turn! [LUCKY *turns.*] Done it! He can walk. [*Turning towards* VLADIMIR *and* ESTRAGON.] Thank you gentlemen, and let me . . . [*He fumbles in his pockets*] . . .

let me wish you . . . [*Fumbles*] . . . wish you . . . [*Fumbles*]
. . . what have I done with my watch? [*Fumbles.*] A
genuine half-hunter, gentlemen, with deadbeat
escapement! [*Sobbing.*] 'Twas my granpa gave it to me!
[*He searches on the ground,* VLADIMIR *and* ESTRAGON
likewise. POZZO *turns over with his foot the remains of*
LUCKY'S *hat.*] Well now, isn't that just —

VLADIMIR: Perhaps it's in your fob.

POZZO: Wait! [*He doubles up in an attempt to apply his ear to
his stomach, listens. Silence.*] I hear nothing. [*He beckons
them to approach.* VLADIMIR *and* ESTRAGON *go towards
him, bend over his stomach.*] Surely one should hear the
tick-tick.

VLADIMIR: Silence!

[*All listen, bent double.*]

ESTRAGON: I hear something.

POZZO: Where?

VLADIMIR: It's the heart.

POZZO: [*Disappointed.*] Damnation!

VLADIMIR: Silence!

ESTRAGON: Perhaps it has stopped.

[*They straighten up.*]

POZZO: Which of you smells so bad?

ESTRAGON: He has stinking breath and I have stinking feet.

POZZO: I must go.

ESTRAGON: And your half-hunter?

POZZO: I must have left it at the manor.

[*Silence.*]

ESTRAGON: Then adieu.

POZZO: Adieu.

VLADIMIR: Adieu.

POZZO: Adieu.

[*Silence. No one moves.*]

VLADIMIR: Adieu.

POZZO: Adieu.

ESTRAGON: Adieu.

[*Silence.*]

POZZO: And thank you.

VLADIMIR: Thank *you*.

POZZO: Not at all.

ESTRAGON: Yes yes.

POZZO: No no.

VLADIMIR: Yes yes.

ESTRAGON: No no.

[*Silence.*]

POZZO: I don't seem to be able . . . [*Long hesitation*] . . . to depart.

ESTRAGON: Such is life.

[POZZO *turns, moves away from* LUCKY *towards the wings, paying out the rope as he goes.*]

VLADIMIR: You're going the wrong way.

POZZO: I need a running start. [*Having come to the end of the rope, i.e. off stage, he stops, turns, and cries.*] Stand back! [VLADIMIR *and* ESTRAGON *stand back, look towards* POZZO. *Crack of whip.*] On! On!

ESTRAGON: On!

VLADIMIR: On!

[LUCKY *moves off.*]

POZZO: Faster! [*He appears, crosses the stage preceded by* LUCKY. VLADIMIR *and* ESTRAGON *wave their hats. Exit* LUCKY.] On! On! [*On the point of disappearing in his turn he stops and turns. The rope tautens. Noise of* LUCKY *falling off.*] Stool! [VLADIMIR *fetches stool and gives it to* POZZO, *who throws it to* LUCKY.] Adieu!

VLADIMIR ⎫
ESTRAGON ⎭ [*Waving.*] Adieu! Adieu!

POZZO: Up! Pig! [*Noise of* LUCKY *getting up.*] On! [*Exit* POZZO.] Faster! On! Adieu! Pig! Yip! Adieu!

[*Long silence.*]

VLADIMIR: That passed the time.

ESTRAGON: It would have passed in any case.

VLADIMIR: Yes, but not so rapidly.

[*Pause.*]

ESTRAGON: What do we do now?

VLADIMIR: I don't know.

ESTRAGON: Let's go.

VLADIMIR: We can't.

ESTRAGON: Why not?

VLADIMIR: We're waiting for Godot.
ESTRAGON: [*Despairingly.*] Ah!
    [*Pause.*]
VLADIMIR: How they've changed!
ESTRAGON: Who?
VLADIMIR: Those two.
ESTRAGON: That's the idea, let's make a little conversation.
VLADIMIR: Haven't they?
ESTRAGON: What?
VLADIMIR: Changed.
ESTRAGON: Very likely. They all change. Only we can't.
VLADIMIR: Likely! It's certain. Didn't you see them?
ESTRAGON: I suppose I did. But I don't know them.
VLADIMIR: Yes you do know them.
ESTRAGON: No I don't know them.
VLADIMIR: We know them, I tell you. You forget everything.
    [*Pause. To himself.*] Unless they're not the same . . .
ESTRAGON: Why didn't they recognize us then?
VLADIMIR: That means nothing. I too pretended not to
    recognize them. And then nobody ever recognizes us.
ESTRAGON: Forget it. What we need – Ow! [VLADIMIR *does*
    not react.] Ow!
VLADIMIR: [*To himself.*] Unless they're not the same . . .
ESTRAGON: Didi! It's the other foot!
    [*He goes hobbling towards the mound.*]
VLADIMIR: Unless they're not the same . . .
BOY: [*Off.*] Mister!
    [ESTRAGON *halts. Both look towards the voice.*]
ESTRAGON: Off we go again.
VLADIMIR: Approach, my child.
    [*Enter* BOY, *timidly. He halts.*]
BOY: Mister Albert . . . ?
VLADIMIR: Yes.
ESTRAGON: What do you want?
VLADIMIR: Approach.
    [*The* BOY *does not move.*]
ESTRAGON: [*Forcibly.*] Approach when you're told, can't you?
    [*The* BOY *advances timidly, halts.*]
VLADIMIR: What is it?

BOY: Mr Godot . . .

VLADIMIR: Obviously . . . [*Pause.*] Approach.

ESTRAGON: [*Violently.*] Will you approach! [*The* BOY *advances timidly.*] What kept you so late?

VLADIMIR: You have a message from Mr Godot?

BOY: Yes, sir.

VLADIMIR: Well, what is it?

ESTRAGON: What kept you so late?
[*The* BOY *looks at them in turn, not knowing to which he should reply.*]

VLADIMIR: [*To* ESTRAGON.] Let him alone.

ESTRAGON: [*Violently.*] You let me alone! [*Advancing, to the* BOY.] Do you know what time it is?

BOY: [*Recoiling.*] It's not my fault, sir.

ESTRAGON: And whose is it? Mine?

BOY: I was afraid, sir.

ESTRAGON: Afraid of what? Of us? [*Pause.*] Answer me!

VLADIMIR: I know what it is, he was afraid of the others.

ESTRAGON: How long have you been here?

BOY: A good while, sir.

VLADIMIR: You were afraid of the whip.

BOY: Yes, sir.

VLADIMIR: The roars.

BOY: Yes, sir.

VLADIMIR: The two big men.

BOY: Yes, sir.

VLADIMIR: Do you know them?

BOY: No, sir.

VLADIMIR: Are you a native of these parts? [*Silence.*] Do you belong to these parts?

BOY: Yes, sir.

ESTRAGON: That's all a pack of lies. [*Shaking the* BOY *by the arm.*] Tell us the truth.

BOY: [*Trembling.*] But it is the truth, sir!

VLADIMIR: Will you let him alone! What's the matter with you? [ESTRAGON *releases the* BOY, *moves away, covering his face with his hands.* VLADIMIR *and the* BOY *observe him.* ESTRAGON *drops his hands. His face is convulsed.*] What's the matter with you?

ESTRAGON: I'm unhappy.

VLADIMIR: Not really! Since when?

ESTRAGON: I'd forgotten.

VLADIMIR: Extraordinary the tricks that memory plays!
   [ESTRAGON *tries to speak, renounces, limps to his place,
   sits down and begins to take off his boots. To* BOY.] Well?

BOY: Mr Godot —

VLADIMIR: I've seen you before, haven't I?

BOY: I don't know sir.

VLADIMIR: You don't know me?

BOY: No, sir.

VLADIMIR: It wasn't you came yesterday?

BOY: No, sir.

VLADIMIR: This is your first time?

BOY: Yes, sir.
   [*Silence.*]

VLADIMIR: Words, words. [*Pause.*] Speak.

BOY: [*In a rush.*] Mr Godot told me to tell you he won't come
   this evening but surely tomorrow.
   [*Silence.*]

VLADIMIR: Is that all?

BOY: Yes, sir.
   [*Silence.*]

VLADIMIR: You work for Mr Godot?

BOY: Yes, sir.

VLADIMIR: What do you do?

BOY: I mind the goats, sir.

VLADIMIR: Is he good to you?

BOY: Yes, sir.

VLADIMIR: He doesn't beat you?

BOY: No, sir, not me.

VLADIMIR: Whom does he beat?

BOY: He beats my brother, sir.

VLADIMIR: Ah, you have a brother?

BOY: Yes, sir.

VLADIMIR: What does he do?

BOY: He minds the sheep, sir.

VLADIMIR: And why doesn't he beat you?

BOY: I don't know, sir.

VLADIMIR: He must be fond of you.

BOY: I don't know, sir.

[*Silence.*]

VLADIMIR: Does he give you enough to eat? [*The* BOY *hesitates.*] Does he feed you well?

BOY: Fairly well, sir.

VLADIMIR: You're not unhappy: [*The* BOY *hesitates.*] Do you hear me?

BOY: Yes, sir.

VLADIMIR: Well?

BOY: I don't know, sir.

VLADIMIR: You don't know if you're unhappy or not?

BOY: No, sir.

VLADIMIR: You're as bad as myself. [*Silence.*] Where do you sleep?

BOY: In the loft, sir.

VLADIMIR: With your brother?

BOY: Yes, sir.

VLADIMIR: In the hay?

BOY: Yes, sir.

[*Silence.*]

VLADIMIR: All right, you may go.

BOY: What am I to say to Mr Godot, sir?

VLADIMIR: Tell him . . . [*He hesitates*] . . . tell him you saw us. [*Pause.*] You did see us, didn't you?

BOY: Yes, sir.

[*He steps back, hesitates, turns and exit running. The light suddenly fails. In a moment it is night. The moon rises at back, mounts in the sky, stands still, shedding a pale light on the scene.*]

VLADIMIR: At last! [ESTRAGON *gets up and goes towards* VLADIMIR, *a boot in each hand. He puts them down at the edge of stage, straightens and contemplates the moon.*] What are you doing?

ESTRAGON: Pale for weariness.

VLADIMIR: Eh?

ESTRAGON: Of climbing heaven and gazing on the likes of us.

VLADIMIR: Your boots. What are you doing with your boots?

ESTRAGON: [*Turning to look at the boots.*] I'm leaving them

there. [*Pause.*] Another will come, just as . . . as . . . as
me, but with smaller feet, and they'll make him happy.

VLADIMIR: But you can't go barefoot!

ESTRAGON: Christ did.

VLADIMIR: Christ! What's Christ got to do with it? You're not
going to compare yourself to Christ!

ESTRAGON: All my life I've compared myself to him.

VLADIMIR: But where he lived it was warm, it was dry!

ESTRAGON: Yes. And they crucified quick.
[*Silence.*]

VLADIMIR: We've nothing more to do here.

ESTRAGON: Nor anywhere else.

VLADIMIR: Ah Gogo, don't go on like that. Tomorrow
everything will be better.

ESTRAGON: How do you make that out?

VLADIMIR: Did you not hear what the child said?

ESTRAGON: No.

VLADIMIR: He said that Godot was sure to come tomorrow.
[*Pause.*] What do you say to that?

ESTRAGON: Then all we have to do is to wait on here.

VLADIMIR: Are you mad? We must take cover. [*He takes*
ESTRAGON *by the arm.*] Come on.
[*He draws* ESTRAGON *after him.* ESTRAGON *yields, then
resists. They halt.*]

ESTRAGON: [*Looking at the tree.*] Pity we haven't got a bit of
rope.

VLADIMIR: Come on. It's cold.
[*He draws* ESTRAGON *after him. As before.*]

ESTRAGON: Remind me to bring a bit of rope tomorrow.

VLADIMIR: Yes. Come on.
[*He draws him after him. As before.*]

ESTRAGON: How long have we been together all the time now?

VLADIMIR: I don't know. Fifty years perhaps.

ESTRAGON: Do you remember the day I threw myself into the
Rhône?

VLADIMIR: We were grape-harvesting.

ESTRAGON: You fished me out.

VLADIMIR: That's all dead and buried.

ESTRAGON: My clothes dried in the sun.

VLADIMIR: There's no good harking back on that. Come on.
  [*He draws him after him. As before.*]
ESTRAGON: Wait.
VLADIMIR: I'm cold!
ESTRAGON: Wait! [*He moves away from* VLADIMIR.] I
  wonder if we wouldn't have been better off alone, each
  one for himself. [*He crosses the stage and sits down on the
  mound.*] We weren't made for the same road.
VLADIMIR: [*Without anger.*] It's not certain.
ESTRAGON: No, nothing is certain.
  [VLADIMIR *slowly crosses the stage and sits down beside*
  ESTRAGON.]
VLADIMIR: We can still part, if you think it would be better.
ESTRAGON: It's not worth while now.
  [*Silence.*]
VLADIMIR: No, it's not worth while now.
  [*Silence.*]
ESTRAGON: Well, shall we go?
VLADIMIR: Yes, let's go.
  [*They do not move.*]

CURTAIN

ACT TWO

Next Day. Same Time. Same Place.

Estragon's boots front centre, heels together, toes splayed.
Lucky's hat at same place.
The tree has four or five leaves.
Enter VLADIMIR *agitatedly. He halts and looks long at the*
tree, then suddenly begins to move feverishly about the stage.
He halts before the boots, picks one up, examines it, sniffs it,
manifests disgust, puts it back carefully. Comes and goes. Halts
extreme right and gazes into distance off, shading his eyes with
his hand. Comes and goes. Halts extreme left, as before.
Comes and goes. Halts suddenly and begins to sing loudly.
VLADIMIR: A dog came in –
[*Having begun too high he stops, clears his throat, resumes.*]

> A dog came in the kitchen
> And stole a crust of bread.
> Then cook up with a ladle
> And beat him till he was dead.
>
> Then all the dogs came running
> And dug the dog a tomb –
> [*He stops, broods, resumes.*]
>
> Then all the dogs came running
> And dug the dog a tomb
> And wrote upon the tombstone
> For the eyes of dogs to come:
>
> A dog came in the kitchen
> And stole a crust of bread.
> Then cook up with a ladle
> And beat him till he was dead.
>
> Then all the dogs came running
> And dug the dog a tomb –
> [*He stops, broods, resumes.*]

Then all the dogs came running
And dug the dog a tomb –
[*He stops, broods. Softly.*]

And dug the dog a tomb . . .

[*He remains a moment silent and motionless, then begins to move feverishly about the stage. He halts before the tree, comes and goes, before the boots, comes and goes, halts extreme right, gazes into distance, extreme left, gazes into distance. Enter* ESTRAGON *right, barefoot, head bowed. He slowly crosses the stage.* VLADIMIR *turns and sees him.*]
You again! [ESTRAGON *halts, but does not raise his head.* VLADIMIR *goes towards him.*] Come here till I embrace you.

ESTRAGON: Don't touch me!
[VLADIMIR *holds back, pained.*]

VLADIMIR: Do you want me to go away? [*Pause.*] Gogo! [*Pause.* VLADIMIR *observes him attentively.*] Did they beat you? [*Pause.*] Gogo! [ESTRAGON *remains silent, head bowed.*] Where did you spend the night?

ESTRAGON: Don't touch me! Don't question me! Don't speak to me! Stay with me!

VLADIMIR: Did I ever leave you?

ESTRAGON: You let me go.

VLADIMIR: Look at me. [ESTRAGON *does not raise his head. Violently.*] Will you look at me!
[ESTRAGON *raises his head. They look long at each other, then suddenly embrace, clapping each other on the back. End of the embrace.* ESTRAGON, *no longer supported, almost falls.*]

ESTRAGON: What a day!

VLADIMIR: Who beat you? Tell me.

ESTRAGON: Another day done with.

VLADIMIR: Not yet.

ESTRAGON: For me it's over and done with, no matter what happens. [*Silence.*] I heard you singing.

VLADIMIR: That's right, I remember.

ESTRAGON: That finished me. I said to myself, he's all alone, he thinks I'm gone for ever, and he sings.

VLADIMIR: One isn't master of one's moods. All day I've felt in great form. [*Pause.*] I didn't get up in the night, not once!

ESTRAGON: [*Sadly.*] You see, you piss better when I'm not there.

VLADIMIR: I missed you . . . and at the same time I was happy. Isn't that a queer thing?

ESTRAGON: [*Shocked.*] Happy?

VLADIMIR: Perhaps it's not the right word.

ESTRAGON: And now?

VLADIMIR: Now? . . . [*Joyous.*] There you are again . . . [*Indifferent.*] There we are again . . . [*Gloomy.*] There I am again.

ESTRAGON: You see, you feel worse when I'm with you. I feel better alone, too.

VLADIMIR: [*Vexed.*] Then why do you always come crawling back?

ESTRAGON: I don't know.

VLADIMIR: No, but I do. It's because you don't know how to defend yourself. I wouldn't have let them beat you.

ESTRAGON: You couldn't have stopped them.

VLADIMIR: Why not?

ESTRAGON: There were ten of them.

VLADIMIR: No, I mean before they beat you. I would have stopped you from doing whatever it was you were doing.

ESTRAGON: I wasn't doing anything.

VLADIMIR: Then why did they beat you?

ESTRAGON: I don't know.

VLADIMIR: Ah no, Gogo, the truth is there are things escape you that don't escape me, you must feel it yourself.

ESTRAGON: I tell you I wasn't doing anything.

VLADIMIR: Perhaps you weren't. But it's the way of doing it that counts, the way of doing it, if you want to go on living.

ESTRAGON: I wasn't doing anything.

VLADIMIR: You must be happy, too, deep down, if you only knew it.

ESTRAGON: Happy about what?

VLADIMIR: To be back with me again.

ESTRAGON: Would you say so?

VLADIMIR: Say you are, even if it's not true.

ESTRAGON: What am I to say?

VLADIMIR: Say, I am happy.

ESTRAGON: I am happy.

VLADIMIR: So am I.

ESTRAGON: So am I.

VLADIMIR: We are happy.

ESTRAGON: We are happy. [*Silence.*] What do we do now, now that we are happy?

VLADIMIR: Wait for Godot. [ESTRAGON *groans. Silence.*] Things have changed since yesterday.

ESTRAGON: And if he doesn't come?

VLADIMIR: [*After a moment of bewilderment.*] We'll see when the time comes. [*Pause.*] I was saying that things have changed here since yesterday.

ESTRAGON: Everything oozes.

VLADIMIR: Look at the tree.

ESTRAGON: It's never the same pus from one second to the next.

VLADIMIR: The tree, look at the tree.
[ESTRAGON *looks at the tree.*]

ESTRAGON: Was it not there yesterday?

VLADIMIR: Yes, of course it was there. Do you not remember? We nearly hanged ourselves from it. But you wouldn't. Do you not remember?

ESTRAGON: You dreamt it.

VLADIMIR: Is it possible that you've forgotten already?

ESTRAGON: That's the way I am. Either I forget immediately or I never forget.

VLADIMIR: And Pozzo and Lucky, have you forgotten them too?

ESTRAGON: Pozzo and Lucky?

VLADIMIR: He's forgotten everything!

ESTRAGON: I remember a lunatic who kicked the shins off me. Then he played the fool.

VLADIMIR: That was Lucky.

ESTRAGON: I remember that. But when was it?

VLADIMIR: And his keeper, do you not remember him?

ESTRAGON: He gave me a bone.

VLADIMIR: That was Pozzo.

ESTRAGON: And all that was yesterday, you say?

VLADIMIR: Yes, of course it was yesterday.

ESTRAGON: And here where we are now?

VLADIMIR: Where else do you think? Do you not recognize the place?

ESTRAGON: [*Suddenly furious.*] Recognize! What is there to recognize? All my lousy life I've crawled about in the mud! And you talk to me about scenery! [*Looking wildly about him.*] Look at this muckheap! I've never stirred from it!

VLADIMIR: Calm yourself, calm yourself.

ESTRAGON: You and your landscapes! Tell me about the worms!

VLADIMIR: All the same, you can't tell me that this [*Gesture*] bears any resemblance to . . . [*He hesitates*] . . . to the Macon country, for example. You can't deny there's a big difference.

ESTRAGON: The Macon country! Who's talking to you about the Macon country?

VLADIMIR: But you were there yourself, in the Macon country.

ESTRAGON: No, I was never in the Macon country. I've puked my puke of a life away here, I tell you! Here! In the Cackon country!

VLADIMIR: But we were there together, I could swear to it! Picking grapes for a man called . . . [*He snaps his fingers*] . . . can't think of the name of the man, at a place called . . . [*Snaps his fingers*] . . . can't think of the name of the place, do you not remember?

ESTRAGON: [*A little calmer.*] It's possible. I didn't notice anything.

VLADIMIR: But down there everything is red!

ESTRAGON: [*Exasperated.*] I didn't notice anything, I tell you! [*Silence.* VLADIMIR *sighs deeply.*]

VLADIMIR: You're a hard man to get on with, Gogo.

ESTRAGON: It'd be better if we parted.

VLADIMIR: You always say that, and you always come crawling back.

ESTRAGON: The best thing would be to kill me, like the other.

VLADIMIR: What other? [*Pause.*] What other?

ESTRAGON: Like billions of others.

VLADIMIR: [*Sententious.*] To every man his little cross. [*He sighs.*] Till he dies. [*Afterthought.*] And is forgotten.

ESTRAGON: In the meantime let us try and converse calmly, since we are incapable of keeping silent.

VLADIMIR: You're right, we're inexhaustible.

ESTRAGON: It's so we won't think.

VLADIMIR: We have that excuse.

ESTRAGON: It's so we won't hear.

VLADIMIR: We have our reasons.

ESTRAGON: All the dead voices.

VLADIMIR: They make a noise like wings.

ESTRAGON: Like leaves.

VLADIMIR: Like sand.

ESTRAGON: Like leaves.

   [*Silence.*]

VLADIMIR: They all speak together.

ESTRAGON: Each one to itself.

   [*Silence.*]

VLADIMIR: Rather they whisper.

ESTRAGON: They rustle.

VLADIMIR: They murmur.

ESTRAGON: They rustle.

   [*Silence.*]

VLADIMIR: What do they say?

ESTRAGON: They talk about their lives.

VLADIMIR: To have lived is not enough for them.

ESTRAGON: They have to talk about it.

VLADIMIR: To be dead is not enough for them.

ESTRAGON: It is not sufficient.

   [*Silence.*]

VLADIMIR: They make a noise like feathers.

ESTRAGON: Like leaves.

VLADIMIR: Like ashes.

ESTRAGON: Like leaves.

[*Long silence.*]

VLADIMIR: Say something!

ESTRAGON: I'm trying.

[*Long silence.*]

VLADIMIR: [*In anguish.*] Say anything at all!

ESTRAGON: What do we do now?

VLADIMIR: Wait for Godot.

ESTRAGON: Ah!

[*Silence.*]

VLADIMIR: This is awful!

ESTRAGON: Sing something.

VLADIMIR: No, no! [*He reflects.*] We could start all over again perhaps.

ESTRAGON: That should be easy.

VLADIMIR: It's the start that's difficult.

ESTRAGON: You can start from anything.

VLADIMIR: Yes, but you have to decide.

ESTRAGON: True.

[*Silence.*]

VLADIMIR: Help me!

ESTRAGON: I'm trying.

[*Silence.*]

VLADIMIR: When you seek you hear.

ESTRAGON: You do.

VLADIMIR: That prevents you from finding.

ESTRAGON: It does.

VLADIMIR: That prevents you from thinking.

ESTRAGON: You think all the same.

VLADIMIR: No, no, impossible.

ESTRAGON: That's the idea, let's contradict each other.

VLADIMIR: Impossible.

ESTRAGON: You think so?

VLADIMIR: We're in no danger of ever thinking any more.

ESTRAGON: Then what are we complaining about?

VLADIMIR: Thinking is not the worst.

ESTRAGON: Perhaps not. But at least there's that.

VLADIMIR: That what?

ESTRAGON: That's the idea, let's ask each other questions.

VLADIMIR: What do you mean, at least there's that?

ESTRAGON: That much less misery.

VLADIMIR: True.

ESTRAGON: Well? If we gave thanks for our mercies?

VLADIMIR: What is terrible is to *have* thought.

ESTRAGON: But did that ever happen to us?

VLADIMIR: Where are all these corpses from?

ESTRAGON: These skeletons.

VLADIMIR: Tell me that.

ESTRAGON: True.

VLADIMIR: We must have thought a little.

ESTRAGON: At the very beginning.

VLADIMIR: A charnel-house! A charnel-house!

ESTRAGON: You don't have to look.

VLADIMIR: You can't help looking.

ESTRAGON: True.

VLADIMIR: Try as one may.

ESTRAGON: I beg your pardon?

VLADIMIR: Try as one may.

ESTRAGON: We should turn resolutely towards Nature.

VLADIMIR: We've tried that.

ESTRAGON: True.

VLADIMIR: Oh, it's not the worst, I know.

ESTRAGON: What?

VLADIMIR: To have thought.

ESTRAGON: Obviously.

VLADIMIR: But we could have done without it.

ESTRAGON: Que voulez-vous?

VLADIMIR: I beg your pardon?

ESTRAGON: Que voulez-vous?

VLADIMIR: Ah! que voulez-vous. Exactly.
    [*Silence.*]

ESTRAGON: That wasn't such a bad little canter.

VLADIMIR: Yes, but now we'll have to find something else.

ESTRAGON: Let me see.
    [*He takes off his hat, concentrates.*]

VLADIMIR: Let me see. [*He takes off his hat, concentrates.*
    Long silence.] Ah!
    [*They put on their hats, relax.*]

ESTRAGON: Well?

VLADIMIR: What was I saying, we could go on from there.

ESTRAGON: What were you saying when?

VLADIMIR: At the very beginning.

ESTRAGON: The beginning of WHAT?

VLADIMIR: This evening . . . I was saying . . . I was saying . . .

ESTRAGON: I'm not a historian.

VLADIMIR: Wait . . . we embraced . . . we were happy . . . happy . . . what do we do now that we're happy . . . go on waiting . . . waiting . . . let me think . . . it's coming . . . go on waiting . . . now that we're happy . . . let me see . . . ah! The tree!

ESTRAGON: The tree?

VLADIMIR: Do you not remember?

ESTRAGON: I'm tired.

VLADIMIR: Look at it.

[*They look at the tree.*]

ESTRAGON: I see nothing.

VLADIMIR: But yesterday evening it was all black and bare. And now it's covered with leaves.

ESTRAGON: Leaves?

VLADIMIR: In a single night.

ESTRAGON: It must be the spring.

VLADIMIR: But in a single night!

ESTRAGON: I tell you we weren't here yesterday. Another of your nightmares.

VLADIMIR: And where were we yesterday evening according to you?

ESTRAGON: How do I know? In another compartment. There's no lack of void.

VLADIMIR: [*Sure of himself.*] Good. We weren't here yesterday evening. Now what did we do yesterday evening?

ESTRAGON: Do?

VLADIMIR: Try and remember.

ESTRAGON: Do . . . I suppose we blathered.

VLADIMIR: [*Controlling himself.*] About what?

ESTRAGON: Oh . . . this and that, I suppose, nothing in particular. [*With assurance.*] Yes, now I remember, yesterday evening we spent blathering about nothing in particular. That's been going on now for half a century.

VLADIMIR: You don't remember any fact, any circumstance?

ESTRAGON: [*Weary.*] Don't torment me, Didi.

VLADIMIR: The sun. The moon. Do you not remember?

ESTRAGON: They must have been there, as usual.

VLADIMIR: You didn't notice anything out of the ordinary?

ESTRAGON: Alas!

VLADIMIR: And Pozzo? And Lucky?

ESTRAGON: Pozzo?

VLADIMIR: The bones.

ESTRAGON: They were like fishbones.

VLADIMIR: It was Pozzo gave them to you.

ESTRAGON: I don't know.

VLADIMIR: And the kick.

ESTRAGON: That's right, someone gave me a kick.

VLADIMIR: It was Lucky gave it to you.

ESTRAGON: And all that was yesterday?

VLADIMIR: Show your leg.

ESTRAGON: Which?

VLADIMIR: Both. Pull up your trousers. [ESTRAGON *gives a leg to* VLADIMIR, *staggers.* VLADIMIR *takes the leg. They stagger.*] Pull up your trousers.

ESTRAGON: I can't.

[VLADIMIR *pulls up the trousers, looks at the leg, lets it go.* ESTRAGON *almost falls.*]

VLADIMIR: The other. [ESTRAGON *gives the same leg.*] The other, pig! [ESTRAGON *gives the other leg. Triumphantly.*] There's the wound! Beginning to fester!

ESTRAGON: And what about it?

VLADIMIR: [*Letting go the leg.*] Where are your boots?

ESTRAGON: I must have thrown them away.

VLADIMIR: When?

ESTRAGON: I don't know.

VLADIMIR: Why?

ESTRAGON: [*Exasperated.*] I don't know why I don't know!

VLADIMIR: No, I mean why did you throw them away?

ESTRAGON: [*Exasperated.*] Because they were hurting me!

VLADIMIR: [*Triumphantly, pointing to the boots.*] There they are! [ESTRAGON *looks at the boots.*] At the very spot where you left them yesterday!

[ESTRAGON *goes towards the boots, inspects them closely.*]

ESTRAGON: They're not mine.

VLADIMIR: [*Stupefied.*] Not yours!

ESTRAGON: Mine were black. These are brown.

VLADIMIR: You're sure yours were black?

ESTRAGON: Well, they were a kind of grey.

VLADIMIR: And these are brown? Show.

ESTRAGON: [*Picking up a boot.*] Well, they're a kind of green.

VLADIMIR: Show. [ESTRAGON *hands him the boot.* VLADIMIR *inspects it, throws it down angrily.*] Well of all the –

ESTRAGON: You see, all that's a lot of bloody –

VLADIMIR: Ah! I see what it is. Yes, I see what's happened.

ESTRAGON: All that's a lot of bloody –

VLADIMIR: It's elementary. Someone came and took yours and left you his.

ESTRAGON: Why?

VLADIMIR: His were too tight for him, so he took yours.

ESTRAGON: But mine were too tight.

VLADIMIR: For you. Not for him.

ESTRAGON: [*Having tried in vain to work it out.*] I'm tired! [*Pause.*] Let's go.

VLADIMIR: We can't.

ESTRAGON: Why not?

VLADIMIR: We're waiting for Godot.

ESTRAGON: Ah! [*Pause. Despairing.*] What'll we do, what'll we do!

VLADIMIR: There's nothing we can do.

ESTRAGON: But I can't go on like this!

VLADIMIR: Would you like a radish?

ESTRAGON: Is that all there is?

VLADIMIR: There are radishes and turnips.

ESTRAGON: Are there no carrots?

VLADIMIR: No. Anyway you overdo it with your carrots.

ESTRAGON: Then give me a radish. [VLADIMIR *fumbles in his pockets, finds nothing but turnips, finally brings out a radish and hands it to* ESTRAGON, *who examines it, sniffs it.*] It's black!

VLADIMIR: It's a radish.

ESTRAGON: I only like the pink ones, you know that!

VLADIMIR: Then you don't want it?

ESTRAGON: I only like the pink ones!

VLADIMIR: Then give it back to me.

[ESTRAGON *gives it back.*]

ESTRAGON: I'll go and get a carrot.

[*He does not move.*]

VLADIMIR: This is becoming really insignificant.

ESTRAGON: Not enough.

[*Silence.*]

VLADIMIR: What about trying them?

ESTRAGON: I've tried everything.

VLADIMIR: No, I mean the boots.

ESTRAGON: Would that be a good thing?

VLADIMIR: It'd pass the time. [ESTRAGON *hesitates.*] I assure you, it'd be an occupation.

ESTRAGON: A relaxation.

VLADIMIR: A recreation.

ESTRAGON: A relaxation.

VLADIMIR: Try.

ESTRAGON: You'll help me?

VLADIMIR: I will of course.

ESTRAGON: We don't manage too badly, eh Didi, between the two of us?

VLADIMIR: Yes yes. Come on, we'll try the left first.

ESTRAGON: We always find something, eh Didi, to give us the impression we exist?

VLADIMIR: [*Impatiently.*] Yes yes, we're magicians. But let us persevere in what we have resolved, before we forget. [*He picks up a boot.*] Come on, give me your foot. [ESTRAGON *raises his foot.*] The other, hog! [ESTRAGON *raises the other foot.*] Higher! [*Wreathed together they stagger about the stage.* VLADIMIR *succeeds finally in getting on the boot.*] Try and walk. [ESTRAGON *walks.*] Well?

ESTRAGON: It fits.

VLADIMIR: [*Taking string from his pocket.*] We'll try and lace it.

ESTRAGON: [*Vehemently.*] No no, no laces, no laces!

VLADIMIR: You'll be sorry. Let's try the other. [*As before.*] Well?

ESTRAGON: [*Grudgingly.*] It fits too.

VLADIMIR: They don't hurt you?

ESTRAGON: Not yet.

VLADIMIR: Then you can keep them.

ESTRAGON: They're too big.

VLADIMIR: Perhaps you'll have socks some day.

ESTRAGON: True.

VLADIMIR: Then you'll keep them?

ESTRAGON: That's enough about these boots.

VLADIMIR: Yes, but —

ESTRAGON: [*Violently.*] Enough! [*Silence.*] I suppose I might as well sit down.
[*He looks for a place to sit down, then goes and sits down on the mound.*]

VLADIMIR: That's where you were sitting yesterday evening.

ESTRAGON: If I could only sleep.

VLADIMIR: Yesterday you slept.

ESTRAGON: I'll try.
[*He resumes his foetal posture, his head between his knees.*]

VLADIMIR: Wait. [*He goes over and sits down beside* ESTRAGON *and begins to sing in a loud voice.*]
Bye bye bye bye
Bye bye —

ESTRAGON: [*Looking up angrily.*] Not so loud!

VLADIMIR: [*Softly.*]
Bye bye bye bye
Bye bye bye bye
Bye bye bye bye
Bye bye . . .
[ESTRAGON *sleeps.* VLADIMIR *gets up softly, takes off his coat and lays it across* ESTRAGON's *shoulders, then starts walking up and down, swinging his arms to keep himself warm.* ESTRAGON *wakes with a start, jumps up, casts about wildly.* VLADIMIR *runs to him, puts his arms round him.*] There . . . there . . . Didi is there . . . don't be afraid . . .

ESTRAGON: Ah!

VLADIMIR: There . . . there . . . it's all over.

ESTRAGON: I was falling —

VLADIMIR: It's all over, it's all over.

ESTRAGON: I was on top of a —

VLADIMIR: Don't tell me! Come, we'll walk it off.

[*He takes* ESTRAGON *by the arm and walks him up and down until* ESTRAGON *refuses to go any further.*]

ESTRAGON: That's enough. I'm tired.

VLADIMIR: You'd rather be stuck there doing nothing?

ESTRAGON: Yes.

VLADIMIR: Please yourself.

[*He releases* ESTRAGON, *picks up his coat and puts it on.*]

ESTRAGON: Let's go.

VLADIMIR: We can't.

ESTRAGON: Why not?

VLADIMIR: We're waiting for Godot.

ESTRAGON: Ah! [VLADIMIR *walks up and down.*] Can you not stay still?

VLADIMIR: I'm cold.

ESTRAGON: We came too soon.

VLADIMIR: It's always at nightfall.

ESTRAGON: But night doesn't fall.

VLADIMIR: It'll fall all of a sudden, like yesterday.

ESTRAGON: Then it'll be night.

VLADIMIR: And we can go.

ESTRAGON: Then it'll be day again. [*Pause. Despairing.*] What'll we do, what'll we do!

VLADIMIR: [*Halting, violently.*] Will you stop whining! I've had about my bellyful of your lamentations!

ESTRAGON: I'm going.

VLADIMIR: [*Seeing Lucky's hat.*] Well!

ESTRAGON: Farewell.

VLADIMIR: Lucky's hat. [*He goes towards it.*] I've been here an hour and never saw it. [*Very pleased.*] Fine!

ESTRAGON: You'll never see me again.

VLADIMIR: I knew it was the right place. Now our troubles are over. [*He picks up the hat, contemplates it, straightens it.*] Must have been a very fine hat. [*He puts it on in place of his own which he hands to* ESTRAGON.] Here.

ESTRAGON: What?

VLADIMIR: Hold that.

[ESTRAGON *takes Vladimir's hat.* VLADIMIR *adjusts Lucky's hat on his head.* ESTRAGON *puts on Vladimir's hat in place of his own which he hands to* VLADIMIR. VLADIMIR *takes Estragon's hat.* ESTRAGON *adjusts Vladimir's hat on his head.* VLADIMIR *puts on Estragon's hat in place of Lucky's which he hands to* ESTRAGON. ESTRAGON *takes Lucky's hat.* VLADIMIR *adjusts Estragon's hat on his head.* ESTRAGON *puts on Lucky's hat in place of Vladimir's which he hands to* VLADIMIR. VLADIMIR *takes his hat.* ESTRAGON *adjusts Lucky's hat on his head.* VLADIMIR *puts on his hat in place of Estragon's which he hands to* ESTRAGON. ESTRAGON *takes his hat.* VLADIMIR *adjusts his hat on his head.* ESTRAGON *puts on his hat in place of Lucky's which he hands to* VLADIMIR. VLADIMIR *takes Lucky's hat.* ESTRAGON *adjusts his hat on his head.* VLADIMIR *puts on Lucky's hat in place of his own which he hands to* ESTRAGON. ESTRAGON *takes Vladimir's hat.* VLADIMIR *adjusts Lucky's hat on his head.* ESTRAGON *hands Vladimir's hat back to* VLADIMIR *who takes it and hands it back to* ESTRAGON *who takes it and hands it back to* VLADIMIR *who takes it and throws it down.*]

How does it fit me?

ESTRAGON: How would I know?

VLADIMIR: No, but how do I look in it?

[*He turns his head coquettishly to and fro, minces like a mannequin.*]

ESTRAGON: Hideous.

VLADIMIR: Yes, but not more so than usual?

ESTRAGON: Neither more nor less.

VLADIMIR: Then I can keep it. Mine irked me. [*Pause.*] How shall I say? [*Pause.*] It itched me.

[*He takes of Lucky's hat, peers into it, shakes it, knocks on the crown, puts it on again.*]

ESTRAGON: I'm going.

[*Silence.*]

VLADIMIR: Will you not play?

ESTRAGON: Play at what?

VLADIMIR: We could play at Pozzo and Lucky.

ESTRAGON: Never heard of it.

VLADIMIR: I'll do Lucky, you do Pozzo. [*He imitates* LUCKY *sagging under the weight of his baggage.* ESTRAGON *looks at him with stupefaction.*] Go on.

ESTRAGON: What am I to do?

VLADIMIR: Curse me!

ESTRAGON: [*After reflection.*] Naughty!

VLADIMIR: Stronger!

ESTRAGON: Gonococcus! Spirochaete!

[VLADIMIR *sways back and forth, doubled in two.*]

VLADIMIR: Tell me to think.

ESTRAGON: What?

VLADIMIR: Say, Think, pig!

ESTRAGON: Think, pig!

[*Silence.*]

VLADIMIR: I can't.

ESTRAGON: That's enough of that.

VLADIMIR: Tell me to dance.

ESTRAGON: I'm going.

VLADIMIR: Dance, hog! [*He writhes. Exit* ESTRAGON *left, precipitately.*] I can't! [*He looks up, misses* ESTRAGON.] Gogo! [*He moves wildly about the stage. Enter* ESTRAGON *left, panting. He hastens towards* VLADIMIR, *falls into his arms.*] There you are again at last!

ESTRAGON: I'm accursed!

VLADIMIR: Where were you! I thought you were gone for ever.

ESTRAGON: They're coming!

VLADIMIR: Who?

ESTRAGON: I don't know.

VLADIMIR: How many?

ESTRAGON: I don't know.

VLADIMIR: [*Triumphantly.*] It's Godot! At last! Gogo! It's Godot! We're saved! Let's go and meet him! [*He drags* ESTRAGON *towards the wings.* ESTRAGON *resists, pulls himself free, exit right.*] Gogo! Come back! [VLADIMIR

runs to extreme left, scans the horizon. Enter ESTRAGON
right, he hastens towards VLADIMIR, *falls into his arms.*]
There you are again again!

ESTRAGON: I'm in hell!

VLADIMIR: Where were you?

ESTRAGON: They're coming there too!

VLADIMIR: We're surrounded! [ESTRAGON *makes a rush
towards back.*] Imbecile! There's no way out there. [*He
takes* ESTRAGON *by the arm and drags him towards front.
Gesture towards front.*] There! Not a soul in sight! Off
you go. Quick! [*He pushes* ESTRAGON *towards
auditorium.* ESTRAGON *recoils in horror.*] You won't? [*He
contemplates auditorium.*] Well, I can understand that.
Wait till I see. [*He reflects.*] Your only hope left is to
disappear.

ESTRAGON: Where?

VLADIMIR: Behind the tree. [ESTRAGON *hesitates.*] Quick!
Behind the tree. [ESTRAGON *goes and crouches behind the
tree, realizes he is not hidden, comes out from behind the
tree.*] Decidedly this tree will not have been of the slightest
use to us.

ESTRAGON: [*Calmer.*] I lost my head. Forgive me. It won't
happen again. Tell me what to do.

VLADIMIR: There's nothing to do.

ESTRAGON: You go and stand there. [*He draws* VLADIMIR *to
extreme right and places him with his back to the stage.*]
There, don't move, and watch out. [VLADIMIR *scans
horizon, screening his eyes with his hand.* ESTRAGON *runs
and takes up same position, extreme left. They turn their
heads and look at each other.*] Back to back like in the
good old days! [*They continue to look at each other for a
moment, then resume their watch. Long silence.*] Do you
see anything coming?

VLADIMIR: [*Turning his head.*] What?

ESTRAGON: [*Louder.*] Do you see anything coming?

VLADIMIR: No.

ESTRAGON: Nor I.

[*They resume their watch. Silence.*]

VLADIMIR: You must have had a vision.

ESTRAGON: [*Turning his head.*] What?

VLADIMIR: [*Louder.*] You must have had a vision!

ESTRAGON: No need to shout!

[*They resume their watch. Silence.*]

VLADIMIR:
ESTRAGON: } [*Turning simulataneously.*] Do you —

VLADIMIR: Oh, pardon!

ESTRAGON: Carry on.

VLADIMIR: No no, after you.

ESTRAGON: No no, you first.

VLADIMIR: I interrupted you.

ESTRAGON: On the contrary.

[*They glare at each other angrily.*]

VLADIMIR: Ceremonious ape!

ESTRAGON: Punctilious pig!

VLADIMIR: Finish your phrase, I tell you!

ESTRAGON: Finish your own!

[*Silence. They draw closer, halt.*]

VLADIMIR: Moron!

ESTRAGON: That's the idea, let's abuse each other.

[*They turn, move apart, turn again and face each other.*]

VLADIMIR: Moron!

ESTRAGON: Vermin!

VLADIMIR: Abortion!

ESTRAGON: Morpion!

VLADIMIR: Sewer-rat!

ESTRAGON: Curate!

VLADIMIR: Cretin!

ESTRAGON: [*With finality.*] Crritic!

VLADIMIR: Oh!

[*He wilts, vanquished, and turns away.*]

ESTRAGON: Now let's make it up.

VLADIMIR: Gogo!

ESTRAGON: Didi!

VLADIMIR: Your hand!

ESTRAGON: Take it!

VLADIMIR: Come to my arms!

ESTRAGON: Your arms?

VLADIMIR: My breast!

ESTRAGON: Off we go!

[*They embrace. They separate. Silence.*]

VLADIMIR: How time flies when one has fun!

[*Silence.*]

ESTRAGON: What do we do now?

VLADIMIR: While waiting.

ESTRAGON: While waiting.

[*Silence.*]

VLADIMIR: We could do our exercises.

ESTRAGON: Our movements.

VLADIMIR: Our elevations.

ESTRAGON: Our relaxations.

VLADIMIR: Our elongations.

ESTRAGON: Our relaxations.

VLADIMIR: To warm us up.

ESTRAGON: To calm us down.

VLADIMIR: Off we go.

[VLADIMIR *hops from one foot to the other.* ESTRAGON *imitates him.*]

ESTRAGON: [*Stopping.*] That's enough. I'm tired.

VLADIMIR: [*Stopping.*] We're not in form. What about a little deep breathing?

ESTRAGON: I'm tired breathing.

VLADIMIR: You're right. [*Pause.*] Let's just do the tree, for the balance.

ESTRAGON: The tree?

[VLADIMIR *does the tree, staggering about on one leg.*]

VLADIMIR: [*Stopping.*] Your turn.

[ESTRAGON *does the tree, staggers.*]

ESTRAGON: Do you think God sees me?

VLADIMIR: You must close your eyes.

[ESTRAGON *closes his eyes, staggers worse.*]

ESTRAGON: [*Stopping, brandishing his fists, at the top of his voice.*] God have pity on me!

VLADIMIR: [*Vexed.*] And me?

ESTRAGON: On me! On me! Pity! On me!

[*Enter* POZZO *and* LUCKY. POZZO *is blind.* LUCKY *burdened as before. Rope as before, but much shorter, so that* POZZO *may follow more easily.* LUCKY *wearing a different hat. At the sight of* VLADIMIR *and* ESTRAGON *he stops short.* POZZO, *continuing on his way, bumps into him.*]

VLADIMIR: Gogo!

POZZO: [*Clutching on to* LUCKY *who staggers.*] What is it? Who is it?

[LUCKY *falls, drops everything and brings down* POZZO *with him. They lie helpless among the scattered baggage.*]

ESTRAGON: Is it Godot?

VLADIMIR: At last! [*He goes towards the heap.*] Reinforcements at last!

POZZO: Help!

ESTRAGON: Is it Godot?

VLADIMIR: We were beginning to weaken. Now we're sure to see the evening out.

POZZO: Help!

ESTRAGON: Do you hear him?

VLADIMIR: We are no longer alone, waiting for the night, waiting for Godot, waiting for . . . waiting. All evening we have struggled, unassisted. Now it's over. It's already tomorrow.

POZZO: Help!

VLADIMIR: Time flows again already. The sun will set, the moon will rise, and we away . . . from here.

POZZO: Pity!

VLADIMIR: Poor Pozzo!

ESTRAGON: I knew it was him.

VLADIMIR: Who?

ESTRAGON: Godot.

VLADIMIR: But it's not Godot.

ESTRAGON: It's not Godot?

VLADIMIR: It's not Godot.

ESTRAGON: Then who is it?

VLADIMIR: It's Pozzo.

POZZO: Here! Here! Help me up!

VLADIMIR: He can't get up.

ESTRAGON: Let's go.

VLADIMIR: We can't.

ESTRAGON: Why not?

VLADIMIR: We're waiting for Godot.

ESTRAGON: Ah!

VLADIMIR: Perhaps he has another bone for you.

ESTRAGON: Bone?

VLADIMIR: Chicken. Do you not remember?

ESTRAGON: It was him?

VLADIMIR: Yes.

ESTRAGON: Ask him.

VLADIMIR: Perhaps we should help him first.

ESTRAGON: To do what?

VLADIMIR: To get up.

ESTRAGON: He can't get up?

VLADIMIR: He wants to get up.

ESTRAGON: Then let him get up.

VLADIMIR: He can't.

ESTRAGON: Why not?

VLADIMIR: I don't know.

    [POZZO *writhes, groans, beats the ground with his fists.*]

ESTRAGON: We should ask him for the bone first. Then if he refuses we'll leave him there.

VLADIMIR: You mean we have him at our mercy?

ESTRAGON: Yes.

VLADIMIR: And that we should subordinate our good offices to certain conditions.

ESTRAGON: What?

VLADIMIR: That seems intelligent all right. But there's one thing I'm afraid of.

POZZO: Help!

ESTRAGON: What?

VLADIMIR: That Lucky might get going all of a sudden. Then we'd be ballocksed.

ESTRAGON: Lucky?

VLADIMIR: He's the one who went for you yesterday.

ESTRAGON: I tell you there was ten of them.

VLADIMIR: No, before that, the one that kicked you.

ESTRAGON: Is he there?

VLADIMIR: As large as life. [*Gesture towards* LUCKY.] For the moment he is inert. But he might run amuck any minute.

POZZO: Help!

ESTRAGON: And suppose we gave him a good beating, the two
of us?

VLADIMIR: You mean if we fell on him in his sleep?

ESTRAGON: Yes.

VLADIMIR: That seems a good idea all right. But could we do
it? Is he really asleep? [*Pause.*] No, the best would be to
take advantage of Pozzo's calling for help —

POZZO: Help!

VLADIMIR: To help him —

ESTRAGON: *We* help *him*?

VLADIMIR: In anticipation of some tangible return.

ESTRAGON: And suppose he —

VLADIMIR: Let us not waste our time in idle discourse! [*Pause.
Vehemently.*] Let us do something, while we have the
chance! It is not every day that we are needed. Not indeed
that we personally are needed. Others would meet the case
equally well, if not better. To all mankind they were
addressed, those cries for help still ringing in our ears! But
at this place, at this moment of time, all mankind is us,
whether we like it or not. Let us make the most of it,
before it is too late! Let us represent worthily for once the
foul brood to which a cruel fate consigned us! What do
you say? [ESTRAGON *says nothing.*] It is true that when
with folded arms we weigh the pros and cons we are no
less a credit to our species. The tiger bounds to the help of
his congeners without the least reflection, or else he slinks
away into the depths of the thickets. But that is not the
question. What are we doing here, *that* is the question.
And we are blessed in this, that we happen to know the
answer. Yes, in this immense confusion one thing alone is
clear. We are waiting for Godot to come —

ESTRAGON: Ah!

POZZO: Help!

VLADIMIR: Or for night to fall. [*Pause.*] We have kept our
appointment, and that's an end to that. We are not saints,
but we have kept our appointment. How many people can
boast as much?

ESTRAGON: Billions.

VLADIMIR: You think so?

ESTRAGON: I don't know.

VLADIMIR: You may be right.

POZZO: Help!

VLADIMIR: All I know is that the hours are long, under these conditions, and constrain us to beguile them with proceedings which – how shall I say – which may at first sight seem reasonable, until they become a habit. You may say it is to prevent our reason from foundering. No doubt. But has it not long been straying in the night without end of the abyssal depths? That's what I sometimes wonder. You follow my reasoning?

ESTRAGON: [*Aphoristic for once.*] We all are born mad. Some remain so.

POZZO: Help! I'll pay you!

ESTRAGON: How much?

POZZO: One hundred francs!

ESTRAGON: It's not enough.

VLADIMIR: I wouldn't go so far as that.

ESTRAGON: You think it's enough?

VLADIMIR: No, I mean so far as to assert that I was weak in the head when I came into the world. But that is not the question.

POZZO: Two hundred!

VLADIMIR: We wait. We are bored. [*He throws up his hand.*] No, don't protest, we are bored to death, there's no denying it. Good. A diversion comes along and what do we do? We let it go to waste. Come, let's get to work! [*He advances towards the heap, stops in his stride.*] In an instant all will vanish and we'll be alone once more, in the midst of nothingness!
[*He broods.*]

POZZO: Two hundred!

VLADIMIR: We're coming!
[*He tries to pull* POZZO *to his feet, fails, tries again, stumbles, falls, tries to get up, fails.*]

ESTRAGON: What's the matter with you all?

VLADIMIR: Help!

ESTRAGON: I'm going.

VLADIMIR: Don't leave me! They'll kill me!

POZZO: Where am I?

VLADIMIR: Gogo!

POZZO: Help!

VLADIMIR: Help!

ESTRAGON: I'm going.

VLADIMIR: Help me up first. Then we'll go together.

ESTRAGON: You promise?

VLADIMIR: I swear it!

ESTRAGON: And we'll never come back?

VLADIMIR: Never!

ESTRAGON: We'll go to the Pyrenees.

VLADIMIR: Wherever you like.

ESTRAGON: I've always wanted to wander in the Pyrenees.

VLADIMIR: You'll wander in them.

ESTRAGON: [*Recoiling.*] Who farted?

VLADIMIR: Pozzo.

POZZO: Here! Here! Pity!

ESTRAGON: It's revolting!

VLADIMIR: Quick! Give me your hand.

ESTRAGON: I'm going. [*Pause. Louder.*] I'm going.

VLADIMIR: Well I suppose in the end I'll get up by myself. [*He tries, fails.*] In the fullness of time.

ESTRAGON: What's the matter with you?

VLADIMIR: Go to hell.

ESTRAGON: Are you staying there?

VLADIMIR: For the time being.

ESTRAGON: Come on, get up, you'll catch a chill.

VLADIMIR: Don't worry about me.

ESTRAGON: Come on, Didi, don't be pig-headed.

    [*He stretches out his hand which* VLADIMIR *makes haste to seize.*]

VLADIMIR: Pull!

    [ESTRAGON *pulls, stumbles, falls. Long silence.*]

POZZO: Help!

VLADIMIR: We've arrived.

POZZO: Who are you?

VLADIMIR: We are men.

    [*Silence.*]

ESTRAGON: Sweet mother earth!

VLADIMIR: Can you get up?

ESTRAGON: I don't know.

VLADIMIR: Try.

ESTRAGON: Not now, not now.

[*Silence.*]

POZZO: What happened?

VLADIMIR: [*Violently.*] Will you stop it, you! Pest! He thinks of nothing but himself!

ESTRAGON: What about a little snooze?

VLADIMIR: Did you hear him? He wants to know what happened!

ESTRAGON: Don't mind him. Sleep.

[*Silence.*]

POZZO: Pity! Pity!

ESTRAGON: [*With a start.*] What is it?

VLADIMIR: Were you asleep?

ESTRAGON: I must have been.

VLADIMIR: It's this bastard Pozzo at it again.

ESTRAGON: Make him stop it. Kick him in the crotch.

VLADIMIR: [*Striking* POZZO.] Will you stop it! Crablouse!

[POZZO *extricates himself with cries of pain and crawls away. He stops, saws the air blindly, calling for help.* VLADIMIR, *propped on his elbow, observes his retreat.*] He's off! [POZZO *collapses.*] He's down!

ESTRAGON: What do we do now?

VLADIMIR: Perhaps I could crawl to him.

ESTRAGON: Don't leave me!

VLADIMIR: Or I could call to him.

ESTRAGON: Yes, call to him.

VLADIMIR: Pozzo! [*Silence.*] Pozzo! [*Silence.*] No reply.

ESTRAGON: Together.

ESTRAGON: } Pozzo! Pozzo!
VLADIMIR: }

VLADIMIR: He moved.

ESTRAGON: Are you sure his name is Pozzo?

VLADIMIR: [*Alarmed.*] Mr Pozzo! Come back! We won't hurt you!

[*Silence.*]

ESTRAGON: We might try him with other names.

VLADIMIR: I'm afraid he's dying.

ESTRAGON: It'd be amusing.

VLADIMIR: What'd be amusing?

ESTRAGON: To try with other names, one after the other. It'd pass the time. And we'd be bound to hit on the right one sooner or later.

VLADIMIR: I tell you his name is Pozzo.

ESTRAGON: We'll soon see. [*He reflects.*] Abel! Abel!

POZZO: Help!

ESTRAGON: Got it in one!

VLADIMIR: I begin to weary of this motif.

ESTRAGON: Perhaps the other is called Cain. Cain! Cain!

POZZO: Help!

ESTRAGON: He's all humanity. [*Silence.*] Look at the little cloud.

VLADIMIR: [*Raising his eyes.*] Where?

ESTRAGON: There. In the zenith.

VLADIMIR: Well? [*Pause.*] What is there so wonderful about it? [*Silence.*]

ESTRAGON: Let's pass on now to something else, do you mind?

VLADIMIR: I was just going to suggest it.

ESTRAGON: But to what?

VLADIMIR: Ah!
  [*Silence.*]

ESTRAGON: Suppose we got up to begin with.

VLADIMIR: No harm in trying.
  [*They get up.*]

ESTRAGON: Child's play.

VLADIMIR: Simple question of will-power.

ESTRAGON: And now?

POZZO: Help!

ESTRAGON: Let's go.

VLADIMIR: We can't.

ESTRAGON: Why not?

VLADIMIR: We're waiting for Godot.

ESTRAGON: Ah! [*Despairing.*] What'll we do, what'll we do!

POZZO: Help!

VLADIMIR: What about helping him?

ESTRAGON: What does he want?

VLADIMIR: He wants to get up.

ESTRAGON: Then why doesn't he?

VLADIMIR: He wants us to help him to get up.

ESTRAGON: Then why don't we? What are we waiting for?
  [*They help* POZZO *to his feet, let him go. He falls.*]

VLADIMIR: We must hold him. [*They get him up again.*
  POZZO *sags between them, his arms round their necks.*]
  Feeling better?

POZZO: Who are you?

VLADIMIR: Do you not recognize us?

POZZO: I am blind.
  [*Silence.*]

ESTRAGON: Perhaps he can see into the future.

VLADIMIR: Since when?

POZZO: I used to have wonderful sight – but are you friends?

ESTRAGON: [*Laughing noisily.*] He wants to know if we are
  friends!

VLADIMIR: No, he means friends of his.

ESTRAGON: Well?

VLADIMIR: We've proved we are, by helping him.

ESTRAGON: Exactly. Would we have helped him if we weren't
  his friends?

VLADIMIR: Possibly.

ESTRAGON: True.

VLADIMIR: Don't let's quibble about that now.

POZZO: You are not highwaymen?

ESTRAGON: Highwaymen! Do we look like highwaymen?

VLADIMIR: Damn it, can't you see the man is blind!

ESTRAGON: Damn it, so he is. [*Pause.*] So he says.

POZZO: Don't leave me!

VLADIMIR: No question of it.

ESTRAGON: For the moment.

POZZO: What time is it?

VLADIMIR: [*Inspecting the sky.*] Seven o'clock . . . eight
  o'clock . . .

ESTRAGON: That depends what time of year it is.

POZZO: Is it evening?
  [*Silence.* VLADIMIR *and* ESTRAGON *scrutinize the sunset.*]

ESTRAGON: It's rising.

VLADIMIR: Impossible.

ESTRAGON: Perhaps it's the dawn.

VLADIMIR: Don't be a fool. It's the west over there.

ESTRAGON: How do you know?

POZZO: [*Anguished.*] Is it evening?

VLADIMIR: Anyway it hasn't moved.

ESTRAGON: I tell you it's rising.

POZZO: Why don't you answer me?

ESTRAGON: Give us a chance.

VLADIMIR: [*Reassuring.*] It's evening, sir, it's evening, night is drawing nigh. My friend here would have me doubt it and I must confess he shook me for a moment. But it is not for nothing I have lived through this long day and I can assure you it is very near the end of its repertory. [*Pause.*] How do you feel now?

ESTRAGON: How much longer must we cart him round? [*They half release him, catch him again as he falls.*] We are not caryatids!

VLADIMIR: You were saying your sight used to be good, if I heard you right.

POZZO: Wonderful! Wonderful, wonderful sight!
[*Silence.*]

ESTRAGON: [*Irritably.*] Expand! Expand!

VLADIMIR: Let him alone. Can't you see he's thinking of the days when he was happy? [*Pause.*] *Memoria praeteritorum bonorum* – that must be unpleasant.

ESTRAGON: We wouldn't know.

VLADIMIR: And it came on you all of a sudden?

POZZO: Quite wonderful!

VLADIMIR: I'm asking you if it came on you all of a sudden.

POZZO: I woke up one fine day as blind as Fortune. [*Pause.*] Sometimes I wonder if I'm not still asleep.

VLADIMIR: And when was that?

POZZO: I don't know.

VLADIMIR: But no later than yesterday –

POZZO: [*Violently.*] Don't question me! The blind have no notion of time. The things of time are hidden from them too.

VLADIMIR: Well just fancy that! I could have sworn it was just the opposite.

ESTRAGON: I'm going.

POZZO: Where are we?

VLADIMIR: I couldn't tell you.

POZZO: It isn't by any chance the place known as the Board?

VLADIMIR: Never heard of it.

POZZO: What is it like?

VLADIMIR: [*Looking round.*] It's indescribable. It's like nothing. There's nothing. There's a tree.

POZZO: Then it's not the Board.

ESTRAGON: [*Sagging.*] Some diversion!

POZZO: Where is my menial?

VLADIMIR: He's about somewhere.

POZZO: Why doesn't he answer when I call?

VLADIMIR: I don't know. He seems to be sleeping. Perhaps he's dead.

POZZO: What happened exactly?

ESTRAGON: Exactly!

VLADIMIR: The two of you slipped. [*Pause.*] And fell.

POZZO: Go and see is he hurt.

VLADIMIR: We can't leave you.

POZZO: You needn't both go.

VLADIMIR: [*To* ESTRAGON.] You go.

ESTRAGON: After what he did to me? Never!

POZZO: Yes yes, let your friend go, he stinks so. [*Silence.*] What is he waiting for?

VLADIMIR: What are you waiting for?

ESTRAGON: I'm waiting for Godot.
[*Silence.*]

VLADIMIR: What exactly should he do?

POZZO: Well to begin with he should pull on the rope, as hard as he likes so long as he doesn't strangle him. He usually responds to that. If not he should give him a taste of his boot, in the face and the privates as far as possible.

VLADIMIR: [*To* ESTRAGON.] You see, you've nothing to be afraid of. It's even an opportunity to revenge yourself.

ESTRAGON: And if he defends himself?

POZZO: No no, he never defends himself.

VLADIMIR: I'll come flying to the rescue.

ESTRAGON: Don't take your eyes off me.

[*He goes towards* LUCKY.]

VLADIMIR: Make sure he's alive before you start. No point in exerting yourself if he's dead.

ESTRAGON: [*Bending over* LUCKY]. He's breathing.

VLADIMIR: Then let him have it.

[*With sudden fury* VLADIMIR *starts kicking* LUCKY, *hurling abuse at him as he does so. But he hurts his foot and moves away limping and groaning.* LUCKY *stirs.*]

ESTRAGON: Oh the brute!

[*He sits down on the mound and tries to take off his boot. But he soon desists and disposes himself for sleep, his arms on his knees and his head on his arms.*]

POZZO: What's gone wrong now?

VLADIMIR: My friend has hurt himself.

POZZO: And Lucky?

VLADIMIR: So it is he?

POZZO: What?

VLADIMIR: It is Lucky?

POZZO: I don't understand.

VLADIMIR: And you are Pozzo?

POZZO: Certainly I am Pozzo.

VLADIMIR: The same as yesterday?

POZZO: Yesterday?

VLADIMIR: We met yesterday. [*Silence.*] Do you not remember?

POZZO: I don't remember having met anyone yesterday. But tomorrow I won't remember having met anyone today. So don't count on me to enlighten you.

VLADIMIR: But —

POZZO: Enough. Up pig!

VLADIMIR: You were bringing him to the fair to sell him. You spoke to us. He danced. He thought. You had your sight.

POZZO: As you please. Let me go! [VLADIMIR *moves away.*] Up!

[LUCKY *gets up, gathering up his burdens.*]

VLADIMIR: Where do you go from here?

POZZO: On. [LUCKY, *laden down, takes his place before*

POZZO.] Whip! [LUCKY *puts everything down, looks for whip, finds it, puts it into* POZZO's *hand, takes up everything again.*] Rope!
[LUCKY *puts everything down, puts end of the rope into* POZZO's *hand, takes up everything again.*]

VLADIMIR: What is there in the bag?

POZZO: Sand. [*He jerks the rope.*] On!

VLADIMIR: Don't go yet!

POZZO: I'm going.

VLADIMIR: What do you do when you fall far from help?

POZZO: We wait till we can get up. Then we go on. On!

VLADIMIR: Before you go tell him to sing!

POZZO: Who?

VLADIMIR: Lucky.

POZZO: To sing?

VLADIMIR: Yes. Or to think. Or to recite.

POZZO: But he's dumb.

VLADIMIR: Dumb!

POZZO: Dumb. He can't even groan.

VLADIMIR: Dumb! Since when?

POZZO: [*Suddenly furious.*] Have you not done tormenting me with your accursed time! It's abominable! When! When! One day, is that not enough for you, one day like any other day, one day he went dumb, one day I went blind, one day we'll go deaf, one day we were born, one day we shall die, the same day, the same second, is that not enough for you? [*Calmer.*] They give birth astride of a grave, the light gleams an instant, then it's night once more. [*He jerks the rope.*] On!
[*Exeunt* POZZO *and* LUCKY. VLADIMIR *follows them to the edge of the stage, looks after them. The noise of falling, reinforced by mimic of* VLADIMIR, *announces that they are down again. Silence.* VLADIMIR *goes towards* ESTRAGON, *contemplates him a moment, then shakes him awake.*]

ESTRAGON: [*Wild gestures, incoherent words. Finally.*] Why will you never let me sleep?

VLADIMIR: I felt lonely.

ESTRAGON: I was dreaming I was happy.

VLADIMIR: That passed the time.

ESTRAGON: I was dreaming that —

VLADIMIR: [*Violently.*] Don't tell me! [*Silence.*] I wonder is he really blind.

ESTRAGON: Blind? Who?

VLADIMIR: Pozzo.

ESTRAGON: Blind?

VLADIMIR: He told us he was blind.

ESTRAGON: Well what about it?

VLADIMIR: It seemed to me he saw us.

ESTRAGON: You dreamt it. [*Pause.*] Let's go. We can't. Ah! [*Pause.*] Are you sure it wasn't him?

VLADIMIR: Who?

ESTRAGON: Godot.

VLADIMIR: But who?

ESTRAGON: Pozzo.

VLADIMIR: Not at all! [*Less sure.*] Not at all! [*Still less sure.*] Not at all!

ESTRAGON: I suppose I might as well get up. [*He gets up painfully.*] Ow! Didi!

VLADIMIR: I don't know what to think any more.

ESTRAGON: My feet! [*He sits down, tries to take off his boots.*] Help me!

VLADIMIR: Was I sleeping, while the others suffered? Am I sleeping now? Tomorrow, when I wake, or think I do, what shall I say of today? That with Estragon my friend, at this place until the fall of night, I waited for Godot? That Pozzo passed, with his carrier, and that he spoke to us? Probably. But in all that what truth will there be? [*ESTRAGON, having struggled with his boots in vain, is dozing off again. VLADIMIR stares at him.*] He'll know nothing. He'll tell me about the blows he received and I'll give him a carrot. [*Pause.*] Astride of a grave and a difficult birth. Down in the hole, lingeringly, the grave-digger puts on the forceps. We have time to grow old. The air is full of our cries. [*He listens.*] But habit is a great deadener. [*He looks again at ESTRAGON.*] At me too someone is looking, of me too someone is saying, he is sleeping, he knows nothing, let him sleep on. [*Pause.*] I can't go on! [*Pause.*] What have I said?

[*He goes feverishly to and fro, halts finally at extreme left, broods. Enter* BOY *right. He halts. Silence.*]

BOY: Mister . . . [VLADIMIR *turns.*] Mr Albert . . .

VLADIMIR: Off we go again. [*Pause.*] Do you not recognize me?

BOY: No, sir.

VLADIMIR: It wasn't you came yesterday.

BOY: No, sir.

VLADIMIR: This is your first time.

BOY: Yes, sir.

　[*Silence.*]

VLADIMIR: You have a message from Mr Godot.

BOY: Yes, sir.

VLADIMIR: He won't come this evening.

BOY: No, sir.

VLADIMIR: But he'll come tomorrow.

BOY: Yes, sir.

VLADIMIR: Without fail.

BOY: Yes, sir.

　[*Silence.*]

VLADIMIR: Did you meet anyone?

BOY: No, sir.

VLADIMIR: Two other . . . [*He hesitates*] . . . men?

BOY: I didn't see anyone, sir.

　[*Silence.*]

VLADIMIR: What does he do, Mr Godot? [*Silence.*] Do you hear me?

BOY: Yes, sir.

VLADIMIR: Well?

BOY: He does nothing, sir.

　[*Silence.*]

VLADIMIR: How is your brother?

BOY: He's sick, sir.

VLADIMIR: Perhaps it was he came yesterday.

BOY: I don't know, sir.

　[*Silence.*]

VLADIMIR: [*Softly.*] Has he a beard, Mr Godot?

BOY: Yes, sir.

VLADIMIR: Fair or . . . [*He hesitates*] . . . or black?

BOY: I think it's white, sir.

 [*Silence.*]

VLADIMIR: Christ have mercy on us!

 [*Silence.*]

BOY: What am I to tell Mr Godot, sir?

VLADIMIR: Tell him . . . [*He hesitates*] . . . tell him you saw
 me and that . . . [*He hesitates*] . . . that you saw me.
 [*Pause.* VLADIMIR *advances, the* BOY *recoils.* VLADIMIR
 halts, the* BOY *halts. With sudden violence.*] You're sure
 you saw me, you won't come and tell me tomorrow that
 you never saw me!
 [*Silence.* VLADIMIR *makes a sudden spring forward, the*
 BOY *avoids him and exit running. Silence. The sun sets,
 the moon rises. As in Act One.* VLADIMIR *stands
 motionless and bowed.* ESTRAGON *wakes, takes off his
 boots, gets up with one in each hand and goes and puts
 them down centre front, then goes towards* VLADIMIR.]

ESTRAGON: What's wrong with you?

VLADIMIR: Nothing.

ESTRAGON: I'm going.

VLADIMIR: So am I.

ESTRAGON: Was I long asleep?

VLADIMIR: I don't know.

 [*Silence.*]

ESTRAGON: Where shall we go?

VLADIMIR: Not far.

ESTRAGON: Oh yes, let's go far away from here.

VLADIMIR: We can't.

ESTRAGON: Why not?

VLADIMIR: We have to come back tomorrow.

ESTRAGON: What for?

VLADIMIR: To wait for Godot.

ESTRAGON: Ah! [*Silence.*] He didn't come?

VLADIMIR: No.

ESTRAGON: And now it's too late.

VLADIMIR: Yes, now it's night.

ESTRAGON: And if we dropped him? [*Pause.*] If we dropped him?

VLADIMIR: He'd punish us. [*Silence. He looks at the tree.*] Everything's dead but the tree.

ESTRAGON: [*Looking at the tree.*] What is it?

VLADIMIR: It's the tree.

ESTRAGON: Yes, but what kind?

VLADIMIR: I don't know. A willow.

[ESTRAGON *draws* VLADIMIR *towards the tree. They stand motionless before it. Silence.*]

ESTRAGON: Why don't we hang ourselves?

VLADIMIR: With what?

ESTRAGON: You haven't got a bit of rope?

VLADIMIR: No.

ESTRAGON: Then we can't.

[*Silence.*]

VLADIMIR: Let's go.

ESTRAGON: Wait, there's my belt.

VLADIMIR: It's too short.

ESTRAGON: You could hang on to my legs.

VLADIMIR: And who'd hang on to mine?

ESTRAGON: True.

VLADIMIR: Show all the same. [ESTRAGON *loosens the cord that holds up his trousers which, much too big for him, fall about his ankles. They look at the cord.*] It might do at a pinch. But is it strong enough?

ESTRAGON: We'll soon see. Here.

[*They each take an end of the cord and pull. It breaks. They almost fall.*]

VLADIMIR: Not worth a curse.

[*Silence.*]

ESTRAGON: You say we have to come back tomorrow?

VLADIMIR: Yes.

ESTRAGON: Then we can bring a good bit of rope.

VLADIMIR: Yes.

[*Silence.*]

ESTRAGON: Didi.

VLADIMIR: Yes.

ESTRAGON: I can't go on like this.

VLADIMIR: That's what you think.

ESTRAGON: If we parted? That might be better for us.

VLADIMIR: We'll hang ourselves tomorrow. [*Pause.*] Unless Godot comes.

ESTRAGON: And if he comes?

VLADIMIR: We'll be saved.

[VLADIMIR *takes off his hat (Lucky's), peers inside it, feels about inside it, shakes it, knocks on the crown, puts it on again.*]

ESTRAGON: Well? Shall we go?

VLADIMIR: Pull on your trousers.

ESTRAGON: What?

VLADIMIR: Pull on your trousers.

ESTRAGON: You want me to pull off my trousers?

VLADIMIR: Pull ON your trousers.

ESTRAGON: [*Realizing his trousers are down.*] True.
[*He pulls up his trousers.*]

VLADIMIR: Well? Shall we go?

ESTRAGON: Yes, let's go.
[*They do not move.*]

CURTAIN

Endgame

A play in one act

For Roger Blin

First performed in Great Britain in French as *Fin de partie* on 3 April 1957 at the Royal Court Theatre, London. English translation by the author first published in 1958 by Faber and Faber Limited.

CAST

HAMM
CLOV
NAGG
NELL

Bare interior.

Grey light.

Left and right back, high up, two small windows, curtains drawn.

Front right, a door. Hanging near door, its face to wall, a picture.

Front left, touching each other, covered with an old sheet, two ashbins.

Centre, in an armchair on castors, covered with an old sheet, HAMM.

Motionless by the door, his eyes fixed on HAMM, CLOV. *Very red face.*

Brief tableau.

CLOV *goes and stands under window left. Stiff, staggering walk. He looks up at window left. He turns and looks at window right. He goes and stands under window right. He looks up at window right. He turns and looks at window left. He goes out, comes back immediately with a small step-ladder, carries it over and sets it down under window left, gets up on it, draws back curtain. He gets down, takes six steps [for example] towards window right, goes back for ladder, carries it over and sets it down under window right, gets up on it, draws back curtain. He gets down, takes three steps towards window left, goes back for ladder, carries it over and sets it down under window left, gets up on it, looks out of window. Brief laugh. He gets down, takes one step towards window right, goes back for ladder, carries it over and sets it down under window right, gets up on it, looks out of window. Brief laugh. He gets down, goes with ladder towards ashbins, halts, turns, carries back ladder and sets it down under window right, goes to ashbins, removes sheet covering them, folds it over his arm. He raises one lid, stoops and looks into bin. Brief laugh. He closes lid. Same with other bin. He goes to* HAMM, *removes sheet*

*covering him, folds it over his arm. In a dressing-gown, a stiff
toque on his head, a large blood-stained handkerchief over his
face, a whistle hanging from his neck, a rug over his knees,
thick socks on his feet,* HAMM *seems to be asleep.* CLOV *looks
him over. Brief laugh. He goes to door, halts, turns towards
auditorium.*

CLOV: [*Fixed gaze, tonelessly.*] Finished, it's finished, nearly
finished, it must be nearly finished. [*Pause.*] Grain upon
grain, one by one, and one day, suddenly, there's a heap, a
little heap, the impossible heap. [*Pause.*] I can't be
punished any more. [*Pause.*] I'll go now to my kitchen, ten
feet by ten feet by ten feet, and wait for him to whistle me.
[*Pause.*] Nice dimensions, nice proportions, I'll lean on the
table, and look at the wall, and wait for him to whistle me.
[*He remains a moment motionless, then goes out. He
comes back immediately, goes to window right, takes up
the ladder and carries it out. Pause.* HAMM *stirs. He yawns
under the handkerchief. He removes the handkerchief from
his face. Very red face. Black glasses.*]

HAMM: Me — [*he yawns*] — to play. [*He holds the handkerchief
spread out before him.*] Old stancher! [*He takes off his
glasses, wipes his eyes, his face, the glasses, puts them on
again, folds the handkerchief and puts it neatly in the
breast-pocket of his dressing-gown. He clears his throat,
joins the tips of his fingers.*] Can there be misery — [*he
yawns*] — loftier than mine? No doubt. Formerly. But
now? [*Pause.*] My father? [*Pause.*] My mother? [*Pause.*]
My . . . dog? [*Pause.*] Oh I am willing to believe they suffer
as much as such creatures can suffer. But does that mean
their sufferings equal mine? No doubt. [*Pause.*] No, all is
a — [*he yawns*] — bsolute, [*proudly*] the bigger a man is the
fuller he is. [*Pause. Gloomily.*] And the emptier. [*He
sniffs.*] Clov! [*Pause.*] No, alone. [*Pause.*] What dreams!
Those forests! [*Pause.*] Enough, it's time it ended, in the
refuge too. [*Pause.*] And yet I hesitate, I hesitate to . . . to
end. Yes, there it is, it's time it ended and yet I hesitate
to — [*he yawns*] — to end. [*Yawns.*] God, I'm tired, I'd be
better off in bed. [*He whistles. Enter* CLOV *immediately.
He halts beside the chair.*] You pollute the air! [*Pause.*] Get

me ready, I'm going to bed.

CLOV: I've just got you up.

HAMM: And what of it?

CLOV: I can't be getting you up and putting you to bed every five minutes, I have things to do.
[*Pause.*]

HAMM: Did you ever see my eyes?

CLOV: No.

HAMM: Did you never have the curiosity, while I was sleeping, to take off my glasses and look at my eyes?

CLOV: Pulling back the lids? [*Pause.*] No.

HAMM: One of these days I'll show them to you. [*Pause.*] It seems they've gone all white. [*Pause.*] What time is it?

CLOV: The same as usual.

HAMM: [*Gesture towards window right.*] Have you looked?

CLOV: Yes.

HAMM: Well?

CLOV: Zero.

HAMM: It'd need to rain.

CLOV: It won't rain.
[*Pause.*]

HAMM: Apart from that, how do you feel?

CLOV: I don't complain.

HAMM: You feel normal?

CLOV: [*Irritably.*] I tell you I don't complain!

HAMM: I feel a little queer. [*Pause.*] Clov!

CLOV: Yes.

HAMM: Have you not had enough?

CLOV: Yes! [*Pause.*] Of what?

HAMM: Of this . . . this . . . thing.

CLOV: I always had. [*Pause.*] Not you?

HAMM: [*Gloomily.*] Then there's no reason for it to change.

CLOV: It may end. [*Pause.*] All life long the same questions, the same answers.

HAMM: Get me ready. [CLOV *does not move.*] Go and get the sheet. [CLOV *does not move.*] Clov!

CLOV: Yes.

HAMM: I'll give you nothing more to eat.

CLOV: Then we'll die.

HAMM: I'll give you just enough to keep you from dying. You'll be hungry all the time.

CLOV: Then we shan't die. [*Pause.*] I'll go and get the sheet. [*He goes towards the door.*]

HAMM: No! [CLOV *halts.*] I'll give you one biscuit per day. [*Pause.*] One and a half. [*Pause.*] Why do you stay with me?

CLOV: Why do you keep me?

HAMM: There's no one else.

CLOV: There's nowhere else.
[*Pause.*]

HAMM: You're leaving me all the same.

CLOV: I'm trying.

HAMM: You don't love me.

CLOV: No.

HAMM: You loved me once.

CLOV: Once!

HAMM: I've made you suffer too much. [*Pause.*] Haven't I?

CLOV: It's not that.

HAMM: [*Shocked.*] I haven't made you suffer too much?

CLOV: Yes!

HAMM: [*Relieved.*] Ah you gave me a fright! [*Pause. Coldly.*] Forgive me. [*Pause. Louder.*] I said, Forgive me.

CLOV: I heard you. [*Pause.*] Have you bled?

HAMM: Less. [*Pause.*] Is it not time for my pain-killer?

CLOV: No.
[*Pause.*]

HAMM: How are your eyes?

CLOV: Bad.

HAMM: How are your legs?

CLOV: Bad.

HAMM: But you can move.

CLOV: Yes.

HAMM: [*Violently.*] Then move! [CLOV *goes to back wall, leans against it with his forehead and hands.*] Where are you?

CLOV: Here.

HAMM: Come back! [CLOV *returns to his place beside the chair.*] Where are you?

CLOV: Here.

HAMM: Why don't you kill me?

CLOV: I don't know the combination of the larder.
[*Pause.*]

HAMM: Go and get two bicycle-wheels.

CLOV: There are no more bicycle-wheels.

HAMM: What have you done with your bicycle?

CLOV: I never had a bicycle.

HAMM: The thing is impossible.

CLOV: When there were still bicycles I wept to have one. I
crawled at your feet. You told me to get out to hell. Now
there are none.

HAMM: And your rounds? When you inspected my paupers.
Always on foot?

CLOV: Sometimes on horse. [*The lid of one of the bins lifts and
the hands of* NAGG *appear, gripping the rim. Then his
head emerges. Nightcap. Very white face.* NAGG *yawns,
then listens.*] I'll leave you, I have things to do.

HAMM: In your kitchen?

CLOV: Yes.

HAMM: Outside of here it's death. [*Pause.*] All right, be off.
[*Exit* CLOV. *Pause.*] We're getting on.

NAGG: Me pap!

HAMM: Accursed progenitor!

NAGG: Me pap!

HAMM: The old folks at home! No decency left! Guzzle,
guzzle, that's all they think of. [*He whistles. Enter* CLOV.
He halts beside the chair.] Well! I thought you were
leaving me.

CLOV: Oh not just yet, not just yet.

NAGG: Me pap!

HAMM: Give him his pap.

CLOV: There's no more pap.

HAMM: [*To* NAGG.] Do you hear that? There's no more pap.
You'll never get any more pap.

NAGG: I want me pap!

HAMM: Give him a biscuit. [*Exit* CLOV.] Accursed fornicator!
How are your stumps?

NAGG: Never mind me stumps.
[*Enter* CLOV *with biscuit.*]

CLOV: I'm back again, with the biscuit.

[*He gives the biscuit to* NAGG *who fingers it, sniffs it.*]

NAGG: [*Plaintively.*] What is it?

CLOV: Spratt's medium.

NAGG: [*As before.*] It's hard! I can't!

HAMM: Bottle him!

[CLOV *pushes* NAGG *back into the bin, closes the lid.*]

CLOV: [*Returning to his place beside the chair.*] If age but knew!

HAMM: Sit on him!

CLOV: I can't sit.

HAMM: True. And I can't stand.

CLOV: So it is.

HAMM: Every man his speciality. [*Pause.*] No phone calls? [*Pause.*] Don't we laugh?

CLOV: [*After reflection.*] I don't feel like it.

HAMM: [*After reflection.*] Nor I. [*Pause.*] Clov!

CLOV: Yes.

HAMM: Nature has forgotten us.

CLOV: There's no more nature.

HAMM: No more nature! You exaggerate.

CLOV: In the vicinity.

HAMM: But we breathe, we change! We lose our hair, our teeth! Our bloom! Our ideals!

CLOV: Then she hasn't forgotten us.

HAMM: But you say there is none.

CLOV: [*Sadly.*] No one that ever lived ever thought so crooked as we.

HAMM: We do what we can.

CLOV: We shouldn't.

[*Pause.*]

HAMM: You're a bit of all right, aren't you?

CLOV: A smithereen.

[*Pause.*]

HAMM: This is slow work. [*Pause.*] Is it not time for my painkiller?

CLOV: No. [*Pause.*] I'll leave you, I have things to do.

HAMM: In your kitchen?

CLOV: Yes.

HAMM: What, I'd like to know.

CLOV: I look at the wall.

HAMM: The wall! And what do you see on your wall? Mene, mene? Naked bodies?

CLOV: I see my light dying.

HAMM: Your light dying! Listen to that! Well, it can die just as well here, *your* light. Take a look at me and then come back and tell me what you think of *your* light.
[*Pause.*]

CLOV: You shouldn't speak to me like that.
[*Pause.*]

HAMM: [*Coldly.*] Forgive me. [*Pause. Louder.*] I said, Forgive me.

CLOV: I heard you.
[*The lid of* NAGG's *bin lifts. His hands appear, gripping the rim. Then his head emerges. In his mouth the biscuit. He listens.*]

HAMM: Did your seeds come up?

CLOV: No.

HAMM: Did you scratch round them to see if they had sprouted?

CLOV: They haven't sprouted.

HAMM: Perhaps it's still too early.

CLOV: If they were going to sprout they would have sprouted.
[*Violently.*] They'll never sprout.
[*Pause.* NAGG *takes biscuit in his hand.*]

HAMM: This is not much fun. [*Pause.*] But that's always the way at the end of the day, isn't it, Clov?

CLOV: Always.

HAMM: It's the end of the day like any other day, isn't it, Clov?

CLOV: Looks like it.
[*Pause.*]

HAMM: [*Anguished.*] What's happening, what's happening?

CLOV: Something is taking its course.
[*Pause.*]

HAMM: All right, be off. [*He leans back in his chair, remains motionless.* CLOV *does not move, heaves a great groaning sigh.* HAMM *sits up.*] I thought I told you to be off.

CLOV: I'm trying. [*He goes to door, halts.*] Ever since I was whelped.

[*Exit* CLOV.]

HAMM: We're getting on.

[*He leans back in his chair, remains motionless.* NAGG *knocks on the lid of the other bin. Pause. He knocks harder. The lid lifts and the hands of* NELL *appear, gripping the rim. Then her head emerges. Lace cap. Very white face.*]

NELL: What is it, my pet? [*Pause.*] Time for love?

NAGG: Were you asleep?

NELL: Oh no!

NAGG: Kiss me.

NELL: We can't.

NAGG: Try.

[*Their heads strain towards each other, fail to meet, fall apart again.*]

NELL: Why this farce, day after day?

[*Pause.*]

NAGG: I've lost me tooth.

NELL: When?

NAGG: I had it yesterday.

NELL: [*Elegiac.*] Ah yesterday!

[*They turn painfully towards each other.*]

NAGG: Can you see me?

NELL: Hardly. And you?

NAGG: What?

NELL: Can you see me?

NAGG: Hardly.

NELL: So much the better, so much the better.

NAGG: Don't say that. [*Pause.*] Our sight has failed.

NELL: Yes.

[*Pause. They turn away from each other.*]

NAGG: Can you hear me?

NELL: Yes. And you?

NAGG: Yes. [*Pause.*] Our hearing hasn't failed.

NELL: Our what?

NAGG: Our hearing.

NELL: No. [*Pause.*] Have you anything else to say to me?

NAGG: Do you remember —

NELL: No.

NAGG: When we crashed on our tandem and lost our shanks.
[*They laugh heartily.*]

NELL: It was in the Ardennes.
[*They laugh less heartily.*]

NAGG: On the road to Sedan. [*They laugh still less heartily.*]
Are you cold?

NELL: Yes, perished. And you?

NAGG: I'm freezing. [*Pause.*] Do you want to go in?

NELL: Yes.

NAGG: Then go in. [NELL *does not move.*] Why don't you go
in?

NELL: I don't know.
[*Pause.*]

NAGG: Has he changed your sawdust?

NELL: It isn't sawdust. [*Pause. Wearily.*] Can you not be a little
accurate, Nagg?

NAGG: Your sand then. It's not important.

NELL: It is important.
[*Pause.*]

NAGG: It was sawdust once.

NELL: Once!

NAGG: And now it's sand. [*Pause.*] From the shore.
[*Pause. Impatiently.*] Now it's sand he fetches from the
shore.

NELL: Now it's sand.

NAGG: Has he changed yours?

NELL: No.

NAGG: Nor mine. [*Pause.*] I won't have it! [*Pause. Holding up
the biscuit.*] Do you want a bit?

NELL: No. [*Pause.*] Of what?

NAGG: Biscuit. I've kept you half. [*He looks at the biscuit.
Proudly.*] Three quarters. For you. Here. [*He proffers the
biscuit.*] No? [*Pause.*] Do you not feel well?

HAMM: [*Wearily.*] Quiet, quiet, you're keeping me awake.
[*Pause.*] Talk softer. [*Pause.*] If I could sleep I might make
love. I'd go into the woods. My eyes would see . . . the sky,
the earth. I'd run, run, they wouldn't catch me. [*Pause.*]
Nature! [*Pause.*] There's something dripping in my head.
[*Pause.*] A heart, a heart in my head.

[*Pause.*]

NAGG: [*Soft.*] Do you hear him? A heart in his head!
[*He chuckles cautiously.*]

NELL: One mustn't laugh at those things, Nagg. Why must you always laugh at them?

NAGG: Not so loud!

NELL: [*Without lowering her voice.*] Nothing is funnier than unhappiness, I grant you that. But —

NAGG: [*Shocked.*] Oh!

NELL: Yes, yes, it's the most comical thing in the world. And we laugh, we laugh, with a will, in the beginning. But it's always the same thing. Yes, it's like the funny story we have heard too often, we still find it funny, but we don't laugh any more. [*Pause.*] Have you anything else to say to me?

NAGG: No.

NELL: Are you quite sure? [*Pause.*] Then I'll leave you.

NAGG: Do you not want your biscuit? [*Pause.*] I'll keep it for you. [*Pause.*] I thought you were going to leave me.

NELL: I am going to leave you.

NAGG: Could you give me a scratch before you go?

NELL: No. [*Pause.*] Where?

NAGG: In the back.

NELL: No. [*Pause.*] Rub yourself against the rim.

NAGG: It's lower down. In the hollow.

NELL: What hollow?

NAGG: The hollow! [*Pause.*] Could you not? [*Pause.*] Yesterday you scratched me there.

NELL: [*Elegiac.*] Ah yesterday!

NAGG: Could you not? [*Pause.*] Would you like me to scratch you? [*Pause.*] Are you crying again?

NELL: I was trying.
[*Pause.*]

HAMM: Perhaps it's a little vein.
[*Pause.*]

NAGG: What was that he said?

NELL: Perhaps it's a little vein.

NAGG: What does that mean? [*Pause.*] That means nothing. [*Pause.*] Will I tell you the story of the tailor?

NELL: No. [*Pause.*] What for?

NAGG: To cheer you up.

NELL: It's not funny.

NAGG: It always made you laugh. [*Pause.*] The first time I thought you'd die.

NELL: It was on Lake Como. [*Pause.*] One April afternoon. [*Pause.*] Can you believe it?

NAGG: What?

NELL: That we once went out rowing on Lake Como. [*Pause.*] One April afternoon.

NAGG: We had got engaged the day before.

NELL: Engaged!

NAGG: You were in such fits that we capsized. By rights we should have been drowned.

NELL: It was because I felt happy.

NAGG: [*Indignant.*] It was not, it was not, it was my story and nothing else. Happy! Don't you laugh at it still? Every time I tell it. Happy!

NELL: It was deep, deep. And you could see down to the bottom. So white. So clean.

NAGG: Let me tell it again. [*Raconteur's voice.*] An Englishman, needing a pair of striped trousers in a hurry for the New Year festivities, goes to his tailor who takes his measurements. [*Tailor's voice.*] 'That's the lot, come back in four days, I'll have it ready.' Good. Four days later. [*Tailor's voice.*] 'So sorry, come back in a week, I've made a mess of the seat.' Good, that's all right, a neat seat can be very ticklish. A week later. [*Tailor's voice.*] 'Frightfully sorry, come back in ten days, I've made a hash of the crutch.' Good, can't be helped, a snug crutch is always a teaser. Ten days later. [*Tailor's voice.*] 'Dreadfully sorry, come back in a fortnight, I've made a balls of the fly.' Good, at a pinch, a smart fly is a stiff proposition. [*Pause. Normal voice.*] I never told it worse. [*Pause. Gloomy.*] I tell this story worse and worse. [*Pause. Raconteur's voice.*] Well, to make it short, the bluebells are blowing and he ballockses the buttonholes. [*Customer's voice.*] 'God damn you to hell, Sir, no, it's indecent, there are limits! In six days, do you hear me, six days, God made

the world. Yes Sir, no less Sir, the WORLD! And you are
not bloody well capable of making me a pair of trousers in
three months!' [*Tailor's voice, scandalized.*] 'But my dear
Sir, my dear Sir, look – [*disdainful gesture, disgustedly*] –
at the world – [*pause*] – and look – [*loving gesture,
proudly*] – at my TROUSERS!'
[*Pause. He looks at* NELL *who has remained impassive,
her eyes unseeing, breaks into a high forced laugh, cuts it
short, pokes his head towards* NELL, *launches his laugh
again.*]

HAMM: Silence!

[NAGG *starts, cuts short his laugh.*]

NELL: You could see down to the bottom.

HAMM: [*Exasperated.*] Have you not finished? Will you never
finish? [*With sudden fury.*] Will this never finish? [NAGG
disappears into his bin, closes the lid behind him. NELL
does not move. Frenziedly.] My kingdom for a nightman!
[*He whistles. Enter* CLOV.] Clear away this muck! Chuck
it in the sea! [CLOV *goes to bins, halts.*]

NELL: So white.

HAMM: What? What's she blathering about?

[CLOV *stoops, takes* NELL's *hand, feels her pulse.*]

NELL: [*To* CLOV.] Desert!

[CLOV *lets go her hand, pushes her back in the bin, closes
the lid.*]

CLOV: [*Returning to his place beside the chair.*] She has no
pulse.

HAMM: What was she drivelling about?

CLOV: She told me to go away, into the desert.

HAMM: Damn busybody! Is that all?

CLOV: No.

HAMM: What else?

CLOV: I didn't understand.

HAMM: Have you bottled her?

CLOV: Yes.

HAMM: Are they both bottled?

CLOV: Yes.

HAMM: Screw down the lids. [CLOV *goes towards door.*] Time
enough. [CLOV *halts.*] My anger subsides, I'd like to pee.

CLOV: [*With alacrity.*] I'll go and get the catheter.
[*He goes towards the door.*]

HAMM: Time enough. [CLOV *halts.*] Give me my pain-killer.

CLOV: It's too soon. [*Pause.*] It's too soon on top of your tonic, it wouldn't act.

HAMM: In the morning they brace you up and in the evening they calm you down. Unless it's the other way round. [*Pause.*] That old doctor, he's dead, naturally?

CLOV: He wasn't old.

HAMM: But he's dead?

CLOV: Naturally. [*Pause.*] You ask *me* that?
[*Pause.*]

HAMM: Take me for a little turn. [CLOV *goes behind the chair and pushes it forward.*] Not too fast! [CLOV *pushes chair.*] Right round the world! [CLOV *pushes chair.*] Hug the walls, then back to the centre again. [CLOV *pushes chair.*] I was right in the centre, wasn't I?

CLOV: [*Pushing.*] Yes.

HAMM: We'd need a proper wheel-chair. With big wheels. Bicycle wheels! [*Pause.*] Are you hugging?

CLOV: [*Pushing.*] Yes.

HAMM: [*Groping for wall.*] It's a lie! Why do you lie to me?

CLOV: [*Bearing closer to wall.*] There! There!

HAMM: Stop! [CLOV *stops chair close to back wall.* HAMM *lays his hand against wall.*] Old wall! [*Pause.*] Beyond is the . . . other hell. [*Pause. Violently.*] Closer! Closer! Up against!

CLOV: Take away your hand. [HAMM *withdraws his hand.* CLOV *rams chair against wall.*] There!
[HAMM *leans towards wall, applies his ear to it.*]

HAMM: Do you hear? [*He strikes the wall with his knuckles.*] Do you hear? Hollow bricks! [*He strikes again.*] All that's hollow! [*Pause. He straightens up. Violently.*] That's enough. Back!

CLOV: We haven't done the round.

HAMM: Back to my place! [CLOV *pushes chair back to centre.*] Is that my place?

CLOV: Yes, that's your place.

HAMM: Am I right in the centre?

CLOV: I'll measure it.

HAMM: More or less! More or less!

CLOV: [*Moving chair slightly.*] There!

HAMM: I'm more or less in the centre?

CLOV: I'd say so.

HAMM: You'd say so! Put me right in the centre!

CLOV: I'll go and get the tape.

HAMM: Roughly! Roughly! [CLOV *moves chair slightly.*] Bang in the centre!

CLOV: There!

[*Pause.*]

HAMM: I feel a little too far to the left. [CLOV *moves chair slightly.*] Now I feel a little too far to the right. [CLOV *moves chair slightly.*] I feel a little too far forward. [CLOV *moves chair slightly.*] Now I feel a little too far back. [CLOV *moves chair slightly.*] Don't stay there [*i.e. behind the chair*], you give me the shivers.

[CLOV *returns to his place beside the chair.*]

CLOV: If I could kill him I'd die happy.

[*Pause.*]

HAMM: What's the weather like?

CLOV: The same as usual.

HAMM: Look at the earth.

CLOV: I've looked.

HAMM: With the glass?

CLOV: No need of the glass.

HAMM: Look at it with the glass.

CLOV: I'll go and get the glass.

[*Exit* CLOV.]

HAMM: No need of the glass!

[*Enter* CLOV *with telescope.*]

CLOV: I'm back again, with the glass. [*He goes to window right, looks up at it.*] I need the steps.

HAMM: Why? Have you shrunk? [*Exit* CLOV *with telescope.*] I don't like that, I don't like that.

[*Enter* CLOV *with ladder, but without telescope.*]

CLOV: I'm back again, with the steps. [*He sets down ladder under window right, gets up on it, realizes he has not the telescope, gets down.*] I need the glass.

[*He goes towards the door.*]

HAMM: [*Violently.*] But you have the glass!

CLOV: [*Halting, violently.*] No I haven't the glass!

[*Exit* CLOV.]

HAMM: This is deadly.

[*Enter* CLOV *with telescope. He goes towards ladder.*]

CLOV: Things are livening up. [*He gets up on ladder, raises the telescope, lets it fall.*] I did it on purpose. [*He gets down, picks up the telescope, turns it on auditorium.*] I see . . . a multitude . . . in transports . . . of joy. [*Pause.*] That's what I call a magnifier. [*He lowers the telescope, turns towards* HAMM.] Well? Don't we laugh?

HAMM: [*After reflection.*] I don't.

CLOV: [*After reflection.*] Nor I. [*He gets up on ladder, turns the telescope on the without.*] Let's see. [*He looks, moving the telescope.*] Zero . . . [*he looks*] . . . zero . . . [*he looks*] . . . and zero.

HAMM: Nothing stirs. All is —

CLOV: Zer —

HAMM: [*Violently.*] Wait till you're spoken to! [*Normal voice.*] All is . . . all is . . . all is what? [*Violently.*] All is what?

CLOV: What all is? In a word? Is that what you want to know? Just a moment. [*He turns the telescope on the without, looks, lowers the telescope, turns towards* HAMM.] Corpsed. [*Pause.*] Well? Content?

HAMM: Look at the sea.

CLOV: It's the same.

HAMM: Look at the ocean!

[CLOV *gets down, take a few steps towards window left, goes back for ladder, carries it over and sets it down under window left, gets up on it, turns the telescope on the without, looks at length. He starts, lowers the telescope, examines it, turns it again on the without.*]

CLOV: Never seen anything like that!

HAMM: [*Anxious.*] What? A sail? A fin? Smoke?

CLOV: [*Looking.*] The light is sunk.

HAMM: [*Relieved.*] Pah! We all knew that.

CLOV: [*Looking.*] There was a bit left.

HAMM: The base.

CLOV: [*Looking.*] Yes.

HAMM: And now?

CLOV: [*Looking.*] All gone.

HAMM: No gulls?

CLOV: [*Looking.*] Gulls!

HAMM: And the horizon? Nothing on the horizon?

CLOV: [*Lowering the telescope, turning towards* HAMM, *exasperated.*] What in God's name could there be on the horizon?
    [*Pause.*]

HAMM: The waves, how are the waves?

CLOV: The waves? [*He turns the telescope on the waves.*] Lead.

HAMM: And the sun?

CLOV: [*Looking.*] Zero.

HAMM: But it should be sinking. Look again.

CLOV: [*Looking.*] Damn the sun.

HAMM: Is it night already then?

CLOV: [*Looking.*] No.

HAMM: Then what is it?

CLOV: [*Looking.*] Grey. [*Lowering the telescope, turning towards* HAMM, *louder.*] Grey! [*Pause. Still louder.*] GRREY! [*Pause. He gets down, approaches* HAMM *from behind, whispers in his ear.*]

HAMM: [*Starting.*] Grey! Did I hear you say grey?

CLOV: Light black. From pole to pole.

HAMM: You exaggerate. [*Pause.*] Don't stay there, you give me the shivers.
    [CLOV *returns to his place beside the chair.*]

CLOV: Why this farce, day after day?

HAMM: Routine. One never knows. [*Pause.*] Last night I saw inside my breast. There was a big sore.

CLOV: Pah! You saw your heart.

HAMM: No, it was living. [*Pause. Anguished.*] Clov!

CLOV: Yes.

HAMM: What's happening?

CLOV: Something is taking its course.
    [*Pause.*]

HAMM: Clov!

CLOV: [*Impatiently.*] What is it?

HAMM: We're not beginning to . . . to . . . mean something?

CLOV: Mean something! You and I, mean something! [*Brief laugh.*] Ah that's a good one!

HAMM: I wonder. [*Pause.*] Imagine if a rational being came back to earth, wouldn't he be liable to get ideas into his head if he observed us long enough. [*Voice of rational being.*] Ah, good, now I see what it is, yes, now I understand what they're at! [CLOV *starts, drops the telescope and begins to scratch his belly with both hands. Normal voice.*] And without going so far as that, we ourselves . . . [*with emotion*] . . . we ourselves . . . at certain moments . . . [*Vehemently.*] To think perhaps it won't all have been for nothing!

CLOV: [*Anguished, scratching himself.*] I have a flea!

HAMM: A flea! Are there still fleas?

CLOV: On me there's one. [*Scratching.*] Unless it's a crablouse.

HAMM: [*Very perturbed.*] But humanity might start from there all over again! Catch him, for the love of God!

CLOV: I'll go and get the powder.

[*Exit* CLOV.]

HAMM: A flea! This is awful! What a day!

[*Enter* CLOV *with a sprinkling-tin.*]

CLOV: I'm back again, with the insecticide.

HAMM: Let him have it!

[CLOV *loosens the top of his trousers, pulls it forward and shakes powder into the aperture. He stoops, looks, waits, starts, frenziedly shakes more powder, stoops, looks, waits.*]

CLOV: The bastard!

HAMM: Did you get him?

CLOV: Looks like it. [*He drops the tin and adjusts his trousers.*] Unless he's laying doggo.

HAMM: Laying! Lying you mean. Unless he's *lying* doggo.

CLOV: Ah? One says lying? One doesn't say laying?

HAMM: Use your head, can't you. If he was laying we'd be bitched.

CLOV: Ah. [*Pause.*] What about that pee?

HAMM: I'm having it.

CLOV: Ah that's the spirit, that's the spirit!

[*Pause.*]

HAMM: [*With ardour.*] Let's go from here, the two of us! South! You can make a raft and the currents will carry us away, far away, to other . . . mammals!

CLOV: God forbid!

HAMM: Alone, I'll embark alone! Get working on that raft immediately. Tomorrow I'll be gone for ever.

CLOV: [*Hastening towards door.*] I'll start straight away.

HAMM: Wait! [CLOV *halts.*] Will there be sharks, do you think?

CLOV: Sharks? I don't know. If there are there will be.
[*He goes towards door.*]

HAMM: Wait! [CLOV *halts.*] Is it not yet time for my pain-killer?

CLOV: [*Violently.*] No!
[*He goes towards door.*]

HAMM: Wait! [CLOV *halts.*] How are your eyes?

CLOV: Bad.

HAMM: But you can see.

CLOV: All I want.

HAMM: How are your legs?

CLOV: Bad.

HAMM: But you can walk.

CLOV: I come . . . and go.

HAMM: In my house. [*Pause. With prophetic relish.*] One day you'll be blind, like me. You'll be sitting there, a speck in the void, in the dark, for ever, like me. [*Pause.*] One day you'll say to yourself, I'm tired, I'll sit down, and you'll go and sit down. Then you'll say, I'm hungry, I'll get up and get something to eat. But you won't get up. You'll say, I shouldn't have sat down, but since I have I'll sit on a little longer, then I'll get up and get something to eat. But you won't get up and you won't get anything to eat. [*Pause.*] You'll look at the wall a while, then you'll say, I'll close my eyes, perhaps have a little sleep, after that I'll feel better, and you'll close them. And when you open them again there'll be no wall any more. [*Pause.*] Infinite emptiness will be all around you, all the resurrected dead of all the ages wouldn't fill it, and there you'll be like a little bit of grit in the middle of the steppe. [*Pause.*] Yes, one day you'll know what it is, you'll be like me, except that you won't have anyone with you, because you won't have had pity on anyone and because there won't be anyone left to have pity on.

[*Pause.*]

CLOV: It's not certain. [*Pause.*] And there's one thing you forget.

HAMM: Ah?

CLOV: I can't sit down.

HAMM: [*Impatiently.*] Well, you'll lie down then, what the hell! Or you'll come to a standstill, simply stop and stand still, the way you are now. One day you'll say, I'm tired, I'll stop. What does the attitude matter?

[*Pause.*]

CLOV: So you all want me to leave you.

HAMM: Naturally.

CLOV: Then I'll leave you.

HAMM: You can't leave us.

CLOV: Then I shan't leave you.

[*Pause.*]

HAMM: Why don't you finish us? [*Pause.*] I'll tell you the combination of the larder if you promise to finish me.

CLOV: I couldn't finish you.

HAMM: Then you shan't finish me.

[*Pause.*]

CLOV: I'll leave you, I have things to do.

HAMM: Do you remember when you came here?

CLOV: No. Too small, you told me.

HAMM: Do you remember your father?

CLOV: [*Wearily.*] Same answer. [*Pause.*] You've asked me these questions millions of times.

HAMM: I love the old questions. [*With fervour.*] Ah the old questions, the old answers, there's nothing like them! [*Pause.*] It was I was a father to you.

CLOV: Yes. [*He looks at* HAMM *fixedly.*] You were that to me.

HAMM: My house a home for you.

CLOV: Yes. [*He looks about him.*] This was that for me.

HAMM: [*Proudly.*] But for me [*gesture towards himself*] no

father. But for Hamm [*gesture towards surroundings*] no
home.
[*Pause.*]

CLOV: I'll leave you.

HAMM: Did you ever think of one thing?

CLOV: Never.

HAMM: That here we're down in a hole. [*Pause.*] But beyond
the hills? Eh? Perhaps it's still green. Eh? [*Pause.*] Flora!
Pomona! [*Ecstatically.*] Ceres! [*Pause.*] Perhaps you won't
need to go very far.

CLOV: I can't go very far. [*Pause.*] I'll leave you.

HAMM: Is my dog ready?

CLOV: He lacks a leg.

HAMM: Is he silky?

CLOV: He's a kind of Pomeranian.

HAMM: Go and get him.

CLOV: He lacks a leg.

HAMM: Go and get him! [*Exit* CLOV.] We're getting on.
[*Enter* CLOV *holding by one of its three legs a black toy
dog.*]

CLOV: Your dogs are here.
[*He hands the dog to* HAMM *who feels it, fondles it.*]

HAMM: He's white, isn't he?

CLOV: Nearly.

HAMM: What do you mean, nearly? Is he white or isn't he?

CLOV: He isn't.
[*Pause.*]

HAMM: You've forgotten the sex.

CLOV: [*Vexed.*] But he isn't finished. The sex goes on at the
end.
[*Pause.*]

HAMM: You haven't put on his ribbon.

CLOV: [*Angrily.*] But he isn't finished, I tell you! First you
finish your dog and then you put on his ribbon!
[*Pause.*]

HAMM: Can he stand?

CLOV: I don't know.

HAMM: Try. [*He hands the dog to* CLOV *who places it on the
ground.*] Well?

CLOV: Wait!

[*He squats down and tries to get the dog to stand on its three legs, fails, lets it go. The dog falls on its side.*]

HAMM: [*Impatiently.*] Well?

CLOV: He's standing.

HAMM: [*Groping for the dog.*] Where? Where is he?

[CLOV *holds up the dog in a standing position.*]

CLOV: There.

[*He takes* HAMM's *hand and guides it towards the dog's head.*]

HAMM: [*His hand on the dog's head.*] Is he gazing at me?

CLOV: Yes.

HAMM: [*Proudly.*] As if he were asking me to take him for a walk?

CLOV: If you like.

HAMM: [*As before.*] Or as if he were begging me for a bone. [*He withdraws his hand.*] Leave him like that, standing there imploring me.

[CLOV *straightens up. The dog falls on its side.*]

CLOV: I'll leave you.

HAMM: Have you had your visions?

CLOV: Less.

HAMM: Is Mother Pegg's light on?

CLOV: Light! How could anyone's light be on?

HAMM: Extinguished!

CLOV: Naturally it's extinguished. If it's not on it's extinguished.

HAMM: No, I mean Mother Pegg.

CLOV: But naturally she's extinguished! [*Pause.*] What's the matter with you today?

HAMM: I'm taking my course. [*Pause.*] Is she buried?

CLOV: Buried! Who would have buried her?

HAMM: You.

CLOV: Me! Haven't I enough to do without burying people?

HAMM: But you'll bury me.

CLOV: No I shan't bury you.

[*Pause.*]

HAMM: She was bonny once, like a flower of the field. [*With reminiscent leer.*] And a great one for the men!

CLOV: We too were bonny — once. It's a rare thing not to have
    been bonny — once.
    [*Pause.*]

HAMM: Go and get the gaff.
    [CLOV *goes to door, halts.*]

CLOV: Do this, do that, and I do it. I never refuse. Why?

HAMM: You're not able to.

CLOV: Soon I won't do it any more.

HAMM: You won't be able to any more. [*Exit* CLOV.] Ah the
    creatures, the creatures, everything has to be explained to
    them.
    [*Enter* CLOV *with gaff.*]

CLOV: Here's your gaff. Stick it up.
    [*He gives the gaff to* HAMM *who, wielding it like a punt-
    pole, tries to move his chair.*]

HAMM: Did I move?

CLOV: No.
    [HAMM *throws down the gaff.*]

HAMM: Go and get the oilcan.

CLOV: What for?

HAMM: To oil the castors.

CLOV: I oiled them yesterday.

HAMM: Yesterday! What does that mean? Yesterday!

CLOV: [*Violently.*] That means that bloody awful day, long
    ago, before this bloody awful day. I use the words you
    taught me. If they don't mean anything any more, teach
    me others. Or let me be silent.
    [*Pause.*]

HAMM: I once knew a madman who thought the end of the
    world had come. He was a painter — and engraver. I had a
    great fondness for him. I used to go and see him, in the
    asylum. I'd take him by the hand and drag him to the
    window. Look! There! All that rising corn! And there!
    Look! The sails of the herring fleet! All that loveliness!
    [*Pause.*] He'd snatch away his hand and go back into his
    corner. Appalled. All he had seen was ashes. [*Pause.*] He
    alone had been spared. [*Pause.*] Forgotten. [*Pause.*] It
    appears the case is . . . was not so . . . so unusual.

CLOV: A madman? When was that?

HAMM: Oh way back, way back, you weren't in the land of the living.

CLOV: God be with the days!

[*Pause.* HAMM *raises his toque.*]

HAMM: I had a great fondness for him. [*Pause. He puts on his toque again.*] He was a painter — and engraver.

CLOV: There are so many terrible things.

HAMM: No, no, there are not so many now. [*Pause.*] Clov!

CLOV: Yes.

HAMM: Do you not think this has gone on long enough?

CLOV: Yes! [*Pause.*] What?

HAMM: This . . . this . . . thing.

CLOV: I've always thought so. [*Pause.*] You not?

HAMM: [*Gloomily.*] Then it's a day like any other day.

CLOV: As long as it lasts. [*Pause.*] All life long the same inanities.

[*Pause.*]

HAMM: I can't leave you.

CLOV: I know. And you can't follow me.

[*Pause.*]

HAMM: If you leave me how shall I know?

CLOV: [*Briskly.*] Well you simply whistle me and if I don't come running it means I've left you.

[*Pause.*]

HAMM: You won't come and kiss me good-bye?

CLOV: Oh I shouldn't think so.

[*Pause.*]

HAMM: But you might be merely dead in your kitchen.

CLOV: The result would be the same.

HAMM: Yes, but how would I know, if you were merely dead in your kitchen?

CLOV: Well . . . sooner or later I'd start to stink.

HAMM: You stink already. The whole place stinks of corpses.

CLOV: The whole universe.

HAMM: [*Angrily.*] To hell with the universe! [*Pause.*] Think of something.

CLOV: What?

HAMM: An idea, have an idea. [*Angrily.*] A bright idea!

CLOV: Ah good. [*He starts pacing to and fro, his eyes fixed on*

the ground, his hands behind his back. He halts.] The
pains in my legs! It's unbelievable! Soon I won't be able to
think any more.

HAMM: You won't be able to leave me. [CLOV *resumes his
pacing.*] What are you doing?

CLOV: Having an idea. [*He paces.*] Ah!
[*He halts.*]

HAMM: What a brain! [*Pause.*] Well?

CLOV: Wait! [*He meditates. Not very convinced.*] Yes . . .
[*Pause. More convinced.*] Yes! [*He raises his head.*] I have
it! I set the alarm.
[*Pause.*]

HAMM: This is perhaps not one of my bright days, but
frankly —

CLOV: You whistle me. I don't come. The alarm rings. I'm
gone. It doesn't ring. I'm dead.
[*Pause.*]

HAMM: Is it working? [*Pause. Impatiently.*] The alarm, is it
working?

CLOV: Why wouldn't it be working?

HAMM: Because it's worked too much.

CLOV: But it's hardly worked at all.

HAMM: [*Angrily.*] Then because it's worked too little!

CLOV: I'll go and see. [*Exit* CLOV. *Brief ring of alarm off.
Enter* CLOV *with alarm-clock. He holds it against* HAMM'S
*ear and releases alarm. They listen to it ringing to the end.
Pause.*] Fit to wake the dead! Did you hear it?

HAMM: Vaguely.

CLOV: The end is terrific!

HAMM: I prefer the middle. [*Pause.*] Is it not time for my pain-
killer?

CLOV: No! [*He goes to the door, turns.*] I'll leave you.

HAMM: It's time for my story. Do you want to listen to my
story?

CLOV: No.

HAMM: Ask my father if he wants to listen to my story.
[CLOV *goes to bins, raises the lid of* NAGG'S, *stoops, looks
into it. Pause. He straightens up.*]

CLOV: He's asleep.

HAMM: Wake him.

[CLOV *stoops, wakes* NAGG *with the alarm. Unintelligible words.* CLOV *straightens up.*]

CLOV: He doesn't want to listen to your story.

HAMM: I'll give him a bon-bon.

[CLOV *stoops. As before.*]

CLOV: He wants a sugar-plum.

HAMM: He'll get a sugar-plum.

[CLOV *stoops. As before.*]

CLOV: It's a deal. [*He goes towards door.* NAGG's *hands appear, gripping the rim. Then the head emerges.* CLOV *reaches door, turns.*] Do you believe in the life to come?

HAMM: Mine was always that. [*Exit* CLOV.] Got him that time!

NAGG: I'm listening.

HAMM: Scoundrel! Why did you engender me?

NAGG: I didn't know.

HAMM: What? What didn't you know?

NAGG: That it'd be you. [*Pause.*] You'll give me a sugar-plum?

HAMM: After the audition.

NAGG: You swear?

HAMM: Yes.

NAGG: On what?

HAMM: My honour.

[*Pause. They laugh heartily.*]

NAGG: Two.

HAMM: One.

NAGG: One for me and one for —

HAMM: One! Silence! [*Pause.*] Where was I? [*Pause. Gloomily.*] It's finished, we're finished. [*Pause.*] Nearly finished. [*Pause.*] There'll be no more speech. [*Pause.*] Something dripping in my head, ever since the fontanelles. [*Stifled hilarity of* NAGG.] Splash, splash, always on the same spot. [*Pause.*] Perhaps it's a little vein. [*Pause.*] A little artery. [*Pause. More animated.*] Enough of that, it's story time, where was I? [*Pause. Narrative tone.*] The man came crawling towards me, on his belly. Pale, wonderfully pale and thin, he seemed on the point of — [*Pause. Normal tone.*] No, I've done that bit. [*Pause. Narrative tone.*] I calmly filled my pipe — the meerschaum, lit it with . . . let us say a vesta, drew a few puffs. Aah! [*Pause.*] Well, what is it *you* want? [*Pause.*] It was an extra-ordinarily bitter day, I remember, zero by the thermometer. But considering it was Christmas Eve there was nothing . . . extra-ordinary about that. Seasonable weather, for once in a way. [*Pause.*] Well, what ill wind blows you my way? He raised his face to me, black with mingled dirt and tears. [*Pause. Normal tone.*] That should do it. [*Narrative tone.*] No, no, don't look at me, don't look at me. He dropped his eyes and mumbled something, apologies I presume. [*Pause.*] I'm a busy man, you know, the final touches, before the festivities, you know what it is. [*Pause. Forcibly.*] Come on now, what is the object of this invasion? [*Pause.*] It was a glorious bright day, I remember, fifty by the heliometer, but already the sun was sinking down into the . . . down among the dead. [*Normal tone.*] Nicely put, that. [*Narrative tone.*] Come on now, come on, present your petition and let me resume my labours. [*Pause. Normal tone.*] There's English for you. Ah well . . . [*Narrative tone.*] It was then he took the plunge. It's my little one, he said. Tsstss, a little one, that's bad. My little boy, he said, as if the sex mattered. Where did he come from? He named the hole. A good half-day, on horse. What are you insinuating? That the place is still inhabited? No no, not a soul, except himself and the child — assuming he existed. Good. I inquired about the situation at Kov, beyond the gulf. Not a sinner. Good. And you expect me to believe you have left your little one back there, all alone, and alive into the bargain? Come now! [*Pause.*] It was a howling wild day, I remember, a hundred by the anemometer. The wind was tearing up the dead pines and sweeping them . . . away. [*Pause. Normal tone.*] A bit feeble, that. [*Narrative tone.*] Come on, man, speak up, what is it you want from me, I have to put up my holly. [*Pause.*] Well to make it short it finally transpired that what he wanted from me was . . . bread for his brat. Bread? But I have no bread, it doesn't agree with me. Good. Then perhaps a little corn? [*Pause. Normal tone.*] That should do it. [*Narrative tone.*]

Corn, yes, I have corn, it's true, in my granaries. But use your head. I give you some corn, a pound, a pound and a half, you bring it back to your child and you make him — if he's still alive — a nice pot of porridge [NAGG *reacts*], a nice pot and a half of porridge, full of nourishment. Good. The colours come back into his little cheeks — perhaps. And then? [*Pause.*] I lost patience. [*Violently.*] Use your head, can't you, use your head, you're on earth, there's no cure for that! [*Pause.*] It was an exceedingly dry day, I remember, zero by the hygrometer. Ideal weather, for my lumbago. [*Pause. Violently.*] But what in God's name do you imagine? That the earth will awake in spring? That the rivers and seas will run with fish again? That there's manna in heaven still for imbeciles like you? [*Pause.*] Gradually I cooled down, sufficiently at least to ask him how long he had taken on the way. Three whole days. Good. In what condition he had left the child. Deep in sleep. [*Forcibly.*] But deep in what sleep, deep in what sleep already? [*Pause.*] Well to make it short I finally offered to take him into my service. He had touched a chord. And then I imagined already that I wasn't much longer for this world. [*He laughs. Pause.*] Well? [*Pause.*] Well? Here if you were careful you might die a nice natural death, in peace and comfort. [*Pause.*] Well? [*Pause.*] In the end he asked me would I consent to take in the child as well — if he were still alive. [*Pause.*] It was the moment I was waiting for. [*Pause.*] Would I consent to take in the child . . . [*Pause.*] I can see him still, down on his knees, his hands flat on the ground, glaring at me with his mad eyes, in defiance of my wishes. [*Pause. Normal tone.*] I'll soon have finished with this story. [*Pause.*] Unless I bring in other characters. [*Pause.*] But where would I find them? [*Pause.*] Where would I look for them? [*Pause. He whistles. Enter* CLOV.] Let us pray to God.

NAGG: Me sugar-plum!

CLOV: There's a rat in the kitchen!

HAMM: A rat! Are there still rats?

CLOV: In the kitchen there's one.

HAMM: And you haven't exterminated him?

CLOV: Half. You disturbed us.

HAMM: He can't get away?

CLOV: No.

HAMM: You'll finish him later. Let us pray to God.

CLOV: Again!

NAGG: Me sugar-plum!

HAMM: God first! [*Pause.*] Are you right?

CLOV: [*Resigned.*] Off we go.

HAMM: [*To* NAGG.] And you?

NAGG: [*Clasping his hands, closing his eyes, in a gabble.*] Our
    Father which art —

HAMM: Silence! In silence! Where are your manners? [*Pause.*]
    Off we go. [*Attitudes of prayer. Silence. Abandoning his
    attitude, discouraged.*] Well?

CLOV: [*Abandoning his attitude.*] What a hope! And you?

HAMM: Sweet damn all! [*To* NAGG.] And you?

NAGG: Wait! [*Pause. Abandoning his attitude.*] Nothing doing!

HAMM: The bastard! He doesn't exist!

CLOV: Not yet.

NAGG: Me sugar-plum!

HAMM: There are no more sugar-plums!
    [*Pause.*]

NAGG: It's natural. After all I'm your father. It's true if it
    hadn't been me it would have been someone else. But
    that's no excuse. [*Pause.*] Turkish Delight, for example,
    which no longer exists, we all know that, there is nothing
    in the world I love more. And one day I'll ask you for
    some, in return for a kindness, and you'll promise it to me.
    One must live with the times. [*Pause.*] Whom did you call
    when you were a tiny boy, and were frightened, in the
    dark? Your mother? No. Me. We let you cry. Then we
    moved you out of earshot, so that we might sleep in peace.
    [*Pause.*] I was asleep, as happy as a king, and you woke
    me up to have me listen to you. It wasn't indispensable,
    you didn't really need to have me listen to you. Besides I
    didn't listen to you. [*Pause.*] I hope the day will come
    when you'll really need to have me listen to you, and need
    to hear my voice, any voice. [*Pause.*] Yes, I hope I'll live till
    then, to hear you calling me like when you were a tiny

boy, and were frightened, in the dark, and I was your only hope. [*Pause.* NAGG *knocks on lid of* NELL's *bin. Pause.*] Nell! [*Pause. He knocks louder. Pause. Louder.*] Nell! [*Pause.* NAGG *sinks back into his bin, closes the lid behind him. Pause.*]

HAMM: Our revels now are ended. [*He gropes for the dog.*] The dog's gone.

CLOV: He's not a real dog, he can't go.

HAMM: [*Groping.*] He's not there.

CLOV: He's lain down.

HAMM: Give him up to me. [CLOV *picks up the dog and gives it to* HAMM. HAMM *holds it in his arms. Pause.* HAMM *throws away the dog.*] Dirty brute! [CLOV *begins to pick up the objects lying on the ground.*] What are you doing?

CLOV: Putting things in order. [*He straightens up. Fervently.*] I'm going to clear everything away!
[*He starts picking up again.*]

HAMM: Order!

CLOV: [*Straightening up.*] I love order. It's my dream. A world where all would be silent and still and each thing in its last place, under the last dust.
[*He starts picking up again.*]

HAMM: [*Exasperated.*] What in God's name do you think you are doing?

CLOV: [*Straightening up.*] I'm doing my best to create a little order.

HAMM: Drop it!
[CLOV *drops the objects he has picked up.*]

CLOV: After all, there or elsewhere.
[*He goes towards door.*]

HAMM: [*Irritably.*] What's wrong with your feet?

CLOV: My feet?

HAMM: Tramp! Tramp!

CLOV: I must have put on my boots.

HAMM: Your slippers were hurting you?
[*Pause.*]

CLOV: I'll leave you.

HAMM: No!

CLOV: What is there to keep me here?

HAMM: The dialogue. [*Pause.*] I've got on with my story. [*Pause.*] I've got on with it well. [*Pause. Irritably.*] Ask me where I've got to.

CLOV: Oh, by the way, your story?

HAMM: [*Surprised.*] What story?

CLOV: The one you've been telling yourself all your . . . days.

HAMM: Ah you mean my chronicle?

CLOV: That's the one.

[*Pause.*]

HAMM: [*Angrily.*] Keep going, can't you, keep going!

CLOV: You've got on with it, I hope.

HAMM: [*Modestly.*] Oh not very far, not very far. [*He sighs.*] There are days like that, one isn't inspired. [*Pause.*] Nothing you can do about it, just wait for it to come. [*Pause.*] No forcing, no forcing, it's fatal. [*Pause.*] I've got on with it a little all the same. [*Pause.*] Technique, you know. [*Pause. Irritably.*] I say I've got on with it a little all the same.

CLOV: [*Admiringly.*] Well I never! In spite of everything you were able to get on with it!

HAMM: [*Modestly.*] Oh not very far, you know, not very far, but nevertheless, better than nothing.

CLOV: Better than nothing! Is it possible?

HAMM: I'll tell you how it goes. He comes crawling on his belly —

CLOV: Who?

HAMM: What?

CLOV: Who do you mean, he?

HAMM: Who do I mean! Yet another.

CLOV: Ah him! I wasn't sure.

HAMM: Crawling on his belly, whining for bread for his brat. He's offered a job as gardener. Before — [CLOV *bursts out laughing.*] What is there so funny about that?

CLOV: A job as gardener!

HAMM: Is that what tickles you?

CLOV: It must be that.

HAMM: It wouldn't be the bread?

CLOV: Or the brat.

[*Pause.*]

HAMM: The whole thing is comical, I grant you that. What about having a good guffaw the two of us together?

CLOV: [*After reflection.*] I couldn't guffaw again today.

HAMM: [*After reflection.*] Nor I. [*Pause.*] I continue then. Before accepting with gratitude he asks if he may have his little boy with him.

CLOV: What age?

HAMM: Oh tiny.

CLOV: He would have climbed the trees.

HAMM: All the little odd jobs.

CLOV: And then he would have grown up.

HAMM: Very likely.

[*Pause.*]

CLOV: Keep going, can't you, keep going!

HAMM: That's all. I stopped there.

[*Pause.*]

CLOV: Do you see how it goes on.

HAMM: More or less.

CLOV: Will it not soon be the end?

HAMM: I'm afraid it will.

CLOV: Pah! You'll make up another.

HAMM: I don't know. [*Pause.*] I feel rather drained. [*Pause.*] The prolonged creative effort. [*Pause.*] If I could drag myself down to the sea! I'd make a pillow of sand for my head and the tide would come.

CLOV: There's no more tide.

[*Pause.*]

HAMM: Go and see is she dead.

[CLOV *goes to bins, raises the lid of* NELL's, *stoops, looks into it. Pause.*]

CLOV: Looks like it.

[*He closes the lid, straightens up.* HAMM *raises his toque. Pause. He puts it on again.*]

HAMM: [*With his hand to his toque.*] And Nagg?

[CLOV *raises lid of* NAGG's *bin, stoops, looks into it. Pause.*]

CLOV: Doesn't look like it.

[*He closes the lid, straightens up.*]

HAMM: [*Letting go his toque.*] What's he doing?

[CLOV *raises lid of* NAGG's *bin, stoops, looks into it.*
Pause.]

CLOV: He's crying.

[*He closes the lid, straightens up.*]

HAMM: Then he's living. [*Pause.*] Did you ever have an instant
of happiness?

CLOV: Not to my knowledge.

[*Pause.*]

HAMM: Bring me under the window. [CLOV *goes towards*
chair.] I want to feel the light on my face. [CLOV *pushes*
chair.] Do you remember, in the beginning, when you took
me for a turn? You used to hold the chair too high. At
every step you nearly tipped me out. [*With senile quaver.*]
Ah great fun, we had, the two of us, great fun! [*Gloomily.*]
And then we got into the way of it. [CLOV *stops the chair*
under window right.] There already? [*Pause. He tilts back*
his head.] Is it light?

CLOV: It isn't dark.

HAMM: [*Angrily.*] I'm asking you is it light?

CLOV: Yes.

[*Pause.*]

HAMM: The curtain isn't closed?

CLOV: No.

HAMM: What window is it?

CLOV: The earth.

HAMM: I knew it! [*Angrily.*] But there's no light there! The
other! [CLOV *pushes chair towards window left.*] The
earth! [CLOV *stops the chair under window left.* HAMM
tilts back his head.] That's what I call light! [*Pause.*] Feels
like a ray of sunshine. [*Pause.*] No?

CLOV: No.

HAMM: It isn't a ray of sunshine I feel on my face?

CLOV: No.

[*Pause.*]

HAMM: Am I very white? [*Pause. Angrily.*] I'm asking you am I
very white!

CLOV: Not more so than usual.

[*Pause.*]

HAMM: Open the window.

CLOV: What for?

HAMM: I want to hear the sea.

CLOV: You wouldn't hear it.

HAMM: Even if you opened the window?

CLOV: No.

HAMM: Then it's not worth while opening it?

CLOV: No.

HAMM: [*Violently.*] Then open it! [CLOV *gets up on the ladder, opens the window. Pause.*] Have you opened it?

CLOV: Yes.

    [*Pause.*]

HAMM: You swear you've opened it?

CLOV: Yes.

    [*Pause.*]

HAMM: Well . . . ! [*Pause.*] It must be very calm. [*Pause. Violently.*] I'm asking you is it very calm?

CLOV: Yes.

HAMM: It's because there are no more navigators. [*Pause.*] You haven't much conversation all of a sudden. Do you not feel well?

CLOV: I'm cold.

HAMM: What month are we? [*Pause.*] Close the window, we're going back. [CLOV *closes the window, gets down, pushes the chair back to its place, remains standing behind it, head bowed.*] Don't stay there, you give me the shivers! [CLOV *returns to his place beside the chair.*] Father! [*Pause. Louder.*] Father! [*Pause.*] Go and see did he hear me.
    [CLOV *goes to* NAGG's *bin, raises the lid, stoops. Unintelligible words.* CLOV *straightens up.*]

CLOV: Yes.

HAMM: Both times?

    [CLOV *stoops. As before.*]

CLOV: Once only.

HAMM: The first time or the second?

    [CLOV *stoops. As before.*]

CLOV: He doesn't know.

HAMM: It must have been the second.

CLOV: We'll never know.

[*He closes lid.*]

HAMM: Is he still crying?

CLOV: No.

HAMM: The dead go fast. [*Pause.*] What's he doing?

CLOV: Sucking his biscuit.

HAMM: Life goes on. [CLOV *returns to his place beside the chair.*] Give me a rug, I'm freezing.

CLOV: There are no more rugs.

    [*Pause.*]

HAMM: Kiss me. [*Pause.*] Will you not kiss me?

CLOV: No.

HAMM: On the forehead.

CLOV: I won't kiss you anywhere.

    [*Pause.*]

HAMM: [*Holding out his hand.*] Give me your hand at least. [*Pause.*] Will you not give me your hand?

CLOV: I won't touch you.

    [*Pause.*]

HAMM: Give me the dog. [CLOV *looks round for the dog.*] No!

CLOV: Do you not want your dog?

HAMM: No.

CLOV: Then I'll leave you.

HAMM: [*Head bowed, absently.*] That's right.

    [CLOV *goes to door, turns.*]

CLOV: If I don't kill that rat he'll die.

HAMM: [*As before.*] That's right. [*Exit* CLOV. *Pause.*] Me to play. [*He takes out his handkerchief, unfolds it, holds it spread out before him.*] We're getting on. [*Pause.*] You weep, and weep, for nothing, so as not to laugh, and little by little . . . you begin to grieve. [*He folds the handkerchief, puts it back in his pocket, raises his head.*] All those I might have helped. [*Pause.*] Helped! [*Pause.*] Saved. [*Pause.*] Saved! [*Pause.*] The place was crawling with them! [*Pause. Violently.*] Use your head, can't you, use your head, you're on earth, there's no cure for that! [*Pause.*] Get out of here and love one another! Lick your neighbour as yourself! [*Pause. Calmer.*] When it wasn't bread they wanted it was crumpets. [*Pause. Violently.*] Out of my sight and back to your petting parties! [*Pause.*] All that, all that! [*Pause.*] Not even a real dog! [*Calmer.*] The end is in the beginning and yet you go on. [*Pause.*] Perhaps I could go on with my story, end it and begin another. [*Pause.*] Perhaps I could throw myself out on the floor. [*He pushes himself painfully off his seat, falls back again.*] Dig my nails into the cracks and drag myself forward with my fingers. [*Pause.*] It will be the end and there I'll be, wondering what can have brought it on and wondering what can have . . . [*he hesitates*] . . . why it was so long coming. [*Pause.*] There I'll be, in the old refuge, alone against the silence and . . . [*he hesitates*] . . . the stillness. If I can hold my peace, and sit quiet, it will be all over with sound, and motion, all over and done with. [*Pause.*] I'll have called my father and I'll have called my . . . [*he hesitates*] . . . my son. And even twice, or three times, in case they shouldn't have heard me, the first time, or the second. [*Pause.*] I'll say to myself, He'll come back. [*Pause.*] And then? [*Pause.*] And then? [*Pause.*] He couldn't, he has gone too far. [*Pause.*] And then? [*Pause. Very agitated.*] All kinds of fantasies! That I'm being watched! A rat! Steps! Breath held and then . . . [*he breathes out.*] Then babble, babble, words, like the solitary child who turns himself into children, two, three, so as to be together, and whisper together, in the dark. [*Pause.*] Moment upon moment, pattering down, like the millet grains of . . . [*he hesitates*] . . . that old Greek, and all life long you wait for that to mount up to a life. [*Pause. He opens his mouth to continue, renounces.*] Ah let's get it over! [*He whistles. Enter* CLOV *with alarm-clock. He halts beside the chair.*] What? Neither gone nor dead?

CLOV: In spirit only.

HAMM: Which?

CLOV: Both.

HAMM: Gone from me you'd be dead.

CLOV: And *vice versa*.

HAMM: Outside of here it's death! [*Pause.*] And the rat?

CLOV: He's got away.

HAMM: He can't go far. [*Pause. Anxious.*] Eh?

CLOV: He doesn't need to go far.

[*Pause.*]

HAMM: Is it not time for my pain-killer?

CLOV: Yes.

HAMM: Ah! At last! Give it to me! Quick!

[*Pause.*]

CLOV: There's no more pain-killer.

[*Pause.*]

HAMM: [*Appalled.*] Good . . . ! [*Pause.*] No more pain-killer!

CLOV: No more pain-killer. You'll never get any more
pain-killer.

[*Pause.*]

HAMM: But the little round box. It was full!

CLOV: Yes. But now it's empty.

[*Pause.* CLOV *starts to move about the room. He is
looking for a place to put down the alarm-clock.*]

HAMM: [*Soft.*] What'll I do? [*Pause. In a scream.*] What'll I do?
[CLOV *sees the picture, takes it down, stands it on the
floor with its face to wall, hangs up the alarm-clock in its
place.*]
What are you doing?

CLOV: Winding up.

HAMM: Look at the earth.

CLOV: Again!

HAMM: Since it's calling to you.

CLOV: Is your throat sore? [*Pause.*] Would you like a lozenge?
[*Pause.*] No? [*Pause.*] Pity.
[CLOV *goes, humming, towards window right, halts before
it, looks up at it.*]

HAMM: Don't sing.

CLOV: [*Turning towards* HAMM.] One hasn't the right to sing
any more?

HAMM: No.

CLOV: Then how can it end?

HAMM: You want it to end?

CLOV: I want to sing.

HAMM: I can't prevent you.

[*Pause.* CLOV *turns towards window right.*]

CLOV: What did I do with that steps? [*He looks round for
ladder.*] You didn't see that steps? [*He sees it.*] Ah, about

time. [*He goes towards window left.*] Sometimes I wonder
if I'm in my right mind. Then it passes over and I'm as
lucid as before. [*He gets up on ladder, looks out of
window.*] Christ, she's under water! [*He looks.*] How can
that be? [*He pokes forward his head, his hand above his
eyes.*] It hasn't rained. [*He wipes the pane, looks. Pause.*]
Ah what a mug I am! I'm on the wrong side! [*He gets
down, take a few steps towards window right.*] Under
water! [*He goes back for ladder.*] What a mug I am! [*He
carries ladder towards window right.*] Sometimes I wonder
if I'm in my right senses. Then it passes off and I'm as
intelligent as ever. [*He sets down ladder under window
right, gets up on it, looks out of window. He turns
towards* HAMM.] Any particular sector you fancy? Or
merely the whole thing?

HAMM: Whole thing.

CLOV: The general effect? Just a moment.
[*He looks out of window. Pause.*]

HAMM: Clov.

CLOV: [*Absorbed.*] Mmm.

HAMM: Do you know what it is?

CLOV: [*As before.*] Mmm.

HAMM: I was never there. [*Pause.*] Clov!

CLOV: [*Turning towards* HAMM, *exasperated.*] What is it?

HAMM: I was never there.

CLOV: Lucky for you.
[*He looks out of window.*]

HAMM: Absent, always. It all happened without me. I don't
know what's happened. [*Pause.*] Do you know what's
happened? [*Pause.*] Clov!

CLOV: [*Turning towards* HAMM, *exasperated.*] Do you want
me to look at this muckheap, yes or no?

HAMM: Answer me first.

CLOV: What?

HAMM: Do you know what's happened?

CLOV: When? Where?

HAMM: [*Violently.*] When! What's happened! Use your head,
can't you! What has happened?

CLOV: What for Christ's sake does it matter?

[*He looks out of window.*]

HAMM: I don't know.

[*Pause.* CLOV *turns towards* HAMM.]

CLOV: [*Harshly.*] When old Mother Pegg asked you for oil for her lamp and you told her to get out to hell, you knew what was happening then, no? [*Pause.*] You know what she died of, Mother Pegg? Of darkness.

HAMM: [*Feebly.*] I hadn't any.

CLOV: [*As before.*] Yes, you had.

[*Pause.*]

HAMM: Have you the glass?

CLOV: No, it's clear enough as it is.

HAMM: Go and get it.

[*Pause.* CLOV *casts up his eyes, brandishes his fists. He loses balance, clutches on to the ladder. He starts to get down, halts.*]

CLOV: There's one thing I'll never understand. [*He gets down.*] Why I always obey you. Can you explain that to me?

HAMM: No . . . Perhaps it's compassion. [*Pause.*] A kind of great compassion. [*Pause.*] Oh you won't find it easy, you won't find it easy.

[*Pause.* CLOV *begins to move about the room in search of the telescope.*]

CLOV: I'm tired of our goings on, very tired. [*He searches.*] You're not sitting on it?

[*He moves the chair, looks at the place where it stood, resumes his search.*]

HAMM: [*Anguished.*] Don't leave me there! [*Angrily* CLOV *restores the chair to its place.*] Am I right in the centre?

CLOV: You'd need a microscope to find this – [*He sees the telescope.*] Ah, about time.

[*He picks up the telescope, gets up on the ladder, turns the telescope on the without.*]

HAMM: Give me the dog.

CLOV: [*Looking.*] Quiet!

HAMM: [*Angrily.*] Give me the dog!

[CLOV *drops the telescope, clasps his hands to his head. Pause. He gets down precipitately, looks for the dog, sees it, picks it up, hastens towards* HAMM *and strikes him on the head violently with the dog.*]

CLOV: There's your dog for you!

[*The dog falls to the ground. Pause.*]

HAMM: He hit me!

CLOV: You drive me mad, I'm mad!

HAMM: If you must hit me, hit me with the axe. [*Pause.*] Or with the gaff, hit me with the gaff. Not with the dog. With the gaff. Or with the axe.

[CLOV *picks up the dog and gives it to* HAMM *who takes it in his arms.*]

CLOV: [*Imploringly.*] Let's stop playing!

HAMM: Never! [*Pause.*] Put me in my coffin.

CLOV: There are no more coffins.

HAMM: Then let it end! [CLOV *goes towards ladder.*] With a bang! [CLOV *gets up on ladder, gets down again, looks for telescope, sees it, picks it up, gets up ladder, raises telescope.*] Of darkness! And me? Did anyone ever have pity on me?

CLOV: [*Lowering the telescope, turning towards* HAMM.] What? [*Pause.*] Is it me you're referring to?

HAMM: [*Angrily.*] An aside, ape! Did you never hear an aside before? [*Pause.*] I'm warming up for my last soliloquy.

CLOV: I warn you. I'm going to look at this filth since it's an order. But it's the last time. [*He turns the telescope on the without.*] Let's see. [*He moves the telescope.*] Nothing . . . nothing . . . good . . . good . . . nothing . . . goo —
[*He starts, lowers the telescope, examines it, turns it again on the without. Pause.*] Bad luck to it!

HAMM: More complications! [CLOV *gets down.*] Not an underplot, I trust.

[CLOV *moves ladder nearer window, gets up on it, turns telescope on the without.*]

CLOV: [*Dismayed.*] Looks like a small boy!

HAMM: [*Sarcastic.*] A small . . . boy!

CLOV: I'll go and see. [*He gets down, drops the telescope, goes towards door, turns.*] I'll take the gaff.

[*He looks for the gaff, sees it, picks it up, hastens towards door.*]

HAMM: No!

[CLOV *halts*.]

CLOV: No? A potential procreator?

HAMM: If he exists he'll die there or he'll come here. And if he doesn't . . .
[*Pause*.]

CLOV: You don't believe me? You think I'm inventing?
[*Pause*.]

HAMM: It's the end, Clov, we've come to the end. I don't need you any more.
[*Pause*.]

CLOV: Lucky for you.
[*He goes towards door*.]

HAMM: Leave me the gaff.
[CLOV *gives him the gaff, goes towards door, halts, looks at alarm-clock, takes it down, looks round for a better place to put it, goes to bins, puts it on lid of* NAGG's *bin. Pause*.]

CLOV: I'll leave you.
[*He goes towards door*.]

HAMM: Before you go . . . [CLOV *halts near door*] . . . say something.

CLOV: There is nothing to say.

HAMM: A few words . . . to ponder . . . in my heart.

CLOV: Your heart!

HAMM: Yes. [*Pause. Forcibly*.] Yes! [*Pause*.] With the rest, in the end, the shadows, the murmurs, all the trouble, to end up with. [*Pause*.] Clov . . . He never spoke to me. Then, in the end, before he went, without my having asked him, he spoke to me. He said . . .

CLOV: [*Despairingly*.] Ah . . . !

HAMM: Something . . . from your heart.

CLOV: My heart!

HAMM: A few words . . . from your heart.
[*Pause*.]

CLOV: [*Fixed gaze, tonelessly, towards auditorium*.] They said to me, That's love, yes yes, not a doubt, now you see how –

HAMM: Articulate!

CLOV: [*As before*.] How easy it is. They said to me, That's friendship, yes yes, no question, you've found it. They said to me, Here's the place, stop, raise your head and look at all that beauty. That order! They said to me, Come now, you're not a brute beast, think upon these things and you'll see how all becomes clear. And simple! They said to me, What skilled attention they get, all these dying of their wounds.

HAMM: Enough!

CLOV: [*As before.*] I say to myself — sometimes, Clov, you must learn to suffer better than that if you want them to weary of punishing you — one day. I say to myself — sometimes, Clov, you must be there better than that if you want them to let you go — one day. But I feel too old, and too far, to form new habits. Good, it'll never end, I'll never go. [*Pause.*] Then one day, suddenly, it ends, it changes, I don't understand, it dies, or it's me, I don't understand that either. I ask the words that remain — sleeping, waking, morning, evening. They have nothing to say. [*Pause.*] I open the door of the cell and go. I am so bowed I only see my feet, if I open my eyes, and between my legs a little trail of black dust. I say to myself that the earth is extinguished, though I never saw it lit. [*Pause.*] It's easy going. [*Pause.*] When I fall I'll weep for happiness.

[*Pause. He goes towards door.*]

HAMM: Clov! [CLOV *halts, without turning.*] Nothing. [CLOV *moves on.*] Clov!

[CLOV *halts, without turning.*]

CLOV: This is what we call making an exit.

HAMM: I'm obliged to you, Clov. For your services.

CLOV: [*Turning, sharply.*] Ah pardon, it's I am obliged to you.

HAMM: It's we are obliged to each other. [*Pause.* CLOV *goes towards door.*] One thing more. [CLOV *halts.*] A last favour. [*Exit* CLOV.] Cover me with the sheet. [*Long pause.*] No? Good. [*Pause.*] Me to play. [*Pause. Wearily.*] Old endgame lost of old, play and lose and have done with losing. [*Pause. More animated.*] Let me see. [*Pause.*] Ah yes! [*He tries to move the chair, using the gaff as before. Enter* CLOV, *dressed for the road. Panama hat, tweed coat, raincoat over his arm, umbrella, bag. He halts by the door*

*and stands there, impassive and motionless, his eyes fixed
on* HAMM, *till the end.* HAMM *gives up.*] Good. [*Pause.*]
Discard. [*He throws away the gaff, makes to throw away
the dog, thinks better of it.*] Take it easy. [*Pause.*] And
now? [*Pause.*] Raise hat. [*He raises his toque.*] Peace to
our . . . arses. [*Pause.*] And put on again. [*He puts on his
toque.*] Deuce. [*Pause. He takes off his glasses.*] Wipe. [*He
takes out his handkerchief and, without unfolding it, wipes
his glasses.*] And put on again. [*He puts on his glasses, puts
back the handkerchief in his pocket.*] We're coming. A few
more squirms like that and I'll call. [*Pause.*] A little poetry.
[*Pause.*] You prayed – [*Pause. He corrects himself.*] You
CRIED for night; it comes – [*Pause. He corrects himself.*]
It FALLS: now cry in darkness. [*He repeats, chanting.*]
You cried for night; it falls: now cry in darkness. [*Pause.*]
Nicely put, that. [*Pause.*] And now? [*Pause.*] Moments for
nothing, now as always, time was never and time is over,
reckoning closed and story ended. [*Pause. Narrative tone.*]
If he could have his child with him . . . [*Pause.*] It was the
moment I was waiting for. [*Pause.*] You don't want to
abandon him? You want him to bloom while you are
withering? Be there to solace your last million last
moments? [*Pause.*] He doesn't realize, all he knows is
hunger, and cold, and death to crown it all. But you! You
ought to know what the earth is like, nowadays. Oh, I put
him before his responsibilities! [*Pause. Normal tone.*] Well,
there we are, there I am, that's enough. [*He raises the
whistle to his lips, hesitates, drops it. Pause.*] Yes, truly!
[*He whistles. Pause. Louder. Pause.*] Good. [*Pause.*]
Father! [*Pause. Louder.*] Father! [*Pause.*] Good. [*Pause.*]
We're coming. [*Pause.*] And to end up with? [*Pause.*]
Discard. [*He throws away the dog. He tears the whistle
from his neck.*] With my compliments. [*He throws whistle
towards auditorium. Pause. He sniffs. Soft.*] Clov! [*Long
pause.*] No? Good. [*He takes out the handkerchief.*] Since
that's the way we're playing it . . . [*he unfolds
handkerchief*] . . . let's play it that way . . . [*he unfolds*] . . .
and speak no more about it . . . [*he finishes unfolding*] . . .
speak no more. [*He holds the handkerchief spread out*

before him.] Old stancher! [*Pause.*] You . . . remain.
[*Pause. He covers his face with handkerchief, lowers his
arms to armrests, remains motionless.*]
[*Brief tableau.*]

CURTAIN

Happy Days

A play in two acts

First performed in New York on 17 September 1961 at the Cherry Lane Theatre. First published in 1961 by Grove Press Inc., New York. First published in Great Britain in 1963 by Faber and Faber Limited.

CAST

WINNIE *a woman of about fifty*
WILLIE *a man of about sixty*

ACT ONE

*Expanse of scorched grass rising centre to low mound. Gentle
slopes down to front and either side of stage. Back an abrupter
fall to stage level. Maximum of simplicity and symmetry.*

Blazing light.

*Very pompier trompe-l'oeil backcloth to represent unbroken
plain and sky receding to meet in far distance.*

Embedded up to above her waist in exact centre of mound,
WINNIE. *About fifty, well-preserved, blonde for preference,
plump, arms and shoulders bare, low bodice, big bosom, pearl
necklace. She is discovered sleeping, her arms on the ground
before her, her head on her arms. Beside her on ground to her
left a capacious black bag, shopping variety, and to her right a
collapsible collapsed parasol, beak of handle emerging from
sheath.*

*To her right and rear, lying asleep on ground, hidden by
mound,* WILLIE.

*Long pause. A bell rings piercingly, say ten seconds, stops.
She does not move. Pause. Bell more piercingly, say five
seconds. She wakes. Bell stops. She raises her head, gazes front.
Long pause. She straightens up, lays her hands flat on ground,
throws back her head and gazes at zenith. Long pause.*

WINNIE: [*Gazing at zenith.*] Another heavenly day. [*Pause.
Head back level, eyes front, pause. She clasps hands to
breast, closes eyes. Lips move in inaudible prayer, say ten
seconds. Lips still. Hands remain clasped. Low.*] For Jesus
Christ sake Amen. [*Eyes open, hands unclasp, return to
mound. Pause. She clasps hands to breast again, closes
eyes, lips move again in inaudible addendum, say five
seconds. Low.*] World without end Amen. [*Eyes open,
hands unclasp, return to mound. Pause.*] Begin, Winnie.
[*Pause.*] Begin your day, Winnie. [*Pause. She turns to bag,
rummages in it without moving it from its place, brings*

*out toothbrush, rummages again, brings out flat tube of
toothpaste, turns back front, unscrews cap of tube, lays
cap on ground, squeezes with difficulty small blob of
paste on brush, holds tube in one hand and brushes teeth
with other. She turns modestly aside and back to her
right to spit out behind mound. In this position her eyes
rest on* WILLIE. *She spits out. She cranes a little farther
back and down. Loud.*] Hoo-oo! [*Pause. Louder.*]
Hoo-oo! [*Pause. Tender smile as she turns back front,
lays down brush.*] Poor Willie – [*examines tube, smile
off*] – running out – [*looks for cap*] – ah well – [*finds
cap*] – can't be helped – [*screws on cap*] – just one of
those old things – [*lays down tube*] – another of those
old things – [*turns towards bag*] – just can't be cured –
[*rummages in bag*] – cannot be cured – [*brings out small
mirror, turns back front*] – ah yes – [*inspects teeth in
mirror*] – poor dear Willie – [*testing upper front teeth
with thumb, indistinctly*] – good Lord! – [*pulling back
upper lip to inspect gums, do.*] – good God! – [*pulling
back corner of mouth, mouth open, do.*] – ah well –
[*other corner, do.*] – no worse – [*abandons inspection,
normal speech*] – no better, no worse – [*lays down mirror*]
– no change – [*wipes fingers on grass*] – no pain – [*looks
for toothbrush*] – hardly any – [*takes up toothbrush*] –
great thing that – [*examines handle of brush*] – nothing
like it – [*examines handle, reads*] – pure . . . what? –
[*pause*] – what? – [*lays down brush*] – ah yes – [*turns
towards bag*] – poor Willie – [*rummages in bag*] – no zest
– [*rummages*] – for anything – [*brings out spectacles in
case*] – no interest – [*turns back front*] – in life – [*takes
spectacles from case*] – poor dear Willie – [*lays down
case*] – sleep for ever – [*opens spectacles*] – marvellous
gift – [*puts on spectacles*] – nothing to touch it – [*looks
for toothbrush*] – in my opinion – [*takes up toothbrush*] –
always said so – [*examines handle of brush*] – wish I had
it – [*examines handle, reads*] – genuine . . . pure . . . what?
– [*lays down brush*] – blind next – [*takes off spectacles*] –
ah well – [*lays down spectacles*] – seen enough – [*feels in
bodice for handkerchief*] – I suppose – [*takes out folded*

handkerchief] – by now – [*shakes out handkerchief*] –
what are those wonderful lines – [*wipes one eye*] – woe
woe is me – [*wipes the other*] – to see what I see – [*looks
for spectacles*] – ah yes – [*takes up spectacles*] – wouldn't
miss it – [*starts polishing spectacles, breathing on lenses*] –
or would I? – [*polishes*] – holy light – [*polishes*] – bob up
out of dark – [*polishes*] – blaze of hellish light. [*Stops
polishing, raises face to sky, pause, head back level,
resumes polishing, stops polishing, cranes back to her right
and down.*] Hoo-oo! [*Pause. Tender smile as she turns
back front and resumes polishing. Smile off.*] Marvellous
gift – [*stops polishing, lays down spectacles*] – wish I had
it – [*folds handkerchief*] – ah well – [*puts handkerchief
back in bodice*] – can't complain – [*looks for spectacles*] –
no no – [*takes up spectacles*] – mustn't complain – [*holds
up spectacles, looks through lens*] – so much to be
thankful for – [*looks through other lens*] – no pain – [*puts
on spectacles*] – hardly any – [*looks for toothbrush*] –
wonderful thing that – [*takes up toothbrush*] – nothing
like it – [*examines handle of brush*] – slight headache
sometimes – [*examines handle, reads*] – guaranteed . . .
genuine . . . pure . . . what? – [*looks closer*] – genuine
pure . . . – [*takes handkerchief from bodice*] – ah yes –
[*shakes out handkerchief*] – occasional mild migraine –
[*starts wiping handle of brush*] – it comes – [*wipes*] – then
goes – [*wiping mechanically*] – ah yes – [*wiping*] – many
mercies – [*wiping*] – great mercies – [*stops wiping, fixed
lost gaze, brokenly*] – prayers perhaps not for naught –
[*pause, do.*] – first thing – [*pause, do.*] – last thing – [*head
down, resumes wiping, stops wiping, head up, calmed,
wipes eyes, folds handkerchief, puts it back in bodice,
examines handle of brush, reads*] – fully guaranteed . . .
genuine pure . . . – [*looks closer*] – genuine pure . . .
[*Takes off spectacles, lays them and brush down, gazes
before her.*] Old things. [*Pause.*] Old eyes. [*Long pause.*]
On, Winnie. [*She casts about her, sees parasol, considers it
at length, takes it up and develops from sheath a handle of
surprising length. Holding butt of parasol in right hand she
cranes back and down to her right to hang over* WILLIE.]

Hoo-oo! [*Pause.*] Willie! [*Pause.*] Wonderful gift. [*She strikes down at him with beak of parasol.*] Wish I had it. [*She strikes again. The parasol slips from her grasp and falls behind mound. It is immediately restored to her by* WILLIE's *invisible hand.*] Thank you, dear. [*She transfers parasol to left hand, turns back front and examines right palm.*] Damp. [*Returns parasol to right hand, examines left palm.*] Ah well, no worse. [*Head up, cheerfully.*] No better, no worse, no change. [*Pause. Do.*] No pain. [*Cranes back to look down at* WILLIE, *holding parasol by butt as before.*] Don't go off on me again now dear will you please, I may need you. [*Pause.*] No hurry, no hurry, just don't curl up on me again. [*Turns back front, lays down parasol, examines palms together, wipes them on grass.*] Perhaps a shade off colour just the same. [*Turns to bag, rummages in it, brings out revolver, holds it up, kisses it rapidly, puts it back, rummages, brings out almost empty bottle of red medicine, turns back front, looks for spectacles, puts them on, reads label.*] Loss of spirits . . . lack of keenness . . . want of appetite . . . infants . . . children . . . adults . . . six level . . . tablespoonfuls daily – [*head up, smile*] – the old style! – [*smile off, head down, reads*] – daily . . . before and after . . . meals . . . instantaneous . . . [*looks closer*] . . . improvement. [*Takes off spectacles, lays them down, holds up bottle at arm's length to see level, unscrews cap, swigs it off head well back, tosses cap and bottle away in* WILLIE's *direction. Sound of breaking glass.*] Ah that's better! [*Turns to bag, rummages in it, brings out lipstick, turns back front, examines lipstick.*] Running out. [*Looks for spectacles.*] Ah well. [*Puts on spectacles, looks for mirror.*] Mustn't complain. [*Takes up mirror, starts doing lips.*] What is that wonderful line? [*Lips.*] Oh fleeting joys – [*lips*] – oh something lasting woe. [*Lips. She is interrupted by disturbance from* WILLIE. *He is sitting up. She lowers lipstick and mirror and cranes back and down to look at him. Pause. Top back of* WILLIE's *bald head, trickling blood, rises to view above slope, comes to rest.* WINNIE *pushes up her spectacles. Pause. His hand appears with*

handkerchief, spreads it on skull, disappears. Pause. The hand appears with boater, club ribbon, settles it on head, rakish angle, disappears. Pause. WINNIE *cranes a little further back and down.*] Slip on your drawers, dear, before you get singed. [*Pause.*] No? [*Pause.*] Oh I see, you still have some of that stuff left. [*Pause.*] Work it well in, dear. [*Pause.*] Now the other. [*Pause. She turns back front, gazes before her. Happy expression.*] Oh this is going to be another happy day! [*Pause. Happy expression off. She pulls down spectacles and resumes lips.* WILLIE *opens newspaper, hands invisible. Tops of yellow sheets appear on either side of his head.* WINNIE *finishes lips, inspects them in mirror held a little further away.*] Ensign crimson. [WILLIE *turns page.* WINNIE *lays down lipstick and mirror, turns towards bag.*] Pale flag.
[WILLIE *turns page.* WINNIE *rummages in bag, brings out small ornate brimless hat with crumpled feather, turns back front, straightens hat, smooths feather, raises it towards head, arrests gesture as* WILLIE *reads.*]

WILLIE: His Grace and Most Reverend Father in God Dr Carolus Hunter dead in tub.
[*Pause.*]

WINNIE: [*Gazing front, hat in hand, tone of fervent reminiscence.*] Charlie Hunter! [*Pause.*] I close my eyes – [*she takes off spectacles and does so, hat in one hand, spectacles in other,* WILLIE *turns page*] – and am sitting on his knees again, in the back garden at Borough Green, under the horse-beech. [*Pause. She opens eyes, puts on spectacles, fiddles with hat.*] Oh the happy memories! [*Pause. She raises hat towards head, arrests gesture as* WILLIE *reads.*]

WILLIE: Opening for smart youth.
[*Pause. She raises hat towards head, arrests gesture, takes off spectacles, gazes front, hat in one hand, spectacles in other.*]

WINNIE: My first ball! [*Long pause.*] My second ball! [*Long pause. Closes eyes.*] My first kiss! [*Pause.* WILLIE *turns page.* WINNIE *opens eyes.*] A Mr Johnson, or Johnston, or perhaps I should say Johnstone. Very bushy moustache,

very tawny. [*Reverently.*] Almost ginger! [*Pause.*] Within a
toolshed, though whose I cannot conceive. We had no
toolshed and he most certainly had no toolshed. [*Closes
eyes.*] I see the piles of pots. [*Pause.*] The tangles of bast.
[*Pause.*] The shadows deepening among the rafters.
[*Pause. She opens eyes, puts on spectacles, raises hat
towards head, arrests gesture as* WILLIE *reads.*]

WILLIE: Wanted bright boy.
    [*Pause.* WINNIE *puts on hat hurriedly, looks for mirror.*
WILLIE *turns page.* WINNIE *takes up mirror, inspects hat,
lays down mirror, turns towards bag. Paper disappears.*
WINNIE *rummages in bag, brings out magnifying-glass,
turns back front, looks for toothbrush. Paper reappears,
folded, and begins to fan* WILLIE'*s face, hand invisible.*
WINNIE *takes up toothbrush and examines handle
through glass.*]

WINNIE: Fully guaranteed . . . [WILLIE *stops fanning*]
    . . . genuine pure . . . [*Pause.* WILLIE *resumes fanning.*
WINNIE *looks closer, reads.*] Fully guaranteed . . .
[WILLIE *stops fanning*] . . . genuine pure . . . [*Pause.*
WILLIE *resumes fanning.* WINNIE *lays down glass and
brush, takes handkerchief from bodice, takes off and
polishes spectacles, puts on spectacles, looks for glass,
takes up and polishes glass, lays down glass, looks for
brush, takes up brush and wipes handle, lays down brush,
puts handkerchief back in bodice, looks for glass, takes up
glass, looks for brush, takes up brush and examines handle
through glass.*] Fully guaranteed . . . [WILLIE *stops
fanning*] . . . genuine pure . . . [*pause,* WILLIE *resumes
fanning*] . . . hog's . . . [WILLIE *stops fanning, pause*]
    . . . setae. [*Pause.* WINNIE *lays down glass and brush,
paper disappears,* WINNIE *takes off spectacles, lays them
down, gazes front.*] Hog's setae. [*Pause.*] That is what I
find so wonderful, that not a day goes by – [*smile*] – to
speak in the old style – [*smile off*] – hardly a day, without
some addition to one's knowledge however trifling, the
addition I mean, provided one takes the pains. [WILLIE'*s
hand reappears with a postcard which he examines close
to eyes.*] And if for some strange reason no further pains

are possible, why then just close the eyes – [*she does so*] – and wait for the day to come – [*opens eyes*] – the happy day to come when flesh melts at so many degrees and the night of the moon has so many hundred hours. [*Pause.*] That is what I find so comforting when I lose heart and envy the brute beast. [*Turning towards* WILLIE.] I hope you are taking in – [*She sees postcard, bends lower.*] What is that you have there, Willie, may I see? [*She reaches down with hand and* WILLIE *hands her card. The hairy forearm appears above slope, raised in gesture of giving, the hand open to take back, and remains in this position till card is returned.* WINNIE *turns back front and examines card.*] Heavens what are they up to! [*She looks for spectacles, puts them on and examines card.*] No but this is just genuine pure filth! [*Examines card.*] Make any nice-minded person want to vomit! [*Impatience of* WILLIE's *fingers. She looks for glass, takes it up and examines card through glass. Long pause.*] What does that creature in the background think he's doing? [*Looks closer.*] Oh no really! [*Impatience of fingers. Last long look. She lays down glass, takes edge of card between right forefinger and thumb, averts head, takes nose between left forefinger and thumb.*] Pah! [*Drops card.*] Take it away! [WILLIE's *arm disappears. His hand reappears immediately, holding card.* WINNIE *takes off spectacles, lays them down, gazes before her. During what follows* WILLIE *continues to relish card, varying angles and distance from his eyes.*] Hog's setae. [*Puzzled expression.*] What exactly is a hog? [*Pause. Do.*] A sow of course I know, but a hog . . . [*Puzzled expression off.*] Oh well what does it matter, that is what I always say, it will come back, that is what I find so wonderful, all comes back. [*Pause.*] All? [*Pause.*] No, not all. [*Smile.*] No no. [*Smile off.*] Not quite. [*Pause.*] A part. [*Pause.*] Floats up, one fine day, out of the blue. [*Pause.*] That is what I find so wonderful. [*Pause. She turns towards bag. Hand and card disappear. She makes to rummage in bag, arrests gesture.*] No. [*She turns back front. Smile.*] No no. [*Smile off.*] Gently Winnie. [*She gazes front.* WILLIE's *hand reappears, takes off hat, disappears*

with hat.] What then? [*Hand reappears, takes
handkerchief from skull, disappears with handkerchief.
Sharply, as to one not paying attention.*] Winnie! [WILLIE
bows head out of sight.] What *is* the alternative? [*Pause.*]
What *is* the al – [WILLIE *blows nose loud and long, head
and hands invisible. She turns to look at him. Pause. Head
reappears. Pause. Hand reappears with handkerchief,
spreads it on skull, disappears. Pause. Hand reappears
with boater, settles it on head, rakish angle, disappears.
Pause.*] Would I had let you sleep on. [*She turns back
front. Intermittent plucking at grass, head up and down, to
animate following.*] Ah yes, if only I could bear to be
alone, I mean prattle away with not a soul to hear.
[*Pause.*] Not that I flatter myself you hear much, no Willie,
God forbid. [*Pause.*] Days perhaps when you hear nothing.
[*Pause.*] But days too when you answer. [*Pause.*] So that I
may say at all times, even when you do not answer and
perhaps hear nothing, something of this is being heard, I
am not merely talking to myself, that is in the wilderness, a
thing I could never bear to do – for any length of time.
[*Pause.*] That is what enables me to go on, go on talking
that is. [*Pause.*] Whereas if you were to die – [*smile*] – to
speak in the old style – [*smile off*] – or go away and leave
me, then what would I do, what *could* I do, all day long, I
mean between the bell for waking and the bell for sleep?
[*Pause.*] Simply gaze before me with compressed lips.
[*Long pause while she does so. No more plucking.*] Not
another word as long as I drew breath, nothing to break
the silence of this place. [*Pause.*] Save possibly, now and
then, every now and then, a sigh into my looking-glass.
[*Pause.*] Or a brief . . . gale of laughter, should I happen to
see the old joke again. [*Pause. Smile appears, broadens and
seems about to culminate in laugh when suddenly replaced
by expression of anxiety.*] My hair! [*Pause.*] Did I brush
and comb my hair? [*Pause.*] I may have done. [*Pause.*]
Normally I do. [*Pause.*] There is so little one *can* do.
[*Pause.*] One does it all. [*Pause.*] All one can. [*Pause.*] 'Tis
only human. [*Pause.*] Human nature. [*She begins to
inspect mound, looks up.*] Human weakness. [*She resumes

inspection of mound, looks up.] Natural weakness. [*She resumes inspection of mound.*] I see no comb. [*Inspects.*] Nor any hairbrush. [*Looks up. Puzzled expression. She turns to bag, rummages in it.*] The comb is here. [*Back front. Puzzled expression. Back to bag. Rummages.*] The brush is here. [*Back front. Puzzled expression.*] Perhaps I put them back, after use. [*Pause. Do.*] But normally I do not put things back, after use, no, I leave them lying about and put them back all together, at the end of the day. [*Smile.*] To speak in the old style. [*Pause.*] The sweet old style. [*Smile off.*] And yet . . . I seem . . . to remember . . . [*Suddenly careless.*] Oh well, what does it matter, that is what I always say, I shall simply brush and comb them later on, purely and simply, I have the whole – [*Pause. Puzzled.*] Them? [*Pause.*] Or it? [*Pause.*] Brush and comb it? [*Pause.*] Sounds improper somehow. [*Pause. Turning a little towards* WILLIE.] What would you say, Willie? [*Pause. Turning a little further.*] What would you say, Willie, speaking of your hair, them or it? [*Pause.*] The hair on your head, I mean. [*Pause. Turning a little further.*] The hair on your head, Willie, what would you say speaking of the hair on your head, them or it? [*Long pause.*]

WILLIE: It.

WINNIE: [*Turning back front, joyful.*] Oh you are going to talk to me today, this is going to be a happy day! [*Pause. Joy off.*] Another happy day. [*Pause.*] Ah well, where was I, my hair, yes, later on, I shall be thankful for it later on. [*Pause.*] I have my – [*raises hands to hat*] – yes, on, my hat on – [*lowers hands*] – I cannot take it off now. [*Pause.*] To think there are times one cannot take off one's hat, not if one's life were at stake. Times one cannot put it on, times one cannot take it off. [*Pause.*] How often I have said, Put on your hat now, Winnie, there is nothing else for it, take off your hat now, Winnie, like a good girl, it will do you good, and did not. [*Pause.*] Could not. [*Pause. She raises hand, frees a strand of hair from under hat, draws it towards eye, squints at it, lets it go, hand down.*] Golden you called it, that day, when the last guest was gone – [*hand up in gesture of raising a glass*] – to your golden . . .

may it never . . . [*voice breaks*] . . . may it never . . . [*Hand
down. Head down. Pause. Low.*] That day. [*Pause. Do.*]
What day? [*Pause. Head up. Normal voice.*] What now?
[*Pause.*] Words fail, there are times when even they fail.
[*Turning a little towards* WILLIE.] Is that not so, Willie?
[*Pause. Turning a little further.*] Is not that so, Willie, that
even words fail, at times? [*Pause. Back front.*] What is one
to do then, until they come again? Brush and comb the
hair, if it has not been done, or if there is some doubt, trim
the nails if they are in need of trimming, these things tide
one over. [*Pause.*] That is what I mean. [*Pause.*] That is all
I mean. [*Pause.*] That is what I find so wonderful, that not
a day goes by — [*smile*] — to speak in the old style — [*smile
off*] — without some blessing — [WILLIE *collapses behind
slope, his head disappears,* WINNIE *turns towards event*] —
in disguise. [*She cranes back and down.*] Go back into
your hole now, Willie, you've exposed yourself enough.
[*Pause.*] Do as I say, Willie, don't lie sprawling there in
this hellish sun, go back into your hole. [*Pause.*] Go on
now, Willie. [WILLIE *invisible starts crawling left towards
hole.*] That's the man. [*She follows his progress with her
eyes.*] Not head first, stupid, how are you going to turn?
[*Pause.*] That's it . . . right round . . . now . . . back in.
[*Pause.*] Oh I know it is not easy, dear, crawling
backwards, but it is rewarding in the end. [*Pause.*] You
have left your vaseline behind. [*She watches as he crawls
back for vaseline.*] The lid! [*She watches as he crawls back
towards hole. Irritated.*] Not head first, I tell you! [*Pause.*]
More to the right. [*Pause.*] The *right*, I said. [*Pause.
Irritated.*] Keep your tail down, can't you! [*Pause.*] Now.
[*Pause.*] There! [*All these directions loud. Now in her
normal voice, still turned towards him.*] Can you hear me?
[*Pause.*] I beseech you, Willie, just yes or no, can you hear
me, just yes or nothing.
[*Pause.*]

WILLIE: Yes.

WINNIE: [*Turning front, same voice.*] And now?

WILLIE: [*Irritated.*] Yes.

WINNIE: [*Less loud.*] And now?

WILLIE: [*More irritated.*] Yes.

WINNIE: [*Still less loud.*] And now? [*A little louder.*] And now?

WILLIE: [*Violently.*] Yes!

WINNIE: [*Same voice.*] Fear no more the heat o' the sun. [*Pause.*] Did you hear that?

WILLIE: [*Irritated.*] Yes.

WINNIE: [*Same voice.*] What? [*Pause.*] What?

WILLIE: [*More irritated.*] Fear no more.
[*Pause.*]

WINNIE: [*Same voice.*] No more what? [*Pause.*] Fear no more what?

WILLIE: [*Violently.*] Fear no more!

WINNIE: [*Normal voice, gabbled.*] Bless you Willie I do appreciate your goodness I know what an effort it costs you, now you may relax I shall not trouble you again unless I am obliged to, by that I mean unless I come to the end of my own resources which is most unlikely, just to know that in theory you can hear me even though in fact you don't is all I need, just to feel you there within earshot and conceivably on the qui vive is all I ask, not to say anything I would not wish you to hear or liable to cause you pain, not to be just babbling away on trust as it is were not knowing and something gnawing at me. [*Pause for breath.*] Doubt. [*Places index and second finger on heart area, moves them about, brings them to rest.*] Here. [*Moves them slightly.*] Abouts. [*Hand away.*] Oh no doubt the time will come when before I can utter a word I must make sure you heard the one that went before and then no doubt another come another time when I must learn to talk to myself a thing I could never bear to do such wilderness. [*Pause.*] Or gaze before me with compressed lips. [*She does so.*] All day long. [*Gaze and lips again.*] No. [*Smile.*] No no. [*Smile off.*] There is of course the bag. [*Turns towards it.*] There will always be the bag. [*Back front.*] Yes, I suppose so. [*Pause.*] Even when you are gone, Willie. [*She turns a little towards him.*] You *are* going, Willie, aren't you? [*Pause. Louder.*] You *will* be going soon, Willie, won't you? [*Pause. Louder.*] Willie! [*Pause. She cranes back and down to look at him.*] So you have

taken off your straw, that is wise. [*Pause.*] You do look
snug, I must say, with your chin on your hands and the old
blue eyes like saucers in the shadows. [*Pause.*] Can you see
me from there I wonder, I still wonder. [*Pause.*] No? [*Back
front.*] Oh I know it does not follow when two are
gathered together — [*faltering*] — in this way — [*normal*] —
that because one sees the other the other sees the one, life
has taught me that . . . too. [*Pause.*] Yes, life I suppose,
there is no other word. [*She turns a little towards him.*]
Could you see me, Willie, do you think, from where you
are, if you were to raise your eyes in my direction? [*Turns
a little further.*] Lift up your eyes to me, Willie, and tell me
can you see me, do that for me, I'll lean back as far as I
can. [*Does so. Pause.*] No? [*Pause.*] Well never mind.
[*Turns back painfully front.*] The earth is very tight today,
can it be I have put on flesh, I trust not. [*Pause. Absently,
eyes lowered.*] The great heat possibly. [*Starts to pat and
stroke ground.*] All things expanding, some more than
others. [*Pause. Patting and stroking.*] Some less. [*Pause.
Do.*] Oh I can well imagine what is passing through your
mind, it is not enough to have to listen to the woman, now
I must look at her as well. [*Pause. Do.*] Well it is very
understandable. [*Pause. Do.*] Most understandable.
[*Pause. Do.*] One does not appear to be asking a great
deal, indeed at times it would seem hardly possible —
[*voice breaks, falls to a murmur*] — to ask less — of a
fellow-creature — to put it mildly — whereas actually —
when you think about it — look into your heart — see the
other — what he needs — peace — to be left in peace — then
perhaps the moon — all this time — asking for the moon.
[*Pause. Stroking hand suddenly still. Lively.*] Oh I say,
what have we here? [*Bending head to ground,
incredulous.*] Looks like life of some kind! [*Looks for
spectacles, puts them on, bends closer. Pause.*] An emmet!
[*Recoils. Shrill.*] Willie, an emmet, a live emmet! [*Seizes
magnifying-glass, bends to ground again, inspects through
glass.*] Where's it gone? [*Inspects.*] Ah! [*Follows its
progress through grass.*] Has like a little white ball in its
arms. [*Follows progress. Hand still. Pause.*] It's gone in.

[*Continues a moment to gaze at spot through glass, then slowly straightens up, lays down glass, takes off spectacles and gazes before her, spectacles in hand. Finally.*] Like a little white ball. [*Long pause. Gesture to lay down spectacles.*]

WILLIE: Eggs.

WINNIE: [*Arresting gesture.*) What?
[*Pause.*]

WILLIE: Eggs. [*Pause. Gesture to lay down glasses.*] Formication.

WINNIE: [*Arresting gesture.*] What?
[*Pause.*]

WILLIE: Formication.
[*Pause. She lays down spectacles, gazes before her. Finally.*]

WINNIE: [*Murmur.*] God. [*Pause.* WILLIE *laughs quietly. After a moment she joins in. They laugh quietly together.* WILLIE *stops. She laughs on a moment alone.* WILLIE *joins in. They laugh together. She stops.* WILLIE *laughs on a moment alone. He stops. Pause. Normal voice.*] Ah well what a joy in any case to hear you laugh again, Willie, I was convinced I never would, you never would. [*Pause.*] I suppose some people might think us a trifle irreverent, but I doubt it. [*Pause.*] How can one better magnify the Almighty than by sniggering with him at his little jokes, particularly the poorer ones? [*Pause.*] I think you would back me up there, Willie. [*Pause.*] Or were we perhaps diverted by two quite different things? [*Pause.*] Oh well, what does it matter, that is what I always say, so long as one . . . you know . . . what is that wonderful line . . . laughing wild . . . something something laughing wild amid severest woe. [*Pause.*] And now? [*Long pause.*] Was I lovable once, Willie? [*Pause.*] Was I ever lovable? [*Pause.*] Do not misunderstand my question, I am not asking you if you loved me, we know all about that, I am asking you if you found me lovable – at one stage. [*Pause.*] No? [*Pause.*] You can't? [*Pause.*] Well I admit it is a teaser. And you have done more than your bit already, for the time being, just lie back now and relax, I shall not trouble you again unless I am compelled to, just to know you are there

within hearing and conceivably on the semi-alert is . . .
er . . . paradise enow. [*Pause.*] The day is now well
advanced. [*Smile.*] To speak in the old style. [*Smile off.*]
And yet it is perhaps a little soon for my song. [*Pause.*] To
sing too soon is a great mistake, I find. [*Turning towards
bag.*] There is of course the bag. [*Looking at bag.*] The bag.
[*Back front.*] Could I enumerate its contents? [*Pause.*] No.
[*Pause.*] Could I, if some kind person were to come along
and ask, What all have you got in that big black bag,
Winnie? give an exhaustive answer? [*Pause.*] No. [*Pause.*]
The depths in particular, who knows what treasures.
[*Pause.*] What comforts. [*Turns to look at bag.*] Yes, there is
the bag. [*Back front.*] But something tells me, Do not
overdo the bag, Winnie, make use of it of course, let it help
you . . . along, when stuck, by all means, but cast your mind
forward, something tells me, cast your mind forward,
Winnie, to the time when words must fail – [*she closes eyes,
pause, opens eyes*] – and do not overdo the bag. [*Pause. She
turns to look at bag.*] Perhaps just one quick dip. [*She turns
back front, closes eyes, throws out left arm, plunges hand in
bag and brings out revolver. Disgusted.*] You again! [*She
opens eyes, brings revolver front and contemplates it. She
weighs it in her palm.*] You'd think the weight of this thing
would bring it down among the . . . last rounds. But no. It
doesn't. Ever uppermost, like Browning. [*Pause.*]
Brownie . . . [*Turning a little towards* WILLIE.] Remember
Brownie, Willie? [*Pause.*] Remember how you used to keep
on at me to take it away from you? Take it away, Winnie,
take it away, before I put myself out of my misery. [*Back
front. Derisive.*] Your misery! [*To revolver.*] Oh I suppose
it's a comfort to know you're there, but I'm tired of you.
[*Pause.*] I'll leave you out, that's what I'll do. [*She lays
revolver on ground to her right.*] There, that's your home
from this day out. [*Smile.*] The old style! [*Smile off.*] And
now? [*Long pause.*] Is gravity what it was, Willie, I fancy
not. [*Pause.*] Yes, the feeling more and more that if I were
not held – [*gesture*] – in this way, I would simply float up
into the blue. [*Pause.*] And that perhaps some day the
earth will yield and let me go, the pull is so great, yes,

crack all round me and let me out. [*Pause.*] Don't you ever
have that feeling, Willie, of being sucked up? [*Pause.*]
Don't you have to cling on sometimes, Willie? [*Pause. She
turns a little towards him.*] Willie.
[*Pause.*]

WILLIE: *Sucked* up?

WINNIE: Yes love, up into the blue, like gossamer. [*Pause.*]
No? [*Pause.*] You don't? [*Pause.*] Ah well, natural laws,
natural laws, I suppose it's like everything else, it all
depends on the creature you happen to be. All I can say is
for my part is that for me they are not what they were
when I was young and . . . foolish and . . . [*faltering, head
down*] . . . beautiful . . . possibly . . . lovely . . . in a
way . . . to look at. [*Pause. Head up.*] Forgive me, Willie,
sorrow keeps breaking in. [*Normal voice.*] Ah well what a
joy in any case to know you are there, as usual, and
perhaps awake, and perhaps taking all this in, some of all
this, what a happy day for me . . . it will have been.
[*Pause.*] So far. [*Pause.*] What a blessing nothing grows,
imagine if all this stuff were to start growing. [*Pause.*]
Imagine. [*Pause.*] Ah yes, great mercies. [*Long pause.*] I
can say no more. [*Pause.*] For the moment. [*Pause. Turns
to look at bag. Back front. Smile.*] No no. [*Smile off.
Looks at parasol.*] I suppose I might – [*takes up parasol*] –
yes, I suppose I might . . . hoist this thing now. [*Begins to
unfurl it. Following punctuated by mechanical difficulties
overcome.*] One keeps putting off – putting up – for fear
of putting up too soon – and the day goes by – quite by –
without one's having put up – at all. [*Parasol now fully
open. Turned to her right she twirls it idly this way and
that.*] Ah yes, so little to say, so little to do, and the fear so
great, certain days, of finding oneself . . . left, with hours
still to run, before the bell for sleep, and nothing more to
say, nothing more to do, that the days go by, certain days
go by, quite by, the bell goes, and little or nothing said,
little or nothing done. [*Raising parasol.*] That is the
danger. [*Turning front.*] To be guarded against. [*She gazes
front, holding up parasol with right hand. Maximum
pause.*] I used to perspire freely. [*Pause.*] Now hardly at

all. [*Pause.*] The heat is much greater. [*Pause.*] The perspiration much less. [*Pause.*] That is what I find so wonderful. [*Pause.*] The way man adapts himself. [*Pause.*] To changing conditions. [*She transfers parasol to left hand. Long pause.*] Holding up wearies the arm. [*Pause.*] Not if one is going along. [*Pause.*] Only if one is at rest. [*Pause.*] That is a curious observation. [*Pause.*] I hope you heard that, Willie, I should be grieved to think you had not heard that. [*She takes parasol in both hands. Long pause.*] I am weary, holding it up, and I cannot put it down. [*Pause.*] I am worse off with it up than with it down, and I cannot put it down. [*Pause.*] Reason says, Put it down, Winnie, it is not helping you, put the thing down and get on with something else. [*Pause.*] I cannot. [*Pause.*] I cannot move. [*Pause.*] No, something must happen, in the world, take place, some change, I cannot, if I am to move again. [*Pause.*] Willie. [*Mildly.*] Help. [*Pause.*] No? [*Pause.*] Bid me put this thing down, Willie, I would obey you instantly, as I have always done, honoured and obeyed. [*Pause.*] Please, Willie. [*Mildly.*] For pity's sake. [*Pause.*] No? [*Pause.*] You can't? [*Pause.*]. Well I don't blame you, no, it would ill become me, who cannot move, to blame my Willie because he cannot speak. [*Pause.*] Fortunately I am in tongue again. [*Pause.*] That is what I find so wonderful, my two lamps, when one goes out the other burns brighter. [*Pause.*] Oh yes, great mercies. [*Maximum pause. The parasol goes on fire. Smoke, flames if feasible. She sniffs, looks up, throws parasol to her right behind mound, cranes back to watch it burning. Pause.*] Ah earth you old extinguisher. [*Back front.*] I presume this has occurred before, though I cannot recall it. [*Pause.*] Can you, Willie? [*Turns a little towards him.*] Can you recall this having occurred before? [*Pause. Cranes back to look at him.*] Do you know what has occurred, Willie? [*Pause.*] Have you gone off on me again? [*Pause.*] I do not ask if you are alive to all that is going on, I merely ask if you have not gone off on me again. [*Pause.*] Your eyes appear to be closed, but that has no particular significance we know. [*Pause.*] Raise a finger, dear, will you please, if you are not quite senseless. [*Pause.*] Do that for me, Willie please, just the little finger, if you are still conscious. [*Pause. Joyful.*] Oh all five, you are a darling today, now I may continue with an easy mind. [*Back front.*] Yes, what ever occurred that did not occur before and yet . . . I wonder, yes, I confess I wonder. [*Pause.*] With the sun blazing so much fiercer down, and hourly fiercer, is it not natural things should go on fire never known to do so, in this way I mean, spontaneous like. [*Pause.*] Shall I myself not melt perhaps in the end, or burn, oh I do not mean necessarily burst into flames, no, just little by little be charred to a black cinder, all this – [*ample gesture of arms*] – visible flesh. [*Pause.*] On the other hand, did I ever know a temperate time? [*Pause.*] No. [*Pause.*] I speak of temperate times and torrid times, they are empty words. [*Pause.*] I speak of when I was not yet caught – in this way – and had my legs and had the use of my legs, and could seek out a shady place, like you, when I was tired of the sun, or a sunny place when I was tired of the shade, like you, and they are all empty words. [*Pause.*] It is no hotter today than yesterday, it will be no hotter tomorrow than today, how could it, and so on back into the far past, forward into the far future. [*Pause.*] And should one day the earth cover my breasts, then I shall never have seen my breasts, no one ever seen my breasts. [*Pause.*] I hope you caught something of that, Willie, I should be sorry to think you had caught nothing of all that, it is not every day I rise to such heights. [*Pause.*] Yes, something seems to have occurred, something has seemed to occur, and nothing has occurred, nothing at all, you are quite right, Willie. [*Pause.*] The sunshade will be there again tomorrow, beside me on this mound, to help me through the day. [*Pause. She takes up mirror.*] I take up this little glass, I shiver it on a stone – [*does so*] – I throw it away – [*does so far behind her*] – it will be in the bag again tomorrow, without a scratch, to help me through the day. [*Pause.*] No, one can do nothing. [*Pause.*] That is what I find so wonderful, the way things . . . [*voice breaks, head down*] . . . things . . . so wonderful. [*Long pause, head down. Finally turns, still bowed, to bag, brings*

*out unidentifiable odds and ends, stuffs them back,
fumbles deeper, brings out finally musical-box, winds it
up, turns it on, listens for a moment holding it in both
hands, huddled over it, turns back front, straightens up
and listens to tune, holding box to breast with both hands.
It plays the Waltz Duet 'I love you so' from The Merry
Widow. Gradually happy expression. She sways to the
rhythm. Music stops. Pause. Brief burst of hoarse song
without words – musical-box tune – from* WILLIE.
Increase of happy expression. She lays down box.] Oh this
will have been a happy day! [*She claps hands.*] Again,
Willie, again! [*Claps.*] Encore, Willie, please! [*Pause.
Happy expression off.*] No? You won't do that for me?
[*Pause.*] Well it is very understandable, very
understandable. One cannot sing just to please someone,
however much one loves them, no, song must come from
the heart, that is what I always say, pour out from the
inmost, like a thrush. [*Pause.*] How often I have said, in
evil hours, Sing now, Winnie, sing your song, there is
nothing else for it, and did not. [*Pause.*] Could not.
[*Pause.*] No, like the thrush, or the bird of dawning, with
no thought of benefit, to oneself or anyone else. [*Pause.*]
And now? [*Long pause. Low.*] Strange feeling. [*Pause.
Do.*] Strange feeling that someone is looking at me. I am
clear, then dim, then gone, then dim again, then clear
again, and so on, back and forth, in and out of someone's
eye. [*Pause. Do.*] Strange? [*Pause. Do.*] No, <u>here</u> all is
strange. [*Pause. Normal voice.*] Something says, Stop
talking now, Winnie, for a minute, don't squander all your
words for the day, stop talking and do something for a
change, will you? [*She raises hands and holds them open
before her eyes. Apostrophic.*] Do something! [*She closes
hands.*] What claws! [*She turns to bag, rummages in it,
brings out finally a nailfile, turns back front and begins to
file nails. Files for a time in silence, then the following
punctuated by filing.*] There floats up – into my thoughts –
a Mr Shower – a Mr and perhaps a Mrs Shower – no –
they are holding hands – his fiancée then more likely – or
just some – loved one. [*Looks closer at nails.*] Very brittle

today. [*Resumes filing.*] Shower – Shower – does the name
mean anything – to you, Willie – evoke any reality, I mean
– for you, Willie – don't answer if you don't – feel up to it
– you have done more – than your bit – already – Shower
– Shower. [*Inspects filed nails.*] Bit more like it. [*Raises
head, gazes front.*] Keep yourself nice, Winnie, that's what
I always say, come what may, keep yourself nice. [*Pause.
Resumes filing.*] Yes – Shower – Shower – [*stops filing,
raises head, gazes front, pause*] – or Cooker, perhaps I
should say Cooker. [*Turning a little towards* WILLIE.]
Cooker, Willie, does Cooker strike a chord? [*Pause. Turns
a little further. Louder.*] Cooker, Willie, does Cooker ring
a bell, the name Cooker? [*Pause. She cranes back to look
at him. Pause.*] Oh really! [*Pause.*] Have you no
handkerchief, darling? [*Pause.*] Have you no delicacy?
[*Pause.*] Oh, Willie, you're not eating it! Spit it out, dear,
spit it out! [*Pause. Back front.*] Ah well, I suppose it's only
natural. [*Break in voice.*] Human. [*Pause. Do.*] What *is*
one to do? [*Head down. Do.*] All day long. [*Pause. Do.*]
Day after day. [*Pause. Head up. Smile. Calm.*] The old
style! [*Smile off. Resumes nails.*] No, done him. [*Passes on
to next.*] Should have put on my glasses. [*Pause.*] Too late
now. [*Finishes left hand, inspects it.*] Bit more human.
[*Starts right hand. Following punctuated as before.*] Well
anyway – this man Shower – or Cooker – no matter –
and the woman – hand in hand – in the other hands bags
– kind of big brown grips – standing there gaping at me –
and at last this man Shower – or Cooker – ends in 'er
anyway – stake my life on that – What's she doing? he
says – What's the idea? he says – stuck up to her diddies
in the bleeding ground – coarse fellow – What does it
mean? he says – What's it meant to mean? – and so on –
lot more stuff like that – usual drivel – Do you hear me?
he says – I do, she says, God help me – What do you
mean, he says, God help you? [*Stops filing, raises head,
gazes front.*] And you, she says, what's the idea of you, she
says, what are you meant to mean? Is it because you're still
on your two flat feet, with your old ditty full of tinned
muck and changes of underwear, dragging me up and

down this fornicating wilderness, coarse creature, fit mate
– [*with sudden violence*] – let go of my hand and drop for
God's sake, she says, drop! [*Pause. Resumes filing.*] Why
doesn't he dig her out? he says – referring to you, my dear
– What good is she to him like that? – What good is he to
her like that? – and so on – usual tosh – Good! she says,
have a heart for God's sake – Dig her out, he says, dig her
out, no sense in her like that – Dig her out with what? she
says – I'd dig her out with my bare hands, he says – must
have been man and – wife. [*Files in silence.*] Next thing
they're away – hand in hand – and the bags – dim – then
gone – last human kind – to stray this way. [*Finishes right
hand, inspects it, lays down file, gazes front.*] Strange
thing, time like this, drift up into the mind. [*Pause.*]
Strange? [*Pause.*] No, here all is strange. [*Pause.*] Thankful
for it in any case. [*Voice breaks.*] Most thankful. [*Head
down. Pause. Head up. Calm.*] Bow and raise the head,
bow and raise, always that. [*Pause.*] And now? [*Long
pause. Starts putting things back in bag, toothbrush last.
This operation, interrupted by pauses as indicated,
punctuates following.*] It is perhaps a little soon – to make
ready – for the night – [*stops tidying, head up, smile*] –
the old style! – [*smile off, resumes tidying*] – and yet I do
– make ready for the night – feeling it at hand – the bell
for sleep – saying to myself – Winnie – it will not be long
now, Winnie – until the bell for sleep. [*Stops tidying, head
up.*] Sometimes I am wrong. [*Smile.*] But not often. [*Smile
off.*] Sometimes all is over, for the day, all done, all said,
all ready for the night, and the day not over, far from over,
the night not ready, far, far from ready. [*Smile.*] But not
often. [*Smile off.*] Yes, the bell for sleep, when I feel it at
hand, and so make ready for the night – [*gesture*] – in this
way, sometimes I am wrong – [*smile*] – but not often.
[*Smile off. Resumes tidying.*] I used to think – I say I used
to think – that all these things – put back into the bag – if
too soon – put back too soon – could be taken out again
– if necessary – if needed – and so on – indefinitely –
back into the bag – back out of the bag – until the bell –
went. [*Stops tidying, head up, smile.*] But no. [*Smile

broader.] No no. [*Smile off. Resumes tidying.*] I suppose
this – might seem strange – this – what shall I say – this
what I have said – yes – [*she takes up revolver*] – strange
– [*she turns to put revolver in bag*] – were it not – [*about
to put revolver in bag she arrests gesture and turns back
front*] – were it not – [*she lays down revolver to her right,
stops tidying, head up*] – that all seems strange. [*Pause.*]
Most strange. [*Pause.*] Never any change. [*Pause.*] And
more and more strange [*Pause. She bends to mound again,
takes up last object, i.e. toothbrush, and turns to put it in
bag when her attention is drawn to disturbance from
WILLIE. She cranes back and to her right to see. Pause.*]
Weary of your hole, dear? [*Pause.*] Well I can understand
that. [*Pause.*] Don't forget your straw. [*Pause.*] Not the
crawler you were, poor darling. [*Pause.*] No, not the
crawler I gave my heart to. [*Pause.*] The hands and knees,
love, try the hands and knees. [*Pause.*] The knees! The
knees! [*Pause.*] What a curse, mobility! [*She follows with
eyes his progress towards her behind mound, i.e. towards
place he occupied at beginning of act.*] Another foot,
Willie, and you're home. [*Pause as she observes last foot.*]
Ah! [*Turns back front laboriously, rubs neck.*] Crick in my
neck admiring you. [*Rubs neck.*] But it's worth it, well
worth it. [*Turning slightly towards him.*] Do you know
what I dream sometimes? [*Pause.*] What I dream
sometimes, Willie. [*Pause.*] That you'll come round and
live this side where I could see you. [*Pause. Back front.*] I'd
be a different woman. [*Pause.*] Unrecognizable. [*Turning
slightly towards him.*] Or just now and then, come round
this side just every now and then and let me feast on you.
[*Back front.*] But you can't, I know. [*Head down.*] I know.
[*Pause. Head up.*] Well anyway – [*looks at toothbrush in
her hand*] – can't be long now – [*looks at brush*] – until
the bell. [*Top back of WILLIE's head appears above slope.
WINNIE looks closer at brush.*] Fully guaranteed . . . [*head
up*] . . . what's this it was? [*WILLIE's hand appears with
handkerchief, spreads it on skull, disappears.*] Genuine
pure . . . fully guaranteed . . . [*WILLIE's hand appears with
boater, settles it on head, rakish angle, disappears*]

. . . genuine pure . . . ah! hog's setae. [*Pause.*] What is a hog exactly? [*Pause. Turns slightly towards* WILLIE.] What exactly is a hog, Willie, do you know, I can't remember. [*Pause. Turning a little further, pleading.*] What *is* a hog, Willie, please! [*Pause.*]

WILLIE: Castrated male swine. [*Happy expression appears on* WINNIE's *face.*] Reared for slaughter. [*Happy expression increases.* WILLIE *opens newspaper, hands invisible. Tops of yellow sheets appear on either side of his head.* WINNIE *gazes before her with happy expression.*]

WINNIE: Oh this *is* a happy day! This will have been another happy day! [*Pause.*] After all. [*Pause.*] So far.
[*Pause. Happy expression off.* WILLIE *turns page. Pause. He turns another page. Pause.*]

WILLIE: Opening for smart youth.
[*Pause.* WINNIE *takes off hat, turns to put it in bag, arrests gesture, turns back front. Smile.*]

WINNIE: No. [*Smile broader.*] No no. [*Smile off. Puts on hat again, gazes front, pause.*] And now? [*Pause.*] Sing. [*Pause.*] Sing your song, Winnie. [*Pause.*] No? [*Pause.*] Then pray. [*Pause.*] Pray your prayer, Winnie.
[*Pause.* WILLIE *turns page. Pause.*]

WILLIE: Wanted bright boy.
[*Pause.* WILLIE *gazes before her.* WILLIE *turns page. Pause. Newspaper disappears. Long pause.*]

WINNIE: Pray your old prayer, Winnie.
[*Long pause.*]

CURTAIN

ACT TWO

Scene as before.

WINNIE *embedded up to neck, hat on head, eyes closed. Her head, which she can no longer turn, nor bow, nor raise, faces front motionless throughout act. Movements of eyes as indicated.*

Bag and parasol as before. Revolver conspicuous to her right on mound.

Long pause.

Bell rings loudly. She opens eyes at once. Bell stops. She gazes front. Long pause.

WINNIE: Hail, holy light. [*Long pause. She closes her eyes. Bell rings loudly. She opens eyes at once. Bell stops. She gazes front. Long smile. Smile off. Long pause.*] Someone is looking at me still. [*Pause.*] Caring for me still. [*Pause.*] That is what I find so wonderful. [*Pause.*] Eyes on my eyes. [*Pause.*] What is that unforgettable line? [*Pause. Eyes right.*] Willie. [*Pause. Louder.*] Willie. [*Pause. Eyes front.*] May one still speak of time? [*Pause.*] Say it is a long time now, Willie, since I saw you. [*Pause.*] Since I heard you. [*Pause.*] May one? [*Pause.*] One does. [*Smile.*] The old style! [*Smile off.*] There is so little one can speak of. [*Pause.*] One speaks of it all. [*Pause.*] All one can. [*Pause.*] I used to think . . . [*pause*] . . . I say I used to think that I would learn to talk alone. [*Pause.*] By that I mean to myself, the wilderness. [*Smile.*] But no. [*Smile broader.*] No no. [*Smile off.*] Ergo you are there. [*Pause.*] Oh no doubt you are dead, like the others, no doubt you have died, or gone away and left me, like the others, it doesn't matter, you are there. [*Pause. Eyes left.*] The bag too is there, the same as ever, I can see it. [*Pause. Eyes right. Louder.*] The bag is there, Willie, as good as ever, the one you gave me that day . . . to go to market. [*Pause. Eyes*

front.] That day. [*Pause.*] What day? [*Pause.*] I used to pray.
[*Pause.*] I say I used to pray. [*Pause.*] Yes, I must confess I did.
[*Smile.*] Not now. [*Smile broader.*] No no. [*Smile off. Pause.*]
Then . . . now . . . what difficulties here, for the mind.
[*Pause.*] To have been always what I am – and so changed
from what I was. [*Pause.*] I am the one, I say the one, then the
other. [*Pause.*] Now the one, then the other. [*Pause.*] There is
so little one can say, one says it all. [*Pause.*] All one can.
[*Pause.*] And no truth in it anywhere. [*Pause.*] My arms.
[*Pause.*] My breasts. [*Pause.*] What arms? [*Pause.*] What
breasts? [*Pause.*] Willie. [*Pause.*] What Willie? [*Sudden
vehement affirmation.*] My Willie! [*Eyes right, calling.*]
Willie! [*Pause. Louder.*] Willie! [*Pause. Eyes front.*] Ah well,
not to know, not to know for sure, great mercy, all I ask.
[*Pause.*] Ah yes . . . then . . . now . . . beechen green . . .
this . . . Charlie . . . kisses . . . this . . . all that . . . deep
trouble for the mind. [*Pause.*] But it does not trouble mine.
[*Smile.*] Not now. [*Smile broader.*] No no. [*Smile off. Long
pause. She closes eyes. Bell rings loudly. She opens eyes.
Pause.*] Eyes float up that seem to close in peace . . . to see . . .
in peace. [*Pause.*] Not mine. [*Smile.*] Not now. [*Smile
broader.*] No no. [*Smile off. Long pause.*] Willie. [*Pause.*] Do
you think the earth has lost its atmosphere, Willie? [*Pause.*]
Do you, Willie? [*Pause.*] You have no opinion? [*Pause.*] Well
that is like you, you never had any opinion about anything.
[*Pause.*] It's understandable. [*Pause.*] Most. [*Pause.*] The
earth ball. [*Pause.*] I sometimes wonder. [*Pause.*] Perhaps not
quite all. [*Pause.*] There always remains something. [*Pause.*]
Of everything. [*Pause.*] Some remains. [*Pause.*] If the mind
were to go. [*Pause.*] It won't of course. [*Pause.*] Not quite.
[*Pause.*] Not mine. [*Smile.*] Not now. [*Smile broader.*] No
no. [*Smile off. Long pause.*] It might be the eternal cold.
[*Pause.*] Everlasting perishing cold. [*Pause.*] Just chance, I
take it, happy chance. [*Pause.*] Oh yes, great mercies, great
mercies. [*Pause.*] And now? [*Long pause.*] The face.
[*Pause.*] The nose. [*She squints down.*] I can see it . . .
[*squinting down*] . . . the tip . . . the nostrils . . . breath of
life . . . that curve you so admired . . . [*pouts*] . . . a hint of
lip . . . [*pouts again*] . . . if I pout them out . . . [*sticks out

tongue] . . . the tongue of course . . . you so admired . . . if
I stick it out . . . [*sticks it out again*] . . . the tip . . . [*eyes
up*] . . . suspicion of brow . . . eyebrow . . . imagination
possibly . . . [*eyes left*] . . . cheek . . . no . . . [*eyes right*] . . .
no . . . [*distends cheeks*] . . . even if I puff them out . . .
[*eyes left, distends cheeks again*] . . . no . . . no damask.
[*Eyes front.*] That is all. [*Pause.*] The bag of course . . .
[*eyes left*] . . . a little blurred perhaps . . . but the bag.
[*Eyes front. Offhand.*] The earth of course and sky. [*Eyes
right.*] The sunshade you gave me . . . that day . . .
[*pause.*] . . . that day . . . the lake . . . the reeds. [*Eyes
front. Pause.*] What day? [*Pause.*] What reeds? [*Long
pause. Eyes close. Bell rings loudly. Eyes open. Pause. Eyes
right.*] Brownie of course. [*Pause.*] You remember Brown-
nie, Willie, I can see him. [*Pause.*] Brownie is there, Willie,
beside me. [*Pause. Loud.*] Brownie is there, Willie. [*Pause.
Eyes front.*] That is all. [*Pause.*] What would I do without
them? [*Pause.*] What would I do without them, when
words fail? [*Pause.*] Gaze before me, with compressed lips.
[*Long pause while she does so.*] I cannot. [*Pause.*] Ah yes,
great mercies, great mercies. [*Long pause. Low.*] Sometimes I hear sounds. [*Listening expression. Normal voice.*]
But not often. [*Pause.*] They are a boon, sounds are a
boon, they help me . . . through the day. [*Smile.*] The old
style! [*Smile off.*] Yes, those are happy days, when there
are sounds. [*Pause.*] When I hear sounds. [*Pause.*] I used to
think . . . [*pause*] . . . I say I used to think they were in my
head. [*Smile.*] But no. [*Smile broader.*] No no. [*Smile off.*]
That was just logic. [*Pause.*] Reason. [*Pause.*] I have not
lost my reason. [*Pause.*] Not yet. [*Pause.*] Not all. [*Pause.*]
Some remains. [*Pause.*] Sounds. [*Pause.*] Like little . . .
sunderings, little falls . . . apart. [*Pause. Low.*] It's things,
Willie. [*Pause. Normal voice.*] In the bag, outside the bag.
[*Pause.*] Ah yes, things have their life, that is what I always
say, *things* have a life. [*Pause.*] Take my looking-glass, it
doesn't need me. [*Pause.*] The bell. [*Pause.*] It hurts like a
knife. [*Pause.*] A gouge. [*Pause.*] One cannot ignore it.
[*Pause.*] How often . . . (*pause*] . . . I say how often I have
said, Ignore it, Winnie, ignore the bell, pay no heed, just

sleep and wake, sleep and wake, as you please, open and close the eyes, as you please, or in the way you find most helpful. [*Pause.*] Open and close the eyes, Winnie, open and close, always that. [*Pause.*] But no. [*Smile.*] Not now. [*Smile broader.*] No no. [*Smile off. Pause.*] What now? [*Pause.*] What now, Willie? [*Long pause.*] There is my story of course, when all else fails. [*Pause.*] A life. [*Smile.*] A long life. [*Smile off.*] Beginning in the womb, where life used to begin, Mildred has memories, she will have memories, of the womb, before she dies, the mother's womb. [*Pause.*] She is now four or five already and has recently been given a big waxen dolly. [*Pause.*] Fully clothed, complete outfit. [*Pause.*] Shoes, socks, undies, complete set, frilly frock, gloves. [*Pause.*] White mesh. [*Pause.*] A little white straw hat with a chin elastic. [*Pause.*] Pearly necklace. [*Pause.*] A little picture-book with legends in real print to go under her arm when she takes her walk. [*Pause.*] China blue eyes that open and shut. [*Pause. Narrative.*] The sun was not well up when Milly rose, descended the steep . . . [*pause*] . . . slipped on her nightgown, descended all alone the steep wooden stairs, backwards on all fours, though she had been forbidden to do so, entered the . . . [*pause*] . . . tiptoed down the silent passage, entered the nursery and began to undress Dolly. [*Pause.*] Crept under the table and began to undress Dolly. [*Pause.*] Scolding her . . . the while. [*Pause.*] Suddenly a mouse – [*Long pause.*] Gently, Winnie. [*Long pause. Calling.*] Willie! [*Pause. Louder.*] Willie! [*Pause. Mild reproach.*] I sometimes find your attitude a little strange, Willie, all this time, it is not like you to be wantonly cruel. [*Pause.*] Strange? [*Pause.*] No. [*Smile.*] Not here. [*Smile broader.*] Not now. [*Smile off.*] And yet . . . [*Suddenly anxious.*] I do hope nothing is amiss. [*Eyes right, loud.*] Is all well, dear? (*Pause. Eyes front. To herself.*] God grant he did not go in head foremost! [*Eyes right, loud.*] You're not stuck, Willie? [*Pause. Do.*] You're not jammed, Willie? [*Eyes front, distressed.*] Perhaps he is crying out for help all this time and I do not hear him! [*Pause.*] I do of course hear cries. [*Pause.*] But they are in

my head surely. [*Pause.*] Is it possible that . . . [*Pause.
With finality.*] No no, my head was always full of cries.
[*Pause.*] Faint confused cries. [*Pause.*] They come. [*Pause.*]
Then go. [*Pause.*] As on a wind. [*Pause.*] That is what I
find so wonderful. [*Pause.*] They cease. [*Pause.*] Ah yes,
great mercies, great mercies. [*Pause.*] The day is now well
advanced. [*Smile. Smile off.*] And yet it is perhaps a little
soon for my song. [*Pause.*] To sing too soon is fatal, I
always find. [*Pause.*] On the other hand it is possible to
leave it too late. [*Pause.*] The bell goes for sleep and one
has not sung. [*Pause.*] The whole day has flown – [*smile,
smile off*] – flown by, quite by, and no song of any class,
kind or description. [*Pause.*] There is a problem here.
[*Pause.*] One cannot sing . . . just like that, no. [*Pause.*] It
bubbles up, for some unknown reason, the time is ill
chosen, one chokes it back. [*Pause.*] One says, Now is the
time, it is now or never, and one cannot. [*Pause.*] Simply
cannot sing. [*Pause.*] Not a note. [*Pause.*] Another thing,
Willie, while we are on this subject. [*Pause.*] The sadness
after song. [*Pause.*] Have you run across that, Willie?
[*Pause.*] In the course of your experience. [*Pause.*] No?
[*Pause.*] Sadness after intimate sexual intercourse one is
familiar with of course. [*Pause.*] You would concur with
Aristotle there, Willie, I fancy. [*Pause.*] Yes, that one
knows and is prepared to face. [*Pause.*] But after song . . .
[*Pause.*] It does not last of course. [*Pause.*] That is what I
find so wonderful. [*Pause.*] It wears away. [*Pause.*] What
are those exquisite lines? [*Pause.*] Go forget me why
should something o'er that something shadow fling . . . go
forget me . . . why should sorrow . . . brightly smile . . . go
forget me . . . never hear me . . . sweetly smile . . . brightly
sing . . . [*Pause. With a sigh.*] One loses one's classics.
[*Pause.*] Oh not all. [*Pause.*] A part. [*Pause.*] A part
remains. [*Pause.*] That is what I find so wonderful, a part
remains, of one's classics, to help one through the day.
[*Pause.*] Oh yes, many mercies, many mercies. [*Pause.*]
And now? [*Pause.*] And now, Willie? [*Long pause.*] I call
to the eye of the mind . . . Mr Shower – or Cooker. [*She
closes her eyes. Bell rings loudly. She opens her eyes.*

Pause.] Hand in hand, in the other hands bags. [*Pause.*]
Getting on . . . in life. [*Pause.*] No longer young, not yet
old. [*Pause.*] Standing there gaping at me. [*Pause.*] Can't
have been a bad bosom, he says, in its day. [*Pause.*] Seen
worse shoulders, he says, in my time. [*Pause.*] Does she
feel her legs? he says. [*Pause.*] Is there any life in her legs?
he says. [*Pause.*] Has she anything on underneath? he says.
[*Pause.*] Ask her, he says, I'm shy. [*Pause.*] Ask her what?
she says. [*Pause.*] Is there any life in her legs. [*Pause.*] Has
she anything on underneath. [*Pause.*] Ask her yourself, she
says. [*Pause. With sudden violence.*] Let go of me for
Christ sake and drop! [*Pause. Do.*] Drop dead! [*Smile.*]
But no. [*Smile broader.*] No no. [*Smile off.*] I watch them
recede. [*Pause.*] Hand in hand – and the bags. [*Pause.*]
Dim. [*Pause.*] Then gone. [*Pause.*] Last human kind – to
stray this way. [*Pause.*] Up to date. [*Pause.*] And now?
[*Pause. Low.*] Help. [*Pause. Do.*] Help, Willie. [*Pause.
Do.*] No? [*Long pause. Narrative.*] Suddenly a mouse . . .
[*Pause.*] Suddenly a mouse ran up her little thigh and
Mildred, dropping Dolly in her fright, began to scream –
[WINNIE *gives a sudden piercing scream*] – and screamed
and screamed – [WINNIE *screams twice*] – screamed and
screamed and screamed and screamed till all came running,
in their night attire, papa, mamma, Bibby and . . . old
Annie, to see what was the matter . . . [*pause*] . . . what on
earth could possibly be the matter. [*Pause.*] Too late.
[*Pause.*] Too late. [*Long pause. Just audible.*] Willie.
[*Pause. Normal voice.*] Ah well, not long now, Winnie,
can't be long now, until the bell for sleep. [*Pause.*] Then
you may close your eyes, then you *must* close your eyes –
and keep them closed. [*Pause.*] Why say that again?
[*Pause.*] I used to think . . . [*pause*] . . . I say I used to think
there was no difference between one fraction of a second
and the next. [*Pause.*] I used to say . . . [*pause*] . . . I say I
used to say, Winnie, you are changeless, there is never any
difference between one fraction of a second and the next.
[*Pause.*] Why bring that up again? [*Pause.*] There is so
little one can bring up, one brings up all. [*Pause.*] All one
can. [*Pause.*] My neck is hurting me. [*Pause. With sudden*

violence.] My neck is hurting me! [*Pause.*] Ah that's better.
[*With mild irritation.*] Everything within reason. [*Long
pause.*] I can do no more. [*Pause.*] Say no more. [*Pause.*]
But I must say more. [*Pause.*] Problem here. [*Pause.*] No,
something must move, in the world, I can't any more.
[*Pause.*] A zephyr. [*Pause.*] A breath. [*Pause.*] What are
those immortal lines? [*Pause.*] It might be the eternal dark.
[*Pause.*] Black night without end. [*Pause.*] Just chance, I
take it, happy chance. [*Pause.*] Oh yes, abounding mercies.
[*Long pause.*] And now? [*Pause.*] And now, Willie? [*Long
pause.*] That day. [*Pause.*] The pink fizz. [*Pause.*] The flute
glasses. [*Pause.*] The last guest gone. [*Pause.*] The last
bumper with the bodies nearly touching. [*Pause.*] The
look. [*Long pause.*] What day? [*Long pause.*] What look?
[*Long pause.*] I hear cries. [*Pause.*] Sing. [*Pause.*] Sing your
old song, Winnie.
[*Long pause. Suddenly alert expression. Eyes switch right.*
WILLIE'*s head appears to her right round corner of mound.
He is on all fours, dressed to kill – top hat, morning coat,
striped trousers, etc., white gloves in hand. Very long
bushy white Battle of Britain moustache. He halts, gazes
front, smooths moustache. He emerges completely from
behind mound, turns to his left, halts, looks up at* WINNIE.
*He advances on all fours towards centre, halts, turns head
front, gazes front, strokes moustache, straightens tie,
adjusts hat, advances a little further, halts, takes off hat
and looks up at* WINNIE. *He is now not far from centre
and within her field of vision. Unable to sustain effort of
looking up he sinks head to ground.*]

WINNIE: [*Mondaine*]. Well this is an unexpected pleasure!
[*Pause.*] Reminds me of the day you came whining for my
hand. [*Pause.*] I worship you, Winnie, be mine. [*He looks
up.*] Life a mockery without Win. [*She goes off into a
giggle.*] What a get up, you do look a sight! [*Giggles.*]
Where are the flowers? [*Pause.*] That smile today. [WILLIE
sinks head.] What's that on your neck, an anthrax?
[*Pause.*] Want to watch that, Willie, before it gets a hold
on you. [*Pause.*] Where were you all this time? [*Pause.*]
What were you doing all this time? [*Pause.*] Changing?

[*Pause.*] Did you not hear me screaming for you? [*Pause.*]
Did you get stuck in your hole? [*Pause. He looks up.*] That's
right, Willie, look at me. [*Pause.*] Feast your old eyes, Willie. [*Pause.*] Does anything remain? [*Pause.*] Any remains?
[*Pause.*] No? [*Pause.*] I haven't been able to look after it,
you know. [*He sinks his head.*] You are still recognizable, in
a way. [*Pause.*] Are you thinking of coming to live this side
now . . . for a bit maybe? [*Pause.*] No? [*Pause.*] Just a brief
call? [*Pause.*] Have you gone deaf, Willie? [*Pause.*] Dumb?
[*Pause.*] Oh I know you were never one to talk, I worship
you Winnie be mine and then nothing from that day forth
only titbits from *Reynolds' News*. [*Eyes front. Pause.*] Ah
well, what matter, that's what I always say, it will have been
a happy day, after all, another happy day. [*Pause.*] Not long
now, Winnie. [*Pause.*] I hear cries. [*Pause.*] Do you ever
hear cries, Willie? [*Pause.*] No? [*Eyes back on* WILLIE.]
Willie. [*Pause.*] Look at me again, Willie. [*Pause.*] Once
more, Willie. [*He looks up. Happily.*] Ah! [*Pause. Shocked.*]
What ails you, Willie, I never saw such an expression!
[*Pause.*] Put on your hat, dear, it's the sun, don't stand on
ceremony, I won't mind. [*He drops hat and gloves and
starts to crawl up mound towards her. Gleeful.*] Oh I say,
this is terrific! [*He halts, clinging to mound with one hand,
reaching up with the other.*] Come on, dear, put a bit of jizz
into it, I'll cheer you on. [*Pause.*] Is it me you're after, Willie . . . or is it something else? [*Pause.*] Do you want to
touch my face . . . again? [*Pause.*] Is it a kiss you're after,
Willie . . . or is it something else? [*Pause.*] There was a time
when I could have given you a hand. [*Pause.*] And then a
time before that again when I did give you a hand. [*Pause.*]
You were always in dire need of a hand, Willie. [*He slithers
back to foot of mound and lies with face to ground.*] Brrum!
[*Pause. He rises to hands and knees, raises his face towards
her.*] Have another go, Willie, I'll cheer you on. [*Pause.*]
Don't look at me like that! [*Pause. Vehement.*] Don't look
at me like that! [*Pause. Low.*] Have you gone off your head,
Willie? [*Pause. Do.*] Out of your poor old wits, Willie?
[*Pause.*]

WILLIE: [*Just audible.*] Win.

[*Pause.* WINNIE's *eyes front. Happy expression appears, grows.*]

WINNIE: Win! [*Pause.*] Oh this *is* a happy day, this will have been another happy day! [*Pause.*] After all. [*Pause.*] So far. [*Pause. She hums tentatively beginning of song, then sings softly, musical-box tune.*]

> Though I say not
> What I may not
> Let you hear,
> Yet the swaying
> Dance is saying,
> Love me dear!
> Every touch of fingers
> Tells me what I know,
> Says for you,
> It's true, it's true,
> You love me so!

(*Pause. Happy expression off. She closes her eyes. Bell rings loudly. She opens her eyes. She smiles, gazing front. She turns her eyes, smiling, to* WILLIE, *still on his hands and knees looking up at her. Smile off. They look at each other. Long pause.*]

CURTAIN

All That Fall

A play for radio

Written in English in July-September 1956. First published by Grove Press, New York, in 1957. First published in Britain by Faber and Faber, London, also in 1957. First broadcast by the BBC Third Programme on 13 January 1957.

CAST

MRS ROONEY (Maddy)	a lady in her seventies
CHRISTY	a carter
MR TYLER	a retired bill-broker
MR SLOCUM	Clerk of the Racecourse
TOMMY	a porter
MR BARRELL	a station-master
MISS FITT	a lady in her thirties
A FEMALE VOICE	
DOLLY	a small girl
MR ROONEY (Dan)	husband of Mrs Rooney, blind
JERRY	a small boy

Rural sounds. Sheep, bird, cow, cock, severally, then together.
Silence.
MRS ROONEY *advances along country road towards railway*
station. Sound of her dragging feet.
Music faint from house by way. "Death and the Maiden."
The steps slow down, stop.

MRS ROONEY: Poor woman. All alone in that ruinous old
    house. [*Music louder. Silence but for music playing.*
    The steps resume. Music dies. MRS ROONEY *murmurs,*
    melody. Her murmur dies.
    Sound of approaching cartwheels. The cart stops.
    The steps slow down, stop.]
    Is that you, Christy?
CHRISTY: It is, Ma'am.
MRS ROONEY: I thought the hinny was familiar. How is your
    poor wife?
CHRISTY: No better, Ma'am.
MRS ROONEY: Your daughter then?
CHRISTY: No worse, Ma'am.
    [*Silence.*]
MRS ROONEY: Why do you halt? [*Pause.*] But why do I halt?
    [*Silence.*]
CHRISTY: Nice day for the races, Ma'am.
MRS ROONEY: No doubt it is. [*Pause.*] But will it hold up?
    [*Pause. With emotion.*] Will it hold up?
    [*Silence.*]
CHRISTY: I suppose you wouldn't—
MRS ROONEY: Hist! [*Pause.*] Surely to goodness that cannot
    be the up mail I hear already.
    [*Silence. The hinny neighs. Silence.*]
CHRISTY: Damn the mail.
MRS ROONEY: Oh thank God for that! I could have sworn I

heard it, thundering up the track in the far distance.
[*Pause.*] So hinnies whinny. Well, it is not surprising.

CHRISTY: I suppose you wouldn't be in need of a small load
of dung?

MRS ROONEY: Dung? What class of dung?

CHRISTY: Stydung.

MRS ROONEY: Stydung... I like your frankness, Christy.
[*Pause.*] I'll ask the master. [*Pause.*] Christy.

CHRISTY: Yes, Ma'am.

MRS ROONEY: Do you find anything... bizarre about my way
of speaking? [*Pause.*] I do not mean the voice. [*Pause.*]
No, I mean the words. [*Pause. More to herself.*] I use none
but the simplest words, I hope, and yet I sometimes find
my way of speaking very... bizarre. [*Pause.*] Mercy! What
was that?

CHRISTY: Never mind her, Ma'am, she's very fresh in herself
today.
[*Silence.*]

MRS ROONEY: Dung? What would we want with dung, at our
time of life? [*Pause.*] Why are you on your feet down on
the road? Why do you not climb up on the crest of your
manure and let yourself be carried along? Is it that you
have no head for heights?
[*Silence.*]

CHRISTY: [*To the hinny.*] Yep! [*Pause. Louder.*] Yep wiyya to
hell owwa that!
[*Silence.*]

MRS ROONEY: She does not move a muscle. [*Pause.*] I too
should be getting along, if I do not wish to arrive late at
the station. [*Pause.*] But a moment ago she neighed and
pawed the ground. And now she refuses to advance. Give
her a good welt on the rump. [*Sound of welt. Pause.*]
Harder! [*Sound of welt. Pause.*] Well! If someone were to
do that for me I should not dally. [*Pause.*] How she gazes
at me to be sure, with her great moist cleg-tormented eyes!
Perhaps if I were to move on, down the road, out of her
field of vision.... [*Sound of welt.*] No, no, enough! Take
her by the snaffle and pull her eyes away from me. Oh this
is awful! [*She moves on. Sound of her dragging feet.*]

What have I done to deserve all this, what, what? [*Dragging feet.*] So long ago .... No! No! [*Dragging feet. Quotes.*] "Sigh out a something something tale of things, Done long ago and ill done." [*She halts.*] How can I go on, I cannot. Oh let me just flop down flat on the road like a big fat jelly out of a bowl and never move again! A great big slop thick with grit and dust and flies, they would have to scoop me up with a shovel. [*Pause.*] Heavens, there is that up mail again, what will become of me! [*The dragging steps resume.*] Oh I am just a hysterical old hag I know, destroyed with sorrow and pining and gentility and church-going and fat and rheumatism and childlessness. [*Pause. Brokenly.*] Minnie! Little Minnie! [*Pause.*] Love, that is all I asked, a little love, daily, twice daily, fifty years of twice daily love like a Paris horse-butcher's regular, what normal woman wants affection? A peck on the jaw at morning, near the ear, and another at evening, peck, peck, till you grow whiskers on you. There is that lovely laburnum again.

[*Dragging feet. Sound of bicycle-bell. It is old* MR TYLER *coming up behind her on his bicycle, on his way to the station. Squeak of brakes. He slows down and rides abreast of her.*]

MR TAYLOR: Mrs Rooney! Pardon me if I do not doff my cap, I'd fall off. Divine day for the meeting.

MRS ROONEY: Oh, Mr Tyler, you startled the life out of me stealing up behind me like that like a deer-stalker! Oh!

MR TYLER: [*Playfully.*] I rang my bell, Mrs Rooney, the moment I sighted you I started tinkling my bell, now don't you deny it.

MRS ROONEY: Your bell is one thing, Mr Tyler, and you are another. What news of your poor daughter?

MR TYLER: Fair, fair. They removed everything, you know, the whole ... er ... bag of tricks. Now I am grandchildless. [*Dragging feet.*]

MRS ROONEY: Gracious how you wobble! Dismount, for mercy's sake, or ride on.

MR TYLER: Perhaps if I were to lay my hand lightly on your

shoulder, Mrs Rooney, how would that be?
[*Pause.*] Would you permit that?

MRS ROONEY: No, Mr Rooney, Mr Tyler I mean, I am tired of
light old hands on my shoulders and other senseless places,
sick and tired of them. Heavens, here comes Connolly's
van! [*She halts. Sound of motor-van. It approaches, passes
with thunderous rattles, recedes.*] Are you all right, Mr
Tyler? [*Pause.*] Where is he? [*Pause.*] Ah there you are!
[*The dragging steps resume.*] That was a narrow squeak.

MR TYLER: I alit in the nick of time.

MRS ROONEY: It is suicide to be abroad. But what is it to be at
home, Mr Tyler, what is it to be at home? A lingering
dissolution. Now we are white with dust from head to
foot. I beg your pardon?

MR TYLER: Nothing, Mrs Rooney, nothing, I was merely
cursing, under my breath, God and man, under my breath,
and the wet Saturday afternoon of my conception. My
back tyre has gone down again. I pumped it hard as iron
before I set out. And now I am on the rim.

MRS ROONEY: Oh what a shame!

MR TYLER: Now if it were the front I should not so much
mind. But the back. The back! The chain! The oil! The
grease! The hub! The brakes! The gear! No! It is too much!
[*Dragging steps.*]

MRS ROONEY: Are we very late, Mr Tyler? I have not the
courage to look at my watch.

MR TYLER: [*Bitterly.*] Late! I on my bicycle as I bowled along
was already late. Now therefore we are doubly late, trebly,
quadrupedly late. Would I had shot by you, without a
word.
[*Dragging feet.*]

MRS ROONEY: Whom are you meeting, Mr Tyler?

MR TYLER: Hardy. [*Pause.*] We used to climb together. [*Pause.*]
I saved his life once. [*Pause.*] I have not forgotten it.
[*Dragging feet. They stop.*]

MRS ROONEY: Let us halt a moment and let this vile dust fall
back upon the viler worms.
[*Silence. Rural sounds.*]

MR TYLER: What sky! What light! Ah in spite of all it is a

blessed thing to be alive in such weather, and out of hospital.

MRS ROONEY: Alive?

MR TYLER: Well half alive shall we say?

MRS ROONEY: Speak for yourself, Mr Tyler. I am not half alive nor anything approaching it. [*Pause.*] What are we standing here for? This dust will not settle in our time. And when it does some great roaring machine will come and whirl it all skyhigh again.

MR TYLER: Well, shall we be getting along in that case?

MRS ROONEY: No.

MR TYLER: Come, Mrs Rooney—

MRS ROONEY: Go, Mr Tyler, go on and leave me, listening to the cooing of the ringdoves. [*Cooing.*] If you see my poor blind Dan tell him I was on my way to meet him when it all came over me again, like a flood. Say to him, Your poor wife, She told me to tell you it all came flooding over her again and ... [*The voice breaks.*] ... she simply went back home ... straight back home ....

MR TYLER: Come, Mrs Rooney, come, the mail has not yet gone up, just take my free arm and we'll be there with time and to spare.

MRS ROONEY: [*Sobbing.*] What? What's all this now? [*Calmer.*] Can't you see I'm in trouble? [*With anger.*] Have you no respect for misery? [*Sobbing.*] Minnie! Little Minnie!

MR TYLER: Come, Mrs Rooney, come, the mail has not yet gone up, just take my free arm and we'll be there with time and to spare.

MRS ROONEY: [*Brokenly.*] In her forties now she'd be, I don't know, fifty, girding up her lovely little loins, getting ready for the change ....

MR TYLER: Come, Mrs Rooney, come, the mail—

MRS ROONEY: [*Exploding.*] Will you get along with you, Mr Rooney, Mr Tyler I mean, will you get along with you now and cease molesting me? What kind of a country is this where a woman can't weep her heart out on the highways and byways without being tormented by retired bill-brokers! [*Mr Tyler prepares to mount his bicycle.*] Heavens you're not going to ride her flat! [*Mr Tyler mounts.*] You'll tear your tube to ribbons! [*Mr Tyler rides off. Receding sound of bumping bicycle. Silence. Cooing.*] Venus birds! Billing in the woods all the long summer long. [*Pause.*] Oh cursed corset! If I could let it out, without indecent exposure. Mr Tyler! Mr Tyler! Come back and unlace me behind the hedge! [*She laughs wildly, ceases.*] What's wrong with me, what's wrong with me, never tranquil, seething out of my dirty old pelt, out of my skull, oh to be in atoms, in atoms! [*Frenziedly.*] ATOMS! [*Silence. Cooing. Faintly.*] Jesus! [*Pause.*] Jesus! [*Sound of car coming up behind her. It slows down and draws up beside her, engine running. It is MR SLOCUM, the Clerk of the Racecourse.*]

MR SLOCUM: Is anything wrong, Mrs Rooney? You are bent all double. Have you a pain in the stomach?
[*Silence.* MRS ROONEY *laughs wildly. Finally.*]

MRS ROONEY: Well if it isn't my old admirer the Clerk of the Course, in his limousine.

MR SLOCUM: May I offer you a lift, Mrs Rooney? Are you going in my direction?

MRS ROONEY: I am, Mr Slocum, we all are. [*Pause.*] How is your poor mother?

MR SLOCUM: Thank you, she is fairly comfortable. We manage to keep her out of pain. That is the great thing, Mrs Rooney, is it not?

MRS ROONEY: Yes, indeed, Mr Slocum, that is the great thing, I don't know how you do it. [*Pause. She slaps her cheek violently.*] Ah these wasps!

MR SLOCUM: [*Coolly.*] May I then offer you a seat, Madam?

MRS ROONEY: [*With exaggerated enthusiasm.*] Oh that would be heavenly, Mr Slocum, just simply heavenly. [*Dubiously.*] But would I ever get in, you look very high off the ground today, these new balloon tyres I presume. [*Sound of door opening and* MRS ROONEY *trying to get in.*] Does this roof never come off? No? [*Efforts of* MRS ROONEY.] No .... I'll never do it ... you'll have to get down, Mr Slocum, and help me from the rear. [*Pause.*] What was that? [*Pause. Aggrieved.*] This is all your suggestion, Mr Slocum, not mine. Drive on, Sir, drive on.

MR SLOCUM: [*Switching off engine.*] I'm coming, Mrs Rooney, I'm coming, give me time, I'm as stiff as yourself. [*Sound of* MR SLOCUM *extracting himself from driver's seat.*]

MRS ROONEY: Stiff! Well I like that! And me heaving all over back and front. [*To herself.*] The dry old reprobate!

MR SLOCUM: [*In position behind her.*] Now, Mrs Rooney, how shall we do this?

MRS ROONEY: As if I were a bale, Mr Slocum, don't be afraid. [*Pause. Sounds of effort.*] That's the way! [*Effort.*] Lower! [*Effort.*] Wait! [*Pause.*] No, don't let go! [*Pause.*] Suppose I do get up, will I ever get down?

MR SLOCUM: [*Breathing hard.*] You'll get down, Mrs Rooney, you'll get down. We may not get you up, but I warrant you we'll get you down. [*He resumes his efforts. Sound of these.*]

MRS ROONEY: Oh! ... Lower! ... Don't be afraid! ... We're past the age when .... There! ... Now! ... Get your shoulder under it .... Oh! ... [*Giggles.*] Oh glory! ... Up! Up! ... Ah! ... I'm in! [*Panting of* MR SLOCUM. *He slams the door. In a scream.*] My frock! You've nipped my frock! [MR SLOCUM *opens the door.* MRS ROONEY *frees her frock.* MR SLOCUM *slams the door. His violent unintelligible muttering as he walks round to the other door. Tearfully.*] My nice frock! Look what you've done to my nice frock! [MR SLOCUM *gets into his seat, slams driver's door, presses starter. The engine does not start. He releases starter.*] What will Dan say when he sees me?

MR SLOCUM: Has he then recovered his sight?

MRS ROONEY: No, I mean when he knows, what will he say when he feels the hole? [MR SLOCUM *presses starter. As before. Silence.*] What are you doing, Mr Slocum?

MR SLOCUM: Gazing straight before me, Mrs Rooney, through the windscreen, into the void.

MRS ROONEY: Start her up, I beseech you, and let us be off. This is awful!

MR SLOCUM: [*Dreamily.*] All morning she went like a dream and now she is dead. That is what you get for a good deed. [*Pause. Hopefully.*] Perhaps if I were to choke her. [*He*

does so, presses the starter. The engine roars. Roaring to
make himself heard.] She was getting too much air!
[*He throttles down, grinds in his first gear, moves off,*
changes up in a grinding of gears.]

MRS ROONEY: [*In anguish.*] Mind the hen! [*Scream of brakes.*
Squawk of hen.] Oh, mother, you have squashed her, drive
on, drive on! [*The car accelerates. Pause.*] What a death!
One minute picking happy at the dung, on the road, in the
sun, with now and then a dust bath, and then—bang!—all
her troubles over. [*Pause.*] All the laying and the hatching.
[*Pause.*] Just one great squawk and then ... peace. [*Pause.*]
They would have slit her weasand in any case. [*Pause.*]
Here we are, let me down. [*The car slows down, stops,*
engine running. MR SLOCUM *blows his horn. Pause. Louder.*
Pause.] What are you up to now, Mr Slocum? We are at a
standstill, all danger is past and you blow your horn. Now
if instead of blowing it now you had blown it at that
unfortunate—
[*Horn violently.* TOMMY *the porter appears at top of*
station steps.]

MR SLOCUM: [*Calling.*] Will you come down, Tommy, and help
this lady out, she's stuck.
[TOMMY *descends the steps.*]
Open the door, Tommy, and ease her out.
[TOMMY *opens the door.*]

TOMMY: Certainly, sir. Nice day for the races, sir. What would
you fancy for—

MRS ROONEY: Don't mind me. Don't take any notice of me. I
do not exist. The fact is well known.

MR SLOCUM: Do as you're asked, Tommy, for the love of God.

TOMMY: Yessir. Now, Mrs Rooney.
[*He starts pulling her out.*]

MRS ROONEY: Wait, Tommy, wait now, don't bustle me, just
let me wheel round and get my feet to the ground. [*Her*
efforts to achieve this.] Now.

TOMMY: [*Pulling her out.*] Mind your feather, Ma'am.
[*Sounds of effort.*] Easy now, easy.

MRS ROONEY: Wait, for God's sake, you'll have me beheaded.

TOMMY: Crouch down, Mrs Rooney, crouch down, and get your

head in the open.

MRS ROONEY: Crouch down! At my time of life! This is lunacy!

TOMMY: Press her down, sir.

[*Sounds of combined efforts.*]

MRS ROONEY: Pity!

TOMMY: Now! She's coming! Straighten up, Ma'am! There!

[MR SLOCUM *slams the door.*]

MRS ROONEY: Am I out?

[*The voice of* MR BARRELL, *the station-master, raised in anger.*]

MR BARRELL: Tommy! Tommy! Where the hell is he?

[MR SLOCUM *grinds in his gear.*]

TOMMY: [*Hurriedly.*] You wouldn't have something for the Ladies Plate, sir? I was given Flash Harry.

MR SLOCUM: [*Scornfully.*] Flash Harry! That carthorse!

MR BARRELL: [*At top of steps, roaring.*] Tommy! Blast your bleeding bloody— [*He sees* MRS ROONEY.] Oh, Mrs Rooney.... [MR SLOCUM *drives away in a grinding of gears.*] Who's that crucifying his gearbox, Tommy?

TOMMY: Old Cissy Slocum.

MRS ROONEY: Cissy Slocum! That's a nice way to refer to your betters. Cissy Slocum! And you an orphan!

MR BARRELL: [*Angrily to* TOMMY.] What are you doing stravaging down here on the public road? This is no place for you at all! Nip up there on the platform now and whip out the truck! Won't the twelve thirty be on top of us before we can turn round?

TOMMY: [*Bitterly.*] And that's the thanks you get for a Christian act.

MR BARRELL: [*Violently.*] Get on with you now before I report you! [*Slow feet of* TOMMY *climbing steps.*] Do you want me to come down to you with the shovel? [*The feet quicken, recede, cease.*] Ah God forgive me, it's a hard life. [*Pause.*] Well, Mrs Rooney, it's nice to see you up and about again. You were laid up there a long time.

MRS ROONEY: Not long enough, Mr Barrell. [*Pause.*] Would I were still in bed, Mr Barrell. [*Pause.*] Would I were lying stretched out in my comfortable bed, Mr Barrell, just

wasting slowly, painlessly away, keeping up my strength
with arrowroot and calves-foot jelly, till in the end you
wouldn't see me under the blankets any more than a
board. [*Pause.*] Oh no coughing or spitting or bleeding or
vomiting, just drifting gently down into the higher life, and
remembering, remembering . . . [*The voice breaks.*] . . . all
the silly unhappiness . . . as though . . . it had never
happened . . . . What did I do with that handkerchief?
[*Sound of handkerchief loudly applied.*] How long have
you been master of this station now, Mr Barrell?

MR BARRELL: Don't ask me, Mrs Rooney, don't ask me.

MRS ROONEY: You stepped into your father's shoes, I believe,
when he took them off.

MR BARRELL: Poor Pappy! [*Reverent pause.*] He didn't live
long to enjoy his ease.

MRS ROONEY: I remember him clearly. A small ferrety purple-
faced widower, deaf as a doornail, very testy and snappy.
[*Pause.*] I suppose you'll be retiring soon yourself, Mr
Barrell, and growing your roses. [*Pause.*] Did I understand
you to say the twelve thirty would soon be upon us?

MR BARRELL: Those were my words.

MRS ROONEY: But according to my watch which is more or less
right—or was—by the eight o'clock news the time is now
coming up to twelve . . . [*Pause as she consults her watch.*]
. . . thirty-six. [*Pause.*] And yet upon the other hand the up
mail has not yet gone through. [*Pause.*] Or has it sped by
unbeknown to me? [*Pause.*] For there was a moment
there, I remember now, I was so plunged in sorrow I
wouldn't have heard a steam roller go over me.
[*Pause.* MR BARRELL *turns to go.*] Don't go, Mr Barrell!
[MR BARRELL *goes. Loud.*] Mr Barrell! [*Pause. Louder.*]
Mr Barrell! [MR BARRELL *comes back.*]

MR BARRELL: [*Testily.*] What is it, Mrs Rooney, I have my
work to do.
[*Silence. Sound of wind.*]

MRS ROONEY: The wind is getting up. [*Pause. Wind.*] The best
of the day is over. [*Pause. Wind. Dreamily.*] Soon the rain
will begin to fall and go on falling, all afternoon.
[MR BARRELL *goes.*] Then at evening the clouds will part,

the setting sun will shine an instant, then sink, behind the hills. [*She realizes* MR BARRELL *has gone.*] Mr Barrell! Mr Barrell! [*Silence.*] I estrange them all. They come towards me, uninvited, bygones bygones, full of kindness, anxious to help ... [*The voice breaks.*] ... genuinely pleased ... to see me again ... looking so well .... [*Handkerchief.*] A few simple words ... from my heart ... and I am all alone ... once more .... [*Handkerchief. Vehemently.*] I should not be out at all! I should never leave the grounds! [*Pause.*] Oh there is that Fitt woman, I wonder will she bow to me. [*Sound of* MISS FITT *approaching, humming a hymn. She starts climbing the steps.*] Miss Fitt! [MISS FITT *halts, stops humming.*] Am I then invisible, Miss Fitt? Is this cretonne so becoming to me that I merge into the masonry? [MISS FITT *descends a step.*] That is right, Miss Fitt, look closely and you will finally distinguish a once female shape.

MISS FITT: Mrs Rooney! I saw you, but I did not know you.

MRS ROONEY: Last Sunday we worshipped together. We knelt side by side at the same altar. We drank from the same chalice. Have I so changed since then?

MISS FITT: [*Shocked.*] Oh but in church, Mrs Rooney, in church I am alone with my Maker. Are not you? [*Pause.*] Why even the sexton himself, you know, when he takes up the collection, knows it is useless to pause before me. I simply do not see the plate, or bag, whatever it is they use, how could I? [*Pause.*] Why even when all is over and I go out into the sweet fresh air, why even then for the first furlong or so I stumble in a kind of daze as you might say, oblivious to my co-religionists. And they are very kind I must admit—the vast majority—very kind and under-standing. They know me now and take no umbrage. There she goes, they say, there goes the dark Miss Fitt, alone with her Maker, take no notice of her. And they step down off the path to avoid my running into them. [*Pause.*] Ah yes, I am distray, very distray, even on week-days. Ask Mother, if you do not believe me. Hetty, she says, when I start eating my doily instead of the thin bread and butter, Hetty, how can you be so distray? [*Sighs.*] I suppose the truth is I am not there, Mrs Rooney, just not really there at all. I see, hear, smell, and so on, I go through the usual motions, but my heart is not in it, Mrs Rooney, my heart is in none of it. Left to myself, with no one to check me, I would soon be flown... home. [*Pause.*] So if you think I cut you just now, Mrs Rooney, you do me an injustice. All I saw was a big pale blur, just another big pale blur. [*Pause.*] Is anything amiss, Mrs Rooney, you do not look normal somehow. So bowed and bent.

MRS ROONEY: [*Ruefully.*] Maddy Rooney, née Dunne, the big pale blur. [*Pause.*] You have piercing sight, Miss Fitt, if you only knew it, literally piercing. [*Pause.*]

MISS FITT: Well... is there anything I can do, now that I am here?

MRS ROONEY: If you would help me up the face of this cliff, Miss Fitt, I have little doubt your Maker would requite you, if no one else.

MISS FITT: Now, now, Mrs Rooney, don't put your teeth in me. Requite! I make these sacrifices for nothing—or not at all. [*Pause. Sound of her descending steps.*] I take it you want to lean on me, Mrs Rooney.

MRS ROONEY: I asked Mr Barrell to give me his arm, just give me his arm. [*Pause.*] He turned on his heel and strode away.

MISS FITT: Is it my arm you want then? [*Pause. Impatiently.*] Is it my arm you want, Mrs Rooney, or what is it?

MRS ROONEY: [*Exploding.*] Your arm! Any arm! A helping hand! For five seconds! Christ what a planet!

MISS FITT: Really.... Do you know what it is, Mrs Rooney, I do not think it is wise of you to be going about at all.

MRS ROONEY: [*Violently.*] Come down here, Miss Fitt, and give me your arm, before I scream down the parish! [*Pause. Wind. Sound of* MISS FITT *descending last steps.*]

MISS FITT: [*Resignedly.*] Well, I suppose it is the Protestant thing to do.

MRS ROONEY: Pismires do it for one another. [*Pause.*] I have seen slugs do it. [MISS FITT *proffers her arm.*] No, the other side, my dear, if it's all the same to you, I'm left-handed on top of everything else. [*She takes* MISS FITT'*s right arm.*] Heavens, child, you're just a bag of bones, you need building up. [*Sound of her toiling up steps on* MISS FITT*'s arm.*] This is worse than the Matterhorn, were you ever up the Matterhorn, Miss Fitt, great honeymoon resort. [*Sound of toiling.*] Why don't they have a handrail? [*Panting.*] Wait till I get some air. [*Pause.*] Don't let me go! [MISS FITT *hums her hymn. After a moment* MRS ROONEY *joins in with the words.*] . . . the encircling gloo-oom . . . [MISS FITT *stops humming.*] . . . tum tum me on. [*Forte.*] The night is dark and I am far from ho-ome, tum tum—

MISS FITT: [*Hysterically.*] Stop it, Mrs Rooney, stop it, or I'll drop you!

MRS ROONEY: Wasn't it that they sung on the *Lusitania*? Or Rock of Ages? Most touching it must have been. Or was it the *Titanic*?

[*Attracted by the noise a group, including* MR TYLER, MR BARRELL *and* TOMMY, *gathers at top of steps.*]

MR BARRELL: What the—
[*Silence.*]

MR TYLER: Lovely day for the fixture.
[*Loud titter from* TOMMY *cut short by* MR BARRELL *with backhanded blow in the stomach. Appropriate noise from* TOMMY.]

A FEMALE VOICE: [*Shrill.*] Oh look, Dolly, look!

DOLLY: What, Mamma?

A FEMALE VOICE: They are stuck! [*Cackling laugh.*] They are stuck!

MRS ROONEY: Now we are the laughing-stock of the twenty-six counties. Or is it thirty-six?

MR TYLER: That is a nice way to treat your defenceless subordinates, Mr Barrell, hitting them without warning in the pit of the stomach.

MISS FITT: Has anyone seen my mother?

MR BARRELL: Who is that?

TOMMY: The dark Miss Fitt.

MR BARRELL: Where is her face?

MRS ROONEY: Now, deary, I am ready if you are. [*They toil up remaining steps.*] Stand back, you cads! [*Shuffle of feet.*]

A FEMALE VOICE: Mind yourself, Dolly!

MRS ROONEY: Thank you, Miss Fitt, thank you, that will do, just prop me up against the wall like a roll of tarpaulin and that will be all, for the moment. [*Pause.*] I am sorry for all this ramdam, Miss Fitt, had I known you were looking for your mother I should not have importuned you, I know what it is.

MISS FITT: [*In marvelling aside.*] Ramdam!

A FEMALE VOICE: Come, Dolly darling, let us take up our stand before the first class smokers. Give me your hand and hold me tight, one can be sucked under.

MR TYLER: You have lost your mother, Miss Fitt?

MISS FITT: Good morning, Mr Tyler.

MR TYLER: Good morning, Miss Fitt.

MR BARRELL: Good morning, Miss Fitt.

MISS FITT: Good morning, Mr Barrell.

MR TYLER: You have lost your mother, Miss Fitt?

MISS FITT: She said she would be on the last train.

MRS ROONEY: Do not imagine, because I am silent, that I am not present, and alive, to all that is going on.

MR TYLER: [*To* MISS FITT.] When you say the last train—

MRS ROONEY: Do not flatter yourselves for one moment, because I hold aloof, that my sufferings have ceased. No. The entire scene, the hills, the plain, the racecourse with its miles and miles of white rails and three red stands, the pretty little wayside station, even you yourselves, yes, I mean it, and over all the clouding blue, I see it all, I stand here and see it all with eyes . . . [*The voice breaks.*] . . . through eyes . . . oh if you had my eyes . . . you would understand . . . the things they have seen . . . and not looked away . . . this is nothing . . . nothing . . . what did I do with that handkerchief? [*Pause.*]

MR TYLER: [*To* MISS FITT.] When you say the last train— [MRS ROONEY *blows her nose violently and long.*] —when you say the last train, Miss Fitt, I take it you mean the twelve thirty.

MISS FITT: What else could I mean, Mr Tyler, what else could I *conceivably* mean?

MR TYLER: Then you have no cause for anxiety, Miss Fitt, for the twelve thirty has not yet arrived. Look. [MISS FITT

looks.] No, up the line. [MISS FITT *looks. Patiently.*]
No, Miss Fitt, follow the direction of my index. [MISS
FITT *looks.*] There. You see now. The signal. At the
bawdy hour of nine. [*In rueful afterthought.*] Or three
alas! [MR BARRELL *stifles a guffaw.*] Thank you, Mr
Barrell.

MISS FITT: But the time is now getting on for—

MR TYLER: [*Patiently.*] We all know, Miss Fitt, we all know
only too well what the time is now getting on for, and
yet the cruel fact remains that the twelve thirty has not
yet arrived.

MISS FITT: Not an accident, I trust! [*Pause.*] Do not tell me she
has left the track! [*Pause.*] Oh darling mother! With the
fresh sole for lunch!
[*Loud titter from* TOMMY, *checked as before by* MR
BARRELL.]

MR BARRELL: That's enough old guff out of you. Nip up to the
box now and see has Mr Case anything for me.
[TOMMY *goes.*]

MRS ROONEY: Poor Dan!

MISS FITT: [*In anguish.*] What terrible thing has happened?

MR TYLER: Now now, Miss Fitt, do not—

MRS ROONEY: [*With vehement sadness.*] Poor Dan!

MR TYLER: Now now, Miss Fitt, do not give way ... to despair,
all will come right ... in the end. [*Aside to* MR BARRELL.]
What *is* the situation, Mr Barrell? Not a collision surely?

MRS ROONEY: [*Enthusiastically.*] A collision! Oh that would
be wonderful!

MISS FITT: [*Horrified.*] A collision! I knew it!

MR TYLER: Come, Miss Fitt, let us move a little up the platform.

MRS ROONEY: Yes, let us all do that. [*Pause.*] No? [*Pause.*]
You have changed your mind? [*Pause.*] I quite agree, we
are better here, in the shadow of the waiting-room.

MR BARRELL: Excuse me a moment.

MRS ROONEY: Before you slink away, Mr Barrell, please, a
statement of some kind, I insist. Even the slowest train
on this brief line is not ten minutes and more behind its
scheduled time without good cause, one imagines. [*Pause.*]
We all know your station is the best kept of the entire net-

work, but there are times when that is not enough, just not
enough. [*Pause.*] Now, Mr Barrell, leave off chewing your
whiskers, we are waiting to hear from you—we the unfortunate ticket-holders' nearest if not dearest.
[*Pause.*]

MR TYLER: [*Reasonably.*] I do think we are owed some kind
of explanation, Mr Barrell, if only to set our minds at rest.

MR BARRELL: I know nothing. All I know is there has been a
hitch. All traffic is retarded.

MRS ROONEY: [*Derisively.*] Retarded! A hitch! Ah these celi-
bates! Here we are eating our hearts out with anxiety for
our loved ones and he calls that a hitch! Those of us like
myself with heart and kidney trouble may collapse at any
moment and he calls that a hitch! In our ovens the Saturday roast is burning to a shrivel and he calls that—

MR TYLER: Here comes Tommy, running! I am glad I have
been spared to see this.

TOMMY: [*Excitedly, in the distance.*] She's coming. [*Pause.
Nearer.*] She's at the level-crossing!
[*Immediately exaggerated station sounds. Falling signals.
Bells. Whistles. Crescendo of train whistle approaching.
Sound of train rushing through station.*]

MRS ROONEY: [*Above rush of train.*] The up mail! The up mail!
[*The up mail recedes, the down train approaches, enters the
station, pulls up with great hissing of steam and clashing of
couplings. Noise of passengers descending, doors banging,
MR BARRELL shouting "Boghill! Boghill!", etc. Piercingly.*]
Dan! . . . Are you all right? . . . Where is he? . . . Dan! . . .
Did you see my husband? . . . Dan! . . . [*Noise of station
emptying. Guard's whistle. Train departing, receding.
Silence.*] He isn't on it! The misery I have endured to get
here, and he isn't on it! . . . Mr Barrell! . . . Was he not on it?
[*Pause.*] Is anything the matter, you look as if you had
seen a ghost. [*Pause.*] Tommy! . . . Did you see the master?

TOMMY: He'll be along, Ma'am, Jerry is minding him.
[*MR ROONEY suddenly appears on platform, advancing
on small boy JERRY's arm. He is blind, thumps the ground
with his stick and pants incessantly.*]

MRS ROONEY: Oh, Dan! There you are! [*Her dragging feet as she*

hastens towards him. She reaches him. They halt.] Where
in the world were you?

MR ROONEY: [*Coolly.*] Maddy.

MRS ROONEY: Where were you all this time?

MR ROONEY: In the men's.

MRS ROONEY: Kiss me!

MR ROONEY: Kiss you? In public? On the platform? Before the
boy? Have you taken leave of your senses?

MRS ROONEY: Jerry wouldn't mind. Would you, Jerry?

JERRY: No, Ma'am.

MRS ROONEY: How is your poor father?

JERRY: They took him away, Ma'am.

MRS ROONEY: Then you are all alone?

JERRY: Yes, Ma'am.

MR ROONEY: Why are you here? You did not notify me.

MRS ROONEY: I wanted to give you a surprise. For your birthday.

MR ROONEY: My birthday?

MRS ROONEY: Don't you remember? I wished you your happy
returns in the bathroom.

MR ROONEY: I did not hear you.

MRS ROONEY: But I gave you a tie! You have it on!
[*Pause.*]

MR ROONEY: How old am I now?

MRS ROONEY: Now never mind about that. Come.

MR ROONEY: Why did you not cancel the boy? Now we shall
have to give him a penny.

MRS ROONEY: [*Miserably.*] I forgot! I had such a time getting
here! Such horrid nasty people! [*Pause. Pleading.*] Be nice
to me, Dan, be nice to me today!

MR ROONEY: Give the boy a penny.

MRS ROONEY: Here are two halfpennies, Jerry. Run along now
and buy yourself a nice gobstopper.

JERRY: Yes, Ma'am.

MR ROONEY: Come for me on Monday, if I am still alive.

JERRY: Yessir.
[*He runs off.*]

MR ROONEY: We could have saved sixpence. We have saved
fivepence. [*Pause.*] But at what cost?
[*They move off along platform arm in arm. Dragging feet,*

panting, thudding stick.]

MRS ROONEY: Are you not well?

[*They halt, on* MR ROONEY's *initiative.*]

MR ROONEY: Once and for all, do not ask me to speak and move at the same time. I shall not say this in this life again. [*They move off. Dragging feet, etc. They halt at top of steps.*]

MRS ROONEY: Are you not—

MR ROONEY: Let us get this precipice over.

MRS ROONEY: Put your arm around me.

MR ROONEY: Have you been drinking again? [*Pause.*] You are quivering like a blancmange. [*Pause.*] Are you in a condition to lead me? [*Pause.*] We shall fall into the ditch.

MRS ROONEY: Oh, Dan! It will be like old times!

MR ROONEY: Pull yourself together or I shall send Tommy for the cab. Then instead of having saved sixpence, no, fivepence, we shall have lost ... [*Calculating mumble.*] ... two and three less six one and no plus one one and no plus three one and nine and one ten and three two and one ... [*Normal voice.*] two and one, we shall be the poorer to the tune of two and one. [*Pause.*] Curse that sun, it has gone in. What is the day doing?

[*Wind.*]

MRS ROONEY: Shrouding, shrouding, the best of it is past. [*Pause.*] Soon the first great drops will fall splashing in the dust.

MR ROONEY: And yet the glass was firm. [*Pause.*] Let us hasten home and sit before the fire. We shall draw the blinds. You will read to me. I think Effie is going to commit adultery with the Major. [*Brief drag of feet.*] Wait! [*Feet cease. Stick tapping at steps.*] I have been up and down these steps five thousand times and still I do not know how many there are. When I think there are six there are four or five or seven or eight and when I remember there are five there three or four or six or seven and when finally I realize there are seven there are five or six or eight or nine. Sometimes I wonder if they do not change them in the night. [*Pause. Irritably.*] Well? How many do you make them today?

MRS ROONEY: Do not ask me to count, Dan, not now.

MR ROONEY: Not count! One of the few satisfactions in life!

MRS ROONEY: Not steps, Dan, please, I always get them wrong. Then you might fall on your wound and I would have that on my manure-heap on top of everything else. No, just cling to me and all will be well.

[Confused noise of their descent. Panting, stumbling, ejaculations, curses. Silence.]

MR ROONEY: Well! That is what you call well!

MRS ROONEY: We are down. And little the worse. [Silence. A donkey brays. Silence.] That was a true donkey. Its father and mother were donkeys.

[Silence.]

MR ROONEY: Do you know what it is, I think I shall retire.

MRS ROONEY: [Appalled.] Retire! And live at home? On your grant!

MR ROONEY: Never tread these cursed steps again. Trudge this hellish road for the last time. Sit at home on the remnants of my bottom counting the hours—till the next meal. [Pause.] The very thought puts life in me! Forward, before it dies!

[They move on. Dragging feet, panting, thudding stick.]

MRS ROONEY: Now mind, here is the path .... Up! ... Well done! Now we are in safety and a straight run home.

MR ROONEY: [Without halting, between gasps.] A straight ... run! ... She calls that ... a straight ... run! ...

MRS ROONEY: Hush! Do not speak as you go along, you know it is not good for your coronary. [Dragging steps, etc.] Just concentrate on putting one foot before the next or whatever the expression is. [Dragging feet, etc.] That is the way, now we are doing nicely. [Dragging feet, etc. They suddenly halt, on MRS ROONEY's initiative.] Heavens! I knew there was something! With all the excitement! I forgot!

MR ROONEY: [Quietly.] Good God!

MRS ROONEY: But you must know, Dan, of course, you were on it. Whatever happened? Tell me!

MR ROONEY: I have never known anything to happen.

MRS ROONEY: But you must—

MR ROONEY: [*Violently.*] All this stopping and starting again is devilish, devilish! I get a little way on me and begin to be carried along when suddenly you stop dead! Two hundred pounds of unhealthy fat! What possessed you to come out at all? Let go of me!

MRS ROONEY: [*In great agitation.*] No, I must know, we won't stir from here till you tell me. Fifteen minutes late! On a thirty minute run! It's unheard of!

MR ROONEY: I know nothing. Let go of me before I shake you off.

MRS ROONEY: But you must know! You were on it! Was it at the terminus? Did you leave on time? Or was it on the line? [*Pause.*] Did something happen on the line? [*Pause.*] Dan! [*Brokenly.*] Why won't you tell me!
[*Silence. They move off. Dragging feet, etc. They halt. Pause.*]

MR ROONEY: Poor Maddy! [*Pause. Children's cries.*] What was that?
[*Pause for* MRS ROONEY *to ascertain.*]

MRS ROONEY: The Lynch twins jeering at us.
[*Cries.*]

MR ROONEY: Will they pelt us with mud today, do you suppose?
[*Cries.*]

MRS ROONEY: Let us turn and face them. [*Cries. They turn. Silence.*] Threaten them with your stick. [*Silence.*] They have run away.
[*Pause.*]

MR ROONEY: Did you ever wish to kill a child? [*Pause.*] Nip some young doom in the bud. [*Pause.*] Many a time at night, in winter, on the black road home, I nearly attacked the boy. [*Pause.*] Poor Jerry! [*Pause.*] What restrained me then? [*Pause.*] Not fear of man. [*Pause.*] Shall we go on backwards now a little?

MRS ROONEY: Backwards?

MR ROONEY: Yes. Or you forwards and I backwards. The perfect pair. Like Dante's damned, with their faces arsy-versy. Our tears will water our bottoms.

MRS ROONEY: What is the matter, Dan? Are you not well?

MR ROONEY: Well! Did you ever know me to be well? The day

you met me I should have been in bed. The day you
proposed to me the doctors gave me up. You knew that,
did you not? The night you married me they came for me
with an ambulance. You have not forgotten that, I
suppose? [*Pause.*] No, I cannot be said to be well. But I
am no worse. Indeed I am better than I was. The loss of
my sight was a great fillip. If I could go deaf and dumb I
think I might pant on to be a hundred. Or have I done so?
[*Pause.*] Was I a hundred today? [*Pause.*] Am I a hundred,
Maddy?
[*Silence.*]

MRS ROONEY: All is still. No living soul in sight. There is no
one to ask. The world is feeding. The wind—[*Brief wind.*]
—scarcely stirs the leaves and the birds—[*Brief chirp.*]—are
tired singing. The cows—[*Brief moo.*]—and sheep—[*Brief
baa.*]—ruminate in silence. The dogs—[*Brief bark.*]—are
hushed and the hens—[*Brief cackle.*]—sprawl torpid in the
dust. We are alone. There is no one to ask.
[*Silence.*]

MR ROONEY: [*Clearing his throat, narrative tone.*] We drew out
on the tick of time, I can vouch for that. I was—

MRS ROONEY: How can you vouch for it?

MR ROONEY: [*Normal tone, angrily.*] I can vouch for it, I tell
you! Do you want my relation or don't you? [*Pause.
Narrative tone.*] On the tick of time. I had the compartment to myself, as usual. At least I hope so, for I made
no attempt to restrain myself. My mind—[*Normal tone.*]
But why do we not sit down somewhere? Are we afraid
we should never rise again?

MRS ROONEY: Sit down on what?

MR ROONEY: On a bench, for example.

MRS ROONEY: There is no bench.

MR ROONEY: Then on a bank, let us sink down upon a bank.

MRS ROONEY: There is no bank.

MR ROONEY: Then we cannot. [*Pause.*] I dream of other roads,
in other lands. Of another home, another—[*He hesitates.*]
—another home. [*Pause.*] What was I trying to say?

MRS ROONEY: Something about your mind.

MR ROONEY: [*Startled.*] My mind? Are you sure? [*Pause.*

Incredulous.] My mind? . . . [*Pause.*] Ah yes. [*Narrative tone.*] Alone in the compartment my mind began to work, as so often after office hours, on the way home, in the train, to the lilt of the bogeys. Your season-ticket, I said, costs you twelve pounds a year and you earn, on an average, seven and six a day, that is to say barely enough to keep you alive and twitching with the help of food, drink, tobacco and periodicals until you finally reach home and fall into bed. Add to this—or subtract from it—rent, stationery, various subscriptions, tramfares to and fro, light and heat, permits and licences, hairtrims and shaves, tips to escorts, upkeep of premises and appearances, and a thousand unspecifiable sundries, and it is clear that by lying at home in bed, day and night, winter and summer, with a change of pyjamas once a fortnight, you would add very considerably to your income. Business, I said—[*A cry. Pause. Again. Normal tone.*] Did I hear a cry?

MRS ROONEY: Mrs Tully I fancy. Her poor husband is in constant pain and beats her unmercifully.
[*Silence.*]

MR ROONEY: That was a short knock. [*Pause.*] What was I trying to get at?

MRS ROONEY: Business.

MR ROONEY: Ah yes, business. [*Narrative tone.*] Business, old man, I said, retire from business, it has retired from you. [*Normal tone.*] One has these moments of lucidity.

MRS ROONEY: I feel very cold and weak.

MR ROONEY: [*Narrative tone.*] On the other hand, I said, there are the horrors of home life, the dusting, sweeping, airing, scrubbing, waxing, waning, washing, mangling, drying, mowing, clipping, raking, rolling, scuffling, shovelling, grinding, tearing, pounding, banging and slamming. And the brats, the happy little healthy little howling neighbours' brats. Of all this and much more the week-end, the Saturday intermission and then the day of rest, have given you some idea. But what must it be like on a working-day? A Wednesday? A Friday? What must it be like on a Friday! And I fell to thinking of my silent, backstreet, basement office, with its obliterated plate, rest-couch and velvet hangings, and what it means to be buried there alive, if only from ten to five, with convenient to the one hand a bottle of light pale ale and to the other a long ice-cold fillet of hake. Nothing, I said, not even fully certified death, can ever take the place of that. It was then I noticed that we were at a standstill. [*Pause. Normal tone. Irritably.*] Why are you hanging out of me like that? Have you swooned away?

MRS ROONEY: I feel very cold and faint. The wind—[*Whistling wind.*]—is whistling through my summer frock as if I had nothing on over my bloomers. I have had no solid food since my elevenses.

MR ROONEY: You have ceased to care. I speak—and you listen to the wind.

MRS ROONEY: No, no, I am agog, tell me all, then we shall press on and never pause, never pause, till we come safe to haven.
[*Pause.*]

MR ROONEY: Never pause . . . safe to haven . . . . Do you know, Maddy, sometimes one would think you were struggling with a dead language.

MRS ROONEY: Yes indeed, Dan, I know full well what you mean, I often have that feeling, it is unspeakably excruciating.

MR ROONEY: I confess I have it sometimes myself, when I happen to overhear what I am saying.

MRS ROONEY: Well, you know, it will be dead in time, just like our own poor dear Gaelic, there is that to be said.
[*Urgent baa.*]

MR ROONEY: [*Startled.*] Good God!

MRS ROONEY: Oh the pretty little woolly lamb, crying to suck its mother! Theirs has not changed, since Arcady.
[*Pause.*]

MR ROONEY: Where was I in my composition?

MRS ROONEY: At a standstill.

MR ROONEY: Ah yes. [*Clears his throat. Narrative tone.*] I concluded naturally that we had entered a station and would soon be on our way again, and I sat on, without misgiving. Not a sound. Things are very dull today, I said, nobody getting down, nobody getting on. Then as time flew by and nothing happened I realized my error. We had not entered a station.

MRS ROONEY: Did you not spring up and poke your head out of the window?

MR ROONEY: What good would that have done me?

MRS ROONEY: Why to call out to be told what was amiss.

MR ROONEY: I did not care what was amiss. No, I just sat on, saying, If this train were never to move again I should not greatly mind. Then gradually a—how shall I say—a growing desire to—er—you know—welled up within me. Nervous probably. In fact now I am sure. You know, the feeling of being confined.

MRS ROONEY: Yes yes, I have been through that.

MR ROONEY: If we sit here much longer, I said, I really do not know what I shall do. I got up and paced to and fro between the seats, like a caged beast.

MRS ROONEY: That is a help sometimes.

MR ROONEY: After what seemed an eternity we simply moved off. And the next thing was Barrell bawling the abhorred name. I got down and Jerry led me to the men's, or Fir as they call it now, from Vir Viris I suppose, the V becoming F, in accordance with Grimm's Law. [*Pause.*] The rest you know. [*Pause.*] You say nothing? [*Pause.*] Say something. Maddy. Say you believe me.

MRS ROONEY: I remember once attending a lecture by one of these new mind doctors. I forget what you call them. He spoke—

MR ROONEY: A lunatic specialist?

MRS ROONEY: No no, just the troubled mind. I was hoping he might shed a little light on my lifelong preoccupation with horses' buttocks.

MR ROONEY: A neurologist.

MRS ROONEY: No no, just mental distress, the name will come back to me in the night. I remember his telling us the story of a little girl, very strange and unhappy in her ways, and how he treated her unsuccessfully over a period of years and was finally obliged to give up the case. He could find nothing wrong with her, he said. The only thing wrong

with her as far as he could see was that she was dying.
And she did in fact die, shortly after he had washed his
hands of her.

MR ROONEY: Well? What is there so wonderful about that?

MRS ROONEY: No, it was just something he said, and the way
he said it, that have haunted me ever since.

MR ROONEY: You lie awake at night, tossing to and fro and
brooding on it.

MRS ROONEY: On it and other . . . wretchedness. [*Pause.*] When
he had done with the little girl he stood there motionless
for some time, quite two minutes I should say, looking
down at his table. Then he suddenly raised his head and
exclaimed, as if he had had a revelation, The trouble with
her was she had never really been born! [*Pause.*] He spoke
throughout without notes. [*Pause.*] I left before the end.

MR ROONEY: Nothing about your buttocks? [MRS ROONEY
weeps. In affectionate remonstrance.] Maddy!

MRS ROONEY: There is nothing to be done for those people!

MR ROONEY: For which is there? [*Pause.*] That does not sound
right somehow. [*Pause.*] What way am I facing?

MRS ROONEY: What?

MR ROONEY: I have forgotten what way I am facing.

MRS ROONEY: You have turned aside and are bowed down
over the ditch.

MR ROONEY: There is a dead dog down there.

MRS ROONEY: No no, just the rotting leaves.

MR ROONEY: In June? Rotting leaves in June?

MRS ROONEY: Yes, dear, from last year, and from the year
before last, and from the year before that again. [*Silence.
Rainy wind. They move on. Dragging steps, etc.*] There is
that lovely laburnum again. Poor thing, it is losing all its
tassels. [*Dragging steps, etc.*] There are the first drops.
[*Rain. Dragging steps, etc.*] Golden drizzle. [*Dragging steps,
etc.*] Do not mind me, dear, I am just talking to myself.
[*Rain heavier. Dragging steps, etc.*] Can hinnies procreate,
I wonder? [*They halt.*]

MR ROONEY: Say that again.

MRS ROONEY: Come on, dear, don't mind me, we are getting
drenched.

MR ROONEY: [*Forcibly.*] Can what what?

MRS ROONEY: Hinnies procreate. [*Silence.*] You know, hinnies, or jinnies, aren't they barren, or sterile, or whatever it is? [*Pause.*] It wasn't an ass's colt at all, you know, I asked the Regius Professor.
[*Pause.*]

MR ROONEY: He should know.

MRS ROONEY: Yes, it was a hinny, he rode into Jerusalem or wherever it was on a hinny. [*Pause.*] That must mean something. [*Pause.*] It's like the sparrows, than many of which we are of more value, they weren't sparrows at all.

MR ROONEY: Than many of which! . . . You exaggerate, Maddy.

MRS ROONEY: [*With emotion.*] They weren't sparrows at all!

MR ROONEY: Does that put our price up?
[*Silence. They move on. Wind and rain. Dragging feet, etc. They halt.*]

MRS ROONEY: Do you want some dung? [*Silence. They move on. Wind and rain, etc. They halt.*] Why do you stop? Do you want to say something?

MR ROONEY: No.

MRS ROONEY: Then why do you stop?

MR ROONEY: It is easier.

MRS ROONEY: Are you very wet?

MR ROONEY: To the buff.

MRS ROONEY: The buff?

MR ROONEY: The buff. From buffalo.

MRS ROONEY: We shall hang up all our things in the hot-cupboard and get into our dressing-gowns. [*Pause.*] Put your arm round me. [*Pause.*] Be nice to me! [*Pause. Gratefully.*] Ah, Dan! [*They move on. Wind and rain. Dragging feet, etc. Faintly same music as before. They halt. Music clearer. Silence but for music playing. Music dies.*] All day the same old record. All alone in that great empty house. She must be a very old woman now.

MR ROONEY: [*Indistinctly.*] Death and the Maiden.
[*Silence.*]

MRS ROONEY: You are crying. [*Pause.*] Are you crying?

MR ROONEY: [*Violently.*] Yes! [*They move on. Wind and rain. Dragging feet, etc. They halt. They move on. Wind and rain. Dragging feet, etc. They halt.*] Who is the preacher tomorrow? The incumbent?

MRS ROONEY: No.

MR ROONEY: Thank God for that. Who?

MRS ROONEY: Hardy.

MR ROONEY: "How to be Happy though Married"?

MRS ROONEY: No no, he died, you remember. No connexion.

MR ROONEY: Has he announced his text?

MRS ROONEY: "The Lord upholdeth all that fall and raiseth up all those that be bowed down." [*Silence. They join in wild laughter. They move on. Wind and rain. Dragging feet, etc.*] Hold me tighter, Dan! [*Pause.*] Oh yes!
[*They halt.*]

MR ROONEY: I hear something behind us.
[*Pause.*]

MRS ROONEY: It looks like Jerry. [*Pause.*] It is Jerry.
[*Sound of* JERRY*'s running steps approaching. He halts beside them, panting.*]

JERRY: [*Panting.*] You dropped—

MRS ROONEY: Take your time, my little man, you will burst a blood-vessel.

JERRY: [*Panting.*] You dropped something, sir. Mr Barrell told me to run after you.

MRS ROONEY: Show. [*She takes the object.*] What is it? [*She examines it.*] What is this thing, Dan?

MR ROONEY: Perhaps it is not mine at all.

JERRY: Mr Barrell said it was, sir.

MRS ROONEY: It looks like a kind of ball. And yet it is not a ball.

MR ROONEY: Give it to me.

MRS ROONEY: [*Giving it.*] What *is* it, Dan?

MR ROONEY: It is a thing I carry about with me.

MRS ROONEY: Yes, but what—

MR ROONEY: [*Violently.*] It is a thing I carry about with me!
[*Silence.* MRS ROONEY *looks for a penny.*]

MRS ROONEY: I have no small money. Have you?

MR ROONEY: I have none of any kind.

MRS ROONEY: We are out of change, Jerry. Remind Mr Rooney on Monday and he will give you a penny for your pains.

JERRY: Yes, Ma'am.

MR ROONEY: If I am alive.

JERRY: Yessir.

[JERRY *starts running back towards the station.*]

MRS ROONEY: Jerry! [JERRY *halts.*] Did you hear what the hitch was? [*Pause.*] Did you hear what kept the train so late?

MR ROONEY: How would he have heard? Come on.

MRS ROONEY: What was it, Jerry?

JERRY: It was a—

MR ROONEY: Leave the boy alone, he knows nothing! Come on!

MRS ROONEY: What was it, Jerry?

JERRY: It was a little child, Ma'am.

[MR ROONEY *groans.*]

MRS ROONEY: What do you mean, it was a little child?

JERRY: It was a little child fell out of the carriage, Ma'am. [*Pause.*] On to the line, Ma'am. [*Pause.*] Under the wheels, Ma'am.

[*Silence.* JERRY *runs off. His steps die away. Tempest of wind and rain. It abates. They move on. Dragging steps, etc. They halt. Tempest of wind and rain.*]

END

Act Without Words I

A mime for one player

Written in French in 1956, with music by John Beckett, the author's cousin. First published in Paris in 1957. Translated by the author and first published in English by Grove Press, New York, in 1958. First performed at the Royal Court Theatre, London, on 3 April 1957.

Desert. Dazzling light.

The man is flung backwards on stage from right wing. He falls, gets up immediately, dusts himself, turns aside, reflects.

Whistle from right wing.

He reflects, goes out right.

Immediately flung back on stage he falls, gets up immediately, dusts himself, turns aside, reflects.

Whistle from left wing.

He reflects, goes out left.

Immediately flung back on stage he falls, gets up immediately, dusts himself, turns aside, reflects.

Whistle from left wing.

He reflects, goes towards left wing, hesitates, thinks better of it, halts, turns aside, reflects.

A little tree descends from flies, lands. It has a single bough some three yards from ground and at its summit a meagre tuft of palms casting at its foot a circle of shadow.

He continues to reflect.

Whistle from above.

He turns, sees tree, reflects, goes to it, sits down in its shadow, looks at his hands.

A pair of tailor's scissors descends from flies, comes to rest before tree, a yard from ground.

He continues to look at his hands.

Whistle from above.

He looks up, sees scissors, takes them and starts to trim his nails.

The palms close like a parasol, the shadow disappears.

He drops scissors, reflects.

A tiny carafe, to which is attached a huge label inscribed
WATER, descends from flies, comes to rest some three yards
from ground.

He continues to reflect.

Whistle from above.

He looks up, sees carafe, reflects, gets up, goes and stands
under it, tries in vain to reach it, renounces, turns aside, reflects.

A big cube descends from flies, lands.

He continues to reflect.

Whistle from above.

He turns, sees cube, looks at it, at carafe, reflects, goes to
cube, takes it up, carries it over and sets it down under carafe,
tests its stability, gets up on it, tries in vain to reach carafe,
renounces, gets down, carries cube back to its place, turns aside,
reflects.

A second smaller cube descends from flies, lands.

He continues to reflect.

Whistle from above.

He turns, sees second cube, looks at it, at carafe, goes to
second cube, takes it up, carries it over and sets it down under
carafe, tests its stability, gets up on it, tries in vain to reach
carafe, renounces, gets down, takes up second cube to carry it
back to its place, hesitates, thinks better of it, sets it down,
goes to big cube, takes it up, carries it over and puts it on small
one, tests their stability, gets up on them, the cubes collapse, he
falls, gets up immediately, brushes himself, reflects.

He takes up small cube, puts it on big one, tests their stability,
gets up on them and is about to reach carafe when it is pulled
up a little way and comes to rest beyond his reach.

He gets down, reflects, carries cubes back to their place, one
by one, turns aside, reflects.

A third still smaller cube descends from flies, lands.

He continues to reflect.

Whistle from above.

He turns, sees third cube, looks at it, reflects, turns aside,
reflects.

The third cube is pulled up and disappears in flies.

Beside carafe a rope descends from flies, with knots to
facilitate ascent.

He continues to reflect.

Whistle from above.

He turns, sees rope, reflects, goes to it, climbs up it and is about to reach carafe when rope is let out and deposits him back on ground.

He reflects, looks around for scissors, sees them, goes and picks them up, returns to rope and starts to cut it with scissors.

The rope is pulled up, lifts him off ground, he hangs on, succeeds in cutting rope, falls back on ground, drops scissors, gets up again immediately, brushes himself, reflects.

The rope is pulled up quickly and disappears in flies.

With length of rope in his possession he makes a lasso with which he tries to lasso the carafe.

The carafe is pulled up quickly and disappears in flies.

He turns aside, reflects.

He goes with lasso in his hand to tree, looks at bough, turns and looks at cubes, looks again at bough, drops lasso, goes to cubes, takes up small one, carries it over and sets it down under bough, goes back for big one, takes it up and carries it over under bough, makes to put it on small one, hesitates, thinks better of it, sets it down, takes up small one and puts it on big one, tests their stability, turns aside and stoops to pick up lasso.

The bough folds down against trunk.

He straightens up with lasso in his hand, turns and sees what has happened.

He drops lasso, turns aside, reflects.

He carries back cubes to their place, one by one, goes back for lasso, carries it over to the cubes and lays it in a neat coil on small one.

He turns aside, reflects.

Whistle from right wing.

He reflects, goes out right.

Immediately flung back on stage he falls, gets up immediately, brushes himself, turns aside, reflects.

Whistle from left wing.

He does not move.

He looks at his hands, looks round for scissors, sees them, goes and picks them up, starts to trim his nails, stops, reflects, runs his finger along blade of scissors, goes and lays them on small cube, turns aside, opens his collar, frees his neck and fingers it.

The small cube is pulled up and disappears in flies, carrying away rope and scissors.

He turns to take scissors, sees what has happened.

He turns aside, reflects.

He goes and sits down on big cube.

The big cube is pulled from under him. He falls. The big cube is pulled up and disappears in flies.

He remains lying on his side, his face towards auditorium, staring before him.

The carafe descends from flies and comes to rest a few feet from his body.

He does not move.

Whistle from above.

He does not move.

The carafe descends further, dangles and plays about his face.

He does not move.

The carafe is pulled up and disappears in flies.

The bough returns to horizontal, the palms open, the shadow returns.

Whistle from above.

He does not move.

The tree is pulled up and disappears in flies.

He looks at his hands.

CURTAIN

Act Without Words II

A mime for two players

Written, according to Beckett, at about the same time as *Act Without Words I* (1956). Translated from the French by the author and first published in *New Departures*, vol. 1 (Summer, 1959). First performed probably at the Institute of Contemporary Arts, London, on 25 January 1960.

This mime should be played on a low and narrow platform at back of stage, violently lit in its entire length, the rest of the stage being in darkness. Frieze effect.

A is slow, awkward (gags dressing and undressing), absent. B brisk, rapid, precise. The two actions therefore, though B has more to do than A, should have approximately the same duration.

ARGUMENT

Beside each other on ground, two yards from right wing, two sacks, A's and B's, A's being to right (as seen from auditorium) of B's, i.e. nearer right wing. On ground beside sack B a little pile of clothes (C) neatly folded (coat and trousers surmounted by boots and hat).

Enter goad right, strictly horizontal. The point stops a foot short of sack A. Pause. The point draws back, pauses, darts forward into sack, withdraws, recoils to a foot short of sack. Pause. The sack does not move. The point draws back again, a little further than before, pauses, darts forward again into sack, withdraws, recoils to a foot short of sack. Pause. The sack moves. Exit goad.

A, wearing shirt, crawls out of sack, halts, broods, prays, broods, gets to his feet, broods, takes a little bottle of pills from his shirt pocket, broods, swallows a pill, puts bottle back, broods, goes to clothes, broods, puts on clothes, broods, takes a large partly-eaten carrot from coat pocket, bites off a piece, chews an instant, spits it out with disgust, puts carrot back, broods, picks up two sacks, carries them bowed and staggering half-way to left wing, sets them down, broods, takes off clothes (except shirt), lets them fall in an untidy heap, broods, takes another pill, broods, kneels, prays, crawls into sack and lies still, sack A being now to left of sack B.

Pause.

Enter goad right on wheeled support (one wheel). The point stops a foot short of sack B. Pause. The point draws back, pauses, darts forward into sack, withdraws, recoils to a foot short of sack. Pause. The sack moves. Exit goad.

B, wearing shirt, crawls out of sack, gets to his feet, takes from shirt pocket and consults a large watch, puts watch back, does exercises, consults watch, takes a tooth brush from shirt pocket and brushes teeth vigorously, puts brush back, rubs scalp vigorously, takes a comb from shirt pocket and combs hair, puts comb back, consults watch, goes to clothes, puts them on, consults watch, takes a brush from coat pocket and brushes clothes vigorously, brushes hair vigorously, puts brush back, takes a little mirror from coat pocket and inspects appearance, puts mirror back, takes carrot from coat pocket, bites off a piece, chews and swallows with appetite, puts carrot back, consults watch, takes a map from coat pocket and consults it, puts map back, consults watch, takes a compass from coat pocket and consults it, puts compass back, consults watch, picks up two sacks and carries them bowed and staggering to two yards short of left wing, sets them down, consults watch, takes off clothes (except shirt), folds them in a neat pile, consults watch, does exercises, consults watch, rubs scalp, combs hair, brushes teeth, consults and winds watch, crawls into sack and lies still, sack B being now to left of sack A as originally.

Pause.

Enter goad right on wheeled support (two wheels). The point stops a foot short of sack A. Pause. The point draws back, pauses, darts forward into sack, withdraws, recoils to a foot short of sack. Pause. The sack does not move. The point draws back again, a little further than before, pauses, darts forward again into sack, withdraws, recoils to a foot short of sack.

Pause. The sack moves. Exit goad.
 A crawls out of sack, halts, broods, prays.

CURTAIN

POSITION I

C B A ←

POSITION II

C A B ← ⊙

POSITION III

C B A ← ⊙   ⊙

STAGE FRONT

Krapp's Last Tape

again, but ~~not dead~~
his death not
prevented, * - the doom
is not the coming death,
but the life.

Written in English in early 1958. First published in *Evergreen Review* (Summer 1958). First performed at the Royal Court Theatre, London, on 28 October 1958.

A late evening in the future.

    KRAPP'S *den.*

    Front centre a small table, the two drawers of which open towards the audience.

    Sitting at the table, facing front, i.e. across from the drawers, a wearish old man: KRAPP.

    Rusty black narrow trousers too short for him. Rusty black sleeveless waistcoat, four capacious pockets. Heavy silver watch and chain. Grimy white shirt open at neck, no collar. Surprising pair of dirty white boots, size ten at least, very narrow and pointed.

    White face. Purple nose. Disordered grey hair. Unshaven.

    Very near-sighted (but unspectacled). Hard of hearing.

    Cracked voice. Distinctive intonation.

    Laborious walk.

    On the table a tape-recorder with microphone and a number of cardboard boxes containing reels of recorded tapes.

    Table and immediately adjacent area in strong white light. Rest of stage in darkness.

    KRAPP *remains a moment motionless, heaves a great sigh, looks at his watch, fumbles in his pockets, takes out an envelope, puts it back, fumbles, takes out a small bunch of keys, raises it to his eyes, chooses a key, gets up and moves to front of table. He stoops, unlocks first drawer, peers into it, feels about inside it, takes out a reel of tape, peers at it, puts it back, locks drawer, unlocks second drawer, peers into it, feels about inside it, takes out a large banana, peers at it, locks drawer, puts keys back in his pocket. He turns, advances to edge of stage, halts, strokes banana, peels it, drops skin at his feet, puts end of*

*banana in his mouth and remains motionless, staring vacuously
before him. Finally he bites off the end, turns aside and begins
pacing to and fro at edge of stage, in the light, i.e. not more
than four or five paces either way, meditatively eating banana.
He treads on skin, slips, nearly falls, recovers himself, stoops
and peers at skin and finally pushes it, still stooping, with his
foot over edge of stage into pit. He resumes his pacing, finishes
banana, returns to table, sits down, remains a moment motionless, heaves a great sigh, takes keys from his pockets, raises
them to his eyes, chooses key, gets up and moves to front of
table, unlocks second drawer, takes out a second large banana,
peers at it, locks drawer, puts back keys in his pocket, turns,
advances to edge of stage, halts, strokes banana, peels it, tosses
skin into pit, puts end of banana in his mouth and remains
motionless, staring vacuously before him. Finally he has an
idea, puts banana in his waistcoat pocket, the end emerging,
and goes with all the speed he can muster backstage into darkness. Ten seconds. Loud pop of cork. Fifteen seconds. He
comes back into light carrying an old ledger and sits down at
table. He lays ledger on table, wipes his mouth, wipes his hands
on the front of his waistcoat, brings them smartly together and
rubs them.*

KRAPP: [*Briskly.*] Ah! [*He bends over ledger, turns the pages,
finds the entry he wants, reads.*] Box . . . thrree . . . spool . . .
five. [*He raises his head and stares front. With relish.*]
Spool! [*Pause.*] Spooool! [*Happy smile. Pause. He bends
over table, starts peering and poking at the boxes.*] Box . . .
thrree . . . thrree . . . four . . . two . . . [*with surprise*] nine!
good God! . . . seven . . . ah! the little rascal! [*He takes up
box, peers at it.*] Box thrree. [*He lays it on table, opens it
and peers at spools inside.*] Spool . . . [*he peers at ledger*]
. . . five . . . [*he peers at spools*] . . . five . . . five . . . ah!
the little scoundrel! [*He takes out a spool, peers at it.*]
Spool five. [*He lays it on table, closes box three, puts it
back with the others, takes up the spool.*] Box thrree,
spool five. [*He bends over the machine, looks up. With
relish.*] Spooool! [*Happy smile. He bends, loads spool on
machine, rubs his hands.*] Ah! [*He peers at ledger, reads*

entry at foot of page.] Mother at rest at last .... Hm ....
The black ball .... [*He raises his head, stares blankly front.
Puzzled.*] Black ball? ... [*He peers again at ledger, reads.*]
The dark nurse .... [*He raises his head, broods, peers again
at ledger, reads.*] Slight improvement in bowel condition.
... Hm .... Memorable ... what? [*He peers closer.*]
Equinox, memorable equinox. [*He raises his head, stares
blankly front. Puzzled.*] Memorable equinox? ... [*Pause.
He shrugs his shoulders, peers again at ledger, reads.*]
Farewell to—[*he turns page*]—love.
[*He raises his head, broods, bends over machine, switches
on and assumes listening posture, i.e. leaning forward,
elbows on table, hand cupping ear towards machine, face
front.*]

TAPE: [*Strong voice, rather pompous, clearly Krapp's at a much
earlier time.*] Thirty-nine today, sound as a—[*Settling
himself more comfortably he knocks one of the boxes off
the table, curses, switches off, sweeps boxes and ledger
violently to the ground, winds tape back to beginning,
switches on, resumes posture.*] Thirty-nine today, sound
as a bell, apart from my old weakness, and intellectually
I have now every reason to suspect at the ... [*hesitates*]
... crest of the wave—or thereabouts. Celebrated the
awful occasion, as in recent years, quietly at the Wine-
house. Not a soul. Sat before the fire with closed eyes,
separating the grain from the husks. Jotted down a few
notes, on the back of an envelope. Good to be back in
my den, in my old rags. Have just eaten I regret to say
three bananas and only with difficulty refrained from a
fourth. Fatal things for a man with my condition.
[*Vehemently.*] Cut'em out! [*Pause.*] The new light above
my table is a great improvement. With all this darkness
round me I feel less alone. [*Pause.*] In a way. [*Pause.*] I
love to get up and move about in it, then back here to
... [*hesitates*] ... me. [*Pause.*] Krapp.
[*Pause.*]
The grain, now what I wonder do I mean by that, I mean
... [*hesitates*] ... I suppose I mean those things worth
having when all the dust has—when all *my* dust has settled.

I close my eyes and try and imagine them.

[*Pause.* KRAPP *closes his eyes briefly.*]

Extraordinary silence this evening, I strain my ears and do not hear a sound. Old Miss McGlome always sings at this hour. But not tonight. Songs of her girlhood, she says. Hard to think of her as a girl. Wonderful woman though. Connaught, I fancy. [*Pause.*] Shall I sing when I am her age, if I ever am? No. [*Pause.*] Did I sing as a boy? No. [*Pause.*] Did I ever sing? No.

[*Pause.*]

Just been listening to an old year, passages at random. I did not check in the book, but it must be at least ten or twelve years ago. At that time I think I was still living on and off with Bianca in Kedar Street. Well out of that, Jesus yes! Hopeless business. [*Pause.*] Not much about her, apart from a tribute to her eyes. Very warm. I suddenly saw them again. [*Pause.*] Incomparable! [*Pause.*] Ah well.... [*Pause.*] These old P.M.s are gruesome, but I often find them—[KRAPP *switches off, broods, switches on.*]—a help before embarking on a new... [*hesitates*] ...retrospect. Hard to believe I was ever that young whelp. The voice! Jesus! And the aspirations! [*Brief laugh in which* KRAPP *joins.*] And the resolutions! [*Brief laugh in which* KRAPP *joins.*] To drink less, in particular. [*Brief laugh of* KRAPP *alone.*] Statistics. Seventeen hundred hours, out of the preceding eight thousand odd, consumed on licensed premises alone. More than 20 per cent, say 40 per cent of his waking life. [*Pause.*] Plans for a less... [*hesitates*] ... engrossing sexual life. Last illness of his father. Flagging pursuit of happiness. Unattainable laxation. Sneers at what he calls his youth and thanks to God that it's over. [*Pause.*] False ring there. [*Pause.*] Shadows of the opus... magnum. Closing with a—[*brief laugh*]—yelp to Providence. [*Prolonged laugh in which* KRAPP *joins.*] What remains of all that misery? A girl in a shabby green coat, on a railway-station platform? No?

[*Pause.*]

When I look—

[KRAPP *switches off, broods, looks at his watch, gets up,*

goes backstage into darkness. Ten seconds. Pop of cork.
Ten seconds. Second cork. Ten seconds. Third cork. Ten
seconds. Brief burst of quavering song.]

KRAPP: [*Sings.*]   Now the day is over,
                       Night is drawing nigh-igh,
                       Shadows—

[*Fit of coughing. He comes back into light, sits down, wipes*
his mouth, switches on, resumes his listening posture.]

TAPE: —back on the year that is gone, with what I hope is perhaps a glint of the old eye to come, there is of course the
house on the canal where mother lay a-dying, in the late
autumn, after her long viduity [KRAPP *gives a start*] and
the—[KRAPP *switches off, winds back tape a little, bends*
his ear closer to machine, switches on]—a-dying, after her
long viduity, and the—

[KRAPP *switches off, raises his head, stares blankly before*
him. His lips move in the syllables of 'viduity'. No sound.
He gets up, goes backstage into darkness, comes back with
an enormous dictionary, lays it on table, sits down and
looks up the word.]

KRAPP: [*Reading from dictionary.*] State—or condition—of
being—or remaining—a widow—or widower. [*Looks up.*
Puzzled.] Being—or remaining?... [*Pause. He peers again*
at dictionary. Reading.] 'Deep weeds of viduity.' ... Also
of an animal, especially a bird ... the vidua or weaver-
bird .... Black plumage of male .... [*He looks up. With*
relish.] The vidua-bird!

[*Pause. He closes dictionary, switches on, resumes listening*
posture.]

TAPE: —bench by the weir from where I could see her window.
There I sat, in the biting wind, wishing she were gone.
[*Pause.*] Hardly a soul, just a few regulars, nursemaids,
infants, old men, dogs. I got to know them quite well—oh
by appearance of course I mean! One dark young beauty I
recollect particularly, all white and starch, incomparable
bosom, with a big black hooded perambulator, most
funereal thing. Whenever I looked in her direction she had
her eyes on me. And yet when I was bold enough to speak
to her—not having been introduced—she threatened to call

a policeman. As if I had designs on her virtue! [*Laugh. Pause.*] The face she had! The eyes! Like ... [*hesitates*] ... chrysolite! [*Pause.*] Ah well.... [*Pause.*] I was there when—[KRAPP *switches off, broods, switches on again.*]— the blind went down, one of those dirty brown roller affairs, throwing a ball for a little white dog as chance would have it. I happened to look up and there it was. All over and done with, at last. I sat on for a few moments with the ball in my hand and the dog yelping and pawing at me. [*Pause.*] Moments. Her moments, my moments. [*Pause.*] The dog's moments. [*Pause.*] In the end I held it out to him and he took it in his mouth, gently, gently. A small, old, black, hard, solid rubber ball. [*Pause.*] I shall feel it, in my hand, until my dying day. [*Pause.*] I might have kept it. [*Pause.*] But I gave it to the dog.

[*Pause.*]

Ah well....

[*Pause.*]

Spiritually a year of profound gloom and indigence until that memorable night in March, at the end of the jetty, in the howling wind, never to be forgotten, when suddenly I saw the whole thing. The vision at last. This I fancy is what I have chiefly to record this evening, against the day when my work will be done and perhaps no place left in my memory, warm or cold, for the miracle that ... [*hesitates*] ... for the fire that set it alight. What I suddenly saw then was this, that the belief I had been going on all my life, namely—[KRAPP *switches off impatiently, winds tape forward, switches on again*]—great granite rocks the foam flying up in the light of the lighthouse and the wind-gauge spinning like a propeller, clear to me at last that the dark I have always struggled to keep under is in reality my most— [KRAPP *curses, switches off, winds tape forward, switches on again*]—unshatterable association until my dissolution of storm and night with the light of the understanding and the fire—[KRAPP *curses louder, switches off, winds tape forward, switches on again*]—my face in her breasts and my hand on her. We lay there without moving. But under us all moved, and moved us, gently, up and down, and from side to side.

[*Pause.*]

Past midnight. Never knew such silence. The earth might be uninhabited.

[*Pause.*]

Here I end—

[KRAPP *switches off, winds tape back, switches on again.*]

—upper lake, with the punt, bathed off the bank, then pushed out into the stream and drifted. She lay stretched out on the floorboards with her hands under her head and her eyes closed. Sun blazing down, bit of a breeze, water nice and lively. I noticed a scratch on her thigh and asked her how she came by it. Picking gooseberries, she said. I said again I thought it was hopeless and no good going on and she agreed, without opening her eyes. [*Pause.*] I asked her to look at me and after a few moments—[*Pause.*]—after a few moments she did, but the eyes just slits, because of the glare. I bent over her to get them in the shadow and they opened. [*Pause. Low.*] Let me in. [*Pause.*] We drifted in among the flags and stuck. The way they went down, sighing, before the stem! [*Pause.*] I lay down across her with my face in her breasts and my hand on her. We lay there without moving. But under us all moved, and moved us, gently, up and down, and from side to side.

[*Pause.*]

Past midnight. Never knew—

[KRAPP *switches off, broods. Finally he fumbles in his pockets, encounters the banana, takes it out, peers at it, puts it back, fumbles, brings out envelope, fumbles, puts back envelope, looks at his watch, gets up and goes backstage into darkness. Ten seconds. Sound of bottle against glass, then brief siphon. Ten seconds. Bottle against glass alone. Ten seconds. He comes back a little unsteadily into light, goes to front of table, takes out keys, raises them to his eyes, chooses key, unlocks first drawer, peers into it, feels about inside, takes out reel, peers at it, locks drawer, puts keys back in his pocket, goes and sits down, takes reel off machine, lays it on dictionary, loads virgin reel on machine, takes envelope from his pocket, consults back of it, lays it on table, switches on, clears his throat and begins to record.*]

KRAPP: Just been listening to that stupid bastard I took myself for thirty years ago, hard to believe I was ever as bad as that. Thank God that's all done with anyway. [*Pause.*] The eyes she had! [*Broods, realizes he is recording silence, switches off, broods. Finally.*] Everything there, everything, all the—[*Realizes this is not being recorded, switches on.*] Everything there, everything on this old muckball, all the light and dark and famine and feasting of . . . [*hesitates*] . . . the ages! [*In a shout.*] Yes! [*Pause.*] Let that go! Jesus! Take his mind off his homework! Jesus! [*Pause. Weary.*] Ah well, maybe he was right. [*Pause.*] Maybe he was right. [*Broods. Realizes. Switches off. Consults envelope.*] Pah! [*Crumples it and throws it away. Broods. Switches on.*] Nothing to say, not a squeak. What's a year now? The sour cud and the iron stool. [*Pause.*] Revelled in the word spool. [*With relish.*] Spooool! Happiest moment of the past half million. [*Pause.*] Seventeen copies sold, of which eleven at trade price to free circulating libraries beyond the seas. Getting known. [*Pause.*] One pound six and something, eight I have little doubt. [*Pause.*] Crawled out once or twice, before the summer was cold. Sat shivering in the park, drowned in dreams and burning to be gone. Not a soul. [*Pause.*] Last fancies. [*Vehemently.*] Keep 'em under! [*Pause.*] Scalded the eyes out of me reading *Effie* again, a page a day, with tears again. Effie . . . . [*Pause.*] Could have been happy with her, up there on the Baltic, and the pines, and the dunes. [*Pause.*] Could I? [*Pause.*] And she? [*Pause.*] Pah! [*Pause.*] Fanny came in a couple of times. Bony old ghost of a whore. Couldn't do much, but I suppose better than a kick in the crutch. The last time wasn't so bad. How do you manage it, she said, at your age? I told her I'd been saving up for her all my life. [*Pause.*] Went to Vespers once, like when I was in short trousers. [*Pause. Sings.*]

> Now the day is over,
> Night is drawing nigh-igh,
> Shadows—[*coughing, then almost inaudible*]—
> of the evening
> Steal across the sky.

[*Gasping.*] Went to sleep and fell off the pew. [*Pause.*]
Sometimes wondered in the night if a last effort mightn't
—[*Pause.*] Ah finish your booze now and get to your bed.
Go on with this drivel in the morning. Or leave it at that.
[*Pause.*] Leave it at that. [*Pause.*] Lie propped up in the
dark—and wander. Be again in the dingle on a Christmas
Eve, gathering holly, the red-berried. [*Pause.*] Be again on
Croghan on a Sunday morning, in the haze, with the bitch,
stop and listen to the bells. [*Pause.*] And so on. [*Pause.*]
Be again, be again. [*Pause.*] All that old misery. [*Pause.*]
Once wasn't enough for you. [*Pause.*] Lie down across her.
[*Long pause. He suddenly bends over machine, switches
off, wrenches off tape, throws it away, puts on the other,
winds it forward to the passage he wants, switches on,
listens staring front.*]

TAPE: —gooseberries, she said. I said again I thought it was
hopeless and no good going on and she agreed, without
opening her eyes. [*Pause.*] I asked her to look at me and
after a few moments—[*Pause.*]—after a few moments she
did, but the eyes just slits, because of the glare. I bent
over to get them in the shadow and they opened. [*Pause.
Low.*] Let me in. [*Pause.*] We drifted in among the flags
and stuck. The way they went down, sighing, before the
stem! [*Pause.*] I lay down across her with my face in her
breasts and my hand on her. We lay there without moving.
But under us all moved, and moved us, gently, up and
down, and from side to side.
[*Pause.* KRAPP'S *lips move. No sound.*]
Past midnight. Never knew such silence. The earth might
be uninhabited.
[*Pause.*]
Here I end this reel. Box—[*Pause.*]—three, spool-[*Pause.*]
—five. [*Pause.*] Perhaps my best years are gone. When
there was a chance of happiness. But I wouldn't want them
back. Not with the fire in me now. No, I wouldn't want
them back.
[KRAPP *motionless staring before him. The tape runs on in
silence.*]

CURTAIN

Rough for Theatre I

Written in French in the late 1950s. First published in English translation by Grove Press, New York, in 1976.

Street corner. Ruins.
A, *blind, sitting on a folding-stool, scrapes his fiddle. Beside him
the case, half open, upended, surmounted by alms bowl. He
stops playing, turns his head audience right, listens.*
Pause.

A : A penny for a poor old man, a penny for a poor old man.
[*Silence. He resumes playing, stops again, turns his head
right, listens. Enter* B *right, in a wheelchair which he
propels by means of a pole. He halts. Irritated.*] A penny
for a poor old man!
[*Pause.*]

B : Music! [*Pause.*] So it is not a dream. At last! Nor a vision,
they are mute and I am mute before them. [*He advances,
halts, looks into bowl. Without emotion.*] Poor wretch.
[*Pause.*] Now I may go back, the mystery is over. [*He
pushes himself backwards, halts.*] Unless we join together,
and live together, till death ensue. [*Pause.*] What would
you say to that, Billy, may I call you Billy, like my son?
[*Pause.*] Do you like company, Billy? [*Pause.*] Do you
like tinned food, Billy?

A : What tinned food?

B : Corned beef, Billy, just corned beef. Enough to keep body and
soul together, till summer, with care. [*Pause.*] No? [*Pause.*]
A few potatoes too, a few pounds of potatoes too.
[*Pause.*] Do you like potatoes, Billy? [*Pause.*] We might
even let them sprout and then, when the time came, put
them in the ground, we might even try that. [*Pause.*] I
would choose the place and you would put them in the
ground. [*Pause.*] No? [*Pause.*]

A: How are the trees doing?

B: Hard to say. It's winter, you know.
   [*Pause.*]

A: Is it day or night?

B: Oh . . . [*he looks at the sky*] . . . day, if you like. No sun of
   course, otherwise you wouldn't have asked. [*Pause.*] Do
   you follow my reasoning? [*Pause.*] Have you your wits
   about you, Billy, have you still some of your wits about
   you?

A: But light?

B: Yes. [*Looks at sky.*] Yes, light, there is no other word for it.
   [*Pause.*] Shall I describe it to you? [*Pause.*] Shall I try to
   give you an idea of this light?

A: It seems to me sometimes I spend the night here, playing
   and listening. I used to feel twilight gather and make myself
   ready. I put away fiddle and bowl and had only to get to
   my feet, when she took me by the hand.
   [*Pause.*]

B: She?

A: My woman. [*Pause.*] A woman. [*Pause.*] But now . . .
   [*Pause.*]

B: Now?

A: When I set out I don't know, and when I get here I don't
   know, and while I am here I don't know, whether it is day
   or night.

B: You were not always as you are. What befell you? Women?
   Gambling? God?

A: I was always as I am.

B: Come!

A: [*Violently.*] I was always as I am, crouched in the dark,
   scratching an old jangle to the four winds!

B: [*Violently.*] We had our women, hadn't we? You yours to
   lead you by the hand and I mine to get me out of the chair
   in the evening and back into it again in the morning and to
   push me as far as the corner when I went out of my mind.

A: Cripple? [*Without emotion.*] Poor wretch.

B: Only one problem: the about-turn. I often felt, as I struggled,
   that it would be quicker to go on, right round the world.
   Till the day I realized I could go home backwards. [*Pause.*]

For example, I am at A. [*He pushes himself forward a little, halts.*] I push on to B. [*He pushes himself back a little, halts.*] And I return to A. [*With élan.*] The straight line! The vacant space! [*Pause.*] Do I begin to move you?

A: Sometimes I hear steps. Voices. I say to myself, They are coming back, some are coming back, to try and settle again, or to look for something they had left behind, or to look for someone they had left behind.

B: Come back! [*Pause.*] Who would want to come back here? [*Pause.*] And you never called out? [*Pause.*] Cried out? [*Pause.*] No?

A: Have you observed nothing?

B: Oh me you know, observe . . . I sit there, in my lair, in my chair, in the dark, twenty-three hours out of the twenty-four. [*Violently.*] What would you have me observe? [*Pause.*] Do you think we would make a match, now you are getting to know me?

A: Corned beef, did you say?

B: Apropos, what have you been living on, all this time? You must be famished.

A: There are things lying around.

B: Edible?

A: Sometimes.

B: Why don't you let yourself die?

A: On the whole I have been lucky. The other day I tripped over a sack of nuts.

B: No!

A: A little sack, full of nuts, in the middle of the road.

B: Yes, all right, but why don't you let yourself die?

A: I have thought of it.

B: [*Irritated.*] But you don't do it!

A: I'm not unhappy enough. [*Pause.*] That was always my unhap, unhappy, but not unhappy enough.

B: But you must be every day a little more so.

A: [*Violently.*] I am not unhappy enough!
[*Pause.*]

B: If you ask me we were made for each other.

A: [*Comprehensive gesture.*] What does it all look like now?

B: Oh me you know . . . I never go far, just a little up and down before my door. I never yet pushed on to here till now.

A: But you look about you?

B: No no.

A: After all those hours of darkness you don't—

B: [*Violently.*] No! [*Pause.*] Of course if you wish me to look about me I shall. And if you care to push me about I shall try to describe the scene, as we go along.

A: You mean you would guide me? I wouldn't get lost any more?

B: Exactly. I would say, Easy, Billy, we're heading for a great muckheap, turn back and wheel left when I give you the word.

A: You'd do that!

B: [*Pressing his advantage.*] Easy, Billy, easy, I see a round tin over there in the gutter, perhaps it's soup, or baked beans.

A: Baked beans!
[*Pause.*]

B: Are you beginning to like me? [*Pause.*] Or is it only my imagination?

A: Baked beans! [*He gets up, puts down fiddle and bowl on the stool and gropes towards* B.] Where are you?

B: Here, dear fellow. [A *lays hold of the chair and starts pushing it blindly.*] Stop!

A: [*Pushing the chair.*] It's a gift! A gift!

B: Stop! [*He strikes behind him with the pole.* A *lets go the chair, recoils. Pause.* A *gropes towards his stool, halts, lost.*] Forgive me! [*Pause.*] Forgive me, Billy!

A: Where am I? [*Pause.*] Where was I?

B: Now I've lost him. He was beginning to like me and I struck him. He'll leave me and I'll never see him again. I'll never see anyone again. We'll never hear the human voice again.

A: Have you not heard it enough? The same old moans and groans from the cradle to the grave.

B: [*Groaning.*] Do something for me, before you go!

A: There! Do you hear it? [*Pause. Groaning.*] I can't go! [*Pause.*] Do you hear it?

B: You can't go?

A: I can't go without my things.

B: What good are they to you?

A: None.

B: And you can't go without them?

A: No. [*He starts groping again, halts.*] I'll find them in the end.
[*Pause.*] Or leave them for ever behind me.
[*He starts groping again.*]

B: Straighten my rug, I feel the cold air on my foot. [*A halts.*]
I'd do it myself, but it would take too long. [*Pause.*] Do
that for me, Billy. Then I may go back, settle in the old
nook again and say, I have seen man for the last time, I
struck him and he succoured me. [*Pause.*] Find a few rags
of love in my heart and die reconciled, with my species.
[*Pause.*] What has you gaping at me like that? [*Pause.*]
Have I said something I shouldn't have? [*Pause.*] What
does my soul look like?
[*A gropes towards him.*]

A: Make a sound.
[*B makes one. A gropes towards it, halts.*]

B: Have you no sense of smell either?

A: It's the same stink everywhere. [*He stretches out his hand.*]
Am I within reach of your hand?
[*He stands motionless with outstretched hand.*]

B: Wait, you're not going to do me a service for nothing?
[*Pause.*] I mean unconditionally? [*Pause.*] Good God!
[*Pause. He takes A's hand and draws it towards him.*]

A: Your foot.

B: What?

A: You said your foot.

B: Had I but known! [*Pause.*] Yes, my foot, tuck it in. [*A stoops,
groping.*] On your knees, on your knees, you'll be more at
your ease. [*He helps him to kneel at the right place.*] There.

A: [*Irritated.*] Let go my hand! You want me to help you and
you hold my hand! [*B lets go his hand. A fumbles in the
rug.*] Have you only one leg?

B: Just the one.

A: And the other?

B: It went bad and was removed.
[*A tucks in the foot.*]

A: Will that do?

B: A little tighter. [*A tucks in tighter.*] What hands you have!
[*Pause.*]

A: [*Groping towards* B's *torso.*] Is all the rest there?

B: You may stand up now and ask me a favour.

A: Is all the rest there?

B: Nothing else has been removed, if that is what you mean. [A's *hand, groping higher, reaches the face, stays.*]

A: Is that your face?

B: I confess it is. [*Pause.*] What else could it be? [A's *fingers stray, stay.*] That? My wen.

A: Red?

B: Purple. [A *withdraws his hand, remains kneeling.*] What hands you have!
[*Pause.*]

A: Is it still day?

B: Day? [*Looks at sky.*] If you like. [*Looks.*] There is no other word for it.

A: Will it not soon be evening?
[B *stoops to* A, *shakes him.*]

B: Come, Billy, get up, you're beginning to incommode me.

A: Will it not soon be night?
[B *looks at sky.*]

B: Day ... night ... [*Looks.*] It seems to me sometimes the earth must have got stuck, one sunless day, in the heart of winter, in the grey of evening. [*Stoops to* A, *shakes him.*] Come on, Billy, up, you're beginning to embarrass me.

A: Is there grass anywhere?

B: I see none.

A: [*Vehement.*] Is there no green anywhere?

B: There's a little moss. [*Pause.* A *clasps his hands on the rug and rests his head on them.*] Good God! Don't tell me you're going to pray?

A: No.

B: Or weep?

A: No. [*Pause.*] I could stay like that for ever, with my head on an old man's knees.

B: Knee. [*Shaking him roughly.*] Get up, can't you!

A: [*Settling himself more comfortably.*] What peace! [B *pushes him roughly away,* A *falls to his hands and knees.*] Dora used to say, the days I hadn't earned enough, You and your harp! You'd do better crawling on all fours, with your

father's medals pinned to your arse and a money box round
your neck. You and your harp! Who do you think you are?
And she made me sleep on the floor. [*Pause.*] Who I
thought I was ... [*Pause.*] Ah that ... I never could ...
[*Pause. He gets up.*] Never could ... [*He starts groping
again for his stool, halts, listens.*] If I listened long enough
I'd hear it, a string would give.

B: Your harp? [*Pause.*] What's all this about a harp?

A: I once had a little harp. Be still and let me listen.
[*Pause.*]

B: How long are you going to stay like that?

A: I can stay for hours listening to all the sounds.
[*They listen.*]

B: What sounds?

A: I don't know what they are.
[*They listen.*]

B: I can see it. [*Pause.*] I can—

A: [*Imploring.*] Will you not be still?

B: No! [A *takes his head in his hands.*] I can see it clearly, over
there on the stool. [*Pause.*] What if I took it, Billy, and
made off with it? [*Pause.*] Eh Billy, what would you say to
that? [*Pause.*] There might be another old man, some day,
would come out of his hole and find you playing the mouth-
organ. And you'd tell him of the little fiddle you once had.
[*Pause.*] Eh Billy? [*Pause.*] Or singing. [*Pause.*] Eh Billy,
what would you say to that? [*Pause.*] There croaking to the
winter wind [*rime with unkind*], having lost his little mouth-
organ. [*He pokes him in the back with the pole.*] Eh Billy?
[A *whirls round, seizes the end of the pole and wrenches it
from* B*'s grasp.*]

Rough for Theatre II

Like *Rough for Theatre I*, written in French in the late 1950s. First published in English translation by Grove Press, New York, in 1976.

Upstage centre high double window open on bright night sky.
Moon invisible.
Downstage audience left, equidistant from wall and axis of
window, small table and chair. On table an extinguished reading-
lamp and a briefcase crammed with documents.
Downstage right, forming symmetry, identical table and chair.
Extinguished lamp only.
Downstage left door.
Standing motionless before left half of window with his back to
stage, C.
Long pause.
Enter A. *He closes door, goes to table on right and sits with his*
back to right wall. Pause. He switches on lamp, takes out his
watch, consults it and lays it on the table. Pause. He switches off.
Long pause.
Enter B. *He closes door, goes to table on left and sits with his*
back to left wall. Pause. He switches on lamp, opens briefcase
and empties contents on table. He looks round, sees A.

B: Well!
A: Hsst! Switch off. [B *switches off. Long pause. Low.*] What a
    night! [*Long pause. Musing.*] I still don't understand.
    [*Pause.*] Why he needs our services. [*Pause.*] A man like
    him. [*Pause.*] And why we give them free. [*Pause.*] Men
    like us. [*Pause.*] Mystery. [*Pause.*] Ah well ... [*Pause. He*
    switches on.] Shall we go? [B *switches on, rummages in his*
    papers.] The crux. [B *rummages.*] We sum up and clear
    out. [B *rummages.*] Set to go?
B: Rearing.

A: We attend.

B: Let him jump.

A: When?

B: Now.

A: From where?

B: From here will do. Three to three and a half metres per floor, say twenty-five in all.
[*Pause.*]

A: I could have sworn we were only on the sixth. [*Pause.*] He runs no risk?

B: He has only to land on his arse, the way he lived. The spine snaps and the tripes explode.
[*Pause.* A *gets up, goes to the window, leans out, looks down. He straightens up, looks at the sky. Pause. He goes back to his seat.*]

A: Full moon.

B: Not quite. Tomorrow.
[A *takes a little diary from his pocket.*]

A: What's the date?

B: Twenty-fourth. Twenty-fifth tomorrow.

A: [*Turning pages.*] Nineteen . . . twenty-two . . . twenty-four. [*Reads.*] 'Our Lady of Succour. Full moon.' [*He puts back the diary in his pocket.*] We were saying then . . . what was it . . . let him jump. Our conclusion. Right?

B: Work, family, third fatherland, cunt, finances, art and nature, heart and conscience, health, housing conditions, God and man, so many disasters.
[*Pause.*]

A: [*Meditative.*] Does it follow? [*Pause.*] Does it follow? [*Pause.*] And his sense of humour? Of proportion?

B: Swamped.
[*Pause.*]

A: May we not be mistaken?

B: [*Indignant.*] We have been to the best sources. All weighed and weighed again, checked and verified. Not a word here [*brandishing sheaf of papers*] that is not cast iron. Tied together like a cathedral. [*He flings down the papers on the table. They scatter on the floor.*] Shit!
[*He picks them up.* A *raises his lamp and shines it about him.*]

A: Seen worse dumps. [*Turning towards window.*] Worse out-
  looks. [*Pause.*] Is that Jupiter we see?
  [*Pause.*]

B: Where?

A: Switch off. [*They switch off.*] It must be.

B: [*Irritated.*] Where?

A: [*Irritated.*] There. [B *cranes.*] There, on the right, in the
  corner.
  [*Pause.*]

B: No. It twinkles.

A: What is it then?

B: [*Indifferent.*] No idea. Sirius. [*He switches on.*] Well? Do we
  work or play? [A *switches on.*] You forget this is not his
  home. He's only here to take care of the cat. At the end of
  the month shoosh back to the barge. [*Pause. Louder.*] You
  forget this is not his home.

A: [*Irritated.*] I forget, I forget! And he, does he not forget?
  [*With passion.*] But that's what saves us!

B: [*Searching through his papers.*] Memory . . . memory . . . [*He
  takes up a sheet.*] I quote: 'An elephant's for the eating
  cares, a sparrow's for the Lydian airs.' Testimony of Mr
  Swell, organist at Seaton Sluice and lifelong friend.
  [*Pause.*]

A: [*Glum.*] Tsstss!

B: I quote: 'Questioned on this occasion'—open brackets—
  '(judicial separation)'—close brackets—'regarding the
  deterioration of our relations, all he could adduce was the
  five or six miscarriages which clouded'—open brackets—'(oh
  through no act of mine!)'—close brackets—'the early days
  of our union and the veto which in consequence I had
  finally to oppose'—open brackets—'(oh not for want of
  inclination!)'—close brackets—'to anything remotely resem-
  bling the work of love. But on the subject of our happiness'
  —open brackets—'(for it too came our way, unavoidably,
  and here my mind goes back to the first vows exchanged at
  Wootton Bassett under the bastard acacias, or again to the
  first fifteen minutes of our wedding night at Littlestone-
  on-Sea, or yet again to those first long studious evenings in
  our nest on Commercial Road East)'—close brackets—'on

the subject of our happiness not a word, Sir, not one word.'
Testimony of Mrs Aspasia Budd-Croker, button designer in
residence, Commercial Road East.

A : [*Glum.*] Tsstss!

B : I quote again: 'Of our national epos he remembered only the
calamities, which did not prevent him from winning a
minor scholarship in the subject.' Testimony of Mr Peaberry,
market gardener in the Deeping Fens and lifelong friend.
[*Pause.*] 'Not a tear was known to fall in our family, and
God knows they did in torrents, that was not caught up
and piously preserved in that inexhaustible reservoir of
sorrow, with the date, the hour and the occasion, and not
a joy, fortunately they were few, that was not on the
contrary irrevocably dissolved, as by a corrosive. In that he
took after me.' Testimony of the late Mrs Darcy-Croker,
woman of letters. [*Pause.*] Care for more?

A : Enough.

B : I quote: 'To hear him talk about his life, after a glass or two,
you would have thought he had never set foot outside hell.
He had us in stitches. I worked it up into a skit that went
down well.' Testimony of Mr Moore, light comedian, c/o
Widow Merryweather-Moore, All Saints on the Wash, and
lifelong friend.
[*Pause.*]

A : [*Stricken.*] Tsstss! [*Pause.*] Tsstsstss!

B : You see. [*Emphatic.*] This is not his home and he knows it
full well.
[*Pause.*]

A : Now let's have the positive elements.

B : Positive? You mean of a nature to make him think . . .
[*hesitates, then with sudden violence*] . . . that some day
things might change? Is that what you want? [*Pause.
Calmer.*] There are none.

A : [*Wearily.*] Oh yes there are, that's the beauty of it.
[*Pause.* B *rummages in his papers.*]

B : [*Looking up.*] Forgive me, Bertrand. [*Pause. Rummages.
Looks up.*] I don't know what came over me. [*Pause.
Rummages. Looks up.*] A moment of consternation.
[*Pause. Rummages.*] There is that incident of the lottery . . .

    possibly. Remember?

A : No.

B : [*Reading.*] 'Two hundred lots . . . winner receives high class watch . . . solid gold, hallmark nineteen carats, marvel of accuracy, showing year, month, date, day, hour, minute and second, super chic, unbreakable hair spring, chrono escapement nineteen rubies, anti-shock, anti-magnetic, airtight, waterproof, stainless, self-winding, centre seconds hand, Swiss parts, de luxe lizard band.'

A : What did I tell you? However unhopefully. The mere fact of chancing his luck. I knew he had a spark left in him.

B : The trouble is he didn't procure it himself. It was a gift. That you forget.

A : [*Irritated.*] I forget, I forget! And he, does he not—[*Pause.*] At least he kept it.

B : If you can call it that.

A : At least he accepted it. [*Pause.*] At least he didn't refuse it.

B : I quote: 'The last time I laid eyes on him I was on my way to the Post Office to cash an order for back-pay. The area before the building is shut off by a row of bollards with chains hung between them. He was seated on one of these with his back to the Thompson works. To all appearances down and out. He sat doubled in two, his hands on his knees, his legs astraddle, his head sunk. For a moment I wondered if he was not vomiting. But on drawing nearer I could see he was merely scrutinizing, between his feet, a lump of dogshit. I moved it slightly with the tip of my umbrella and observed how his gaze followed the movement and fastened on the object in its new position. This at three o'clock in the afternoon if you please! I confess I had not the heart to bid him the time of day, I was overcome. I simply slipped into his hip pocket a lottery ticket I had no use for, while silently wishing him the best of luck. When two hours later I emerged from the Post Office, having cashed my order, he was at the same place and in the same attitude. I sometimes wonder if he is still alive.' Testimony of Mr Feckman, certified accountant and friend for better and for worse.
[*Pause.*]

A: Dated when?

B: Recent.

A: It has such a bygone ring. [*Pause.*] Nothing else?

B: Oh . . . bits and scraps . . . good graces of an heirless aunt . . .
unfinished—

A: Hairless aunt?

B: . . . heirless aunt . . . unfinished game of chess with a corre-
spondent in Tasmania . . . hope not dead of living to see the
extermination of the species . . . literary aspirations incom-
pletely stifled . . . bottom of a dairy-woman in Waterloo
Lane . . . you see the kind of thing.
[*Pause.*]

A: We pack up this evening, right?

B: Without fail. Tomorrow we're at Bury St Edmunds.

A: [*Sadly.*] We'll leave him none the wiser. We'll leave him now,
never to meet again, having added nothing to what he
knew already.

B: All these testimonies were new to him. They will have
finished him off.

A: Not necessarily. [*Pause.*] Any light on that? [*Papers.*] This is
vital. [*Papers.*] Something . . . I seem to remember . . .
something . . . he said himself.

B: [*Papers.*] Under 'Confidences' then. [*Brief laugh.*] Slim file.
[*Papers.*] Confidences . . . confidences . . . ah!

A: [*Impatient.*] Well?

B: [*Reading.*] '. . . sick headaches . . . eye trouble . . . irrational
fear of vipers . . . ear trouble . . .'—nothing for us there—
'. . . fibroid tumours . . . pathological horror of songbirds . . .
throat trouble . . . need of affection . . .'—we're coming to
it—'. . . inner void . . . congenital timidity . . . nose trouble . . .'
—ah! listen to this!—'. . . morbidly sensitive to the opinion
of others . . .' [*Looks up.*] What did I tell you?

A: [*Glum.*] Tsstss!

B: I'll read the whole passage: '. . . morbidly sensitive to the
opinion of others—'[*His lamp goes out.*] Well! The bulb
has blown! [*The lamp goes on again.*] No, it hasn't! Must
be a faulty connection. [*Examines lamp, straightens flex.*]
The flex was twisted, now all is well. [*Reading.*] '. . .mor-
bidly sensitive—' [*The lamp goes out.*] Bugger and shit!

A: Try giving her a shake. [B *shakes the lamp. It goes on again.*]
   See! I picked up that wrinkle in the Band of Hope.
   [*Pause.*]

B: ⎤
   ⎟ [*Together.*]   '. . . morbidly sensitive—'
A: ⎦   Keep your hands off the table.

B: What?

A: Keep your hands off the table. If it's a connection the least
   jog can do it.

B: [*Having pulled back his chair a little way.*] '. . . morbidly
   sensitive—'
   [*The lamp goes out.* B *bangs on the table with his fist. The
   lamp goes on again. Pause.*]

A: Mysterious affair, electricity.

B: [*Hurriedly.*] '. . . morbidly sensitive to the opinion of others
   at the time, I mean as often and for as long as they entered
   my awareness—' What kind of Chinese is that?

A: [*Nervously.*] Keep going, keep going!

B: '. . . for as long as they entered my awareness, and that in
   either case, I mean whether such on the one hand as to
   give me pleasure or on the contrary on the other to cause
   me pain, and truth to tell—' Shit! Where's the verb?

A: What verb?

B: The main!

A: I give up.

B: Hold on till I find the verb and to hell with all this drivel in
   the middle. [*Reading.*] '. . . were I but . . . could I but . . .'
   —Jesus!—'. . . though it be . . . be it but . . .'—Christ!—ah! I
   have it—'. . . I was unfortunately incapable . . .' Done it!

A: How does it run now?

B: [*Solemnly.*] '. . . morbidly sensitive to the opinion of others
   at the time . . .'—drivel drivel drivel—'. . . I was unfortunately
   incapable—'
   [*The lamp goes out. Long pause.*]

A: Would you care to change seats? [*Pause.*] You see what I
   mean? [*Pause.*] That you come over here with your papers
   and I go over there. [*Pause.*] Don't whinge, Morvan, that
   will get us nowhere.

B: It's my nerves. [*Pause.*] Ah if I were only twenty years
   younger I'd put an end to my sufferings!

A: Fie! Never say such horrid things! Even to a well-wisher!

B: May I come to you? [*Pause.*] I need animal warmth. [*Pause.*]

A: [*Coldly.*] As you like. [B *gets up and goes towards* A.] With your files if you don't mind. [B *goes back for papers and briefcase, returns towards* A, *puts them on* A's *table, remains standing. Pause.*] Do you want me to take you on my knees?

   [*Pause.* B *goes back for his chair, returns towards* A, *stops before* A's *table with the chair in his arms. Pause.*]

B: [*Shyly.*] May I sit beside you? [*They look at each other.*] No? [*Pause.*] Then opposite. [*He sits down opposite* A, *looks at him. Pause.*] Do we continue?

A: [*Forcibly.*] Let's get it over and go to bed.

   [B *rummages in his papers.*]

B: I'll take the lamp. [*He draws it towards him.*] Please God it holds out. What would we do in the dark the pair of us? [*Pause.*] Have you matches?

A: Never without. [*Pause.*] What we would do? Go and stand by the window in the starlight. [B's *lamp goes on again.*] That is to say you would.

B: [*Fervently.*] Oh no not alone I wouldn't!

A: Pass me a sheet. [B *passes him a sheet.*] Switch off.

   [B *switches off.*] Oh lord, yours is on again.

B: This gag has gone on long enough for me.

A: Just so. Go and switch it off.

   [B *goes to his table, switches off his lamp. Pause.*]

B: What am I to do now? Switch it on again?

A: Come back.

B: Switch on then till I see where I'm going.

   [A *switches on.* B *goes back and sits down opposite* A. A *switches off, goes to window with sheet, halts, contemplates the sky.*]

A: And to think all that is nuclear combustion! All that faerie! [*He stoops over sheet and reads haltingly.*] 'Aged ten, runs away from home first time, brought back next day, admonished, forgiven.' [*Pause.*] 'Aged fifteen, runs away from home second time, dragged back a week later, thrashed, forgiven.' [*Pause.*] 'Aged seventeen, runs away from home third time, slinks back six months later with his tail between his legs, locked up, forgiven.' [*Pause.*]

'Aged seventeen runs away from home last time, crawls back a year later on his hands and knees, kicked out, forgiven.'

[*Pause. He moves up against window to inspect* C's *face, to do which he has to lean out a little way, with his back to the void.*]

B: Careful!

[*Long pause, all three dead still.*]

A: [*Sadly.*] Tsstss! [*He resumes his equilibrium.*] Switch on.

[B *switches on.* A *goes back to his table, sits, returns the sheet to* B.] It's heavy going, but we're nearly home.

B: How does he look?

A: Not at his best.

B: Has he still got that little smile on his face?

A: Probably.

B: What do you mean, probably, haven't you just been looking at him?

A: He didn't have it then.

B: [*With satisfaction.*] Ah! [*Pause.*] Could never make out what he thought he was doing with that smile on his face. And his eyes? Still goggling?

A: Shut.

B: Shut!

A: Oh it was only so as not to see me. He must have opened them again since. [*Pause. Violently.*] You'd need to stare them in the face day and night! Never take your eyes off them for a week on end! Unbeknownst to them! [*Pause.*]

B: Looks to me we have him.

A: [*Impatiently.*] Come on, we're getting nowhere, get on with it.

[B *rummages in his papers, finds the sheet.*]

B: [*Reading at top speed.*] '... morbidly sensitive to the opinion of others at the time ...'—drivel drivel drivel—'... I was unfortunately incapable of retaining it for more than ten or fifteen minutes at the most, that is to say the time required to take it in. From then on it might as well never have been uttered.' [*Pause.*] Tsstss!

A: [*With satisfaction.*] You see. [*Pause.*] Where does that come in?

B: In a letter presumably never posted to an anonymous admiratrix.

A: An admiratrix? He had admiratrixes?

B: It begins: 'Dear friend and admiratrix . . .' That's all we know.

A: Come, Morvan, calm yourself, letters to admiratrixes, we all know what they're worth. No need to take everything literally.

B: [*Violently, slapping down his hand on the pile of papers.*] There's the record, closed and final. That's what we're going on. Too late now to start saying that [*slapping to his left*] is right and that [*slapping to his right*] wrong. You're a pain in the arse.
[*Pause.*]

A: Good. Let us sum up.

B: We do nothing else.

A: A black future, an unpardonable past—so far as he can remember, inducements to linger on all equally preposterous and the best advice dead letter. Agreed?

B: An heirless aunt preposterous?

A: [*Warmly.*] He's not the interested type. [*Sternly.*] One has to consider the client's temperament. To accumulate documents is not enough.

B: [*Vexed, slapping on his papers.*] Here, as far as I'm concerned the client is here and nowhere else.

A: All right. Is there a single reference there to personal gain? That old aunt, was he ever as much as commonly civil to her? And that dairy-woman, come to that, in all the years he's been going to her for his bit of cheddar, was he ever once wanting in respect? [*Pause.*] No, Morvan, look you— [*Feeble miaow. Pause. Second miaow, louder.*]

B: That must be the cat.

A: Sounds like it. [*Long pause.*] So, agreed? Black future, unpardonable—

B: As you wish. [*He starts to tidy back the papers in the briefcase. Wearily.*] Let him jump.

A: No further exhibit?

B: Let him jump, let him jump. [*He finishes tidying, gets up with the briefcase in his hand.*] Let's go.
[*A consults his watch.*]

A: It is now . . . ten . . . twenty-five. We have no train before eleven twenty. Let us kill the time here, talking of this and that.

B: What do you mean, eleven twenty? Ten fifty.
    [A *takes a time-table from his pocket, opens it at relevant
    page and hands it to* B.]
A: Where it's marked with a cross. [B *consults the time-table,
    hands it back to* A *and sits down again. Long pause.* A
    clears his throat. Pause. Impassionately.] How many
    unfortunates would be so still today if they had known
    in time to what extent they were so? [*Pause.*] Remember
    Smith?
B: Smith? [*Pause.*] Never knew anyone of that name.
A: Yes you did! A big fat redhair. Always to be seen hanging
    round World's End. Hadn't done a hand's turn for years.
    Reputed to have lost his genitals in a shooting accident.
    His own double-barrel that went off between his legs in a
    moment of abstraction, just as he was getting set to let fly
    at a quail.
B: Stranger to me.
A: Well to make a long story short he had his head in the oven
    when they came to tell him his wife had gone under an
    ambulance. Hell, says he, I can't miss that, and now he has
    a steady job in Marks and Spencer's. [*Pause.*] How is
    Mildred?
B: [*Disgustedly.*] Oh you know— [*Brief burst of birdsong.
    Pause.*] Good God!
A: Philomel!
B: Oh that put the heart across me!
A: Hsst! [*Low.*] Hark hark! [*Pause. Second brief burst, louder.
    Pause.*] It's in the room! [*He gets up, moves away on tip-
    toe.*] Come on, let's have a look.
B: I'm scared!
    [*He gets up none the less and follows cautiously in the wake
    of* A. A *advances on tiptoe upstage right,* B *tiptoes after.*]
A: [*Turning.*] Hsst! [*They advance, halt in the corner.* A *strikes
    a match, holds it above his head. Pause. Low.*] She's not
    here. [*He drops the match and crosses the stage on tiptoe
    followed on tiptoe by* B. *They pass before the window,
    halt in the corner upstage left. Match as before. Pause.*]
    Here she is!
B: [*Recoiling.*] Where?

[A *squats. Pause.*]

A: Lend me a hand.

B: Let her be! [A *straightens up painfully, clutching to his belly
a large birdcage covered with a green silk cloth fringed
with beads. He starts to stagger with it towards the table.*]
Give it here.
[B *helps to carry the cage. Holding it between them they
advance warily towards* A*'s table.*]

A: [*Breathing hard.*] Hold on a second. [*They halt. Pause.*]
Let's go. [*They move on, set down cage gently on the
table.* A *lifts cautiously the cloth on the side away from
the audience, peers. Pause.*] Show a light.
[B *takes up the lamp and shines it inside the cage. They
peer, stooped. Long pause.*]

B: There's one dead.
[*They peer.*]

A: Have you a pencil? [B *hands him a long pencil.* A *pokes it
between the bars of the cage. Pause.*] Yes. [*He withdraws
the pencil, puts it in his pocket.*]

B: Hi!
[A *gives him back his pencil. They peer.* A *takes* B*'s hand
and changes its position.*]

A: There.
[*They peer.*]

B: Is it the cock or the hen?

A: The hen. See how drab she is.

B: [*Revolted.*] And he goes on singing! [*Pause.*] There's lovebirds for you!

A: Lovebirds! [*Guffaw.*] Ah Morvan, you'd be the death of me
if I were sufficiently alive! Lovebirds! [*Guffaw.*] Finches,
pinhead! Look at that lovely little green rump! And the
blue cap! And the white bars! And the gold breast!
[*Didactic.*] Note moreover the characteristic warble, there
can be no mistaking it. [*Pause.*] Oh you pretty little pet,
oh you bonny wee birdie! [*Pause. Glum.*] And to think all
that is organic waste! All that splendour!
[*They peer.*]

B: They have no seed. [*Pause.*] No water. [*Pointing.*] What's
that there?

A: That? [*Pause. Slow, toneless.*] An old cuttle-bone.

B: Cuttle-bone?

A: Cuttle-bone.

[*He lets the cloth fall back. Pause.*]

B: Come, Bertrand, don't, there is nothing we can do. [A *takes up the cage and goes with it upstage left.* B *puts down the lamp and hastens after him.*] Give it here.

A: Leave it, leave it! [*He advances to the corner, followed by* B, *and puts down the cage where he found it. He straightens up and moves back towards his table, still followed by* B. A *stops short.*] Will you have done dogging me! Do you want me to jump too? [*Pause.* B *goes to* A*'s table, takes up briefcase and chair, goes to his table and sits with back to window. He switches on his lamp, switches it off again immediately.*] How end? [*Long pause.* A *goes to window, strikes a match, holds it high and inspects* C*'s face. The match burns out, he throws it out of window.*] Hi! Take a look at this! [B *does not move.* A *strikes another match, holds it high and inspects* C*'s face.*] Come on! Quick! [B *does not move. The match burns out,* A *lets it fall.*] Well I'll be . . . !

[A *takes out his handkerchief and raises it timidly towards* C*'s face.*]

CURTAIN

Embers

A piece for radio

Written in English and completed at the beginning of 1959. First published in *Evergreen Review* (Nov./Dec. 1959). First broadcast on the BBC Third Programme on 24 June 1959.

Sea scarcely audible.
HENRY's *boots on shingle. He halts.*
Sea a little louder.

HENRY: On. [*Sea. Voice louder.*] On! [*He moves on. Boots
on shingle. As he goes.*] Stop. [*Boots on shingle. As he
goes, louder.*] Stop! [*He halts. Sea a little louder.*] Down.
[*Sea. Voice louder.*] Down! [*Slither of shingle as he sits.
Sea, still faint, audible throughout what follows whenever
pause indicated.*] Who is beside me now? [*Pause.*] An old
man, blind and foolish. [*Pause.*] My father, back from the
dead, to be with me. [*Pause.*] As if he hadn't died. [*Pause.*]
No, simply back from the dead, to be with me, in this
strange place. [*Pause.*] Can he hear me? [*Pause.*] Yes, he
must hear me. [*Pause.*] To answer me? [*Pause.*] No, he
doesn't answer me. [*Pause.*] Just be with me. [*Pause.*]
That sound you hear is the sea. [*Pause. Louder.*] I say that
sound you hear is the sea, we are sitting on the strand.
[*Pause.*] I mention it because the sound is so strange, so un-
like the sound of the sea, that if you didn't see what it was
you wouldn't know what it was. [*Pause.*] Hooves! [*Pause.
Louder.*] Hooves! [*Sound of hooves walking on hard road.
They die rapidly away. Pause.*] Again! [*Hooves as before.
Pause. Excitedly.*] Train it to mark time! Shoe it with steel
and tie it up in the yard, have it stamp all day! [*Pause.*] A
ten-ton mammoth back from the dead, shoe it with steel and
have it tramp the world down! Listen to it! [*Pause.*] Listen
to the light now, you always loved light, not long past noon
and all the shore in shadow and the sea out as far as the
island. [*Pause.*] You would never live this side of the bay,
you wanted the sun on the water for that evening bathe
you took once too often. But when I got your money I
moved across, as perhaps you may know. [*Pause.*] We never

found your body, you know, that held up probate an unconscionable time, they said there was nothing to prove you hadn't run away from us all and alive and well under a false name in the Argentine for example, that grieved mother greatly. [*Pause.*] I'm like you in that, can't stay away from it, but I never go in, no, I think the last time I went in was with you. [*Pause.*] Just be near it. [*Pause.*] Today it's calm, but I often hear it above in the house and walking the roads and start talking, oh just loud enough to drown it, nobody notices. [*Pause.*] But I'd be talking now no matter where I was, I once went to Switzerland to get away from the cursed thing and never stopped all the time I was there. [*Pause.*] I usen't to need anyone, just to myself, stories, there was a great one about an old fellow called Bolton, I never finished it, I never finished any of them, I never finished anything, everything always went on for ever. [*Pause.*] Bolton [*Pause. Louder.*] Bolton! [*Pause.*] There before the fire. [*Pause.*] Before the fire with all the shutters ... no, hangings, hangings, all the hangings drawn and the light, no light, only the light of the fire, sitting there in the ... no, standing, standing there on the hearthrug in the dark before the fire with his arms on the chimney-piece and his head on his arms, standing there waiting in the dark before the fire in his old red dressing-gown and no sound in the house of any kind, only the sound of the fire. [*Pause.*] Standing there in his old red dressing-gown might go on fire any minute like when he was a child, no, that was his pyjamas, standing there waiting in the dark. no light, only the light of the fire, and no sound of any kind, only the fire, an old man in great trouble. [*Pause.*] Ring then at the door and over he goes to the window and looks out between the hangings, fine old chap, very big and strong, bright winter's night, snow everywhere, bitter cold, white world, cedar boughs bending under load and then as the arm goes up to ring again recognizes ... Holloway ... [*Long pause.*] ... yes, Holloway, recognizes Holloway, goes down and opens. [*Pause.*] Outside all still, not a sound, dog's chain maybe or a bough groaning if you stood there listening long

enough, white world, Holloway with his little black bag,
not a sound, bitter cold, full moon small and white,
crooked trail of Holloway's galoshes, Vega in the Lyre very
green. [*Pause.*] Vega in the Lyre very green. [*Pause.*]
Following conversation then on the step, no, in the room,
back in the room, following conversation then back in the
room, Holloway: 'My dear Bolton, it is now past midnight,
if you would be good enough—', gets no further, Bolton:
'Please! PLEASE!' Dead silence then, not a sound, only
the fire, all coal, burning down now, Holloway on the
hearthrug trying to toast his arse, Bolton, where's Bolton,
no light, only the fire, Bolton at the window his back to
the hangings, holding them a little apart with his hand
looking out, white world, even the spire, white to the vane,
most unusual, silence in the house, not a sound, only the
fire, no flames now, embers. [*Pause.*] Embers. [*Pause.*]
Shifting, lapsing, furtive like, dreadful sound, Holloway
on the rug, fine old chap, six foot, burly, legs apart, hands
behind his back holding up the tails of his old macfarlane,
Bolton at the window, grand old figure in his old red
dressing-gown, back against the hangings, hand stretched
out widening the chink, looking out, white world great
trouble, not a sound, only the embers, sound of dying,
dying glow, Holloway, Bolton, Bolton, Holloway, old
men, great trouble, white world, not a sound. [*Pause.*]
Listen to it! [*Pause.*] Close your eyes and listen to it,
what would you think it was? [*Pause. Vehement.*] A
drip! A drip! [*Sound of drip, rapidly amplified, suddenly
cut off.*] Again! [*Drip again. Amplification begins.*] No!
[*Drip cut off. Pause.*] Father! [*Pause. Agitated.*] Stories,
stories, years and years of stories, till the need came on
me, for someone, to be with me, anyone, a stranger, to
talk to, imagine he hears me, years of that, and then, now,
for someone who . . . knew me, in the old days, anyone, to
be with me, imagine he hears me, what I am, now.
[*Pause.*] No good either. [*Pause.*] Not there either.
[*Pause.*] Try again. [*Pause.*] White world, not a sound.
[*Pause.*] Holloway. [*Pause.*] Holloway says he'll go,
damned if he'll sit up all night before a black grate, doesn't

understand, call a man out, an old friend, in the cold and dark, an old friend, urgent need, bring the bag, then not a word, no explanation no heat, no light, Bolton: 'Please! PLEASE!' Holloway, no refreshment, no welcome, chilled to the medulla, catch his death, can't understand, strange treatment, old friend, says he'll go, doesn't move, not a sound, fire dying, white beam from window, ghastly scene, wishes to God he hadn't come, no good, fire out, bitter cold, great trouble, white world, not a sound, no good. [*Pause.*] No good. [*Pause.*] Can't do it. [*Pause.*] Listen to it! [*Pause.*] Father! [*Pause.*] You wouldn't know me now, you'd be sorry you ever had me, but you were that already, a washout, that's the last I heard from you, a washout. [*Pause. Imitating father's voice.*] 'Are you coming for a dip?' 'No.' 'Come on, come on.' 'No.' Glare, stump to door, turn, glare. 'A washout, that's all you are, a washout!' [*Violent slam of door. Pause.*] Again! [*Slam. Pause.*] Slam life shut like that! [*Pause.*] Washout. [*Pause.*] Wish to Christ she had. [*Pause.*] Never met Ada, did you, or did you, I can't remember, no matter, no one'd know her now. [*Pause.*] What turned her against me do you think, the child I suppose, horrid little creature, wish to God we'd never had her, I use to walk with her in the fields, Jesus that was awful, she wouldn't let go my hand and I mad to talk. 'Run along now, Addie, and look at the lambs.' [*Imitating* ADDIE's *voice.*] 'No papa.' 'Go on now, go on.' [*Plaintive.*] 'No papa.' [*Violent.*] 'Go on with you when you're told and look at the lambs!' [ADDIE's *loud wail. Pause.*] Ada too, conversation with her, that was something, that's what hell will be like, small chat to the babbling of Lethe about the good old days when we wished we were dead. [*Pause.*] Price of margarine fifty years ago. [*Pause.*] And now. [*Pause. With solemn indignation.*] Price of blueband now! [*Pause.*] Father! [*Pause.*] Tired of talking to you. [*Pause.*] That was always the way, walk all over the mountains with you talking and talking and then suddenly mum and home in misery and not a word to a soul for weeks, sulky little bastard, better off dead. [*Long pause.*] Ada. [*Pause. Louder.*] Ada!

ADA: [*Low remote voice throughout.*] Yes.

HENRY: Have you been there long?

ADA: Some little time. [*Pause.*] Why do you stop, don't mind me. [*Pause.*] Do you want me to go away? [*Pause.*] Where is Addie?
[*Pause.*]

HENRY: With her music master. [*Pause.*] Are you going to answer me today?

ADA: You shouldn't be sitting on the cold stones, they're bad for your growths. Raise yourself up till I slip my shawl under you. [*Pause.*] Is that better?

HENRY: No comparison, no comparison. [*Pause.*] Are you going to sit down beside me?

ADA: Yes. [*No sound as she sits.*] Like that? [*Pause.*] Or do you prefer like that? [*Pause.*] You don't care. [*Pause.*] Chilly enough I imagine, I hope you put on your jaegers. [*Pause.*] Did you put on your jaegers, Henry?

HENRY: What happened was this, I put them on and then I took them off again and then I put them on again and then I took them off again and then I took them on again and then I—

ADA: Have you them on now?

HENRY: I don't know. [*Pause.*] Hooves! [*Pause. Louder.*] Hooves! [*Sound of hooves walking on hard road. They die rapidly away.*] Again!
[*Hooves as before. Pause.*]

ADA: Did you hear them?

HENRY: Not well.

ADA: Galloping?

HENRY: No. [*Pause.*] Could a horse mark time?
[*Pause.*]

ADA: I'm not sure that I know what you mean.

HENRY: [*Irritably.*] Could a horse be trained to stand still and mark time with its four legs?

ADA: Oh. [*Pause.*] The ones I used to fancy all did. [*She laughs. Pause.*] Laugh, Henry, it's not every day I crack a joke. [*Pause.*] Laugh, Henry do that for me.

HENRY: You wish *me* to laugh?

ADA: You laughed so charmingly once, I think that's what

first attracted me to you. That and your smile. [*Pause.*] Come on, it will be like old times.
[*Pause. He tries to laugh, fails.*]

HENRY: Perhaps I should begin with the smile. [*Pause for smile.*] Did that attract you? [*Pause.*] Now I'll try again. [*Long horrible laugh.*] Any of the old charm there?

ADA: Oh Henry!
[*Pause.*]

HENRY: Listen to it! [*Pause.*] Lips and claws! [*Pause.*] Get away from it! Where it couldn't get at me! The Pampas! What?

ADA: Calm yourself.

HENRY: And I live on the brink of it! Why? Professional obligations? [*Brief laugh.*] Reasons of health? [*Brief laugh.*] Family ties? [*Brief laugh.*] A woman? [*Laugh in which she joins.*] Some old grave I cannot tear myself away from? [*Pause.*] Listen to it! What is it like?

ADA: It is like an old sound I used to hear. [*Pause.*] It is like another time, in the same place. [*Pause.*] It was rough, the spray came flying over us. [*Pause.*] Strange it should have been rough then [*Pause.*] And calm now.
[*Pause.*]

HENRY: Let us get up and go.

ADA: Go? Where? And Addie? She would be very distressed if she came and found you had gone without her. [*Pause.*] What do you suppose is keeping her?
[*Smart blow of cylindrical ruler on piano case. Unsteadily, ascending and descending, ADDIE plays scale of A Flat Major, hands first together, then reversed. Pause.*]

MUSIC MASTER: [*Italian accent.*] Santa Cecilia!
[*Pause.*]

ADDIE: Will I play my piece now please?
[*Pause. MUSIC MASTER beats two bars of waltz time with ruler on piano case. ADDIE plays opening bars of Chopin's 5th Waltz in A Flat Major, MUSIC MASTER beating time lightly with ruler as she plays. In first chord of bass, bar 5, she plays E instead of F. Resounding blow of ruler on piano case. ADDIE stops playing.*]

MUSIC MASTER: [*Violently.*] Fa!

ADDIE: [*Tearfully.*] What?

MUSIC MASTER: [*Violently.*] Eff! Eff!

ADDIE: [*Tearfully.*] Where?

MUSIC MASTER: [*Violently.*] Qua! [*He thumps note.*] Fa!
[*Pause.* ADDIE *begins again,* MUSIC MASTER *beating
time lightly with ruler. When she comes to bar 5 she makes
same mistake. Tremendous blow of ruler on piano case.*
ADDIE *stops playing, begins to wail.*]

MUSIC MASTER: [*Frenziedly.*] Eff! Eff! [*He hammers note.*] Eff!
[*He hammers note.*] Eff!
[*Hammered note, 'Eff!' and* ADDIE's *wail amplified to
paroxysm, then suddenly cut off. Pause.*]

ADA: You are silent today.

HENRY: It was not enough to drag her into the world, now she
must play the piano.

ADA: She must learn. She shall learn. That—and riding.
[*Hooves walking.*]

RIDING MASTER: Now Miss! Elbows in Miss! Hands down Miss!
[*Hooves trotting.*] Now Miss! Back straight Miss! Knees in
Miss! [*Hooves cantering.*] Now Miss! Tummy in Miss! Chin
up Miss! [*Hooves galloping.*] Now Miss! Eyes front Miss!
[ADDIE *begins to wail.*] Now Miss! Now Miss!
[*Galloping hooves, 'Now Miss!' and* ADDIE's *wail amplified
to paroxysm, then suddenly cut off. Pause.*]

ADA: What are you thinking of? [*Pause.*] I was never taught,
until it was too late. All my life I regretted it.

HENRY: What was your strong point, I forget.

ADA: Oh . . . geometry I suppose, plane and solid. [*Pause.*] First
plane, then solid. [*Shingle as he gets up.*] Why do you get
up?

HENRY: I thought I might try and get as far as the water's edge.
[*Pause. With a sigh.*] And back. [*Pause.*] Stretch my old
bones.
[*Pause.*]

ADA: Well, why don't you? [*Pause.*] Don't stand there thinking
about it. [*Pause.*] Don't stand there staring. [*Pause. He goes
towards sea. Boots on shingle, say ten steps. He halts at
water's edge. Pause. Sea a little louder. Distant.*] Don't wet
your good boots.
[*Pause.*]

HENRY: Don't, don't ....

[*Sea suddenly rough.*]

ADA: [*Twenty years earlier, imploring.*] Don't! Don't!

HENRY: [*Ditto, urgent.*] Darling!

ADA: [*Ditto, more feebly.*] Don't!

HENRY: [*Ditto, exultantly.*] Darling!

[*Rough sea.* ADA *cries out. Cry and sea amplified, cut off. End of evocation. Pause. Sea calm. He goes back up deeply shelving beach. Boots laborious on shingle. He halts. Pause. He moves on. He halts. Pause. Sea calm and faint.*]

ADA: Don't stand there gaping. Sit down. [*Pause. Shingle as he sits.*] On the shawl. [*Pause.*] Are you afraid we might touch? [*Pause.*] Henry.

HENRY: Yes.

ADA: You should see a doctor about your talking, it's worse, what must it be like for Addie? [*Pause.*] Do you know what she said to me once, when she was still quite small, she said, Mummy, why does Daddy keep on talking all the time? She heard you in the lavatory. I didn't know what to answer.

HENRY: Daddy! Addie! [*Pause.*] I told you to tell her I was praying. [*Pause.*] Roaring prayers at God and his saints.

ADA: It's very bad for the child. [*Pause.*] It's silly to say it keeps you from hearing it, it doesn't keep you from hearing it and even if it does you shouldn't be hearing it, there must be something wrong with your brain.

[*Pause.*]

HENRY: That! I shouldn't be hearing that!

ADA: I don't think you are hearing it. And if you are what's wrong with it, it's a lovely peaceful gentle soothing sound, why do you hate it? [*Pause.*] And if you hate it why don't you keep away from it? Why are you always coming down here? [*Pause.*] There's something wrong with your brain, you ought to see Holloway, he's alive still, isn't he? [*Pause.*]

HENRY: [*Wildly.*] Thuds, I want thuds! Like this! [*He fumbles in the shingle, catches up two big stones and starts dashing them together.*] Stone! [*Clash.*] Stone! [*Clash. 'Stone!' and clash amplified, cut off. Pause. He throws one stone away. Sound of its fall.*] That's life! [*He throws the other stone away. Sound of its fall.*] Not this . . . [*Pause.*] . . . sucking!

ADA: And why life? [*Pause.*] Why life, Henry? [*Pause.*] Is there anyone about?

HENRY: Not a living soul.

ADA: I thought as much. [*Pause.*] When we longed to have it to ourselves there was always someone. Now that it does not matter the place is deserted.

HENRY: Yes, you were always very sensitive to being seen in gallant conversation. The least feather of smoke on the horizon and you adjusted your dress and became immersed in the *Manchester Guardian*. [*Pause.*] The hole is still there, after all these years. [*Pause. Louder.*] The hole is still there.

ADA: What hole? The earth is full of holes.

HENRY: Where we did it at last for the first time.

ADA: Ah yes, I think I remember. [*Pause.*] The place has not changed.

HENRY: Oh yes it has, *I* can see it. [*Confidentially.*] There is a levelling going on! [*Pause.*] What age is she now?

ADA: I have lost count of time.

HENRY: Twelve? Thirteen? [*Pause.*] Fourteen?

ADA: I really could not tell you, Henry.

HENRY: It took us a long time to have her. [*Pause.*] Years we kept hammering away at it. [*Pause.*] But we did it in the end. [*Pause. Sigh.*] We had her in the end. [*Pause.*] Listen to it! [*Pause.*] It's not so bad when you get out on it. [*Pause.*] Perhaps I should have gone into the merchant navy.

ADA: It's only on the surface, you know. Underneath all is as quiet as the grave. Not a sound. All day, all night, not a sound. [*Pause.*]

HENRY: Now I walk about with the gramophone. But I forgot it today.

ADA: There is no sense in that. [*Pause.*] There is no sense in trying to drown it. [*Pause.*] See Holloway. [*Pause.*]

HENRY: Let us go for a row.

ADA: A row? And Addie? She would be very distressed if she came and found you had gone for a row without her. [*Pause.*] Who were you with just now? [*Pause.*] Before you spoke to me.

HENRY: I was trying to be with my father.

ADA: Oh. [*Pause.*] No difficulty about that.

HENRY: I mean I was trying to get him to be with me. [*Pause.*] You seem a little cruder than usual today, Ada. [*Pause.*] I was asking him if he had ever met you, I couldn't remember.

ADA: Well?

HENRY: He doesn't answer any more.

ADA: I suppose you have worn him out. [*Pause.*] You wore him out living and now you are wearing him out dead. [*Pause.*] The time comes when one cannot speak to you any more. [*Pause.*] The time will come when no one will speak to you at all, not even complete strangers. [*Pause.*] You will be quite alone with your voice, there will be no other voice in the world but yours. [*Pause.*] Do you hear me? [*Pause.*]

HENRY: I can't remember if he met you.

ADA: You know he met me.

HENRY: No, Ada, I don't know, I'm sorry, I have forgotten almost everything connected with you.

ADA: You weren't there. Just your mother and sister. I had called to fetch you, as arranged. We were to go bathing together. [*Pause.*]

HENRY: [*Irritably.*] Drive on, drive on! Why do people always stop in the middle of what they are saying?

ADA: None of them knew where you were. Your bed had not been slept in. They were all shouting at one another. Your sister said she would throw herself off the cliff. Your father got up and went out, slamming the door. I left soon afterwards and passed him on the road. He did not see me. He was sitting on a rock looking out to sea. I never forgot his posture. And yet it was a common one. You used to have it sometimes. Perhaps just the stillness, as if he had been turned to stone. I could never make it out. [*Pause.*]

HENRY: Keep on, keep on! [*Imploringly.*] Keep it going, Ada, every syllable is a second gained.

ADA: That's all, I'm afraid. [*Pause.*] Go on now with your father or your stories or whatever you were doing, don't mind me any more.

HENRY: I can't! [*Pause.*] I can't do it any more!

ADA: You were doing it a moment ago, before you spoke to me.

HENRY: [*Angrily.*] I can't do it any more now! [*Pause.*] Christ! [*Pause.*]

ADA: Yes, you know what I mean, there are attitudes remain in one's mind for reasons that are clear, the carriage of a head for example, bowed when one would have thought it should be lifted, and vice versa, or a hand suspended in mid-air, as if unowned. That kind of thing. But with your father sitting on the rock that day nothing of the kind, no detail you could put your finger on and say, How very peculiar! No, I could never make it out. Perhaps, as I said, just the great stillness of the whole body, as if all the breath had left it. [*Pause.*] Is this rubbish a help to you, Henry? [*Pause.*] I can try and go on a little if you wish. [*Pause.*] No? [*Pause.*] Then I think I'll be getting back.

HENRY: Not yet! You needn't speak. Just listen. Not even. Be with me. [*Pause.*] Ada! [*Pause. Louder.*] Ada! [*Pause.*] Christ! [*Pause.*] Hooves! [*Pause. Louder.*] Hooves! [*Pause.*] Christ! [*Long pause.*] Left soon afterwards, passed you on the road, didn't see her, looking out to . . . . [*Pause.*] Can't have been looking out to *sea*. [*Pause.*] Unless you had gone round the other side. [*Pause.*] Had you gone round the cliff side? [*Pause.*] Father! [*Pause.*] Must have I suppose. [*Pause.*] Stands watching you a moment, then on down path to tram, up on open top and sits down in front. [*Pause.*] Sits down in front. [*Pause.*] Suddenly feels uneasy and gets down again, conductor: 'Changed your mind, Miss?', goes back up path, no sign of you. [*Pause.*] Very unhappy and uneasy, hangs round a bit, not a soul about, cold wind coming in off sea, goes back down path and takes tram home. [*Pause.*] Takes tram home. [*Pause.*] Christ! [*Pause.*] 'My dear Bolton . . . .' [*Pause.*] 'If it's an injection you want, Bolton, let down your trousers and I'll give you one, I have a panhysterectomy at nine,' meaning of course the anaesthetic. [*Pause.*] Fire out, bitter cold, white world, great trouble, not a sound. [*Pause.*] Bolton starts playing with the curtain, no, hanging, difficult to describe, draws it back no, kind of gathers it towards him and the moon comes

flooding in, then lets it fall back, heavy velvet affair, and
pitch black in the room, then towards him again, white,
black, white, black, Holloway: 'Stop that for the love of
God, Bolton, do you want to finish me?' [*Pause.*] Black,
white, black, white, maddening thing. [*Pause.*] Then he
suddenly strikes a match, Bolton does, lights a candle,
catches it up above his head, walks over and looks Holloway
full in the eye. [*Pause.*] Not a word, just the look, the old
blue eye, very glassy, lids worn thin, lashes gone, whole
thing swimming, and the candle shaking over his head.
[*Pause.*] Tears? [*Pause. Long laugh.*] Good God no!
[*Pause.*] Not a word, just the look, the old blue eye,
Holloway: 'If you want a shot say so and let me get to hell
out of here.' [*Pause.*] 'We've had this before, Bolton,
don't ask me to go through it again.' [*Pause.*] Bolton:
'Please!' [*Pause.*] 'Please!' [*Pause.*] 'Please, Holloway!'
[*Pause.*] Candle shaking and guttering all over the place,
lower now, old arm tired takes it in the other hand and
holds it high again, that's it, that was always it, night, and
the embers cold, and the glim shaking in your old fist,
saying, Please! Please! [*Pause.*] Begging. [*Pause.*] Of the
poor. [*Pause.*] Ada! [*Pause.*] Father! [*Pause.*] Christ!
[*Pause.*] Holds it high again, naughty world, fixes Holloway,
eyes drowned, won't ask again, just the look, Holloway
covers his face, not a sound, white world, bitter cold,
ghastly scene, old men, great trouble, no good. [*Pause.*]
No good. [*Pause.*] Christ! [*Pause. Shingle as he gets up.
He goes towards sea. Boots on shingle. He halts. Pause.
Sea a little louder.*] On. [*Pause. He moves on. Boots
on shingle. He halts at water's edge. Pause. Sea a little
louder.*] Little book. [*Pause.*] This evening.... [*Pause.*]
Nothing this evening. [*Pause.*] Tomorrow ... tomorrow ...
plumber at nine, then nothing. [*Pause. Puzzled.*] Plumber
at nine? [*Pause.*] Ah yes, the waste. [*Pause.*] Words.
[*Pause.*] Saturday ... nothing. Sunday ... Sunday ...
nothing all day. [*Pause.*] Nothing, all day nothing. [*Pause.*]
All day all night nothing. [*Pause.*] Not a sound.

Rough for Radio I

Written in French in late 1961. First published in English as 'Sketch for Radio Play' in *Stereo Headphones*, no. 7 (Spring 1976).

HE: [*Gloomily.*] Madam.

SHE: Are you all right? [*Pause.*] You asked me to come.

HE: I ask no one to come here.

SHE: You suffered me to come.

HE: I meet my debts.
  [*Pause.*]

SHE: I have come to listen.

HE: When you please.
  [*Pause.*]

SHE: May I squat on this hassock? [*Pause.*] Thank you.
  [*Pause.*] May we have a little heat?

HE: No, madam.
  [*Pause.*]

SHE: Is it true the music goes on all the time?

HE: Yes.

SHE: Without cease?

HE: Without cease.

SHE: It's unthinkable! [*Pause.*] And the words too? All the
  time too?

HE: All the time.

SHE: Without cease?

HE: Yes.

SHE: It's unimaginable. [*Pause.*] So you are here all the time?

HE: Without cease.
  [*Pause.*]

SHE: How troubled you look! [*Pause.*] May one see them?

HE: No, madam.

SHE: I may not go and see them?

HE: No, madam.
  [*Pause.*]

SHE: May we have a little light?

HE: No, madam.
  [*Pause.*]

SHE: How cold you are! [*Pause.*] Are these the two knobs?

HE: Yes.

SHE: Just push? [*Pause.*] Is it live? [*Pause.*] I ask you is it live.

HE: No, you must twist. [*Pause.*] To the right.
    [*Click.*]

MUSIC: [*Faint.*] . . . .
    [*Silence.*]

SHE: [*Astonished.*] But there are more than one!

HE: Yes.

SHE: How many?
    [*Pause.*]

HE: To the right, madam, to the right.
    [*Click.*]

VOICE: [*Faint.*] . . . .

SHE: [*With voice.*] Louder!

VOICE: [*No louder.*] . . . .
    [*Silence.*]

SHE: [*Astonished.*] But he is alone!

HE: Yes.

SHE: All alone?

HE: When one is alone one is all alone.
    [*Pause.*]

SHE: What is it like together?
    [*Pause.*]

HE: To the right, madam.
    [*Click.*]

MUSIC: [*Faint, brief.*] . . . .

MUSIC:
VOICE:]   [*Together.*] . . . .

    [*Silence.*]

SHE: They are not together?

HE: No.

SHE: They cannot see each other?

HE: No.

SHE: Hear each other?

HE: No.

SHE: It's inconceivable!
    [*Pause.*]

HE: To the right, madam.

[*Click.*]

VOICE: [*Faint.*] ....

SHE: [*With voice.*] Louder!

VOICE: [*No louder.*] ....

[*Silence.*]

SHE: And– [*Faint stress.*]–*you* like that?

HE: It is a need.

SHE: A need? *That* a need?

HE: It has become a need. [*Pause.*] To the right, madam.

[*Click.*]

MUSIC: [*Faint.*] ....

SHE: [*With music.*] Louder!

MUSIC: [*No louder.*] ....

[*Silence.*]

SHE: That too? [*Pause.*] That a need too?

HE: It has become a need, madam.

SHE: Are they in the same ... situation?

[*Pause.*]

HE: I don't understand.

SHE: Are they ... subject to the same ... conditions?

HE: Yes, madam.

SHE: For instance? [*Pause.*] For instance?

HE: One cannot describe them, madam.

[*Pause.*]

SHE: Well, I'm obliged to you.

HE: Allow me, this way.

[*Pause.*]

SHE: [*A little off.*] Is that a Turkoman?

HE: [*Ditto.*] Allow me.

SHE: [*A little further off.*] How troubled you look! [*Pause.*]
Well, I'll leave you. [*Pause.*] To your needs.

HE: [*Ditto.*] Good-bye, madam. [*Pause.*] To the right, madam,
that's the garbage–[*Faint stress.*]–the *house* garbage.
[*Pause.*] Good-bye, madam.

[*Long pause. Sound of curtains violently drawn, first one,
then the other, clatter of the heavy rings along the rods.
Pause. Faint ping–as sometimes happens–of telephone
receiver raised from cradle. Faint sound of dialling. Pause.*]
Hello ... Miss ... is the doctor ... ah ... yes ... he to call

me ... Macgillycuddy ... Mac-gilly-cuddy ... right ... he'll know ... and Miss ... Miss! ... urgent ... yes! ... [*Shrill.*] ... most urgent!

[*Pause. Receiver put down with same faint ping. Pause. Click.*]

MUSIC: [*Faint.*] ....

HE: [*With music.*] Good God!

MUSIC: [*Faint.*] ....

[*Silence. Pause. Click.*]

VOICE: [*Faint.*] ....

HE: [*With voice, shrill.*] Come on! Come on!

VOICE: [*Faint.*] ....

[*Silence.*]

HE: [*Low.*] What'll I do? [*Pause. Faint ping of receiver raised again. Faint dialling. Pause.*] Hello ... Miss ... Macgilly-cuddy ... Mac-gilly-cuddy ... right ... I'm sorry but ... ah ... yes ... of course ... can't reach him ... no idea ... understand ... right ... immediately ... the moment he gets back ... what? ... [*Shrill.*] ... yes! ... I told you so! ... most urgent! ... most urgent! ... [*Pause. Low.*] Slut!

[*Sound of receiver put down violently. Pause. Click.*]

MUSIC: [*Faint. Brief.*] ....

[*Silence. Click.*]

VOICE: [*Faint. Brief.*] ....

HE: [*With voice, shrill.*] It's crazy! Like one!

MUSIC:⎤
      ⎟ [*Together.*] ....
VOICE:⎦

[*Telephone rings. Receiver raised immediately, not more than a second's ring.*]

HE: [*With music and voice.*] Yes ... wait ... [*Music and voice silent. Very agitated.*] Yes ... yes ... no matter ... what the trouble is? ... they're ending ... ENDING ... this morning ... what? ... no! ... no question! ... ENDING I tell you ... nothing what? ... to be done? ... I know there's nothing to be done ... what? ... no! ... it's me ... ME ... what? I tell you they're ending ... ENDING ... I can't stay like that after ... who? ... but she's left me ... ah for God's sake ... haven't they all left me? ... did you not know that? ... all left me ... sure? ... of course I'm sure ...

what? ... in an hour? ... not before? ... wait ... [*Low.*]
... there's more ... they're together ... TOGETHER ...
yes ... I don't know ... like ... [*Hesitation.*] ... one ...
the breathing ... I don't know ... [*Vehement.*] ... no! ...
never! ... meet? ... how could they meet? ... what? ...
what are all alike? ... last what? ... gasps? ... wait ...
don't go yet ... wait! ... [*Pause. Sound of receiver put
down violently. Low.*] Swine!
[*Pause. Click.*]

MUSIC: [*Failing.*] . . . .

MUSIC: ⎱   [*Together, failing.*] . . . .
VOICE: ⎰

[*Telephone rings. Receiver immediately raised.*]

HE: [*With music and voice.*] Miss ... what? ... [*Music and
voice silent.*] ... a confinement? ... [*Long pause.*] ... two
confinements? ... [*Long pause.*] ... one what? ... what? ...
breech? ... what? ... [*Long pause.*] ... tomorrow noon? ...
[*Long pause. Faint ping as receiver put gently down. Long
pause. Click.*]

MUSIC: [*Brief, failing.*] . . . .

MUSIC: ⎱   [*Together, ending, breaking off together, resuming
VOICE: ⎰   together more and more feebly.*] . . . .

[*Silence. Long pause.*]

HE: [*Whisper.*] Tomorrow ... noon ...

Rough for Radio II

Written in French in the early 1960s. First published in English by Grove Press, New York, in 1976. First broadcast under the title 'Rough for Radio' on BBC Radio 3 on 13 April 1976.

ANIMATOR
STENOGRAPHER
FOX
DICK (mute)

A: Ready, miss?

S: And waiting, sir.

A: Fresh pad, spare pencils?

S: The lot, sir.

A: Good shape?

S: Tiptop, sir.

A: And you, Dick, on your toes? [*Swish of bull's pizzle. Admiringly.*] Wow! Let's hear it land. [*Swish and formidable thud.*] Good. Off with his hood. [*Pause.*] Ravishing face, ravishing! Is it not, miss?

S: Too true, sir. We know it by heart and yet the pang is ever new.

A: The gag. [*Pause.*] The blind. [*Pause.*] The plugs. [*Pause.*] Good. [*He thumps on his desk with a cylindrical ruler.*] Fox, open your eyes, readjust them to the light of day and look about you. [*Pause.*] You see, the same old team. I hope--

S: [*Aflutter.*] Oh!

A: What is it, miss? Vermin in the lingerie?

S: He smiled at me!

A: Good omen. [*Faint hope.*] Not the first time by any chance?

S: Heavens no, sir, what an idea!

A: [*Disappointed.*] I might have known. [*Pause.*] And yet it still affects you?

S: Why yes, sir, it is so sudden! So radiant! So fleeting!

A: You note it?

S: Oh no, sir, the words alone. [*Pause.*] Should one note the play of feature too?

A: I don't know, miss. Depending perhaps.

S: Me you know--

A: [*Trenchant.*] Leave it for the moment. [*Thump with ruler.*] Fox, I hope you have had a refreshing night and will be better inspired today than heretofore. Miss.

S: Sir.

A: Let us hear again the report on yesterday's results, it has
   somewhat slipped my memory.

S: [*Reading.*] 'We the undersigned, assembled under—'

A: Skip.

S: [*Reading.*] '. . . note yet again with pain that these dicta—'

A: Dicta! [*Pause.*] Read on.

S: '. . . with pain that these dicta, like all those communicated
   to date and by reason of the same deficiencies, are totally
   inacceptable. The second half in particular is of such—'

A: Skip.

S: '. . . outlook quite hopeless were it not for our conviction—'

A: Skip. [*Pause.*] Well?

S: That is all, sir.

A: . . . same deficiencies . . . totally inacceptable . . . outlook quite
   hopeless . . . [*Disgusted.*] Well! [*Pause.*] Well!

S: That is all, sir. Unless I am to read the exhortations.

A: Read them.

S: '. . . instantly renew our standing exhortations, namely:
   1. Kindly to refrain from recording mere animal cries, they
   serve only to indispose us.
   2. Kindly to provide a strictly literal transcript, the
   meanest syllable has, or may have, its importance.
   3. Kindly to ensure full neutralization of the subject when
   not in session, especially with regard to the gag, its perma-
   nence and good repair. Thus rigid enforcement of the tube
   feed, be it per buccam or be it on the other hand per
   rectum, is *absolutely*'—one word underlined—'essential.
   The least word let fall in solitude and thereby in danger, as
   Mauthner has shown, of being no longer needed, *may be it*
   —three words underlined.
   '4. Kindly—'

A: Enough! [*Sickened.*] Well! [*Pause.*] Well!

S: It is past two, sir.

A: [*Roused from his prostration.*] It is what?

S: Past two, sir.

A: [*Roughly.*] Then what are you waiting for? [*Pause. Gently.*]
   Forgive me, miss, forgive me, my cup is full. [*Pause.*]
   Forgive me!

S: [*Coldly.*] Shall I open with yesterday's close?

A: If you would be so good.

S: [*Reading.*] 'When I had done soaping the mole, thoroughly rinsing and drying before the embers, what next only out again in the blizzard and put him back in his chamber with his weight of grubs, at that instant his little heart was beating still I swear, ah my God my God.' [*She strikes with her pencil on her desk.*] 'My God.'
[*Pause.*]

A: Unbelievable! And there he jibbed, if I remember aright.

S: Yes, sir, he would say no more.

A: Dick functioned?

S: Let me see . . . Yes, twice.
[*Pause.*]

A: Does not the glare incommode you, miss, what if we should let down the blind?

S: Thank you, sir, not on my account, it can never be too warm, never too bright, for me. But, with your permission, I shall shed my overall.

A: [*With alacrity.*] Please do, miss, please do. [*Pause.*] Staggering! Staggering! Ah were I but . . . forty years younger!

S: [*Rereading.*] 'Ah my God my God.' [*Blow with pencil.*] 'My God.'

A: Crabbed youth! No pity! [*Thump with ruler.*] Do you mark me? On! [*Silence.*] Dick! [*Swish and thud of pizzle on flesh. Faint cry from* FOX.] Off record, miss, remember?

S: Drat it! Where's that eraser?

A: Erase, miss, erase, we're in trouble enough already. [*Ruler.*] On! [*Silence.*] Dick!

F: Ah yes, that for sure, live I did, no denying, all stones all sides—

A: One moment.

F: —walls no further—

A: [*Ruler.*] Silence! Dick! [*Silence. Musing.*] Live I did . . . [*Pause.*] Has he used that turn before, miss?

S: To what turn do you allude, sir?

A: Live I did.

S: Oh yes, sir, it's a notion crops up now and then. Perhaps not in those precise terms, so far, that I could not say

offhand. But allusions to a life, though not common, are
not rare.

A: His own life?

S: Yes, sir, a life all his own.

A: [*Disappointed.*] I might have known. [*Pause.*] What a
memory—mine! [*Pause.*] Have you read the Purgatory,
miss, of the divine Florentine?

S: Alas no, sir. I have merely flipped through the Inferno.

A: [*Incredulous.*] Not read the Purgatory?

S: Alas no, sir.

A: There all sigh, I was, I was. It's like a knell. Strange, is it not?

S: In what sense, sir?

A: Why, one would rather have expected, I shall be. No?

S: [*With tender condescension.*] The creatures! [*Pause.*] It is
getting on for three, sir.

A: [*Sigh.*] Good. Where were we?

S: '. . . walls no further—'

A: Before, that, miss, the house is not on fire.

S: '. . . live I did, no denying, all stones all sides'—inaudible
—'walls—'

A: [*Ruler.*] On! [*Silence.*] Dick!

S: Sir.

A: [*Impatiently.*] What is it, miss, can't you see that old time is
aflying?

S: I was going to suggest a touch of kindness, sir, perhaps just a
hint of kindness.

A: So soon? And then? [*Firmly.*] No, miss, I appreciate your
sentiment. But I have my method. Shall I remind you of
it? [*Pause. Pleading.*] Don't say no! [*Pause.*] Oh you are
an angel! You may sit, Dick. [*Pause.*] In a word, REDUCE
the pressure instead of increasing it. [*Lyrical.*] Caress,
fount of resipescence! [*Calmer.*] Dick, if you would.
[*Swish and thud of pizzle on flesh. Faint cry from* FOX.]
Careful, miss.

S: Have no fear, sir.

A: [*Ruler.*] . . . walls . . . walls what?

S: 'no further', sir.

A: Right. [*Ruler.*] . . . walls no further . . . [*Ruler.*] On! [*Silence.*]
Dick!

F: That for sure, no further, and there gaze, all the way up, all
　　the way down, slow gaze, age upon age, up again, down
　　again, little lichens of my own span, living dead in the
　　stones, and there took to the tunnels. [*Silence. Ruler.*]
　　Oceans too, that too, no denying, I drew near down the
　　tunnels, blue above, blue ahead, that for sure, and there
　　too, no further, ways end, all ends and farewell, farewell
　　and fall, farewell seasons, till I fare again. [*Silence. Ruler.*]
　　Farewell.
　　[*Silence. Ruler. Pause.*]

A: Dick!

F: That for sure, no denying, no further, down in Spring, up in
　　Fall, or inverse, such summers missed, such winters.
　　[*Pause.*]

A: Nice! Nicely put! Such summers missed! So sibilant! Don't
　　you agree, miss?

F: ⎱
　　⎰　[*Together.*]　　Ah that for sure—
S: 　　　　　　　　　　Oh me you know—

A: Hsst!

F: —fatigue, what fatigue, my brother inside me, my old twin,
　　ah to be he and he—but no, no no. [*Pause.*] No no.
　　[*Silence. Ruler.*] Me get up, me go on, what a hope, it was
　　he, for hunger. Have yourself opened, Maud would say,
　　opened up, it's nothing, I'll give him suck if he's still alive,
　　ah but no, no no. [*Pause.*] No no.
　　[*Silence.*]

A: [*Discouraged.*] Ah dear.

S: He is weeping, sir, shall I note it?

A: I really do not know what to advise, miss.

S: Inasmuch as . . . how shall I say? . . . human trait . . . can one
　　say in English?

A: I have never come across it, miss, but no doubt.

F: Scrabble scrabble—

A: Silence! [*Pause.*] No holding him!

S: As such . . . I feel . . . perhaps . . . at a pinch . . .
　　[*Pause.*]

A: Are you familiar with the works of Sterne, miss?

S: Alas no, sir.

A: I may be quite wrong, but I seem to remember, there

somewhere, a tear an angel comes to catch as it falls. Yes, I seem to remember . . . admittedly he was grandchild to an archbishop. [*Half rueful, half complacent.*] Ah these old spectres from the days of book reviewing, they lie in wait for one at every turn. [*Pause. Suddenly decided.*] Note it, miss, note it, and come what may. As well as for a sheep . . . [*Pause.*] Who is this woman . . . what's the name?

s: Maud. I don't know, sir, no previous mention of her has been made.

a: [*Excited.*] Are you sure?

s: Positive, sir. You see, my nanny was a Maud, so that the name would have struck me, had it been pronounced. [*Pause.*]

a: I may be quite wrong, but I somehow have the feeling this is the first time—oh I know it's a far call!—that he has actually . . . *named* anyone. No?

s: That may well be, sir. To make sure I would have to check through from the beginning. That would take time.

a: Kith and kin?

s: Never a word, sir. I have been struck by it. Mine play such a part, in my life!

a: And of a sudden, in the same sentence, a woman, with Christian name to boot, and a brother. I ask you! [*Pause.*]

s: That twin, sir . . .

a: I know, not very convincing.

s: [*Scandalized.*] But it's quite simply impossible! Inside him! Him!

a: No no, such things happen, such things happen. Nature, you know . . . [*Faint laugh.*] Fortunately. A world without monsters, just imagine! [*Pause for imagining.*] No, that is not what troubles me. [*Warmly.*] Look you, miss, what counts is not so much the *thing*, in itself, that would astonish me too. No, it's the word, the notion. The notion brother is not unknown to him! [*Pause.*] But what really matters is this woman—what name did you say?

s: Maud, sir.

a: Maud!

s: And who is in milk, what is more, or about to be.

A: For mercy's sake! [*Pause.*] How does the passage go again?

s: [*Rereading.*] 'Me get up, me go on, what a hope, it was he, for hunger. Have yourself opened, Maud would say, opened up, it's nothing, I'll give him suck if he's still alive, ah but no, no no.' [*Pause.*] 'No no.' [*Pause.*]

A: And then the tear.

s: Exactly, sir. What I call the human trait. [*Pause.*]

A: [*Low, with emotion.*] Miss.

s: Sir.

A: Can it be we near our goal. [*Pause.*] Oh how bewitching you look when you show your teeth! Ah were I but ... thirty years younger.

s: It is well after three, sir.

A: [*Sigh.*] Good. Where he left off. Once more.

s: 'Oh but no, no—'

A: *Ah* but no. No?

s: You are quite right, sir. 'Ah but no, no—'

A: [*Severely.*] Have a care, miss.

s: 'Ah but no, no no.' [*Pause.*] 'No, no.'

A: [*Ruler.*] On! [*Silence.*] Dick!

s: He has gone off, sir.

A: Just a shade lighter, Dick. [*Mild thud of pizzle.*] Ah no, you exaggerate, better than that. [*Swish and violent thud. Faint cry from* FOX. *Ruler.*] Ah but no, no no. On!

F: [*Scream.*] Let me out! Peter out in the stones!

A: Ah dear! There he goes again. Peter out in the stones!

s: It's a mercy he's tied.

A: [*Gently.*] Be reasonable, Fox. Stop—you may sit, Dick—stop jibbing. It's hard on you, we know. It does not lie entirely with us, we know. You might prattle away to your latest breath and still the one ... thing remain unsaid that can give you back your darling solitudes, we know. But this much is sure: the more you say the greater your chances. Is that not so, miss?

s: It stands to reason, sir.

A: [*As to a backward pupil.*] Don't ramble! Treat the subject, whatever it is! [*Snivel.*] More variety! [*Snivel.*] Those

everlasting wilds may have their charm, but there is nothing
there for us, that would astonish me. [*Snivel.*] Those
micaceous schists, if you knew the effect [*Snivel.*] they
can have on one, in the long run. [*Snivel.*] And your fauna!
Those fodient rodents! [*Snivel.*] You wouldn't have a
handkerchief, miss, you could lend me?

s: Here you are, sir.

a: Most kind. [*Blows nose abundantly.*] Much obliged.

s: Oh you may keep it, sir.

a: No no, now I'll be all right. [*To* fox.] Of course we do not
know, any more than you, what exactly it is we are after,
what sign or set of words. But since you have failed so far
to let it escape you, it is not by harking on the same old
themes that you are likely to succeed, that would astonish
me.

s: He has gone off again, sir.

a: [*Warming to his point.*] Someone, perhaps that is what is
wanting, someone who once saw you . . . [*Abating.*] . . . go
by. I may be quite wrong, but try, at least, what do you
stand to lose? [*Beside himself.*] Even though it is not true!

s: [*Shocked.*] Oh sir!

a: A father, a mother, a friend, a . . . Beatrice—no, that is asking
too much. Simply someone, anyone, who once saw you . . .
go by. [*Pause.*] That woman . . . what's the name?

s: Maud, sir.

a: That Maud, for example, perhaps you once brushed against
each other. Think hard!

s: He has gone off, sir.

a: Dick!—no, wait. Kiss him, miss, perhaps that will stir some
fibre.

s: Where, sir?

a: In his heart, in his entrails—or some other part.

s: No, I mean kiss him where, sir?

a: [*Angry.*] Why on his stinker of a mouth, What do you
suppose? [stenographer *kisses* fox. *Howl from* fox.]
Till it bleeds! Kiss it white! [*Howl from* fox.] Suck his
gullet!
[*Silence.*]

s: He has fainted away, sir.

A: Ah ... perhaps I went too far. [*Pause.*] Perhaps I slipped you too soon.

S: Oh no, sir, you could not have waited a moment longer, time is up. [*Pause.*] The fault is mine, I did not go about it as I ought.

A: Come, come, miss! To the marines! [*Pause.*] Up already! [*Pained.*] I chatter too much.

S: Come, come, sir, don't say that, it is part of your rôle, as animator.
   [*Pause.*]

A: That tear, miss, do you remember?

S: Oh yes, sir, distinctly.

A: [*Faint hope.*] Not the first time by any chance?

S: Heavens no, sir, what an idea!

A: [*Disappointed.*] I might have known.

S: Last winter, now I come to think of it, he shed several, do you not remember?

A: Last winter! But, my dear child, I don't remember yesterday, it is down the hatch with love's young dream. Last winter! [*Pause. Low, with emotion.*] Miss.

S: [*Low.*] Sir.

A: That ... Maud.
   [*Pause.*]

S: [*Encouraging.*] Yes, sir.

A: Well ... you know ... I may be wrong ... I wouldn't like to ... I hardly dare say it ... but it seems to me that ... here ... possibly ... we have something at last.

S: Would to God, sir.

A: Particularly with that tear so hard behind. It is not the first, agreed. But in such a context!

S: And the milk, sir, don't forget the milk.

A: The breast! One can almost see it!

S: Who got her in that condition, there's another question for us.

A: What condition, miss, I fail to follow you.

S: Someone has fecundated her. [*Pause. Impatient.*] If she is in milk someone must have fecundated her.

A: To be sure!

S: Who?

A: [*Very excited.*] You mean ...

s: I ask myself.
   [*Pause.*]

a: May we have that passage again, miss?

s: 'Have yourself opened, Maud would say, opened—'

a: [*Delighted.*] That frequentative! [*Pause.*] Sorry, miss.

s: 'Have yourself opened, Maud would say, opened—'

a: Don't skip, miss, the text in its entirety if you please.

s: I skip nothing, sir. [*Pause.*] What have I skipped, sir?

a: [*Emphatically.*] '... between two kisses ...' [*Sarcastic.*] That mere trifle! [*Angry.*] How can we ever hope to get anywhere if you suppress gems of that magnitude?

s: But, sir, he never said anything of the kind.

a: [*Angry.*] '... Maud would say, *between two kisses*, etc.' Amend.

s: But, sir, I—

a: What the devil are you deriding, miss? My hearing? My memory? My good faith? [*Thunderous.*] Amend!

s: [*Feebly.*] As you will, sir.

a: Let us hear how it runs now.

s: [*Tremulous.*] 'Have yourself opened, Maud would say, between two kisses, opened up, it's nothing, I'll give him suck if he's still alive, ah but no, no no.' [*Faint pencil.*] 'No no.'
   [*Silence.*]

a: Don't cry, miss, dry your pretty eyes and smile at me. Tomorrow, who knows, we may be free.

Words and Music

A piece for radio

Written in English and completed towards the end of 1961. First published in *Evergreen Review* (Nov./Dec. 1962). First broadcast on the BBC Third Programme on 13 November 1962.

MUSIC: *Small orchestra softly tuning up.*

WORDS: Please! [*Tuning. Louder.*] Please! [*Tuning dies away.*] How much longer cooped up here in the dark? [*With loathing.*] With you! [*Pause.*] Theme .... [*Pause.*] Theme ... sloth. [*Pause. Rattled off, low.*] Sloth is of all the passions the most powerful passion and indeed no passion is more powerful than the passion of sloth, this is the mode in which the mind is most affected and indeed—[*Burst of tuning. Loud, imploring.*] Please! [*Tuning dies away. As before.*] The mode in which the mind is most affected and indeed in no mode is the mind more affected than in this, by passion we are to understand a movement of the soul pursuing or fleeing real or imagined pleasure or pain pleasure or pain real or imagined pleasure or pain, of all these movements and who can number them of all these movements and they are legion sloth is the most urgent and indeed by no movement is the soul more urged than by this by this by this to and from by no movement the soul more urged than by this to and—[*Pause.*] From. [*Pause.*] Listen! [*Distant sound of rapidly shuffling carpet slippers.*] At last! [*Shuffling louder. Burst of tuning.*] Hsst! [*Tuning dies away. Shuffling louder. Silence.*]

CROAK: Joe.

WORDS: [*Humble.*] My Lord.

CROAK: Bob.

MUSIC: *Humble muted adsum.*

CROAK: My comforts! Be friends! [*Pause.*] Bob.

MUSIC: *As before.*

CROAK: Joe.

WORDS: [*As before.*] My Lord.

CROAK: Be friends! [*Pause.*] I am late, forgive. [*Pause.*] The face. [*Pause.*] On the stairs. [*Pause.*] Forgive. [*Pause.*] Joe.

WORDS: [*As before.*] My Lord.

CROAK: Bob.

MUSIC: *As before.*

CROAK: Forgive. [*Pause.*] In the tower. [*Pause.*] The face.
[*Long pause.*] Theme tonight .... [*Pause.*] Theme
tonight ... love. [*Pause.*] Love. [*Pause.*] My club. [*Pause.*]
Joe.

WORDS: [*As before.*] My Lord.

CROAK: Love. [*Pause. Thump of club on ground.*] Love!

WORDS: [*Orotund.*] Love is of all the passions the most powerful
passion and indeed no passion is more powerful than the
passion of love. [*Clears throat.*] This is the mode in which
the mind is most strongly affected and indeed in no mode
is the mind more strongly affected than in this. [*Pause.*]

CROAK: *Rending sigh. Thump of club.*

WORDS: [*As before.*] By passion we are to understand a movement of the mind pursuing or fleeing real or imagined
pleasure or pain. [*Clears throat.*] Of all—

CROAK: [*Anguished.*] Oh!

WORDS: [*As before.*] Of all these movements then and who can
number them and they are legion sloth is the LOVE is the
most urgent and indeed by no manner of movement is the
soul more urged than by this, to and—
[*Violent thump of club.*]

CROAK: Bob.

WORDS: From.
[*Violent thump of club.*]

CROAK: Bob!

MUSIC: *As before.*

CROAK: Love!

MUSIC: *Rap of baton on stand. Soft music worthy of foregoing,
great expression, with audible groans and protestations—
'No!' 'Please!' etc.—from* WORDS. *Pause.*

CROAK: [*Anguished.*] Oh! [*Thump of club.*] Louder!

MUSIC: *Loud rap of baton and as before fortissimo, all expression
gone, drowning* WORDS' *protestations. Pause.*

CROAK: My comforts! [*Pause.*] Joe sweet.

WORDS: [*As before.*] Arise then and go now the manifest
unanswerable—

CROAK: *Groans.*

WORDS: —to wit this love what is this love that more than all the cursed deadly or any other of its great movers so moves the soul and soul what is this soul that more than by any of its great movers is by love so moved? [*Clears throat. Prosaic.*] Love of woman, I mean, if that is what my Lord means.

CROAK: Alas!

WORDS: What? [*Pause. Very rhetorical.*] Is love the word? [*Pause. Do.*] Is soul the word? [*Pause. Do.*] Do we mean love, when we say love? [*Pause. Pause. Do.*] Soul, when we say soul?

CROAK: [*Anguished.*] Oh! [*Pause.*] Bob dear.

WORDS: Do we? [*With sudden gravity.*] Or don't we?

CROAK: [*Imploring.*] Bob!

MUSIC: *Rap of baton. Love and soul music, with just audible protestations—'No!' 'Please!' 'Peace!' etc.—from* WORDS. *Pause.*

CROAK: [*Anguished.*] Oh! [*Pause.*] My balms! [*Pause.*] Joe.

WORDS: [*Humble.*] My Lord.

CROAK: Bob.

MUSIC: *Adsum as before.*

CROAK: My balms! [*Pause.*] Age. [*Pause.*] Joe. [*Pause. Thump of club.*] Joe.

WORDS: [*As before.*] My Lord.

CROAK: Age!
[*Pause.*]

WORDS: [*Faltering.*] Age is ... age is when ... old age I mean ... if that is what my Lord means ... is when ... if you're a man ... were a man ... huddled ... nodding ... the ingle ... waiting—
[*Violent thump of club.*]

CROAK: Bob. [*Pause.*] Age. [*Pause. Violent thump of club.*] Age!

MUSIC: *Rap of baton. Age music, soon interrupted by violent thump.*

CROAK: Together. [*Pause. Thump.*] Together! [*Pause. Violent thump.*] Together, dogs!

MUSIC: *Long la.*

WORDS: [*Imploring.*] No!

[*Violent thump.*]

CROAK: Dogs!

MUSIC: *La.*

WORDS: [*Trying to sing.*] Age is when ... to a man ...

MUSIC: *Improvement of above.*

WORDS: [*Trying to sing this.*] Age is when to a man ...

MUSIC: *Suggestion for following.*

WORDS: [*Trying to sing this.*] Huddled o'er ... the ingle ....
[*Pause. Violent thump. Trying to sing.*] Waiting for the
hag to put the ... pan in the bed ...

MUSIC: *Improvement of above.*

WORDS: [*Trying to sing this.*] Waiting for the hag to put the
pan in the bed.

MUSIC: *Suggestion for following.*

WORDS: [*Trying to sing this.*] And bring the ... arrowroot ...
[*Pause. Violent thump. As before.*] And bring the toddy....
[*Pause. Tremendous thump.*]

CROAK: Dogs!

MUSIC: *Suggestion for following.*

WORDS: [*Trying to sing this.*] She comes in the ashes ....
[*Imploring.*] No!

MUSIC: *Repeats suggestion.*

WORDS: [*Trying to sing this.*] She comes in the ashes who
loved could not be ... won or ...
[*Pause.*]

MUSIC: *Repeats end of previous suggestion.*

WORDS: [*Trying to sing this.*] Or won not loved ... [*Wearily.*]
... or some other trouble .... [*Pause. Trying to sing.*]
Comes in the ashes like in that old—

MUSIC: *Interrupts with improvement of this and brief
suggestion.*

WORDS: [*Trying to sing this.*] Comes in the ashes like in that
old light ... her face ... in the ashes ....
[*Pause.*]

CROAK: *Groans.*

MUSIC: *Suggestion for following.*

WORDS: [*Trying to sing this.*] That old moonlight ... on the
earth ... again.
[*Pause.*]

MUSIC: *Further brief suggestion.*
  [*Silence.*]
CROAK: *Groans.*
MUSIC: *Plays air through alone, then invites* WORDS *with opening, pause, invites again and finally accompanies very softly.*
WORDS: [*Trying to sing, softly.*]

> Age is when to a man
> Huddled o'er the ingle
> Shivering for the hag
> To put the pan in the bed
> And bring the toddy
> She comes in the ashes
> Who loved could not be won
> Or won not loved
> Or some other trouble
> Comes in the ashes
> Like in that old light
> The face in the ashes
> That old starlight
> On the earth again.

  [*Long pause.*]
CROAK: [*Murmur.*] The face. [*Pause.*] The face. [*Pause.*] The face. [*Pause.*] The face.
MUSIC: *Rap of baton and warmly sentimental, about one minute.*
  [*Pause.*]
CROAK: The face.
WORDS: [*Cold.*] Seen from above in that radiance so cold and faint . . . .
  [*Pause.*]
MUSIC: *Warm suggestion from above for above.*
WORDS: [*Disregarding, cold.*] Seen from above at such close quarters in that radiance so cold and faint with eyes so dimmed by . . . what had passed, its quite . . . piercing beauty is a little . . . .
  [*Pause.*]
MUSIC: *Renews timidly previous suggestion.*
WORDS: [*Interrupting, violently.*] Peace!
CROAK: My comforts! Be friends!

[*Pause.*]

WORDS: ...blunted. Some moments later however, such are the powers of recuperation at this age, the head is drawn back to a distance of two or three feet, the eyes widen to a stare and begin to feast again. [*Pause.*] What then is seen would have been better seen in the light of day, that is incontestable. But how often it has, in recent months, how often, at all hours, under all angles, in cloud and shine, been seen I mean. And there is, is there not, in that clarity of silver... that clarity of silver... is there not... my Lord....
[*Pause.*] Now and then the rye, swayed by a light wind, casts and withdraws its shadow.
[*Pause.*]

CROAK: *Groans.*

WORDS: Leaving aside the features or lineaments proper, matchless severally and in their ordonnance—

CROAK: *Groans.*

WORDS: —flare of the black disordered hair as though spread wide on water, the brows knitted in a groove suggesting pain but simply concentration more likely all things considered on some consummate inner process, the eyes of course closed in keeping with this, the lashes... [*Pause.*] ...the nose... [*Pause.*] ...nothing, a little pinched perhaps, the lips....

CROAK: [*Anguished.*] Lily!

WORDS: ...tight, a gleam of tooth biting on the under, no coral, no swell, whereas normally....

CROAK: *Groans.*

WORDS: ...the whole so blanched and still that were it not for the great white rise and fall of the breasts, spreading as they mount and then subsiding to their natural... aperture—

MUSIC: *Irrepressible burst of spreading and subsiding music with vain protestations—'Peace!' 'No!' 'Please!' etc.—from* WORDS. *Triumph and conclusion.*

WORDS: [*Gently expostulatory.*] My Lord! [*Pause. Faint thump of club.*] I resume, so wan and still and so ravished away that it seems no more of the earth than Mira in the Whale, at her tenth and greatest magnitude on this particular night shining coldly down—as we say, looking up. [*Pause.*] Some moments later however, such are the powers—

CROAK: [*Anguished.*] No!

WORDS: —the brows uncloud, the lips part and the eyes... [*Pause.*] ...the brows uncloud, the nostrils dilate, the lips part and the eyes... [*Pause.*] ...a little colour comes back into the cheeks and the eyes... [*Reverently.*] ...open. [*Pause.*] Then down a little way... [*Pause. Change to poetic tone. Low.*]

> Then down a little way
> Through the trash
> To where... towards where....

[*Pause.*]

MUSIC: *Discreet suggestion for above.*

WORDS: [*Trying to sing this.*]

> Then down a little way
> Through the trash
> Towards where...

[*Pause.*]

MUSIC: *Discreet suggestion for following.*

WORDS: [*Trying to sing this.*]

> All dark no begging
> No giving no words
> No sense no need....

[*Pause.*]

MUSIC: *More confident suggestion for following.*

WORDS: [*Trying to sing this.*]

> Through the scum
> Down a little way
> To where one glimpse
> Of that wellhead.

[*Pause.*]

MUSIC: *Invites with opening, pause, invites again and finally accompanies very softly.*

WORDS: [*Trying to sing, softly.*]

> Then down a little way
> Through the trash
> Towards where

> All dark no begging
> No giving no words
> No sense no need
> Through the scum
> Down a little way
> To whence one glimpse
> Of that wellhead.

[*Pause. Shocked.*] My Lord! [*Sound of club let fall. As before.*] My Lord! [*Shuffling slippers, with halts. They die away. Long pause.*] Bob. [*Pause.*] Bob!

MUSIC: *Brief rude retort.*

WORDS: Music. [*Imploring.*] Music!
    [*Pause.*]

MUSIC: *Rap of baton and statement with elements already used or wellhead alone.*
    [*Pause.*]

WORDS: Again. [*Pause. Imploring.*] Again!

MUSIC: *As before or only very slightly varied.*
    [*Pause.*]

WORDS: *Deep sigh.*

CURTAIN

Cascando

A radio piece for music and voice

Written in French in 1962, with music by Marcel Mihalovici. First published in *Dramatische Dichtungen*, vol. 1 (1963). First published in English in *Evergreen Review* (May/June 1963). First broadcast in French by the ORTF on 13 October 1963. First broadcast in English on the BBC Third Programme on 6 October 1964.

OPENER: [*Cold.*] It is the month of May . . . for me.
  [*Pause.*]
  Correct.
  [*Pause.*]
  I open.
VOICE: [*Low, panting.*] —story . . . if you could finish it . . .
  you could rest . . . sleep . . . not before . . . oh I know . . .
  the ones I've finished . . . thousands and one . . . all I ever
  did . . . in my life . . . with my life . . . saying to myself . . .
  finish this one . . . it's the right one . . . then rest . . . sleep
  . . . no more stories . . . no more words . . . and finished it . . .
  and not the right one . . . couldn't rest . . . straight away
  another . . . to begin . . . to finish . . . saying to myself . . .
  finish this one . . . then rest . . . this time . . . it's the right
  one . . . this time . . . you have it . . . and finished it . . . and
  not the right one . . . couldn't rest . . . straight away another
  . . . but this one . . . it's different . . . I'll finish it . . . I've got
  it . . . Woburn . . . I resume . . . a long life . . . already . . . say
  what you like . . . a few misfortunes . . . that's enough . . .
  five years later . . . ten . . . I don't know . . . Woburn . . . he's
  changed . . . not enough . . . recognizable . . . in the shed . . .
  yet another . . . waiting for night . . . night to fall . . . to go
  out . . . go on . . . elsewhere . . . sleep elsewhere . . . it's slow
  . . . he lifts his head . . . now and then . . . his eyes . . . to the
  window . . . it's darkening . . . earth darkening . . . it's night
  . . . he gets up . . . knees first . . . then up . . . on his feet . . .
  slips out . . . Woburn . . . same old coat . . . right the sea . . .
  left the hills . . . he has the choice . . . he has only—
OPENER: [*With* VOICE.] And I close.
  [*Silence.*]
  I open the other.
MUSIC: . . . .
OPENER: [*With* MUSIC.] And I close.

[*Silence.*]
I open both.

VOICE: ⎤
MUSIC: ⎦ [*Together.*]   —on ... getting on ... finish ... don't
....
give up ... then rest ... sleep ... not before ... finish ...
....
this time ... it's the right one ... you have it ... you've got
....
it ... it's there ... somewhere ... you've got him ... follow
....
him ... don't lose him ... Woburn story ... getting on ...
....
finish ... then sleep ... no more stories ... no more words
....
... come on ... next thing ... he—
....

OPENER: [*With* VOICE *and* MUSIC.] And I close.
[*Silence.*]
I start again.

VOICE: —down ... gentle slopes ... boreen ... giant aspens ...
wind in the boughs ... faint sea ... Woburn ... same old
coat ... he goes on ... stops ... not a soul ... not yet ...
night too bright ... say what you like ... he goes on ...
hugging the bank ... same old stick ... he goes down ...
falls ... on purpose or not ... can't see ... he's down ...
that's what counts ... face in the mud ... arms spread ...
that's the idea ... already ... there already ... no not yet
... he gets up ... knees first ... hands flat ... in the mud ...
head sunk ... then up ... on his feet ... huge bulk ...
come on ... he goes on ... he goes down ... come on ...
in his head ... what's in his head ... a hole ... a shelter ...
a hollow ... in the dunes ... a cave ... vague memory ...
in his head ... of a cave ... he goes down ... no more
trees ... no more bank ... he's changed ... not enough
... night too bright ... soon the dunes ... no more cover
... not a soul ... not—
[*Silence.*]

MUSIC: ....
[*Silence.*]

VOICE: ⎤   —rest . . . sleep . . . no more stories . . .
MUSIC: ⎦ [*Together.*]
. . . .
no more words . . . don't give up . . . this time . . . it's the
. . . .
right one . . . we're there . . . I'm there . . . somewhere . . .
. . . .
Woburn . . . I've got him . . . don't lose him . . . follow him
. . . .
. . . to the end . . . come on . . . this time . . . it's the right one
. . . .
. . . finish . . . sleep . . . Woburn . . . come on—
. . . .
[*Silence.*]

OPENER: So, at will.
They say, It's in his head.
No. I open.

VOICE: —falls . . . again . . . on purpose or not . . . can't see . . .
he's down . . . that's what matters . . . face in the sand . . .
arms spread . . . bare dunes . . . not a scrub . . . same old
coat . . . night too bright . . . say what you like . . . sea
louder . . . thunder . . . manes of foam . . . Woburn . . . his
head . . . what's in his head . . . peace . . . peace again . . . in
his head . . . no further . . . no more searching . . . sleep . . .
no not yet . . . he gets up . . . knees first . . . hands flat . . . in
the sand . . . head sunk . . . then up . . . on his feet . . . huge
bulk . . . same old broadbrim . . . jammed down . . . come on
. . . he goes on . . . ton weight . . . in the sand . . . knee-deep . . .
he goes down . . . sea—

OPENER: [*With* VOICE.] And I close.
[*Silence.*]
I open the other.

MUSIC: . . . .

OPENER: [*With* MUSIC.] And I close.
[*Silence.*]
So, at will.
It's my life, I live on that.
[*Pause.*]
Correct.
[*Pause.*]

What do I open?

They say, He opens nothing, he has nothing to open, it's in his head.

They don't see me, they don't see what I do, they don't see what I have, and they say, He opens nothing, he has nothing to open, it's in his head.

I don't protest any more, I don't say any more,

There is nothing in my head.

I don't answer any more.

I open and close.

VOICE: —lights . . . of the land . . . the island . . . the sky . . . he need only . . . lift his head . . . his eyes . . . he'd see them . . . shine on him . . . but no . . . he—

[Silence.]

MUSIC: [Brief.] . . . .

[Silence.]

OPENER: They say, That is not his life, he does not live on that. They don't see me, they don't see what my life is, they don't see what I live on, and they say, That is not his life, he does not live on that.

[Pause.]

I have lived on it . . . till I'm old.

Old enough.

Listen.

VOICE: [Weakening.] —this time . . . I'm there . . . Woburn . . . it's him . . . I've seen him . . . I've got him . . . come on . . . same old coat . . . he goes down . . . falls . . . falls again . . . on purpose or not . . . can't see . . . he's down . . . that's what counts . . . come on—

OPENER: [With VOICE.] Full strength.

VOICE: —face . . . in the stones . . . no more sand . . . all stones . . . that's the idea . . . we're there . . . this time . . . no not yet . . . he gets up . . . knees first . . . hands flat . . . in the stones . . . head sunk . . . then up . . . on his feet . . . huge bulk . . . Woburn . . . faster . . . he goes on . . . he goes down . . . he—

[Silence.]

MUSIC: [Weakening.] . . . .

OPENER: [With MUSIC.] Full strength.

MUSIC: . . . .

[*Silence.*]

OPENER: That's not all.

I open both.

Listen.

VOICE: ⎱ [*Together.*]   —sleep ... no further ... no more
MUSIC: ⎰
. . . .

searching ... to find him ... in the dark ... to see him ...
. . . .

to say him ... for whom ... that's it ... no matter ...
. . . .

never him ... never right ... start again ... in the dark ...
. . . .

done with that ... this time ... it's the right one ... we're
. . . .

there ... nearly ... finish—
. . . .

[*Silence.*]

OPENER: From one world to another, it's as though they drew
together. We have not much further to go. Good.

VOICE: ⎱ [*Together.*]   —nearly ... I've got him ... I've seen
MUSIC: ⎰
. . . .

him ... I've said him ... we're there ... nearly ... no more
. . . .

stories ... all false ... this time ... it's the right one ... I
. . . .

have it ... finish ... sleep ... Woburn ... it's him ... I've
. . . .

got him ... follow him ... to—
. . . .

[*Silence.*]

OPENER: Good.

[*Pause.*]

Yes, correct, the month of May.

You know, the reawakening.

[*Pause.*]

I open.

VOICE: —no tiller ... no thwarts ... no oars ... afloat ... sucked
out ... then back ... aground ... drags free ... out ...
Woburn ... he fills it ... flat out ... face in the bilge ...

arms spread . . . same old coat . . . hands clutching . . . the
gunnels . . . no . . . I don't know . . . I see him . . . he clings
on . . . out to sea . . . heading nowhere . . . for the island . . .
then no more . . . else—
[*Silence.*]

MUSIC: . . . .
[*Silence.*]

OPENER: They said, It's his own, it's his voice, it's in his head.
[*Pause.*]

VOICE: —faster . . . out . . . driving out . . . rearing . . . plunging
. . . heading nowhere . . . for the island . . . then no more
. . . elsewhere . . . anywhere . . . heading anywhere . . .
lights—
[*Pause.*]

OPENER: No resemblance.
I answered, And that . . .

MUSIC: [*Brief.*] . . . .
[*Silence.*]

OPENER: . . . is that mine too?
But I don't answer any more.
And they don't say anything any more.
They have quit.
Good.
[*Pause.*]
Yes, correct, the month of May, the close of May.
The long days.
[*Pause.*]
I open.
[*Pause.*]
I'm afraid to open.
But I must open.
So I open.

VOICE: —come on . . . Woburn . . . arms spread . . . same old
coat . . . face in the bilge . . . he clings on . . . island gone . . .
far astern . . . heading out . . . open sea . . . land gone . . . his
head . . . what's in his head . . . Woburn—

OPENER: [*With* VOICE.] Come on! Come on!

VOICE: —at last . . . we're there . . . no further . . . no more
searching . . . in the dark . . . elsewhere . . . always elsewhere

... we're there ... nearly ... Woburn ... hang on ... don't
let go ... lights gone ... of the land ... all gone ... nearly
all ... too far ... too late ... of the sky ... those ... if you
like ... he need only ... turn over ... he'd see them ...
shine on him ... but no ... he clings on ... Woburn ... he's
changed ... nearly enough—

[*Silence.*]

MUSIC: ....

OPENER: [*With* MUSIC.] God.

MUSIC: ....

[*Silence.*]

OPENER: God God.

[*Pause.*]

There was a time I asked myself, What is it.

There were times I answered, It's the outing.

Two outings.

Then the return.

Where?

To the village.

To the inn.

Two outings, then at last the return, to the village, to the
inn, by the only road that leads there.

An image, like any other.

But I don't answer any more.

I open.

VOICE: ⎤ [*Together.*]　　—don't let go ... finish ... it's the
MUSIC: ⎦　　　　　　　...

right one ... this time ... I have it ... we're there ...

....

Woburn ... nearly—

....

OPENER: [*With* VOICE *and* MUSIC.] As though they had linked
their arms.

VOICE: ⎤ [*Together.*]　　—sleep ... no more stories ... come on
MUSIC: ⎦　　　　　　　...

... Woburn ... it's him ... see him ... say him ... to the

....

end ... don't let go—

OPENER: [*With* VOICE *and* MUSIC.] Good.

VOICE: ⎤
   [*Together.*] —nearly ... just a few more ... a few
MUSIC: ⎦
 . . . .
more ... I'm there ... nearly ... Woburn ... it's him ... it
. . . .
was him ... I've got him ... nearly—

OPENER: [*With* VOICE *and* MUSIC, *fervently.*] Good!

VOICE: ⎤
   [*Together.*] —this time ... it's the right one ...
MUSIC: ⎦
 . . . .
finish ... no more stories ... sleep ... we're there ... nearly
. . . .
... just a few more ... don't let go ... Woburn ... he clings
. . . .
on ... come on ... come on—
. . . .
[*Silence.*]

CURTAIN

Play

A play in one act

Written in English in late 1962-3. First published in German, as *Spiel*, in *Theater Heute* (July 1963). First published in English by Faber and Faber, London, in 1964. First performance was of, *Spiel*, translated by Erika and Elmar Tophoven, at the Ulmer Theater, Ulm-Donau, on 14 June 1963. First performed in Britain by the National Theatre Company at the Old Vic Theatre, London, on 7 April 1964.

Front centre, touching one another, three identical grey urns (see page 319) about one yard high. From each a head protrudes, the neck held fast in the urn's mouth. The heads are those, from left to right as seen from auditorium, of w2, m and w1. They face undeviatingly front throughout the play. Faces so lost to age and aspect as to seem almost part of urns. But no masks.

Their speech is provoked by a spotlight projected on faces alone (see page 318).

The transfer of light from one face to another is immediate. No blackout, i.e. return to almost complete darkness of opening, except where indicated.

The response to light is immediate.

Faces impassive throughout. Voices toneless except where an expression is indicated.

Rapid tempo throughout.

The curtain rises on a stage in almost complete darkness. Urns just discernible. Five seconds.

Faint spots simultaneously on three faces. Three seconds. Voices faint, largely unintelligible.

w1:		Yes, strange, darkness best, and the darker the worse, till all dark, then all well, for the time, but it will come, the time will come, the thing is there, you'll see it, get off me, keep off me, all dark, all still, all over, wiped out—
w2:	*[Together. See page 319.]*	Yes, perhaps, a shade gone, I suppose, some might say, poor thing, a shade gone, just a shade, in the head—[*Faint wild laugh.*]—just a shade, but I doubt it, *I* doubt it, not really, I'm all right, still all right, do my best, all I can—

M: Yes, peace, one assumed, all out, all the
pain, all as if ... never been, it will
come—[*Hiccup.*]—pardon, no sense in
this, oh I know ... none the less, one
assumed, peace ... I mean ... not merely
all over, but as if ... never been—

[*Spots off. Blackout. Five seconds. Strong spots simultaneously on three faces. Three seconds. Voices normal strength.*]

w1:   I said to him, Give her up—
w2:   [*Together.*]   One morning as I was sitting—
M: We were not long together—

[*Spots off. Blackout. Five seconds. Spot on* w1.]

w1: I said to him, Give her up. I swore by all I held most sacred—

[*Spot from* w1 *to* w2.]

w2: One morning as I was sitting stitching by the open window she burst in and flew at me. Give him up, she screamed, he's mine. Her photographs were kind to her. Seeing her now for the first time full length in the flesh I understood why he preferred me.

[*Spot from* w2 *to* M.]

M: We were not long together when she smelled the rat. Give up that whore, she said, or I'll cut my throat—[*Hiccup.*] pardon—so help me God. I knew she could have no proof. So I told her I did not know what she was talking about.

[*Spot from* M *to* w2.]

w2: What are you talking about? I said, stitching away. Someone yours? Give up whom? I smell you off him, she screamed, he stinks of bitch.

[*Spot from* w2 *to* w1.]

w1: Though I had him dogged for months by a first-rate man, no shadow of proof was forthcoming. And there was no denying that he continued as ... assiduous as ever. This, and his horror of the merely Platonic thing, made me sometimes wonder if I were not accusing him unjustly. Yes.

[*Spot from* w1 *to* M.]

M: What have you to complain of? I said. Have I been neglecting you? How could we be together in the way we are if there were someone else? Loving her as I did, with all my heart,

I could not but feel sorry for her.

[*Spot from* M *to* W2.]

W2: Fearing she was about to offer me violence I rang for
  Erskine and had her shown out. Her parting words, as he
  could testify, if he is still living, and has not forgotten,
  coming and going on the earth, letting people in, showing
  people out, were to the effect that she would settle my
  hash. I confess this did alarm me a little, at the time.

[*Spot from* W2 *to* M.]

M: She was not convinced. I might have known. I smell her off
  you, she kept saying. There was no answer to this. So I
  took her in my arms and swore I could not live without
  her. I meant it, what is more. Yes, I am sure I did. She did
  not repulse me.

[*Spot from* M *to* W1.]

W1: Judge then of my astonishment when one fine morning, as
  I was sitting stricken in the morning room, he slunk in, fell
  on his knees before me, buried his face in my lap and . . .
  confessed.

[*Spot from* W1 *to* M.]

M: She put a bloodhound on me, but I had a little chat with
  him. He was glad of the extra money.

[*Spot from* M *to* W2.]

W2: Why don't you get out, I said, when he started moaning
  about his home life, there is obviously nothing between
  you any more. Or is there?

[*Spot from* W2 *to* W1.]

W1: I confess my first feeling was one of wonderment. What a
  male!

[*Spot from* W1 *to* M. *He opens his mouth to speak. Spot
  from* M *to* W2.]

W2: Anything between us, he said, what do you take me for, a
  something machine? And of course with him no danger of
  the . . . spiritual thing. Then why don't you get out? I said.
  I sometimes wondered if he was not living with her for her
  money.

[*Spot from* W2 *to* M.]

M: The next thing was the scene between them. I can't have her
  crashing in here, she said, threatening to take my life. I

must have looked incredulous. Ask Erskine, she said, if
you don't believe me. But she threatens to take her own, I
said. Not yours? she said. No, I said, hers. We had fun
trying to work this out.
[*Spot from* M *to* w1.]

w1: Then I forgave him. To what will love not stoop! I sugges-
ted a little jaunt to celebrate, to the Riviera or our darling
Grand Canary. He was looking pale. Peaked. But this was
not possible just then. Professional commitments.
[*Spot from* w1 *to* w2.]

w2: She came again. Just strolled in. All honey. Licking her
lips. Poor thing. I was doing my nails, by the open window.
He has told me all about it, she said. Who he, I said filing
away, and what it? I know what torture you must be going
through, she said, and I have dropped in to say I bear you
no ill-feeling. I rang for Erskine.
[*Spot from* w2 *to* M.]

M: Then I got frightened and made a clean breast of it. She was
looking more and more desperate. She had a razor in her
vanity-bag. Adulterers, take warning, never admit.
[*Spot from* M *to* w1.]

w1: When I was satisfied it was all over I went to have a gloat.
Just a common tart. What he could have found in her when
he had me—
[*Spot from* w1 *to* w2.]

w2: When he came again we had it out. I felt like death. He went
on about why he had to tell her. Too risky and so on. That
meant he had gone back to her. Back to that!
[*Spot from* w2 *to* w1.]

w1: Pudding face, puffy, spots, blubber mouth, jowls, no neck,
dugs you could—
[*Spot from* w1 *to* w2.]

w2: He went on and on. I could hear a mower. An old hand
mower. I stopped him and said that whatever I might feel
I had no silly threats to offer—but not much stomach for
her leavings either. He thought that over for a bit.
[*Spot from* w2 *to* w1.]

w1: Calves like a flunkey—
[*Spot from* w1 *to* M.]

M: When I saw her again she knew. She was looking—[*Hiccup.*]
—wretched. Pardon. Some fool was cutting grass. A little
rush, then another. The problem was how to convince her
that no . . . revival of intimacy was involved. I couldn't. I
might have known. So I took her in my arms and said I
could not go on living without her. I don't believe I could
have.
[*Spot from* M *to* W2.]

W2: The only solution was to go away together. He swore we
should as soon as he had put his affairs in order. In the
meantime we were to carry on as before. By that he meant
as best we could.
[*Spot from* W2 *to* W1.]

W1: So he was mine again. All mine. I was happy again. I went
about singing. The world—
[*Spot from* W1 *to* M.]

M: At home all heart to heart, new leaf and bygones bygones. I
ran into your ex-doxy, she said one night, on the pillow,
you're well out of that. Rather uncalled for, I thought. I
am indeed, sweetheart, I said, I am indeed. God what
vermin women. Thanks to you, angel, I said.
[*Spot from* M *to* W1.]

W1: Then I began to smell her off him again. Yes.
[*Spot from* W1 *to* W2.]

W2: When he stopped coming I was prepared. More or less.
[*Spot from* W2 *to* M.]

M: Finally it was all too much. I simply could no longer— |
[*Spot from* M *to* W1.]

W1: Before I could do anything he disappeared. That meant
she had won. That slut! I couldn't credit it. I lay stricken
for weeks. Then I drove over to her place. It was all bolted
and barred. All grey with frozen dew. On the way back by
Ash and Snodland—
[*Spot from* W1 *to* M.]

M: I simply could no longer— |
[*Spot from* M *to* W2.]

W2: I made a bundle of his things and burnt them. It was
November and the bonfire was going. All night I smelt
them smouldering.

[*Spot off* w 2. *Blackout. Five seconds. Spots half previous strength simultaneously on three faces. Three seconds. Voices proportionately lower.*]

w 1:		Mercy, mercy—
w 2:	[*Together.*]	To say I am—
M :		When first this change—

[*Spots off. Blackout. Five seconds. Spot on* M.]

M : When first this change I actually thanked God. I thought, It is done, it is said, now all is going out—
[*Spot from* M *to* w 1.]

w 1: Mercy, mercy, tongue still hanging out for mercy. It will come. You haven't seen me. But you will. Then it will come.
[*Spot from* w 1 *to* w 2.]

w 2: To say I am not disappointed, no, I am. I had anticipated something better. More restful.
[*Spot from* w 2 *to* w 1.]

w 1: Or you will weary of me.
[*Spot from* w 1 *to* M.]

M : Down, all going down, into the dark, peace is coming, I thought, after all, at last, I was right, after all, thank God, when first this change.
[*Spot from* M *to* w 2.]

w 2: Less confused. Less confusing. At the same time I prefer this to ... the other thing. Definitely. There are endurable moments.
[*Spot from* w 2 *to* M.]

M : I thought.
[*Spot from* M *to* w 2.]

w 2: When you go out—and I go out. Some day you will tire of me and go out ... for good.
[*Spot from* w 2 *to* w 1.]

w 1: Hellish half-light.
[*Spot from* w 1 *to* M.]

M : Peace, yes, I suppose, a kind of peace, and all that pain as if ... never been.
[*Spot from* M *to* w 2.]

w 2: Give me up, as a bad job. Go away and start poking and pecking at someone else. On the other hand—
[*Spot from* w 2 *to* w 1.]

w1: Get off me! Get off me!
   [*Spot from* w1 *to* m.]

m: It will come. Must come. There is no future in this.
   [*Spot from* m *to* w2.]

w2: On the other hand things may disimprove, there is that
    danger.
   [*Spot from* w2 *to* m.]

m: Oh of course I know now—
   [*Spot from* m *to* w1.]

w1: Is it that I do not tell the truth, is that it, that some day
    somehow I may tell the truth at last and then no more
    light at last, for the truth?
   [*Spot from* w1 *to* w2.]

w2: You might get angry and blaze me clean out of my wits.
    Mightn't you?
   [*Spot from* w2 *to* m.]

m: I know now, all that was just . . . play. And all this? When
   will all this—
   [*Spot from* m *to* w1.]

w1: Is that it?
   [*Spot from* w1 *to* w2.]

w2: Mightn't you?
   [*Spot from* w2 *to* m.]

m: All this, when will all this have been . . . just play?
   [*Spot from* m *to* w1.]

w1: I can do nothing . . . for anybody . . . any more . . . thank
    God. So it must be something I have to say. How the
    mind works still!
   [*Spot from* w1 *to* w2.]

w2: But I doubt it. It would not be like you somehow. And you
    must know I am doing my best. Or don't you?
   [*Spot from* w2 *to* m.]

m: Perhaps they have become friends. Perhaps sorrow—
   [*Spot from* m *to* w1.]

w1: But I have said all I can. All you let me. All I—
   [*Spot from* w1 *to* m.]

m: Perhaps sorrow has brought them together.
   [*Spot from* m *to* w2.]

w2: No doubt I make the same mistake as when it was the sun

that shone, of looking for sense where possibly there is
none.

[*Spot from* w2 *to* m.]

m: Perhaps they meet, and sit, over a cup of that green tea they
both so loved, without milk or sugar not even a squeeze of
lemon—

[*Spot from* m *to* w2.]

w2: Are you listening to me? Is anyone listening to me? Is anyone looking at me? Is anyone bothering about me at all?

[*Spot from* w2 *to* m.]

m: Not even a squeeze of—

[*Spot from* m *to* w1.]

w1: Is it something I should do with my face, other than utter?
Weep?

[*Spot from* w1 *to* w2.]

w2: Am I taboo, I wonder. Not necessarily, now that all danger
is averted. That poor creature—I can hear her—that poor
creature- -

[*Spot from* w2 *to* w1.]

w1: Bite off my tongue and swallow it? Spit it out? Would that
placate you? How the mind works still to be sure!

[*Spot from* w1 *to* m.]

m: Meet, and sit, now in the one dear place, now in the other,
and sorrow together, and compare—[*Hiccup.*] pardon--
happy memories.

[*Spot from* m *to* w1.]

w1: If only I could think, There is no sense in this ... either,
none whatsoever. I can't.

[*Spot from* w1 *to* w2.]

w2: That poor creature who tried to seduce you, what ever
became of her, do you suppose?—I can hear her. Poor
thing.

[*Spot from* w2 *to* m.]

m: Personally I always preferred Lipton's.

[*Spot from* m *to* w1.]

w1: And that all is falling, all fallen, from the beginning, on
empty air. Nothing being asked at all. No one asking me
for anything at all.

[*Spot from* w1 *to* w2.]

w2: They might even feel sorry for me, if they could see me.
But never so sorry as I for them.
[*Spot from* w2 *to* w1.]

w1: I can't.
[*Spot from* w1 *to* w2.]

w2: Kissing their sour kisses.
[*Spot from* w2 *to* M.]

M: I pity them in any case, yes, compare my lot with theirs,
however blessed, and—
[*Spot from* M *to* w1.]

w1: I can't. The mind won't have it. It would have to go. Yes.
[*Spot from* w1 *to* M.]

M: Pity them.
[*Spot from* M *to* w2.]

w2: What do you do when you go out? Sift?
[*Spot from* w2 *to* M.]

M: Am I hiding something? Have I lost—
[*Spot from* M *to* w1.]

w1: She had means, I fancy, though she lived like a pig.
[*Spot from* w1 *to* w2.]

w2: Like dragging a great roller, on a scorching day. The strain
... to get it moving, momentum coming—
[S*pot off* w2. *Blackout. Three seconds. Spot on* w2.]

w2: Kill it and strain again.
[*Spot from* w2 *to* M.]

M: Have I lost ... the thing you want? Why go out? Why go—
[*Spot from* M *to* w2.]

w2: And you perhaps pitying me, thinking, Poor thing, she
needs a rest.
[*Spot from* w2 *to* w1.]

w1: Perhaps she has taken him away to live ... somewhere in
the sun.
[*Spot from* w1 *to* M.]

M: Why go down? Why not—
[*Spot from* M *to* w2.]

w2: I don't know.
[*Spot from* w2 *to* w1.]

w1: Perhaps she is sitting somewhere, by the open window, her
hands folded in her lap, gazing down out over the olives—

[*Spot from* w1 *to* M.]

M : Why not keep on glaring at me without ceasing? I might start to rave and—[*Hiccup.*]—bring it up for you. Par—
   [*Spot from* M *to* w2.]

w2: No.
   [*Spot from* w2 *to* M.]

M : —don.
   [*Spot from* M *to* w1.]

w1: Gazing down out over the olives, then the sea, wondering what can be keeping him, growing cold. Shadow stealing over everything. Creeping. Yes.
   [*Spot from* w1 *to* M.]

M : To think we were never together.
   [*Spot from* M *to* w2.]

w2: Am I not perhaps a little unhinged already?
   [*Spot from* w2 *to* w1.]

w1: Poor creature. Poor creatures.
   [*Spot from* w1 *to* M.]

M : Never woke together, on a May morning, the first to wake to wake the other two. Then in a little dinghy—
   [*Spot from* M *to* w1.]

w1: Penitence, yes, at a pinch, atonement, one was resigned, but no, that does not seem to be th_ point either.
   [*Spot from* w1 *to* w2.]

w2: I say, Am I not perhaps a little unhinged already? [*Hopefully.*] Just a little? [*Pause.*] I doubt it.
   [*Spot from* w2 *to* M.]

M : A little dinghy—
   [*Spot from* M *to* w1.]

w1: Silence and darkness were all I craved. Well, I get a certain amount of both. They being one. Perhaps it is more wickedness to pray for more.
   [*Spot from* w1 *to* M.]

M : A little dinghy, on the river, I resting on my oars, they lolling on air-pillows in the stern . . . sheets. Drifting. Such fantasies.
   [*Spot from* M *to* w1.]

w1: Hellish half-light.
   [*Spot from* w1 *to* w2.]

w2: A shade gone. In the head. Just a shade. I doubt it.
   [*Spot from* w2 *to* M.]

M: We were not civilized.
   [*Spot from* M *to* w1.]

w1: Dying for dark—and the darker the worse. Strange.
   [*Spot from* w1 *to* M.]

M: Such fantasies. Then. And now—
   [*Spot from* M *to* w2.]

w2: *I* doubt it.
   [*Pause. Peal of wild low laughter from* w2 *cut short as spot from her to* w1.]

w1: Yes, and the whole thing there, all there, staring you in the face. You'll see it. Get off me. Or weary.
   [*Spot from* w1 *to* M.]

M: And now, that you are . . . mere eye. Just looking. At my face. On and off.
   [*Spot from* M *to* w1.]

w1: Weary of playing with me. Get off me. Yes.
   [*Spot from* w1 *to* M.]

M: Looking for something. In my face. Some truth. In my eyes. Not even.
   [*Spot from* M *to* w2. *Laugh as before from* w2 *cut short as spot from her to* M.]

M: Mere eye. No mind. Opening and shutting on me. Am I as much—
   [*Spot off* M. *Blackout. Three seconds. Spot on* M.]
   Am I as much as . . . being seen?
   [*Spot off* M. *Blackout. Five seconds. Faint spots simultaneously on three faces. Three seconds. Voices faint, largely unintelligible.*]

w1: ⎤   Yes, strange, etc.
w2: ⎬ [*Together.*]   Yes, perhaps, etc.
M: ⎦   Yes, peace, etc.
   [*Repeat play*.]

M: [*Closing repeat.*] Am I as much as . . . being seen?
   [*Spot off* M. *Blackout. Five seconds. Strong spots simultaneously on three faces. Three seconds. Voices normal strength.*]

w1:⎫   I said to him, Give her up-
w2:⎬   [*Together.*]   One morning as I was sitting-
m:⎭   We were not long together-
    [*Spots off. Blackout. Five seconds. Spot on* m .]
m : We were not long together—
    [*Spot off* m. *Blackout. Five seconds.*]

CURTAIN

LIGHT

The source of light is single and must not be situated outside the ideal space (stage) occupied by its victims.

The optimum position for the spot is at the centre of the footlights, the faces being thus lit at close quarters and from below.

When exceptionally three spots are required to light the three faces simultaneously, they should be as a single spot branching into three.

Apart from these moments a single mobile spot should be used, swivelling at maximum speed from one face to another as required.

The method consisting in assigning to each face a separate fixed spot is unsatisfactory in that it is less expressive of a unique inquisitor than the single mobile spot.

CHORUS

w1 Yes strange	darkness best	and the darker	the worse
w2 Yes perhaps	a shade gone	I suppose	some might say
M Yes peace	one assumed	all out	all the pain
w1 till all dark	then all well	for the time	but it will come
w2 poor thing	a shade gone	just a shade	in the head
M all as if	never been	it will come	[Hiccup.] pardon
w1 the time will come	the thing is there		you'll see it
w2 [Laugh - - - - - -]	just a shade		but I doubt it
M no sense in this	oh I know		none the less
w1 get off me	keep off me	all dark	all still
w2 I doubt it	not really	I'm all right	still all right
M one assumed	peace I mean	not merely	all over
w1 all over	wiped out—		
w2 do my best	all I can—		
M but as if	never been—		

URNS

In order for the urns to be only one yard high, it is necessary
either that traps be used, enabling the actors to stand below
stage level, or that they kneel throughout play, the urns being
open at the back.

Should traps be not available, and the kneeling posture found
impracticable, the actors should stand, the urns be enlarged to
full length and moved back from front to mid-stage, the tallest
actor setting the height, the broadest the breadth, to which the
three urns should conform.

The sitting posture results in urns of unacceptable bulk and
is not to be considered.

REPEAT

The repeat may be an exact replica of first statement or it may present an element of variation.

In other words, the light may operate the second time exactly as it did the first (exact replica) or it may try a different method (variation).

The London production (and in a lesser degree the Paris production) opted for the variation with following deviations from first statement:

1. Introduction of an abridged chorus, cut short on laugh of w2, to open fragment of second repeat.

2. Light less strong in repeat and voices correspondingly lower, giving the following schema, where A is the highest level of light and voice and E the lowest:

c First chorus.
A First part of 1.   1
B Second part of 1.

D Second chorus.
B First part of Repeat 1.   Repeat 1
c Second part of Repeat 1.

E Abridged chorus.
c Fragment of Repeat 2   Fragment of Repeat 2

3. Breathless quality in voices from beginning of Repeat 1 and increasing to end of play.

4. Changed order of speeches in repeat as far as this is compatible with unchanged continuity for actors. E.g. the order of interrogation w1, w2, M, w2, w1, M at opening of 1 becomes w2, w1, M, w2, M, w1 at opening of repeat, and so on if and as desired.

Film

Written in English in April 1963. Commissioned for the Evergreen Theater, New York. Filmed in New York in the summer of 1964 and first shown publicly in 1965 at the New York Film Festival. First published by Faber and Faber, London, in 1967.

This is the original project for *Film*. No attempt has been made to bring it into line with the finished work. The one considerable departure from what was imagined concerns the opening sequence in the street. This was first shot as given, then replaced by a simplified version in which only the indispensable couple is retained. For the rest the shooting followed closely the indications of the script.

Throughout first two parts all perception is E's. E is the camera. But in third part there is O's perception of room and contents and at the same time E's continued perception of O. This poses a problem of images which I cannot solve without technical help. See below, note 8.

The film is divided into three parts. 1. The street (about eight minutes). 2. The stairs (about five minutes). 3. The room (about seventeen minutes).

The film is entirely silent except for the 'sssh!' in part one.

Climate of film comic and unreal. O should invite laughter throughout by his way of moving. Unreality of street scene (see notes to this section).

GENERAL

Esse est percipi.

All extraneous perception suppressed, animal, human, divine, self-perception maintains in being.

Search of non-being in flight from extraneous perception breaking down in inescapability of self-perception.

No truth value attaches to above, regarded as of merely structural and dramatic convenience.

In order to be figured in this situation the protagonist is sundered into object (O) and eye (E), the former in flight, the latter in pursuit.

It will not be clear until end of film that pursuing perceiver is not extraneous, but self.

Until end of film O is perceived by E from behind and at an angle not exceeding 45°. Convention: O enters *percipi* = experiences anguish of perceivedness, only when this angle is exceeded.

O not in perceivedness:

O in perceivedness:

E is therefore at pains, throughout pursuit, to keep within this 'angle of immunity' and only exceeds it (1) inadvertently at beginning of part one when he first sights O (2) inadvertently at beginning of part two when he follows O into vestibule and (3) deliberately at end of part three when O is cornered. In first two cases he hastily reduces angle.

OUTLINE

1. The street

Dead straight. No sidestreets or intersections. Period: about 1929. Early summer morning. Small factory district. Moderate animation of workers going unhurriedly to work. All going in same direction and all in couples. No automobiles. Two bicycles ridden by men with girl passengers (on crossbar). One cab, cantering nag, driver standing brandishing whip. All persons in opening scene to be shown in some way perceiving—one another, an object, a shop window, a poster, etc., i.e. all contentedly in *percipere* and *percipi*. First view of above is by E motionless and searching with his eyes for O. He may be supposed at street edge of wide (4 yards) sidewalk. O finally comes into view hastening blindly along sidewalk, hugging the wall on his left, in opposite direction to all the others. Long dark overcoat (whereas all others in light summer dress) with collar up, hat pulled down over eyes, briefcase in left hand, right hand shielding exposed side of face. He storms along in comic foundered precipitancy. E's searching eye, turning left from street to sidewalk, picks him up at an angle exceeding that of immunity (O's unperceivedness according to convention) (1). O, entering perceivedness, reacts (after just sufficient onward movement for his gait to be established) by halting and cringing aside towards wall. E immediately draws back to close the angle (2) and O, released from perceivedness, hurries on. E lets him get about 10 yards ahead and then starts after him (3). Street elements from now on incidental (except for episode of couple) in the sense that only registered in so far as they happen to enter field of pursuing eye fixed on O.

Episode of couple (4). In his blind haste O jostles an elderly couple of shabby genteel aspect, standing on sidewalk, peering together at a newspaper. They should be discovered by E a few yards before collision. The woman is holding a pet monkey under her left arm. E follows O an instant as he hastens blindly on, then registers couple recovering from shock, comes up with them, passes them slightly and halts to observe them (5). Having recovered they turn and look after O, the woman raising a lorgnon to her eyes, the man taking off his pince-nez fastened to his coat by a ribbon. They then look at each other, she lowering her lorgnon, he resuming his pince-nez. He opens his mouth to vituperate. She checks him with a gesture and soft 'sssh!' He turns again, taking off his pince-nez, to look after O. She feels the gaze of E upon them and turns, raising her lorgnon, to look at him. She nudges her companion who turns back towards her, resuming his pince-nez, follows direction of her gaze and, taking off his pince-nez, looks at E. As they both stare at E the expression gradually comes over their faces which will be that of the flower-woman in the stairs scene and that of O at the end of film, an expression only to be described as corresponding to an agony of perceivedness. Indifference of monkey, looking up into face of its mistress. They close their eyes, she lowering her lorgnon, and hasten away in direction of all the others, i.e. that opposed to O and E (6).

E turns back towards O by now far ahead and out of sight. Immediate acceleration of E in pursuit (blurred transit of encountered elements). O comes into view, grows rapidly larger until E settles down behind him at same angle and remove as before. O disappears suddenly through open housedoor on his left. Immediate acceleration of E who comes up with O in vestibule at foot of stairs.

2. Stairs

Vestibule about 4 yards square with stairs at inner righthand
angle. Relation of streetdoor to stairs such that E's first perception of O (E near door, O motionless at foot of stairs, right
hand on banister, body shaken by panting) is from an angle a
little exceeding that of immunity. O, entering perceivedness
(according to convention), transfers right hand from banister
to exposed side of face and cringes aside towards wall on his
left. E immediately draws back to close the angle and O,
released, resumes his pose at foot of stairs, hand on banister.
O mounts a few steps (E remaining near door), raises head,
listens, redescends hastily backwards and crouches down in
angle of stairs and wall on his right, invisible to one descending
(7). E registers him there, then transfers to stairs. A frail old
woman appears on bottom landing. She carries a tray of flowers
slung from her neck by a strap. She descends slowly, with
fumbling feet, one hand steadying the tray, the other holding
the banister. Absorbed by difficulty of descent she does not
become aware of E until she is quite down and making for the
door. She halts and looks full at E. Gradually same expression
as that of couple in street. She closes her eyes, then sinks to the
ground and lies with face in scattered flowers. E lingers on this
a moment, then transfers to where O last registered. He is no
longer there, but hastening up the stairs. E transfers to stairs
and picks up O as he reaches first landing. Bound forwards and
up of E who overtakes O on second flight and is literally at his
heels when he reaches second landing and opens with key door
of room. They enter room together, E turning with O as he
turns to lock the door behind him.

3. The room

Here we assume problem of dual perception solved and enter
O's perception (8). E must so manoeuvre throughout what
follows, until investment proper, that O is always seen from
behind, at most convenient remove, and from an angle never
exceeding that of immunity, i.e. preserved from perceivedness.

Small barely furnished room (9). Side by side on floor a
large cat and small dog. Unreal quality. Motionless till ejected.
Cat bigger than dog. On a table against wall a parrot in a cage

and a goldfish in a bowl. This room sequence falls into three parts.

1. Preparation of room (occlusion of window and mirror, ejection of dog and cat, destruction of God's image, occlusion of parrot and goldfish).

2. Period in rocking-chair. Inspection and destruction of photographs.

3. Final investment of O by E and dénouement.

1. O stands near door with case in hand and takes in room. Succession of images: dog and cat, side by side, staring at him; mirror; window; couch with rug; dog and cat staring at him; parrot and goldfish, parrot staring at him; rocking-chair; dog and cat staring at him. He sets down case, approaches window from side and draws curtain. He turns towards dog and cat, still staring at him, then goes to couch and takes up rug. He turns towards dog and cat, still staring at him. Holding rug before him he approaches mirror from side and covers it with rug. He turns towards parrot and goldfish, parrot still staring at him. He goes to rocking-chair, inspects it from front. Insistent image of curiously carved headrest (10). He turns towards dog and cat still staring at him. He puts them out of room (11). He takes up case and is moving towards chair when rug falls from mirror. He drops briefcase, hastens to wall between couch and mirror, follows walls past window, approaches mirror from side, picks up rug and, holding it before him, covers mirror with it again. He returns to briefcase, picks it up, goes to chair, sits down and is opening case when disturbed by print, pinned to wall before him, of the face of God the Father, the eyes staring at him severely. He sets down case on floor to his left, gets up and inspects print. Insistent image of wall, paper hanging off in strips (10). He tears print from wall, tears it in four, throws down the pieces and grinds them underfoot. He turns back to chair, image again of its curious headrest, sits down, image again of tattered wall-paper, takes case on his knees, takes out a folder, sets down case on floor to his left and is opening folder when disturbed by parrot's eye. He lays folder on case, gets up, takes off overcoat, goes to parrot, close up of parrot's eye, covers cage with coat, goes back to chair, image again of headrest, sits down, image again of tattered wall-paper, takes up

folder and is opening it when disturbed by fish's eye. He lays folder on case, gets up, goes to fish, close-up of fish's eye, extends coat to cover bowl as well as cage, goes back to chair, image again of headrest, sits down, image again of wall, takes up folder, takes off hat and lays it on case to his left. Scant hair or bald to facilitate identification of narrow black elastic encircling head.

When O sits up and back his head is framed in headrest which is a narrower extension of backrest. Throughout scene of inspection and destruction of photographs E may be supposed immediately behind chair looking down over O's left shoulder (12).

2. O opens folder, takes from it a packet of photographs (13), lays folder on case and begins to inspect photographs. He inspects them in order 1 to 7. When he has finished with 1 he lays it on his knees, inspects 2, lays it on top of 1, and so on, so that when he has finished inspecting them all 1 will be at the bottom of the pile and 7—or rather 6, for he does not lay down 7—at the top. He gives about six seconds each to 1-4, about twice as long to 5 and 6 (trembling hands). Looking at 6 he touches with forefinger little girl's face. After six seconds of 7 he tears it in four and drops pieces on floor on his left. He takes up 6 from top of pile on his knees, looks at it again for about three seconds, tears it in four and drops pieces on floor to his left. So on for the others, looking at each again for about three seconds before tearing it up. 1 must be on tougher mount for he has difficulty in tearing it across. Straining hands. He finally succeeds, drops pieces on floor and sits, rocking slightly, hands holding armrests (14).

3. Investment proper. Perception from now on, if dual perception feasible, E's alone, except perception of E by O at end. E moves a little back (image of headrest from back), then starts circling to his left, approaches maximum angle and halts. From this open angle, beyond which he will enter *percipi*, O can be seen beginning to doze off. His visible hand relaxes on armrest, his head nods and falls forward, the rock approaches stillness. E advances, opening angle beyond limit of immunity, his gaze pierces the light sleep and O starts awake. The start revives the rock, immediately arrested by foot to floor. Tension of hand on armrest. Turning his head to right, O cringes away from per-

ceivedness. E draws back to reduce the angle and after a moment, reassured, O turns back front and resumes his pose. The rock resumes, dies down slowly as O dozes off again. E now begins a much wider encirclement. Images of curtained window, walls and shrouded mirror to indicate his path and that he is not yet looking at O. Then brief image of O seen by E from well beyond the angle of immunity, i.e. from near the table with shrouded bowl and cage. O is now seen to be fast asleep, his head sunk on his chest and his hands, fallen from the armrests, limply dangling. E resumes his cautious approach. Images of shrouded bowl and cage and tattered wall adjoining, with same indication as before. Halt and brief image, not far short of full-face, of O still fast asleep. E advances last few yards along tattered wall and halts directly in front of O. Long image of O, full-face, against ground of headrest, sleeping. E's gaze pierces the sleep, O starts awake, stares up at E. Patch over O's left eye now seen for the first time. Rock revived by start, stilled at once by foot to ground. Hand clutches armrests. O half starts from chair, then stiffens, staring up at E. Gradually that look. Cut to E, of whom this very first image (face only, against ground of tattered wall). It is O's face (with patch) but with very different expression, impossible to describe, neither severity nor benignity, but rather acute *intentness*. A big nail is visible near left temple (patch side). Long image of the un-blinking gaze. Cut back to O, still half risen, staring up, with that look. O closes his eyes and falls back in chair, starting off rock. He covers his face with his hands. Image of O rocking, his head in his hands but not yet bowed. Cut back to E. As before. Cut back to O. He sits, bowed forward, his head in his hands, gently rocking. Hold it as the rocking dies down.

END

NOTES

1. First sight of O

2. O released from perceivedness

  = 2 yds

3. Relation E—O during pursuit

4. The purpose of this episode, undefendable except as a dramatic convenience, is to suggest as soon as possible unbearable quality of E's scrutiny. Reinforced by episode of flower-woman in stairs sequence.

5.

  = 2 yds

6. Expression of this episode, like that of animals' ejection in part three, should be as precisely stylized as possible. The purpose of the monkey, either unaware of E or indifferent to him, is to anticipate behaviour of animals in part three, attentive to O exclusively.

7. Suggestion for vestibule with (1) O in *percipi* (2) released (3) hiding from flower-woman. Note that even when E exceeds angle of immunity O's face never really seen because of immediate turn aside and (here) hand to shield face.

8. Up till now the perceptions of O, hastening *blindly* to illusory sanctuary, have been neglected and must in fact have been negligible. But in the room, until he falls asleep and the investment begins, they must be recorded. And at the same time E's perceiving of O must continue to be given. E is concerned only with O, not with the room, or only incidentally with the room in so far as its elements happen to enter the field of his gaze fastened on O. We see O in the room thanks to E's perceiving and the room itself thanks to O's perceiving. In other words this room sequence, up to the moment of O's falling asleep, is composed of two independent sets of images. I feel that any attempt to express them in simultaneity (composite images, double frame, superimposition, etc.) must prove unsatisfactory. The presentation in a single image of O's perception of the print, for example, and E's perception of O perceiving it—no doubt feasible technically—would perhaps

make impossible for the spectator a clear apprehension of either. The solution might be in a succession of images of different *quality*, corresponding on the one hand to E's perception of O and on the other to O's perception of the room. This difference of quality might perhaps be sought in different degrees of development, the passage from the one to the other being from greater to lesser and lesser to greater definition or luminosity. The dissimilarity, however obtained, would have to be flagrant. Having been up till now exclusively in the E quality, we would suddenly pass, with O's first survey of the room, into this quite different O quality. Then back to the E quality when O is shown moving to the window. And so on throughout the sequence, switching from the one to the other as required. Were this the solution adopted it might be desirable to establish, by means of brief sequences, the O quality in parts one and two.

This seems to be the chief problem of the film, though I perhaps exaggerate its difficulty through technical ignorance.

9.

Suggestion for room.

This obviously cannot be O's room. It may be supposed it is his mother's room, which he has not visited for many years and is now to occupy momentarily, to look after the pets, until she comes out of hospital. This has no bearing on the film and need not be elucidated.

10. At close of film face E and face O can only be distinguished (1) By different expressions (2) by fact of O looking up and E down and (3) by difference of ground (for O headrest of chair, for E wall). Hence insistence on headrest and tattered wall.

11. Foolish suggestion for eviction of cat and dog. Also see Note 6.

O with dog to door

Door ——————— · Dog   1   ——————←——— 2
              · Cat   · Cat

O with cat to door

Dog out —→ O back for cat   3   ————←——— 4
              · Cat   —→ Dog back

O with dog to door

Cat out —→ O back for dog   5   ————←——— 6
              · Dog   —→ Cat back

O with cat to door

Dog out —→ O back for cat   7   ————←——— 8
              Cat   —→ Dog back

Cat out —→ ⎯ O back for dog ⎯ 9   O with dog to door

             · Dog   ←⎯ 10
                                      ⎯→ Cat back

Dog out —→ ⎯ O back for cat ⎯ 11   O with cat to door

             · Cat   ←⎯ 12
                                      ⎯→ Dog back

Cat out —→ ⎯ O back for dog ⎯ 13   O with dog to door

             · Dog   ←⎯ 14
                                      ⎯→ Cat back

Dog out —→ ⎯ O back for cat ⎯ 15   O with cat to door

             · Cat   ←⎯ 16

—→ ⎯ O picks up case ⎯ 17

Cat and dog
out

12. Chair from front during photo sequence.

13. Description of photographs.

1. Male infant. 6 months. His mother holds him in her arms.
Infant smiles front. Mother's big hands. Her severe eyes de-
vouring him. Her big old-fashioned beflowered hat.

2. The same. 4 years. On a veranda, dressed in loose night-
shirt, kneeling on a cushion, attitude of prayer, hands clasped,
head bowed, eyes closed. Half profile. Mother on chair beside
him, big hands on knees, head bowed towards him, severe eyes,
similar hat to 1.

3. The same. 15 years. Bareheaded. School blazer. Smiling.
Teaching a dog to beg. Dog on its hind legs looking up at him.

4. The same. 20 years. Graduation day. Academic gown.

Mortar-board under arm. On a platform, receiving scroll from
Rector. Smiling. Section of public watching.

5. The same. 21 years. Bareheaded. Smiling. Small moustache.
Arm round fiancée. A young man takes a snap of them.

6. The same. 25 years. Newly enlisted. Bareheaded. Uniform.
Bigger moustache. Smiling. Holding a little girl in his arms. She
looks into his face, exploring it with finger.

7. The same. 30 years. Looking over 40. Wearing hat and
overcoat. Patch over left eye. Cleanshaven. Grim expression.

14. Profit by rocking-chair to emotionalize inspection, e.g.
gentle steady rock for 1 to 4, rock stilled (foot to ground)
after two seconds of 5, rock resumed between 5 and 6, rock
stilled after two seconds of 6, rock resumed after 6 and for 7 as
for 1-4.

The Old Tune

An adaptation

An English adaptation of *La Manivelle*, a play for radio by
Robert Pinget, which was first published in France by Editions
de Minuit, Paris, and by John Calder (Publishers), London, in
1963.

Background of street noises. In the foreground a barrel-organ playing an old tune. 20 seconds. The mechanism jams. Thumps on the box to set it off again. No result.

GORMAN: [*Old man's cracked voice, frequent pauses for breath even in the middle of a word, speech indistinct for want of front teeth, whistling sibilants.*] There we go, bust again. [*Sound of lid raised. Scraping inside box.*] Cursed bloody music! [*Scraping. Creaking of handle. Thumps on box. The mechanism starts off again.*] Ah about time! [*Tune resumes. 10 seconds. Sound of faltering steps approaching.*]

CREAM: [*Old man's cracked voice, stumbling speech, pauses in the middle of sentences, whistling sibilants due to ill-fitting denture.*] —Well, if it isn't—[*The tune stops.*] —Gorman my old friend Gorman, do you recognize me Cream father of the judge, Cream you remember Cream.

GORMAN: Mr Cream! Well, I'll be! Mr Cream! [*Pause.*] Sit you down, sit you down, here, there. [*Pause.*] Great weather for the time of day Mr Cream, eh.

CREAM: My old friend Gorman, it's a sight to see you again after all these years, all these years.

GORMAN: Yes indeed, Mr Cream, yes indeed, that's the way it is. [*Pause.*] And you, tell me.

CREAM: I was living with my daughter and she died, then I came here to live with the other.

GORMAN: Miss Miss what?

CREAM: Bertha. You know she got married, yes, Moody the nurseryman, two children.

GORMAN: Grand match, Mr Cream, grand match, more power to you. But tell me then the poor soul she was taken then was she.

CREAM: Malignant, tried everything, lingered three years, that's how it goes, the young pop off and the old hang on.

GORMAN: Ah dear oh dear Mr Cream, dear oh dear.

[*Pause.*]

CREAM: And you your wife?

GORMAN: Still in it, still in it, but for how long.

CREAM: Poor Daisy yes.

GORMAN: Had she children?

CREAM: Three, three children, Johnny, the eldest, then Ronnie, then a baby girl, Queenie, my favourite, Queenie, a baby girl.

GORMAN: Darling name.

CREAM: She's so quick for her years you wouldn't believe it, do you know what she came out with to me the other day ah only the other day poor Daisy.

GORMAN: And your son-in-law?

CREAM: Eh?

GORMAN: Ah dear oh dear, Mr Cream, dear oh dear. [*Pause.*] Ah yes children that's the way it is. [*Roar of motor engine.*] They'd tear you to flitters with their flaming machines.

CREAM: Shocking crossing, sudden death.

GORMAN: As soon as look at you, tear you to flitters.

CREAM: Ah in our time Gorman this was the outskirts, you remember, peace and quiet.

GORMAN: Do I remember, fields it was, fields, bluebells, over there, on the bank, bluebells. When you think.... [*Suddenly complete silence. 10 seconds. The tune resumes, falters, stops. Silence. The street noises resume.*] Ah the horses, the carriages, and the barouches, ah the barouches, all that's the dim distant past, Mr Cream.

CREAM: And the broughams, remember the broughams, there was style for you, the broughams.

[*Pause.*]

GORMAN: The first car I remember I saw it here, here, on the corner, a Pic-Pic she was.

CREAM: Not a Pic-Pic, Gorman, not a Pic-Pic, a Dee Dyan Button.

GORMAN: A Pic-Pic, a Pic-Pic, don't I remember it well, just as I was coming out of Swan's the bookseller's beyond there on the corner, Swan's the bookseller's that was, just as I was coming out with a rise of fourpence ah there wasn't much money in it in those days.

CREAM: A Dee Dyan, a Dee Dyan.

GORMAN: You had to work for your living in those days, it wasn't at six you knocked off, nor at seven neither, eight it was, eight o'clock, yes by God. [*Pause.*] Where was I? [*Pause.*] Ah yes eight o'clock as I was coming out of Swan's there was the crowd gathered and the car wheeling round the bend.

CREAM: A Dee Dyan Gorman, a Dee Dyan, I can remember the man himself from Wougham he was the vintner what's this his name was.

GORMAN: Bush, Seymour Bush.

CREAM: Bush that's the man.

GORMAN: One way or t'other, Mr Cream, one way or t'other no matter it wasn't the likes of nowadays, their flaming machines they'd tear you to shreds.

CREAM: My dear Gorman do you know what it is I'm going to tell you, all this speed do you know what it is has the whole place ruinated, no living with it any more, the whole place ruinated, even the weather. [*Roar of engine.*] Ah when you think of the springs in our time remember the springs we had, the heat there was in them, and the summers remember the summers would destroy you with the heat.

GORMAN: Do I remember, there was one year back there seems like yesterday must have been round 95 when we were still out at Cruddy, didn't we water the roof of the house every evening with the rubber jet to have a bit of cool in the night, yes summer 95.

CREAM: That would surprise me Gorman, remember in those days the rubber hose was a great luxury a great luxury, wasn't till after the war the rubber hose.

GORMAN: You may be right.

CREAM: No may be about it. I tell you the first we ever had round here was in Drummond's place, old Da Drummond, that was after the war 1920 maybe, still very exorbitant it was at the time, don't you remember watering out of the can you must with that bit of garden you had didn't you, wasn't it your father owned that patch out on the Marston Road.

GORMAN: The Sheen Road Mr Cream but true for you the watering you're right there, me and me hose how are you when we had no running water at the time or had we.

CREAM: The Sheen Road, that's the one out beyond Shackleton's sawpit.

GORMAN: We didn't get it in till 1925 now it comes back to me the wash-hand basin and jug.

[*Roar of engine.*]

CREAM: The Sheen Road you saw what they've done to that I was out on it yesterday with the son-in-law, you saw what they've done our little gardens and the grand sloe hedges.

GORMAN: Yes all those gazebos springing up like thistles there's trash for you if you like, collapse if you look at them am I right.

CREAM: Collapse is the word, when you think of the good stone made the cathedrals nothing to come up to it.

GORMAN: And on top of all no foundations, no cellars, no nothing, how are you going to live without cellars I ask you, on piles if you don't mind, piles, like in the lake age, there's progress for you.

CREAM: Ah Gorman you haven't changed a hair, just the same old wag he always was. Getting on for seventy-five is it?

GORMAN: Seventy-three, seventy-three, soon due for the knock.

CREAM: Now Gorman none of that, none of that, and me turning seventy-six, you're a young man Gorman.

GORMAN: Ah Mr Cream, always a great one for a crack.

CREAM: Here Gorman while we're at it have a fag, here. [*Pause.*] The daughter must have whipped them again, doesn't want me to be smoking, mind her own damn business. [*Pause.*] Ah I have them, here, have one.

GORMAN: I wouldn't leave you short.

CREAM: Short for God's sake, here, have one. [*Pause.*]

GORMAN: They're packed so tight they won't come out.

CREAM: Take hold of the packet. [*Pause.*] Ah what ails me all bloody thumbs. Can you pick it up. [*Pause.*]

GORMAN: Here we are. [*Pause.*] Ah yes a nice puff now and again but it's not what it was their gaspers now not worth a fiddler's, remember in the forces the shag remember the black shag that was tobacco for you.

CREAM: Ah the black shag my dear Gorman the black shag, fit for royalty the black shag fit for royalty. [*Pause.*] Have you a light on you.

GORMAN: Well then I haven't, the wife doesn't like me to be smoking.
[*Pause.*]

CREAM: Must have whipped my lighter too the bitch, my old tinder jizzer.

GORMAN: Well no matter I'll keep it and have a draw later on.

CREAM: The bitch sure as a gun she must have whipped it too that's going beyond the beyonds, beyond the beyonds, nothing you can call your own. [*Pause.*] Perhaps we might ask this gentleman. [*Footsteps approach.*] Beg your pardon Sir trouble you for a light.
[*Footsteps recede.*]

GORMAN: Ah the young nowadays Mr Cream very wrapped up they are the young nowadays, no thought for the old. When you think, when you think .... [*Suddenly complete silence. 10 seconds. The tune resumes, falters, stops. Silence. The street noises resume.*] Where were we? [*Pause.*] Ah yes the forces, you went in in 1900, 1900, 1902, am I right?

CREAM: 1903, 1903, and you 1906 was it?

GORMAN: 1906 yes at Chatham.

CREAM: The Gunners?

GORMAN: The Foot, the Foot.

CREAM: But the Foot wasn't Chatham don't you remember, there it was the Gunners, you must have been at Caterham, Caterham, the Foot.

GORMAN: Chatham I tell you, isn't it like yesterday, Morrison's pub on the corner.

CREAM: Harrison's. Harrison's Oak Lounge, do you think I don't know Chatham. I used to go there on holiday with Mrs Cream, I know Chatham backwards Gorman, inside and out, Harrison's Oak Lounge on the corner of what was the name of the street, on a rise it was, it'll come back to me, do you think I don't know Harrison's Oak Lounge there on the corner of dammit I'll forget my own name next and the square it'll come back to me.

GORMAN: Morrison or Harrison we were at Chatham.

CREAM: That would surprise me greatly, the Gunners were Chatham do you not remember that?

GORMAN: I was in the Foot, at Chatham, in the Foot.

CREAM: The Foot, that's right the Foot at Chatham.

GORMAN: That's what I'm telling you, Chatham the Foot.

CREAM: That would surprise me greatly, you must have it mucked up with the war, the mobilization.

GORMAN: The mobilization have a heart it's as clear in my mind as yesterday the mobilization, we were shifted straight away to Chesham, was it, no, Chester, that's the place, Chester, there was Morrison's pub on the corner and a chamber-maid what was her name, Joan, Jean, Jane, the very start of the war when we still didn't believe it, Chester, ah those are happy memories.

CREAM: Happy memories, happy memories, I wouldn't go so far as that.

GORMAN: I mean the start up, the start up at Chatham, we still didn't believe it, and that chamber-maid what was her name it'll come back to me. [*Pause.*] And your son by the same token.

[*Roar of engine.*]

CREAM: Eh?

GORMAN: Your son the judge.

CREAM: He has rheumatism.

GORMAN: Ah rheumatism, rheumatism runs in the blood Mr Cream.

CREAM: What are you talking about, I never had rheumatism.

GORMAN: When I think of my poor old mother, only sixty and couldn't move a muscle. [*Roar of engine.*] Rheumatism they never found the remedy for it yet, atom rockets is all they care about, I can thank my lucky stars touch wood. [*Pause.*] Your son yes he's in the papers the Carton affair, the way he managed that case he can be a proud man, the wife read it again in this morning's *Lark*.

CREAM: What do you mean the Barton affair.

GORMAN: The Carton affair Mr Cream, the sex fiend, on the Assizes.

CREAM: That's not him, he's not the Assizes my boy isn't, he's the County Courts, you mean Judge ... Judge ... what's this his name was in the Barton affair.

GORMAN: Ah I thought it was him.

CREAM: Certainly not I tell you, the County Courts my boy, not the Assizes, the County Courts.

GORMAN: Oh you know the Courts and the Assizes it was always all six of one to me.

CREAM: Ah but there's a big difference Mr Gorman, a power of difference, a civil case and a criminal one, quite another how d'you do, what would a civil case be doing in the *Lark* now I ask you.

GORMAN: All that machinery you know I never got the swing of it and now it's all six of one to me.

CREAM: Were you never in the Courts?

GORMAN: I was once all right when my niece got her divorce that was when was it now thirty years ago yes thirty years, I was greatly put about I can tell you the poor little thing divorced after two years of married life, my sister was never the same after it.

CREAM: Divorce is the curse of society you can take it from me, the curse of society, ask my boy if you don't believe me.

GORMAN: Ah there I'm with you the curse of society look at what it leads up to, when you think my niece had a little girl as good as never knew her father.

CREAM: Did she get alimony.

GORMAN: She was put out to board and wasted away to a shadow, that's a nice thing for you.

CREAM: Did the mother get alimony.

GORMAN: Divil the money. [*Pause.*] So that's your son ladling out the divorces.

CREAM: As a judge he must, as a father it goes to his heart.

GORMAN: Has he children.

CREAM: Well in a way he had one, little Herbert, lived to be four months then passed away, how long is it now, how long is it now.

GORMAN: Ah dear oh dear, Mr Cream, dear oh dear and did they never have another?

[*Roar of engine.*]

CREAM: Eh?

GORMAN: Other children.

CREAM: Didn't I tell you, I have my daughters' children, my two daughters. [*Pause.*] Talking of that your man there Barton the sex boyo isn't that nice carryings on for you showing himself off like that without a stitch on him to little children might just as well have been ours Gorman, our own little grandchildren.

[*Roar of engine.*]

GORMAN: Mrs Cream must be a proud woman too to be a grandmother.

CREAM: Mrs Cream is in her coffin these twenty years Mr Gorman.

GORMAN: Oh God forgive me what am I talking about, I'm getting you wouldn't know what I'd be talking about, that's right you were saying you were with Miss Daisy.

CREAM: With my daughter Bertha, Mr Gorman, my daughter Bertha, Mrs Rupert Moody.

GORMAN: Your daughter Bertha that's right so she married Moody, gallous garage they have there near the slaughter-house.

CREAM: Not him, his brother the nursery-man.

GORMAN: Grand match, more power to you, have they children?

[*Roar of engine.*]

CREAM: Eh?

GORMAN: Children.

CREAM: Two dotey little boys, little Johnny I mean Hubert and the other, the other.

GORMAN: But tell me your daughter poor soul she was taken then was she. [*Pause.*] That cigarette while we're at it might try this gentleman. [*Footsteps approach.*] Beg your pardon Sir trouble you for a light. [*Footsteps recede.*] Ah the young are very wrapped up Mr Cream.

CREAM: Little Hubert and the other, the other, what's this his name is. [*Pause.*] And Mrs Gorman.

GORMAN: Still in it.

CREAM: Ah you're the lucky jim Gorman, you're the lucky jim, Mrs Gorman by gad, fine figure of a woman Mrs Gorman, fine handsome woman.

GORMAN: Handsome, all right, but you know, age. We have our health thanks be to God touch wood. [*Pause.*] You know what it is Mr Cream, that'd be the way to pop off chatting away like this of a sunny morning.

CREAM: None of that now Gorman, who's talking of popping off with the health you have as strong as an ox and a comfortable wife, ah I'd give ten years of mine to have her back do you hear me, living with strangers isn't the same.

GORMAN: Miss Bertha's so sweet and good you're on the pig's back for God's sake, on the pig's back.

CREAM: It's not the same you can take it from me, can't call your soul your own, look at the cigarettes, the lighter.

GORMAN: Miss Bertha so sweet and good.

CREAM: Sweet and good, all right, but dammit if she doesn't take me for a doddering old drivelling dotard. [*Pause.*] What did I do with those cigarettes?

GORMAN: And tell me your poor dear daughter-in-law what am I saying your daughter-in-law.

CREAM: My daughter-in-law, my daughter-in-law, what about my daughter-in-law.

GORMAN: She had private means, it was said she had private means.

CREAM: Private means ah they were the queer private means, all swallied up in the war every ha'penny do you hear me, all in the bank the private means not as much land as you'd tether a goat. [*Pause.*] Land Gorman there's no security like land but that woman you might as well have been talking to the bedpost, a mule she was that woman was.

GORMAN: Ah well it's only human nature, you can't always pierce into the future.

CREAM: Now now Gorman don't be telling me, land wouldn't you live all your life off a bit of land damn it now wouldn't you any fool knows that unless they take the fantasy to go and build on the moon the way they say, ah that's all fantasy Gorman you can take it from me all fantasy and delusion, they'll smart for it one of these days by God they will.

GORMAN: You don't believe in the moon what they're experimenting at.

CREAM: My dear Gorman the moon is the moon and cheese is cheese what do they take us for, didn't it always exist the moon wasn't it always there as large as life and what did it ever mean only fantasy and delusion Gorman, fantasy and delusion. [*Pause.*] Or is it our forefathers were a lot of old bags maybe now is that on the cards I ask you, Bacon, Wellington, Washington, for them the moon was always in their opinion damn it I ask you you'd think to hear them talk no one ever bothered his arse with the moon before, make a cat swallow his whiskers they think they've discovered the moon as if as if. [*Pause.*] What was I driving at? [*Roar of engine.*]

GORMAN: So you're against progress are you.

CREAM: Progress, progress, progress is all very fine and grand, there's such a thing I grant you, but it's scientific, progress, scientific, the moon's not progress, lunacy, lunacy.

GORMAN: Ah there I'm with you progress is scientific and the moon, the moon, that's the way it is.

CREAM: The wisdom of the ancients that's the trouble they don't give a rap or a snap for it any more, and the world going to rack and ruin, wouldn't it be better now to go back to the old maxims and not be gallivanting off killing one another in China over the moon, ah when I think of my poor father.

GORMAN: Your father that reminds me I knew your father well. [*Roar of engine.*] There was a man for you old Mr Cream, what he had to say he lashed out with it straight from the shoulder and no humming and hawing, now it comes back to me one year there on the town council my father told me must have been wait now till I see 95, 95 or 6, a short while before he resigned, 95 that's it the year of the great frost.

CREAM: Ah I beg your pardon, the great frost was 93 I'd just turned ten, 93 Gorman the great frost.
[*Roar of engine.*]

GORMAN: My father used to tell the story how Mr Cream went

hell for leather for the mayor who was he in those days, must have been Overend, yes Overend.

CREAM: Ah there you're mistaken my dear Gorman, my father went on the council with Overend in 97, January 97.

GORMAN: That may be, that may be, but it must have been 95 or 6 just the same seeing as how my father went off in 96, April 96, there was a set against him and he had to give in his resignation.

CREAM: Well then your father was off when it happened, all I know is mine went on with Overend in 97 the year Marrable was burnt out.

GORMAN: Ah Marrable it wasn't five hundred yards from the door five hundred yards Mr Cream, I can still hear my poor mother saying to us ah poor dear Maria she was saying to me again only last night, January 96 that's right.

CREAM: 97 I tell you, 97, the year my father was voted on.

GORMAN: That may be but just the same the clout he gave Overend that's right now I have it.

CREAM: The clout was Oscar Bliss the butcher in Pollox Street.

GORMAN: The butcher in Pollox Street, there's a memory from the dim distant past for you, didn't he have a daughter do you remember.

CREAM: Helen, Helen Bliss, pretty girl, she'd be my age, 83 saw the light of day.

GORMAN: And Rosie Plumpton bonny Rosie staring up at the lid these thirty years she must be now and Molly Berry and Eva what was her name Eva Hart that's right Eva Hart didn't she marry a Crumplin.

CREAM: Her brother, her brother Alfred married Gertie Crumplin great one for the lads she was you remember, Gertie great one for the lads.

GORMAN: Do I remember, Gertie Crumplin great bit of skirt by God, hee hee hee great bit of skirt.

CREAM: You old dog you!
[Roar of engine.]

GORMAN: And Nelly Crowther there's one came to a nasty end.

CREAM: Simon's daughter that's right, the parents were greatly to blame you can take it from me.

GORMAN: They reared her well then just the same bled themselves white for her so they did, poor Mary used to tell us all we were very close in those days lived on the same landing you know, poor Mary yes she used to say what a drain it was having the child boarding out at Saint Theresa's can you imagine, very classy, daughters of the gentry Mr Cream, even taught French they were the young ladies.

CREAM: Isn't that what I'm telling you, reared her like a princess of the blood they did, French now I ask you, French.

GORMAN: Would you blame them Mr Cream, the best of parents, you can't deny it, education.

CREAM: French, French, isn't that what I'm saying.

[*Roar of engine.*]

GORMAN: They denied themselves everything, take the bits out of their mouths they would for their Nelly.

CREAM: Don't be telling me they had her on a string all the same the said young lady, remember that Holy Week 1912 was it or 13.

[*Roar of engine.*]

GORMAN: Eh?

CREAM: When you think of Simon the man he was don't be telling me that. [*Pause.*] Holy Week 1913 now it all comes back to me is that like as if they had her on a string what she did then.

GORMAN: Peace to her ashes Mr Cream.

CREAM: Principles, Gorman, principles without principles I ask you. [*Roar of engine.*] Wasn't there an army man in it.

GORMAN: Eh?

CREAM: Wasn't there an army man in it?

GORMAN: In the car?

CREAM: Eh?

GORMAN: An army man in the car?

CREAM: In the Crowther blow-up.

[*Roar of engine.*]

GORMAN: You mean the Lootnant St John Fitzball.

CREAM: St John Fitzball that's the man, wasn't he mixed up in it?

GORMAN: They were keeping company all right. [*Pause.*] He died in 14. Wounds.

CREAM: And his aunt Miss Hester.

GORMAN: Dead then these how many years is it now how many.

CREAM: She was a great old one, a little on the high and mighty side perhaps you might say.

GORMAN: Take fire like gunpowder but a heart of gold if you only knew. [*Roar of engine.*] Her niece has a chip of the old block wouldn't you say.

CREAM: Her niece? No recollection.

GORMAN: No recollection, Miss Victoria, come on now, she was to have married an American and she's in the Turrets yet.

CREAM: I thought they'd sold.

GORMAN: Sell the Turrets is it they'll never sell, the family seat three centuries and maybe more, three centuries Mr Cream.

CREAM: You might be their historiographer Gorman to hear you talk, what you don't know about those people.

GORMAN: Histryographer no Mr Cream I wouldn't go so far as that but Miss Victoria right enough I know her through and through we stop and have a gas like when her aunt was still in it, ah yes nothing hoity-toity about Miss Victoria you can take my word she has a great chip of the old block.

CREAM: Hadn't she a brother.

GORMAN: The Lootnant yes, died in 14. Wounds.
[*Deafening roar of engine.*]

CREAM: The bloody cars such a thing as a quiet chat I ask you. [*Pause.*] Well I'll be slipping along I'm holding you back from your work.

GORMAN: Slipping along what would you want slipping along and we only after meeting for once in a blue moon.

CREAM: Well then just a minute and smoke a quick one. [*Pause.*] What did I do with those cigarettes? [*Pause.*] You fire ahead don't mind me.

GORMAN: When you think, when you think ....

[*Suddenly complete silence. 10 seconds. The tune resumes. The street noises resume and submerge tune a moment. Street noises and tune together crescendo. Tune finally rises above them triumphant.*]

Come and Go

A dramaticule

For John Calder

Written in English early in 1965. First published in French by
Editions de Minuit, Paris, in 1966. First published in English by
Calder and Boyars, London, in 1967. First produced as *Kommen
und Gehen*, translated by Elmar Tophoven, at the Schiller-
Theater Werkstatt, Berlin, on 14 January 1966. First performed
in English at the Peacock Theatre, Dublin, on 28 February 1968
and subsequently at the Royal Festival Hall, London, on 9
December 1968.

CHARACTERS:

FLO

VI

RU

(Ages undeterminable)

Sitting centre side by side stage right to left FLO, VI *and* RU. *Very erect, facing front, hands clasped in laps.*
Silence.

VI: When did we three last meet?
RU: Let us not speak.
　　[*Silence.*
　　Exit VI *right.*
　　Silence.]
FLO: Ru.
RU: Yes.
FLO: What do you think of Vi?
RU: I see little change. [FLO *moves to centre seat, whispers in*
　　RU's *ear. Appalled.*] Oh! [*They look at each other.* FLO
　　puts her finger to her lips.] Does she not realize?
FLO: God grant not.
　　[*Enter* VI. FLO *and* RU *turn back front, resume pose.* VI
　　sits right.
　　Silence.]
　　Just sit together as we used to, in the playground at Miss
　　Wade's.
RU: On the log.
　　[*Silence.*
　　Exit FLO *left.*
　　Silence.]
　　Vi.
VI: Yes.
RU: How do you find Flo?
VI: She seems much the same. [RU *moves to centre seat,*
　　whispers in VI's *ear. Appalled.*] Oh! [*They look at each*
　　other. RU *puts her finger to her lips.*] Has she not been
　　told?
RU: God forbid.

[*Enter* FLO. RU *and* VI *turn back front, resume pose.* FLO *sits left.*]

Holding hands ... that way.

FLO: Dreaming of ... love.

[*Silence.*

Exit RU *right.*

Silence.]

VI: Flo.

FLO: Yes.

VI: How do you think Ru is looking?

FLO: One sees little in this light. [VI *moves to centre seat, whispers in* FLO'*s ear. Appalled.*] Oh! [*They look at each other.* VI *puts her finger to her lips.*] Does she not know?

VI: Please God not.

[*Enter* RU. VI *and* FLO *turn back front, resume pose.* RU *sits right.*

Silence.]

May we not speak of the old days? [*Silence.*] Of what came after? [*Silence.*] Shall we hold hands in the old way?

[*After a moment they join hands as follows:* VI'*s right hand with* RU'*s right hand.* VI'*s left hand with* FLO'*s left hand,* FLO'*s right hand with* RU'*s left hand,* VI'*s arms being above* RU'*s left arm and* FLO'*s right arm. The three pairs of clasped hands rest on the three laps.*

Silence.]

FLO: I can feel the rings.

[*Silence.*]

CURTAIN

NOTES

Successive positions

1	FLO	VI	RU
2	FLO		RU
		FLO	RU
3	VI	FLO	RU
4	VI		RU
	VI	RU	
5	VI	RU	FLO
6	VI		FLO
		VI	FLO
7	RU	VI	FLO

Hands

RU   VI   FLO

Lighting

Soft, from above only and concentrated on playing area.
Rest of stage as dark as possible.

Costume

Full-length coats, buttoned high, dull violet (Ru), dull red (Vi),
dull yellow (Flo). Drab nondescript hats with enough brim to
shade faces. Apart from colour differentiation three figures as
alike as possible. Light shoes with rubber soles. Hands made up
to be as visible as possible. No rings apparent.

Seat

Narrow benchlike seat, without back, just long enough to
accommodate three figures almost touching. As little visible as
possible. It should not be clear what they are sitting on.

Exits

The figures are not seen to go off stage. They should disappear a
few steps from lit area. If dark not sufficient to allow this,
recourse should be had to screens or drapes as little visible as
possible. Exits and entrances slow, without sound of feet.

Obs
Three very different sounds.

Voices
As low as compatible with audibility. Colourless except for
three 'ohs' and two lines following.

Eh Joe

A piece for television

Written in English in April-May 1965. First televised on BBC2 on 4 July 1966. First published by Faber and Faber, London, in 1967.

Joe, late fifties, grey hair, old dressing-gown, carpet slippers, in his room.

1. Joe seen from behind sitting on edge of bed, intent pose, getting up, going to window, opening window, looking out, closing window, drawing curtain, standing intent.

2. Joe do. (=from behind) going from window to door, opening door, looking out, closing door, locking door, drawing hanging before door, standing intent.

3. Joe do. going from door to cupboard, opening cupboard, looking in, closing cupboard, locking cupboard, drawing hanging before cupboard, standing intent.

4. Joe do. going from cupboard to bed, kneeling down, looking under bed, getting up, sitting down on edge of bed as when discovered, beginning to relax.

5. Joe seen from front sitting on edge of bed, relaxed, eyes closed. Hold, then dolly slowly in to closeup of face. First word of text stops this movement.

Camera

Joe's opening movements followed by camera at constant remove, Joe full length in frame throughout. No need to record room as whole. After this opening pursuit, between first and final closeup of face, camera has nine slight moves in towards face, say four inches each time. Each move is stopped by voice resuming, never camera move and voice together. This would give position of camera when dolly stopped by first word of text as one yard from maximum closeup of face. Camera does not move between paragraphs till clear that pause (say three seconds) longer than between phrases. Then four inches in say four seconds when movement stopped by voice resuming.

Voice

Low, distinct, remote, little colour, absolutely steady rhythm, slightly slower than normal. Between phrases a beat of one second at least. Between paragraphs about seven, i.e. three before camera starts to advance and four for advance before it is stopped by voice resuming.

Face
Practically motionless throughout, eyes unblinking during paragraphs, impassive except in so far as it reflects mounting tension of *listening*. Brief zones of relaxation between paragraphs when perhaps voice has relented for the evening and intentness may relax variously till restored by voice resuming.

WOMAN'S VOICE:
    Joe...
    [*Eyes open, resumption of intentness.*]
    Joe...
    [*Full intentness.*]
    Thought of everything?... Forgotten nothing?... You're all right now, eh?... No one can see you now.... No one can get at you now.... Why don't you put out that light?... There might be a louse watching you.... Why don't you go to bed?... What's wrong with that bed, Joe?... You changed it, didn't you?... Made no difference?... Or is the heart already?... Crumbles when you lie down in the dark.... Dry rotten at last.... Eh Joe?

Camera move 1

    The best's to come, you said, that last time.... Hurrying me into my coat.... Last I was favoured with from you.... Say it you now, Joe, no one'll hear you.... Come on, Joe, no one can say it like you, say it again now and listen to yourself.... The best's to come.... You were right for once.... In the end.

Camera move 2

    You know that penny farthing hell you call your mind.... That's where you think this is coming from, don't you?...

That's where you heard your father . . . . Isn't that what
you told me? . . . Started in on you one June night and
went on for years . . . . On and off . . . . Behind the eyes . . . .
That's how you were able to throttle him in the end . . . .
Mental thuggee you called it . . . . One of your happiest
fancies . . . . Mental thuggee . . . . Otherwise he'd be plaguing
you yet . . . . Then your mother when her hour came . . . .
'Look up, Joe, look up, we're watching you' . . . . Weaker
and weaker till you laid her too . . . . Others . . . . All the
others . . . . Such love he got . . . . God knows why . . . .
Pitying love . . . . None to touch it . . . . And look at him
now . . . . Throttling the dead in his head.

Camera move 3

Anyone living love you now, Joe? . . . Anyone living sorry
for you now? . . . That slut that comes on Saturday, you
pay her, don't you? . . . Penny a hoist tuppence as long as
you like . . . Watch yourself you don't run short, Joe . . .
Ever think of that? . . . Eh Joe? . . . What it'd be if you ran
out of us . . . . Not another soul to still . . . . Sit there in his
stinking old wrapper hearing himself . . . . That lifelong
adorer . . . . Weaker and weaker till not a gasp left there
either . . . . Is it that you want? . . . Well preserved for his
age and the silence of the grave . . . . That old paradise you
were always harping on . . . . No Joe . . . . Not for the likes
of us.

Camera move 4

I was strong myself when I started . . . . In on you . . . .
Wasn't I, Joe? . . . Normal strength . . . . Like those summer
evenings in the Green . . . . In the early days . . . . Of our
idyll . . . . When we sat watching the ducks . . . . Holding
hands exchanging vows . . . . How you admired my elo-
cution! . . . Among other charms . . . . Voice like flint
glass . . . . To borrow your expression . . . . Powerful grasp of
language you had . . . . Flint glass . . . . You could have
listened to it for ever . . . . And now this . . . . Squeezed

down to this .... How much longer would you say? ... Till
the whisper .... You know .... When you can't hear the
words .... Just the odd one here and there .... That's the
worst .... Isn't it, Joe? ... Isn't that what you told me ....
Before we expire .... The odd word .... Straining to hear
.... Why must you do that? ... When you're nearly home
.... What matter then .... What we mean .... It should be
the best .... Nearly home again .... Another stilled ....
And it's the worst .... Isn't that what you said? ... The
whisper .... The odd word .... Straining to hear .... Brain
tired squeezing .... It stops in the end .... You stop it in
the end .... Imagine if you couldn't .... Ever think of
that? ... If it went on .... The whisper in your head ....
Me whispering at you in your head .... Things you can't
catch .... On and off .... Till you join us .... Eh Joe?

Camera move 5

How's your Lord these days? ... Still worth having? ... Still
lapping it up? ... The passion of our Joe .... Wait till He
starts talking to you .... When you're done with yourself
.... All your dead dead .... Sitting there in your foul old
wrapper .... Very fair health for a man of your years ....
Just that lump in your bubo .... Silence of the grave without
the maggots .... To crown your labours .... Till one night
.... 'Thou fool thy soul' .... Put your thugs on that ....
Eh Joe? ... Ever think of that? ... When He starts in on you
.... When you're done with yourself .... If you ever are.

Camera move 6

Yes, great love God knows why .... Even me .... But I
found a better .... As I hope you heard .... Preferable in
all respects .... Kinder .... Stronger .... More intelligent
.... Better looking .... Cleaner .... Truthful .... Faithful
.... Sane ... Yes .... I did all right.

Camera move 7

> But there was one didn't .... You know the one I mean,
> Joe .... The green one .... The narrow one .... Always
> pale .... The pale eyes .... Spirit made light .... To
> borrow your expression .... The way they opened after
> .... Unique .... Are you with me now? ... Eh Joe? ...
> There was love for you .... The best's to come, you said
> .... Bundling her into her Avoca sack .... Her fingers
> fumbling with the big horn buttons .... Ticket in your
> pocket for the first morning flight .... You've had her,
> haven't you? ... You've laid her? ... Of course he has ....
> She went young .... No more old lip from her.

Camera move 8

> Ever know what happened? ... She didn't say? ... Just the
> announcement in the *Independent* .... 'On Mary's beads we
> plead her needs and in the Holy Mass' .... Will I tell you? ...
> Not interested? ... Well I will just the same .... I think you
> should know .... That's right, Joe, squeeze away ....
> Don't lose heart now .... When you're nearly home ....
> I'll soon be gone .... The last of them .... Unless that
> poor old slut loves you .... Then yourself .... That old
> bonfire .... Years of that stink .... Then the silence ....
> A dollop of that .... To crown all .... Till His Nibs ....
> One dirty winter night .... 'Mud thou art.'

Camera move 9

> All right .... Warm summer night .... All sleeping ....
> Sitting on the edge of her bed in her lavender slip ....
> You know the one .... Ah she knew you, heavenly
> powers! ... Faint lap of sea through open window ....
> Gets up in the end and slips out as she is .... Moon ....
> Stock .... Down the garden and under the viaduct ....

Sees from the seaweed the tide is flowing.... Goes on
down to the edge and lies down with her face in the
wash.... Cut a long story short doesn't work....
Gets up in the end sopping wet and back up to the
house.... Gets out the Gillette.... The make you
recommended for her body hair.... Back down the
garden and under the viaduct.... Takes the blade from the
holder and lies down at the edge on her side.... Cut
another long story short doesn't work either.... You
know how she always dreaded pain.... Tears a strip from
the slip and ties it round the scratch.... Gets up in the
end and back up to the house.... Slip clinging the way
wet silk will.... This all new to you, Joe?... Eh Joe?...
Gets the tablets and back down the garden and under the
viaduct.... Takes a few on the way.... Unconscionable
hour by now.... Moon going off the shore behind the
hill.... Stands a bit looking at the beaten silver.... Then
starts along the edge to a place further down near the
Rock.... Imagine what in her mind to make her do that....
Imagine.... Trailing her feet in the water like a child....
Takes a few more on the way.... Will I go on, Joe?...
Eh Joe?... Lies down in the end with her face a few feet
from the tide.... Clawing at the shingle now.... Has it all
worked out this time.... Finishes the tube.... There's
love for you.... Eh Joe?... Scoops a little cup for her
face in the stones.... The green one.... The narrow one
.... Always pale.... The pale eyes.... The look they
shed before.... The way they opened after.... Spirit
made light.... Wasn't that your description, Joe?...
[*Voice drops to whisper, almost inaudible except words in
italics.*]
All right.... You've had the best.... Now *imagine*....
Before she goes.... Face in the cup.... Lips on a *stone*
.... Taking Joe with her.... Light gone....'*Joe Joe*'....
No sound.... To the *stones*.... Say it you now, no one'll
hear you.... Say 'Joe' it parts the *lips*... *Imagine* the
hands.... The *solitaire*.... Against a *stone*.... Imagine
the *eyes*.... Spiritlight.... Month of June.... What year
of your Lord?... *Breasts* in the stones.... And the *hands*

.... Before they go .... *Imagine* the hands .... What are they at?... In the *stones* ....
[*Image fades, voice as before.*]
What are they fondling?... Till they go .... *There's love for you* .... Isn't it, Joe?... Wasn't it, Joe?... *Eh Joe?*... Wouldn't you say?... Compared to us .... Compared to Him .... *Eh Joe?*...
[*Voice and image out. End.*]

Breath

Written in English some time before it was sent to New York, in 1969, in response to Kenneth Tynan's request for a contribution to his review *Oh! Calcutta!* The original text first published in *Gambit*, vol. 4, no. 16 (1970). First produced at the Eden' Theater, New York, on 16 June 1969. First performed in Britain at the Close Theatre Club, Glasgow, in October 1969.

1. Faint light on stage littered with miscellaneous rubbish. Hold about five seconds.
2. Faint brief cry and immediately inspiration and slow increase of light together reaching maximum together in about ten seconds. Silence and hold about five seconds.
3. Expiration and slow decrease of light together reaching minimum together (light as in 1) in about ten seconds and immediately cry as before. Silence and hold about five seconds.

CURTAIN

RUBBISH
No verticals, all scattered and lying.

CRY
Instant of recorded vagitus. Important that two cries be identical, switching on and off strictly synchronized light and breath.

BREATH
Amplified recording.

MAXIMUM LIGHT
Not bright. If 0 = dark and 10 = bright, light should move from about 3 to 6 and back.

Not I

Written in English in spring 1972. First performed at the Forum Theater of the Lincoln Center, New York, in September 1972. First published by Faber and Faber, London, in 1973. First performed in Britain at the Royal Court Theatre, London, on 16 January 1973.

Note

Movement: this consists in simple sideways raising of arms from sides and their falling back, in a gesture of helpless compassion. It lessens with each recurrence till scarcely perceptible at third. There is just enough pause to contain it as MOUTH recovers from vehement refusal to relinquish third person.

Stage in darkness but for MOUTH, *upstage audience right, about 8 feet above stage level, faintly lit from close-up and below, rest of face in shadow. Invisible microphone.*

AUDITOR, *downstage audience left, tall standing figure, sex undeterminable, enveloped from head to foot in loose black djellaba, with hood, fully faintly lit, standing on invisible podium about 4 feet high shown by attitude alone to be facing diagonally across stage intent on* MOUTH, *dead still throughout but for four brief movements where indicated. See Note.*

As house lights down MOUTH's *voice unintelligible behind curtain. House lights out. Voice continues unintelligible behind curtain, 10 seconds. With rise of curtain ad-libbing from text as required leading when curtain fully up and attention sufficient into:*

MOUTH: .... out... into this world ... this world ... tiny little thing ... before its time ... in a godfor— ... what? .. girl? .. yes ... tiny little girl ... into this ... out into this ... before her time ... godforsaken hole called ... called ... no matter ... parents unknown ... unheard of ... he having vanished ... thin air ... no sooner buttoned up his breeches ... she similarly ... eight months later ... almost to the tick ... so no love ... spared that ... no love such as normally vented on the ... speechless infant ... in the home ... no ... nor indeed for that matter any of any kind ... no love of any kind ... at any subsequent stage ... so typical affair ... nothing of any note till coming up to sixty when— ... what? .. seventy? .. good God! .. coming up to seventy ... wandering in a field ... looking aimlessly for cowslips ... to make a ball ... a few steps then stop ... stare into space ... then on ... a few more ... stop and stare again ... so on ... drifting around ... when suddenly ... gradually ... all went out ... all that early April morn-

ing light . . . and she found herself in the— . . . what? . .
who? . . no! . . she! . . [*Pause and movement 1.*] . . . found
herself in the dark . . . and if not exactly . . . insentient . . .
insentient . . . for she could still hear the buzzing . . . so-
called . . . in the ears . . . and a ray of light came and went . . .
came and went . . . such as the moon might cast . . . drifting
. . . in and out of cloud . . . but so dulled . . . feeling . . .
feeling so dulled . . . she did not know . . . what position she
was in . . . imagine! . . what position she was in! . . whether
standing . . . or sitting . . . but the brain— . . . what? . .
kneeling? . . yes . . . whether standing . . . or sitting . . . or
kneeling . . . but the brain— . . . what? . . lying? . . yes . . .
whether standing . . . or sitting . . . or kneeling . . . or lying . . .
but the brain still . . . still . . . in a way . . . for her first
thought was . . . oh long after . . . sudden flash . . . brought
up as she had been to believe . . . with the other waifs . . . in
a merciful . . . [*Brief laugh.*] . . . God . . . [*Good laugh.*] . . .
first thought was . . . oh long after . . . sudden flash . . . she
was being punished . . . for her sins . . . a number of which
then . . . further proof if proof were needed . . . flashed
through her mind . . . one after another . . . then dismissed
as foolish . . . oh long after . . . this thought dismissed . . . as
she suddenly realized . . . gradually realized . . . she was not
suffering . . . imagine! . . not suffering! . . indeed could not
remember . . . off-hand . . . when she had suffered less . . .
unless of course she was . . . *meant* to be suffering . . .
ha! . . *thought* to be suffering . . . just as the odd time . . . in
her life . . . when clearly intended to be having pleasure . . .
she was in fact . . . having none . . . not the slightest . . . in
which case of course . . . that notion of punishment . . . for
some sin or other . . . or for the lot . . . or no particular
reason . . . for its own sake . . . thing she understood per-
fectly . . . that notion of punishment . . . which had first
occurred to her . . . brought up as she had been to believe . . .
with the other waifs . . . in a merciful . . . [*Brief laugh.*] . . .
God . . . [*Good laugh.*] . . . first occurred to her . . . then
dismissed . . . as foolish . . . was perhaps not so foolish . . .
after all . . . so on . . . all that . . . vain reasonings . . . till
another thought . . . oh long after . . . sudden flash . . . very

foolish really but— . . . what? . . the buzzing? . . yes . . . all
the time the buzzing . . . so-called . . . in the ears . . . though
of course actually . . . not in the ears at all . . . in the skull . . .
dull roar in the skull . . . and all the time this ray or beam
. . . like moonbeam . . . but probably not . . . certainly not . . .
always the same spot . . . now bright . . . now shrouded . . .
but always the same spot . . . as no moon could . . . no . . .
no moon . . . just all part of the same wish to . . . torment
. . . though actually in point of fact . . . not in the least . . .
not a twinge . . . so far . . . ha! . . so far . . . this other thought
then . . . oh long after . . . sudden flash . . . very foolish
really but so like her . . . in a way . . . that she might do well
to . . . groan . . . on and off . . . writhe she could not . . . as if
in actual agony . . . but could not . . . could not bring herself . . . some flaw in her make-up . . . incapable of deceit . . .
or the machine . . . more likely the machine . . . so dis-
connected . . . never got the message . . . or powerless to
respond . . . like numbed . . . couldn't make the sound . . .
not any sound . . . no sound of any kind . . . no screaming
for help for example . . . should she feel so inclined . . .
scream . . . [Screams.] . . . then listen . . . [Silence.]
. . . scream again . . . [Screams again.] . . . then listen again . . .
[Silence.] . . . no . . . spared that . . . all silent as the grave . . .
no part— . . . what? . . the buzzing? . . yes . . . all silent but for
the buzzing . . . so-called . . . no part of her moving . . . that
she could feel . . . just the eyelids . . . presumably . . . on and
off . . . shut out the light . . . reflex they call it . . . no feeling
of any kind . . . but the lids . . . even best of times . . . who
feels them? . . opening . . . shutting . . . all that moisture . . .
but the brain still . . . still sufficiently . . . oh very much
so! . . at this stage . . . in control . . . under control . . . to
question even this . . . for on that April morning . . . so it
reasoned . . . that April morning . . . she fixing with her eye
. . . a distant bell . . . as she hastened towards it . . . fixing it
with her eye . . . lest it elude her . . . had not all gone out . . .
all that light . . . of itself . . . without any . . . any . . . on her
part . . . so on . . . so on it reasoned . . . vain questionings . . .
and all dead still . . . sweet silent as the grave . . . when
suddenly . . . gradually . . . she realiz— . . . what? . . the

buzzing?.. yes ... all dead still but for the buzzing ...
when suddenly she realized ... words were— ... what?..
who?.. no!.. she!.. [*Pause and movement 2.*] ...realized
...words were coming ... imagine!.. words were coming
... a voice she did not recognize ... at first ... so long since
it had sounded ... then finally had to admit ... could be
none other ... than her own ... certain vowel sounds ...
she had never heard ... elsewhere ... so that people would
stare ... the rare occasions ... once or twice a year ...
always winter some strange reason ... stare at her uncom-
prehending ... and now this stream ... steady stream ...
she who had never ... on the contrary ... practically
speechless ... all her days ... how she survived!.. even
shopping ... out shopping ... busy shopping centre ...
supermart ... just hand in the list ... with the bag ... old
black shopping bag ... then stand there waiting ... any
length of time ... middle of the throng ... motionless ...
staring into space ... mouth half open as usual ... till it
was back in her hand ... the bag back in her hand ... then
pay and go ... not as much as good-bye ... how she
survived!.. and now this stream ... not catching the half
of it ... not the quarter ... no idea ... what she was saying
...imagine!.. no idea what she was saying!.. till she began
trying to ... delude herself ... it was not hers at all ... not
her voice at all ... and no doubt would have ... vital she
should ... was on the point ... after long efforts ... when
suddenly she felt ... gradually she felt ... her lips moving
... imagine!.. her lips moving!.. as of course till then she
had not ... and not alone the lips ... the cheeks ... the
jaws ... the whole face ... all those— ... what?.. the
tongue?.. yes ... the tongue in the mouth ... all those
contortions without which ... no speech possible ... and
yet in the ordinary way ... not felt at all ... so intent one
is ... on what one is saying ... the whole being ... hanging
on its words ... so that not only she had ... had she ...
not only had she ... to give up ... admit hers alone ... her
voice alone ... but this other awful thought ... oh long
after ... sudden flash ... even more awful if possible ...
that feeling was coming back ... imagine!.. feeling coming

back! .. starting at the top ... then working down ... the
whole machine ... but no ... spared that ... the mouth
alone ... so far ... ha! .. so far ... then thinking ... oh long
after ... sudden flash ... it can't go on ... all this ... all
that ... steady stream ... straining to hear ... make something of it ... and her own thoughts ... make something of
them ... all— ... what? .. the buzzing? .. yes ... all the time
the buzzing ... so-called ... all that together ... imagine! ..
whole body like gone ... just the mouth ... lips ... cheeks ...
jaws ... never— ... what? .. tongue? .. yes ... lips ... cheeks
... jaws ... tongue ... never still a second ... mouth on
fire ... stream of words ... in her ear ... practically in her
ear ... not catching the half ... not the quarter ... no
idea what she's saying ... imagine! .. no idea what she's
saying! .. and can't stop ... no stopping it ... she who
but a moment before ... but a moment! .. could not
make a sound ... no sound of any kind ... now can't
stop ... imagine! .. can't stop the stream ... and the whole
brain begging ... something begging in the brain ... begging
the mouth to stop ... pause a moment ... if only for a
moment ... and no response ... as if it hadn't heard ... or
couldn't ... couldn't pause a second ... like maddened ...
all that together ... straining to hear ... piece it together
... and the brain ... raving away on its own ... trying to
make sense of it ... or make it stop ... or in the past ...
dragging up the past ... flashes from all over ... walks
mostly ... walking all her days ... day after day ... a few
steps then stop ... stare into space ... then on ... a few
more ... stop and stare again ... so on ... drifting around
... day after day ... or that time she cried ... the one time
she could remember ... since she was a baby ... must have
cried as a baby ... perhaps not ... not essential to life ...
just the birth cry to get her going ... breathing ... then no
more till this ... old hag already ... sitting staring at her
hand ... where was it? .. Croker's Acres ... one evening on
the way home ... home! .. a little mound in Croker's Acres
... dusk ... sitting staring at her hand ... there in her lap ...
palm upward ... suddenly saw it wet ... the palm ... tears
presumably ... hers presumably ... no one else for miles ...

no sound ... just the tears ... sat and watched them dry ...
all over in a second ... or grabbing at straw ... the brain ...
flickering away on its own ... quick grab and on ... nothing
there ... on to the next ... bad as the voice ... worse ...
as little sense ... all that together ... can't— ... what? ..
the buzzing? .. yes ... all the time the buzzing ... dull
roar like falls ... and the beam ... flickering on and off ...
starting to move around ... like moonbeam but not ...
all part of the same ... keep an eye on that too ... corner
of the eye ... all that together ... can't go on ... God is
love ... she'll be purged ... back in the field ... morning
sun ... April ... sink face down in the grass ... nothing
but the larks ... so on ... grabbing at the straw ... straining
to hear ... the odd word ... make some sense of it ...
whole body like gone ... just the mouth ... like maddened
... and can't stop ... no stopping it ... something she— ...
something she had to— ... what? .. who? .. no! .. she! ..
[*Pause and movement 3.*] ... something she had to— ...
what? .. the buzzing? .. yes ... all the time the buzzing ...
dull roar ... in the skull ... and the beam ... ferreting
around ... painless ... so far ... ha! .. so far ... then
thinking ... oh long after ... sudden flash ... perhaps
something she had to ... had to ... tell ... could that be
it? .. something she had to ... tell ... tiny little thing ...
before its time ... godforsaken hole ... no love ... spared
that ... speechless all her days ... practically speechless ...
how she survived! .. that time in court ... what had she
to say for herself ... guilty or not guilty ... stand up
woman ... speak up woman ... stood there staring into
space ... mouth half open as usual ... waiting to be led
away ... glad of the hand on her arm ... now this ... something she had to tell ... could that be it? .. something that
would tell ... how it was ... how she— ... what? .. had
been? .. yes ... something that would tell how it had been
... how she had lived ... lived on and on ... guilty or not
... on and on ... to be sixty ... something she— ... what? ..
seventy? .. good God! .. on and on to be seventy ... something she didn't know herself ... wouldn't know if she
heard ... then forgiven ... God is love ... tender mercies

. . . new every morning . . . back in the field . . . April
morning . . . face in the grass . . . nothing but the larks . . .
pick it up there . . . get on with it from there . . . another
few— . . . what? . . not that? . . nothing to do with that? . .
nothing she could tell? . . all right . . . nothing she could tell
. . . try something else . . . think of something else . . . oh
long after . . . sudden flash . . . not that either . . . all right . . .
something else again . . . so on . . . hit on it in the end . . .
think everything keep on long enough . . . then forgiven . . .
back in the— . . . what? . . not that either? . . nothing to do
with that either? . . nothing she could think? . . all right . . .
nothing she could tell . . . nothing she could think . . .
nothing she— . . . what? . . who? . . no! . . she! . . [*Pause and
movement 4.*] . . . tiny little thing . . . out before its time . . .
godforsaken hole . . . no love . . . spared that . . . speechless
all her days . . . practically speechless . . . even to herself . . .
never out loud . . . but not completely . . . sometimes
sudden urge . . . once or twice a year . . . always winter
some strange reason . . . the long evenings . . . hours of darkness . . . sudden urge to . . . tell . . . then rush out stop the
first she saw . . . nearest lavatory . . . start pouring it out . . .
steady stream . . . mad stuff . . . half the vowels wrong . . .
no one could follow . . . till she saw the stare she was
getting . . . then die of shame . . . crawl back in . . . once or
twice a year . . . always winter some strange reason . . . long
hours of darkness . . . now this . . . this . . . quicker and
quicker . . . the words . . . the brain . . . flickering away like
mad . . . quick grab and on . . . nothing there . . . on somewhere else . . . try somewhere else . . . all the time something begging . . . something in her begging . . . begging it all
to stop . . . unanswered . . . prayer unanswered . . . or unheard
. . . too faint . . . so on . . . keep on . . . trying . . . not knowing
what . . . what she was trying . . . what to try . . . whole
body like gone . . . just the mouth . . . like maddened . . . so
on . . . keep— . . . what? . . the buzzing? . . yes . . . all the time
the buzzing . . . dull roar like falls . . . in the skull . . . and
the beam . . . poking around . . . painless . . . so far . . . ha! . .
so far . . . all that . . . keep on . . . not knowing what . . . what
she was— . . . what? . . who? . . no! . . she! . . SHE! . . [*Pause.*]

... what she was trying ... what to try ... no matter ...
keep on ... [*Curtain starts down.*] ... hit on it in the end
... then back ... God is love ... tender mercies ... new
every morning ... back in the field ... April morning ...
face in the grass ... nothing but the larks ... pick it up—

[*Curtain fully down. House dark. Voice continues behind
curtain, unintelligible, 10 seconds, ceases as house lights
up.*]

That Time

Written in English between June 1974 and August 1975. First published by Grove Press, New York, in 1976. First performed at the Royal Court Theatre, London, on 20 May 1976.

Note

Moments of one and the same voice A B C relay one another without solution of continuity—apart from the two 10-second breaks. Yet the switch from one to another must be clearly faintly perceptible. If threefold source and context prove insufficient to produce this effect it should be assisted mechanically (e.g. threefold pitch).

Curtain. Stage in darkness. Fade up to LISTENER'S FACE *about
10 feet above stage level midstage off centre.*
*Old white face, long flaring white hair as if seen from above
outspread.*
Voices A B C *are his own coming to him from both sides and
above. They modulate back and forth without any break in
general flow except where silence indicated. See note.*
Silence 7 seconds. LISTENER'S EYES *are open. His breath
audible, slow and regular.*

A: that time you went back that last time to look was the ruin
    still there where you hid as a child when was that [*Eyes
    close.*] grey day took the eleven to the end of the line and
    on from there no no trams then all gone long ago that time
    you went back to look was the ruin still there where you
    hid as a child that last time not a tram left in the place
    only the old rails when was that

C: when you went in out of the rain always winter then always
    raining that time in the Portrait Gallery in off the street
    out of the cold and rain slipped in when no one was
    looking and through the rooms shivering and dripping till
    you found a seat marble slab and sat down to rest and dry
    off and on to hell out of there when was that

B: on the stone together in the sun on the stone at the edge of
    the little wood and as far as eye could see the wheat
    turning yellow vowing every now and then you loved each
    other just a murmur not touching or anything of that
    nature you one end of the stone she the other long low
    stone like millstone no looks just there on the stone in
    the sun with the little wood behind gazing at the wheat or
    eyes closed all still no sign of life not a soul abroad no
    sound

A: straight off the ferry and up with the nightbag to the high

street neither right nor left not a curse for the old scenes
the old names straight up the rise from the wharf to the
high street and there not a wire to be seen only the old
rails all rust when was that was your mother ah for God's
sake all gone long ago that time you went back that last
time to look was the ruin still there where you hid as a
child someone's folly

c: was your mother ah for God's sake all gone long ago all dust
the lot you the last huddled up on the slab in the old
green greatcoat with your arms round you whose else
hugging you for a bit of warmth to dry off and on to hell
out of there and on to the next not a living soul in the
place only yourself and the odd attendant drowsing
around in his felt shufflers not a sound to be heard only
every now and then a shuffle of felt drawing near then
dying away

b: all still just the leaves and ears and you too still on the stone
in a daze no sound not a word only every now and then to
vow you loved each other just a murmur one thing could
ever bring tears till they dried up altogether that thought
when it came up among the others floated up that scene

a: Foley was it Foley's Folly bit of a tower still standing all the
rest rubble and nettles where did you sleep no friend all
the homes gone was it that kip on the front where you no
she was with you then still with you then just the one
night in any case off the ferry one morning and back on
her the next to look was the ruin still there where none
ever came where you hid as a child slip off when no one
was looking and hide there all day long on a stone among
the nettles with your picture-book

c: till you hoisted your head and there before your eyes when
they opened a vast oil black with age and dirt someone
famous in his time some famous man or woman or even
child such as a young prince or princess some young prince
or princess of the blood black with age behind the glass
where gradually as you peered trying to make it out
gradually of all things a face appeared had you swivel on
the slab to see who it was there at your elbow

b: on the stone in the sun gazing at the wheat or the sky or the

eyes closed nothing to be seen but the wheat turning
yellow and the blue sky vowing every now and then you
loved each other just a murmur tears without fail till they
dried up altogether suddenly there in whatever thoughts
you might be having whatever scenes perhaps way back in
childhood or the womb worst of all or that old Chinaman
long before Christ born with long white hair

C: never the same after that never quite the same but that was
nothing new if it wasn't this it was that common occur-
rence something you could never be the same after
crawling about year after year sunk in your lifelong mess
muttering to yourself who else you'll never be the same
after this you were never the same after that

A: or talking to yourself who else out loud imaginary con-
versations there was childhood for you ten or eleven on a
stone among the giant nettles making it up now one voice
now another till you were hoarse and they all sounded the
same well on into the night some moods in the black dark
or moonlight and they all out on the roads looking for you

B: or by the window in the dark harking to the owl not a
thought in your head till hard to believe harder and harder
to believe you ever told anyone you loved them or anyone
you till just one of those things you kept making up to
keep the void out just another of those old tales to keep
the void from pouring in on top of you the shroud
[Silence 10 seconds. Breath audible. After 3 seconds eyes
open.]

C: never the same but the same as what for God's sake did you
ever say I to yourself in your life come on now [Eyes close.]
could you ever say I to yourself in your life turning-point
that was a great word with you before they dried up
altogether always having turning-points and never but the
one the first and last that time curled up worm in slime
when they lugged you out and wiped you off and
straightened you up never another after that never looked
back after that was that the time or was that another time

B: muttering that time altogether on the stone in the sun or that
time together on the towpath or that time together in the
sand that time that time making it up from there as best

you could always together somewhere in the sun on the
towpath facing downstream into the sun sinking and the
bits of flotsam coming from behind and drifting on or
caught in the reeds the dead rat it looked like came on
you from behind and went drifting on till you could see
it no more

A : that time you went back to look was the ruin still there
where you hid as a child that last time straight off the
ferry and up the rise to the high street to catch the eleven
neither right nor left only one thought in your head not
a curse for the old scenes the old names just head down
press on up the rise to the top and there stood waiting
with the nightbag till the truth began to dawn

C : when you started not knowing who you were from Adam
trying how that would work for a change not knowing
who you were from Adam no notion who it was saying
what you were saying whose skull you were clapped up
in whose moan had you the way you were was that the
time or was that another time there alone with the
portraits of the dead black with dirt and antiquity and the
dates on the frames in case you might get the century
wrong not believing it could be you till they put you out
in the rain at closing-time

B : no sight of the face or any other part never turned to her nor
she to you always parallel like on an axle-tree never turned
to each other just blurs on the fringes of the field no
touching or anything of that nature always space between
if only an inch no pawing in the manner of flesh and blood
no better than shades no worse if it wasn't for the vows

A : no getting out to it that way so what next no question of
asking not another word to the living as long as you lived
so foot it up in the end to the station bowed half double
get out to it that way all closed down and boarded up Doric
terminus of the Great Southern and Eastern all closed
down and the colonnade crumbling away so what next

C : the rain and the old rounds trying making it up that way as
you went along how it would work that way for a change
never having been how never having been would work the
old rounds trying to wangle you into it tottering and

      muttering all over the parish till the words dried up and the head dried up and the legs dried up whosever they were or it gave up whoever it was

B: stock still always stock still like that time on the stone or that time in the sand stretched out parallel in the sand in the sun gazing up at the blue or eyes closed blue dark blue dark stock still side by side scene float up and there you were wherever it was

A: gave it up gave up and sat down on the steps in the pale morning sun no those steps got no sun somewhere else then gave up and off somewhere else and down on a step in the pale sun a doorstep say someone's doorstep for it to be time to get on the night ferry and out to hell out of there no need sleep anywhere not a curse for the old scenes the old names the passers pausing to gape at you quick gape then pass pass on pass by on the other side

B: stock still side by side in the sun then sink and vanish without your having stirred any more than the two knobs on a dumbbell except the lids and every now and then the lips to vow and all around all still all sides wherever it might be no stir or sound only faintly the leaves in the little wood behind or the ears or the bent or the reeds as the case might be of man no sight of man or beast no sight or sound

C: always winter then always raining always slipping in somewhere when no one would be looking in off the street out of the cold and rain in the old green holeproof coat your father left you places you hadn't to pay to get in like the Public Library that was another great thing free culture far from home or the Post Office that was another another place another time

A: huddled on the doorstep in the old green greatcoat in the pale sun with the nightbag needless on your knees not knowing where you were little by little not knowing where you were or when you were or what for place might have been uninhabited for all you knew like that time on the stone the child on the stone where none ever came [*Silence 10 seconds. Breath audible. After 3 seconds eyes open.*]

B: or alone in the same the same scenes making it up that way
   to keep it going keep it out on the stone [*Eyes close.*]
   alone on the end of the stone with the wheat and blue or
   the towpath alone on the towpath with the ghosts of the
   mules the drowned rat or bird or whatever it was floating
   off into the sunset till you could see it no more nothing
   stirring only the water and the sun going down till it went
   down and you vanished all vanished

A: none ever came but the child on the stone among the giant
   nettles with the light coming in where the wall had
   crumbled away poring on his book well on into the night
   some moods the moonlight and they all out on the roads
   looking for him or making up talk breaking up two or
   more talking to himself being together that way where
   none ever came

C: always winter then endless winter year after year as if it
   couldn't end the old year never end like time could go no
   further that time in the Post Office all bustle Christmas
   bustle in off the street when no one was looking out of the
   cold and rain pushed open the door like anyone else and
   straight for the table neither right nor left with all the
   forms and the pens on their chains sat down first vacant
   seat and were taking a look round for a change before
   drowsing away

B: or that time alone on your back in the sand and no vows to
   break the peace when was that an earlier time a later time
   before she came after she went or both before she came
   after she was gone and you back in the old scene wherever
   it might be might have been the same old scene before as
   then then as after with the rat or the wheat the yellowing
   ears or that time in the sand the glider passing over that
   time you went back soon after long after

A: eleven or twelve in the ruin on the flat stone among the
   nettles in the dark or moonlight muttering away now one
   voice now another there was childhood for you till there
   on the step in the pale sun you heard yourself at it again
   not a curse for the passers pausing to gape at the scandal
   huddled there in the sun where it had no warrant clutching
   the nightbag drooling away out loud eyes closed and the

      white hair pouring out down from under the hat and so sat
      on in that pale sun forgetting it all

c: perhaps fear of ejection having clearly no warrant in the
      place to say nothing of the loathsome appearance so this
      look round for once at your fellow bastards thanking God
      for once bad and all as you were you were not as they till
      it dawned that for all the loathing you were getting you
      might as well not have been there at all the eyes passing
      over you and through you like so much thin air was that
      the time or was that another time another place another
      time

b: the glider passing over never any change same blue skies
      nothing ever changed but she with you there or not on
      your right hand always the right hand on the fringe of the
      field and every now and then in the great peace like a
      whisper so faint she loved you hard to believe you even
      you made up that bit till the time came in the end

a: making it all up on the doorstep as you went along making
      yourself all up again for the millionth time forgetting it all
      where you were and what for Foley's Folly and the lot the
      child's ruin you came to look was it still there to hide in
      again till it was night and time to go till that time came

c: the Library that was another place another time that time
      you slipped in off the street out of the cold and rain
      when no one was looking what was it then you were never
      the same after never again after something to do with dust
      something the dust said sitting at the big round table with
      a bevy of old ones poring on the page and not a sound

b: that time in the end when you tried and couldn't by the
      window in the dark and the owl flown to hoot at someone
      else or back with a shrew to its hollow tree and not
      another sound hour after hour hour after hour not a sound
      when you tried and tried and couldn't any more no words
      left to keep it out so gave it up gave up there by the
      window in the dark or moonlight gave up for good and let
      it in and nothing the worse a great shroud billowing in all
      over you on top of you and little or nothing the worse
      little or nothing

a: back down to the wharf with the nightbag and the old green

greatcoat your father left you trailing the ground and the
white hair pouring out down from under the hat till that
time came on down neither right nor left not a curse for
the old scenes the old names not a thought in your head
only get back on board and away to hell out of it and
never come back or was that another time all that another
time was there ever any other time but that time away to
hell out of it all and never come back

c: not a sound only the old breath and the leaves turning and
then suddenly this dust whole place suddenly full of dust
when you opened your eyes from floor to ceiling nothing
only dust and not a sound only what was it it said come
and gone was that it something like that come and gone
come and gone no one come and gone in no time gone in
no time

[*Silence 10 seconds. Breath audible. After 3 seconds eyes
open. After 5 seconds smile, toothless for preference. Hold
5 seconds till fade out and curtain.*]

Footfalls

Written in English. Begun in March 1975 and substantially completed by November of that year. First published by Grove Press, New York, in 1976. First performed at the Royal Court Theatre, London, on 20 May 1976.

MAY (M), *dishevelled grey hair, worn grey wrap hiding feet, trailing.*
WOMAN'S VOICE (V) *from dark upstage.*
Strip: downstage, parallel with front, length nine steps, width one metre, a little off centre audience right.

L <u>r l r l r l r l r</u> ◄ R
  ► <u>l r l r l r l r l</u>

Pacing: starting with right foot (r), from right (R) to left (L), with left foot (l) from L to R.
Turn: rightabout at L, leftabout at R.
Steps: clearly audible rhythmic tread.
Lighting: dim, strongest at floor level, less on body, least on head.
Voices: both low and slow throughout.

Curtain. Stage in darkness.
Faint single chime. Pause as echoes die.
Fade up to dim on strip. Rest in darkness.
M *discovered pacing towards L. Turns at L. paces three more lengths, halts, facing front at R.*
Pause.

M: Mother. [*Pause. No louder.*] Mother.
   [*Pause.*]
V: Yes, May.
M: Were you asleep?
V: Deep asleep. [*Pause.*] I heard you in my deep sleep. [*Pause.*] There is no sleep so deep I would not hear you there. [*Pause.* M *resumes pacing. Four lengths. After first length, synchronous with steps.*] One two three four five six seven eight nine wheel one two three four five six seven eight nine wheel. [*Free.*] Will you not try to snatch a little sleep? [M *halts facing front at R. Pause.*]

M: Would you like me to inject you again?

V: Yes, but it is too soon.
   [*Pause.*]

M: Would you like me to change your position again?

V: Yes, but it is too soon.
   [*Pause.*]

M: Straighten your pillows? [*Pause.*] Change your drawsheet?
   [*Pause.*] Pass you the bedpan? [*Pause.*] The warming-pan?
   [*Pause.*] Dress your sores? [*Pause.*] Sponge you down?
   [*Pause.*] Moisten your poor lips? [*Pause.*] Pray with you?
   [*Pause.*] For you? [*Pause.*] Again.
   [*Pause.*]

V: Yes, but it is too soon.
   [*Pause.*]

M: What age am I now?

V: And I? [*Pause. No louder.*] And I?

M: Ninety.

V: So much?

M: Eighty-nine, ninety.

V: I had you late. [*Pause.*] In life. [*Pause.*] Forgive me again.
   [*Pause. No louder.*] Forgive me again.
   [M *resumes pacing. After one length halts facing front at L.*
   Pause.]

M: What age am I now?

V: In your forties.

M: So little?

V: I'm afraid so. [*Pause.* M *resumes pacing. After first turn at L.*]
   May. [*Pause. No louder.*] May.

M: [*Pacing.*] Yes, Mother.

V: Will you never have done? [*Pause.*] Will you never have done
   ...revolving it all?

M: [*Halting.*] It?

V: It all. [*Pause.*] In your poor mind. [*Pause.*] It all. [*Pause.*]
   It all.
   [M *resumes pacing. Five seconds. Fade out on strip.*
   All in darkness. Steps cease.
   Pause.
   Chime a little fainter. Pause for echoes.
   Fade up to a little less on strip. Rest in darkness.]

M *discovered facing front at R.*
Pause.]

V: I walk here now. [*Pause.*] Rather I come and stand. [*Pause.*]
At nightfall. [*Pause.*] She fancies she is alone. [*Pause.*] See
how still she stands, how stark, with her face to the wall.
[*Pause.*] How outwardly unmoved. [*Pause.*] She has not
been out since girlhood. [*Pause.*] Not out since girlhood.
[*Pause.*] Where is she, it may be asked. [*Pause.*] Why, in
the old home, the same where she— [*Pause.*] The same
where she began. [*Pause.*] Where it began. [*Pause.*] It all
began. [*Pause.*] But this, this, when did this begin? [*Pause.*]
When other girls of her age were out at . . . lacrosse she was
already here. [*Pause.*] At this. [*Pause.*] The floor here,
now bare, once was— [M *begins pacing. Steps a little
slower.*] But let us watch her move, in silence. [M *paces.
Towards end of second length.*] Watch how feat she
wheels. [M *turns, paces. Synchronous with steps third
length.*] Seven, eight, nine, wheel. [M *turns at L, paces one
more length, halts facing front at R.*] I say the floor here,
now bare, this strip of floor, once was carpeted, a deep
pile. Till one night, while still little more than a child, she
called her mother and said, Mother, this is not enough.
The mother: Not enough? May—the child's given name
—May: Not enough. The mother: What do you mean, May,
not enough, what can you possibly mean, May, not
enough? May: I mean, Mother, that I must hear the feet,
however faint they fall. The mother: The motion alone is
not enough? May: No, Mother, the motion alone is not
enough, I must hear the feet, however faint they fall.
[*Pause.* M *resumes pacing. With pacing.*] Does she still
sleep, it may be asked? Yes, some nights she does, in
snatches, bows her poor head against the wall and snatches
a little sleep. [*Pause.*] Still speak? Yes, some nights she
does, when she fancies none can hear. [*Pause.*] Tells how
it was. [*Pause.*] Tries to tell how it was. [*Pause.*] It all.
[*Pause.*] It all. [M *continues pacing. Five seconds. Fade
out on strip.*
All in darkness, Steps cease.
Pause.

Chime a little fainter still. Pause for echoes.
Fade up to a little less still on strip. Rest in darkness.
M discovered facing front at R.
Pause.]

M : Sequel. [*Pause. Begins pacing. Steps a little slower still. After
two lengths halts facing front at R. Pause.*] Sequel. A little
later, when she was quite forgotten, she began to— [*Pause.*]
A little later, when as though she had never been, it never
been, she began to walk. [*Pause.*] At nightfall. [*Pause.*]
Slip out at nightfall and into the little church by the north
door, always locked at that hour, and walk, up and down,
up and down, His poor arm. [*Pause.*] Some nights she would
halt, as one frozen by some shudder of the mind, and stand
stark still till she could move again. But many also were the
nights when she paced without pause, up and down, up and
down, before vanishing the way she came. [*Pause.*] No
sound. [*Pause.*] None at least to be heard. [*Pause.*] The semblance. [*Pause. Resumes pacing. After two lengths halts
facing front at R. Pause.*] The semblance. Faint, though by
no means invisible, in a certain light. [*Pause.*] Given the
right light. [*Pause.*] Grey rather than white, a pale shade
of grey. [*Pause.*] Tattered. [*Pause.*] A tangle of tatters.
[*Pause.*] Watch it pass—[*Pause.*]—watch her pass before the
candelabrum, how its flames, their light ... like moon
through passing rack. [*Pause.*] Soon then after she was
gone, as though never there, began to walk, up and down,
up and down, that poor arm. [*Pause.*] At nightfall. [*Pause.*]
That is to say, at certain seasons of the year, during
Vespers. [*Pause.*] Necessarily. [*Pause. Resumes pacing.
After one length halts facing front at L. Pause.*] Old Mrs
Winter, whom the reader will remember, old Mrs Winter,
one late autumn Sunday evening, on sitting down to
supper with her daughter after worship, after a few half-
hearted mouthfuls laid down her knife and fork and
bowed her head. What is it, Mother, said the daughter, a
most strange girl, though scarcely a girl any more ...
[*Brokenly.*] ... dreadfully un— ... [*Pause. Normal voice.*]
What is it, Mother, are you not feeling yourself? [*Pause.*]
Mrs W. did not at once reply. But finally, raising her head

and fixing Amy—the daughter's given name, as the reader
will remember—raising her head and fixing Amy full in the
eye she said—[*Pause.*]—she murmured, fixing Amy full in
the eye she murmured, Amy did you observe anything . . .
strange at Evensong? Amy: No, Mother, I did not. Mrs W:
Perhaps it was just my fancy. Amy: Just what exactly,
Mother, did you perhaps fancy it was? [*Pause.*] Just what
exactly, Mother, did you perhaps fancy this . . . strange
thing was you observed? [*Pause.*] Mrs W: You yourself
observed nothing . . . strange? Amy: No, Mother, I myself
did not, to put it mildly. Mrs W: What do you mean, Amy,
to put it mildly, what can you possibly mean, Amy,
to put it mildly? Amy: I mean, Mother, that to say I
observed nothing . . . strange is indeed to put it mildly.
For I observed nothing of any kind, strange or otherwise.
I saw nothing, heard nothing, of any kind. I was not there.
Mrs W: Not there? Amy: Not there. Mrs W: But I heard
you respond. [*Pause.*] I heard you say Amen. [*Pause.*]
How could you have responded if you were not there?
[*Pause.*] How could you possibly have said Amen if, as
you claim, you were not there? [*Pause.*] The love of God,
and the fellowship of the Holy Ghost, be with us all, now,
and for evermore. Amen. [*Pause.*] I heard you distinctly.
[*Pause. Resumes pacing. After three steps halts without
facing front. Long pause. Resumes pacing, halts facing
front at R. Long pause.*] Amy. [*Pause. No louder.*] Amy.
[*Pause.*] Yes, Mother. [*Pause.*] Will you never have done?
[*Pause.*] Will you never have done . . . revolving it all?
[*Pause.*] It? [*Pause.*] It all. [*Pause.*] In your poor mind.
[*Pause.*] It all. [*Pause.*] It all.
[*Pause. Fade out on strip. All in darkness.
Pause.
Chime even a little fainter still. Pause for echoes.
Fade up to even a little less still on strip.
No trace of* MAY.
*Hold ten seconds.
Fade out.*]

CURTAIN

Ghost Trio

A play for television

Written in English in 1975. First published by Grove Press, New York, in 1976. First televised on BBC2 on 17 April 1977.

FEMALE VOICE (V)
MALE FIGURE (F)

I Pre-action
II Action
III Re-action

Room: 6m. x 5m.

1 Door.
2 Window.
3 Mirror.
4 Pallet.
5 F seated by door.
6 F at window.
7 F at head of pallet.
A Position general view.
B Position medium shot.
C Position near shot of 5 and 1, 6 and 2, 7 and 3.

I

1. *Fade up to general view from A. 10 seconds.*
2. v: Good evening. Mine is a faint voice. Kindly tune accordingly. [*Pause.*] Good evening. Mine is a faint voice. Kindly tune accordingly. [*Pause.*] It will not be raised, nor lowered, whatever happens. [*Pause.*] Look. [*Long pause.*] The familiar chamber. [*Pause.*] At the far end a window. [*Pause.*] On the right the indispensable door. [*Pause.*] On the left, against the wall, some kind of pallet. [*Pause.*] The light: faint, omnipresent. No visible source. As if all luminous. Faintly luminous. No shadow. [*Pause.*] No shadow. Colour: none. All grey. Shades of grey. [*Pause.*] The colour grey if you wish, shades of the colour grey. [*Pause.*] Forgive my stating the obvious. [*Pause.*] Keep that sound down. [*Pause.*] Now look closer. [*Pause.*] Floor.
3. *Cut to close-up of floor. Smooth grey rectangle 0.70 m. × 1.50 m. 5 seconds.*
4. v: Dust. [*Pause.*] Having seen that specimen of floor you have seen it all. Wall.
5. *Cut to close-up of wall. Smooth grey rectangle 0.70 m. × 1.50 m. 5 seconds.*
6. v: Dust. [*Pause.*] Knowing this, the kind of wall—
7. *Close-up of wall continued. 5 seconds.*
8. v: The kind of floor—
9. *Cut to close-up of floor. 5 seconds.*
10. v: Look again.
11. *Cut to general view from A. 5 seconds.*
12. v: Door.
13. *Cut to close-up of whole door. Smooth grey rectangle 0.70 m. × 2 m. Imperceptibly ajar. No knob. Faint music. 5 seconds.*
14. v: Window.
15. *Cut to close-up of whole window. Opaque sheet of glass 0.70 m. × 1.50 m. Imperceptibly ajar. No knob. 5 seconds.*

16. v: Pallet.
17. *Cut to close-up from above of whole pallet. 0.70 × 2 m.
    Grey sheet. Grey rectangular pillow at window end. 5
    seconds.*
18. v: Knowing all this, the kind of pallet—
19. *Close-up of whole pallet continued. 5 seconds.*
20. v: The kind of window—
21. *Cut to close-up of whole window. 5 seconds.*
22. v: The kind of door—
23. *Cut to close-up of whole door. Faint music. 5 seconds.*
24. v: The kind of wall—
25. *Cut to close-up of wall as before. 5 seconds.*
26. v: The kind of floor.
27. *Cut to close-up of floor as before. 5 seconds.*
28. v: Look again.
29. *Cut to general view. 5 seconds.*
30. v: Sole sign of life a seated figure.
31. *Move in slowly from A to B whence medium shot of F and
    door. F is seated on a stool, bowed forward, face hidden,
    clutching with both hands a small cassette not identifiable
    as such at this range. Faint music. 5 seconds.*
32. *Move in from B to C whence near shot of F and door.
    Cassette now identifiable. Music slightly louder, 5 seconds.*
33. *Move in from C to close-up of head, hands, cassette.
    Clutching hands, head bowed, face hidden. Music slightly
    louder. 5 seconds.*
34. *Move slowly back to A via C and B (no stops). Music pro-
    gressively fainter till at level of B it ceases to be heard.*
35. *General view from A. 5 seconds.*

II

All from A except 26-29

1. v: He will now think he hears her.
2. F *raises head sharply, turns still crouched to door, fleeting face, tense pose. 5 seconds.*
3. v: No one.
4. F *relapses into opening pose, bowed over cassette. 5 seconds.*
5. v: Again.
6. *Same as 2.*
7. v: Now to door.
8. F *gets up, lays cassette on stool, goes to door, listens with right ear against door, back to camera. 5 seconds.*
9. v: No one. [*Pause 5 seconds.*] Open.
10. *With right hand* F *pushes door open half-way clockwise, looks out, back to camera. 2 seconds.*
11. v: No one.
12. F *removes hand from door which closes slowly of itself, stands irresolute, back to camera. 2 seconds.*
13. v: Now to window.
14. F *goes to window, stands irresolute, back to camera. 5 seconds.*
15. v: Open.
16. *With right hand* F *pushes window open half-way clockwise, looks out, back to camera. 5 seconds.*
17. v: No one.
18. F *removes hand from window which closes slowly of itself, stands irresolute, back to camera. 2 seconds.*
19. v: Now to pallet.
20. F *goes to head of pallet (window end), stands looking down at it. 5 seconds.*
21. F *turns to wall at head of pallet, goes to wall, looks at his face in mirror hanging on wall, invisible from A.*

22. v: [*Surprised.*] Ah!
23. *After 5 seconds F bows his head, stands before mirror with bowed head. 2 seconds.*
24. v: Now to door.
25. *F goes to stool, takes up cassette, sits, settles into opening pose, bowed over cassette. 2 seconds.*
26. *Same as I.31.*
27. *Same as I.32.*
28. *Same as I.33.*
29. *Same as I.34.*
30. *Same as I.35.*
31. v: He will now again think he hears her.
32. *Same as II.2.*
33. *F gets up, lays cassette on stool, goes to door, opens it as before, looks out, stoops forward. 10 seconds.*
34. *F straightens up, releases door which closes slowly of itself, stands irresolute, goes to stool, takes up cassette, sits irresolute, settles finally into opening pose, bowed over cassette. 5 seconds.*
35. *Faint music audible for first time at A. It grows louder. 5 seconds.*
36. v: Stop.
37. *Music stops. General view from A. 5 seconds.*
38. v: Repeat.

III

1. *Immediately after 'Repeat' cut to near shot from C of F and door. Music audible. 5 seconds.*

2. *Move in to close-up of head, hands, cassette. Music slightly louder. 5 seconds.*

3. *Music stops. Action II.2. 5 seconds.*

4. *Action II.4. Music resumes. 5 seconds.*

5. *Move back to near shot from C of F and door. Music audible. 5 seconds.*

6. *Music stops. Action II.2. Near shot from C of F and door. 5 seconds.*

7. *Action II.8. Near shot from C of stool, cassette, F with right ear to door. 5 seconds.*

8. *Action II.10. Crescendo creak of door opening. Near shot from C of stool, cassette, F with right hand holding door open. 5 seconds.*

9. *Cut to view of corridor seen from door. Long narrow (0.70 m.) grey rectangle between grey walls, empty, far end in darkness. 5 seconds.*

10. *Cut back to near shot from C of stool, cassette, F holding door open. 5 seconds.*

11. *Action II.12. Decrescendo creak of door slowly closing. Near shot from C of stool, cassette, F standing irresolute, door. 5 seconds.*

12. *Cut to close-up from above of cassette on stool, small grey rectangle on larger rectangle of seat. 5 seconds.*

13. *Cut back to near shot of stool, cassette, F standing irresolute, door. 5 seconds.*

14. *Action II.14 seen from C. Near shot from C of F and window. 5 seconds.*

15. *Action II.16 seen from C. Crescendo creak of window opening. Faint sound of rain. Near shot from C of F with right hand holding window open. 5 seconds.*

16. *Cut to view from window. Night. Rain falling in dim light. Sound of rain slightly louder. 5 seconds.*

17. *Cut back to near shot from C of* F *with right hand holding window open. Faint sound of rain. 5 seconds.*

18. *Action II.18 seen from C. Decrescendo creak of window slowly closing. Near shot from C of* F *and window. 5 seconds.*

19. *Action II.20 seen from C. Near shot from C of* F*, mirror, head of pallet.*

20. *Cut to close-up from above of whole pallet.*

21. *Move down to tighter close-up of pallet moving slowly from pillow to foot and back to pillow. 5 seconds on pillow.*

22. *Move back to close-up from above of whole pallet. 5 seconds.*

23. *Cut back to near shot from C of* F*, mirror, head of pallet. 5 seconds.*

24. *Cut to close-up of mirror reflecting nothing. Small grey rectangle (same dimensions as cassette) against larger rectangle of wall. 5 seconds.*

25. *Cut back to near shot from C of* F*, mirror, head of pallet. 5 seconds.*

26. *Action II.21 seen from C. Near shot from C of* F *and mirror. 5 seconds.*

27. *Cut to close-up of* F*'s face in mirror. 5 seconds. Eyes close. 5 seconds. Eyes open. 5 seconds. Head bows. Top of head in mirror. 5 seconds.*

28. *Cut back to near shot from C of* F *with bowed head, mirror, head of pallet. 5 seconds.*

29. *Action II.25 seen from C. Near shot from C of* F *settling into opening pose. Music audible once settled. 10 seconds.*

30. *Music stops. Action II.2 seen from C. Faint sound of steps approaching. They stop. Faint sound of knock on door. 5 seconds. Second knock, no louder. 5 seconds.*

31. *Action II.33 seen from C. Crescendo creak of door slowly opening. Near shot from C of stool, cassette,* F *holding door open, stooping forward. 10 seconds.*

32. *Cut to near shot of small boy full length in corridor before open door. Dressed in black oilskin with hood glistening with rain. White face raised to invisible* F*. 5 seconds. Boy shakes head faintly. Face still, raised. 5 seconds. Boy*

shakes head again. Face still, raised. 5 seconds. Boy turns and goes. Sound of receding steps. Register from the same position his slow recession till he vanishes in dark at end of corridor. 5 seconds on empty corridor.

33. *Cut back to near shot from C of stool, cassette,* F *holding door open. 5 seconds.*

34. *Action II.34 seen from C. Decrescendo creak of door slowly closing. 5 seconds.*

35. *Cut to general view from A. 5 seconds.*

36. *Music audible at A. It grows. 10 seconds.*

37. *With growing music move in slowly to close-up of head bowed right down over cassette now held in arms and invisible. Hold till end of Largo.*

38. *Silence.* F *raises head. Face seen clearly for second time. 10 seconds.*

39. *Move slowly back to A.*

40. *General view from A. 5 seconds.*

41. *Fade out.*

MUSIC

From Largo of Beethoven's Fifth Piano Trio (*The Ghost*):

I.13	*beginning bar 47*
I.23	*beginning bar 49*
I.31-34	*beginning bar 19*
II.26-29	*beginning bar 64*
II.35-36	*beginning bar 71*
III.1-2, 4-5	*beginning bar 26*
III.29	*beginning bar 64*
III.36 to end	*beginning bar 82*

. . . but the clouds . . .

A play for television

Written in English in October-November 1976. First televised on BBC2 on 17 April 1977. First published by Faber and Faber, London, in 1977.

M   Near shot from behind of man sitting on invisible stool bowed over invisible table. Light grey robe and skullcap. Dark ground. Same shot throughout.

M1 M in set. Hat and greatcoat dark, robe and skullcap light.

W   Close-up of woman's face reduced as far as possible to eyes and mouth. Same shot throughout.

S   Long shot of set empty or with M1. Same shot throughout.

V   M's voice.

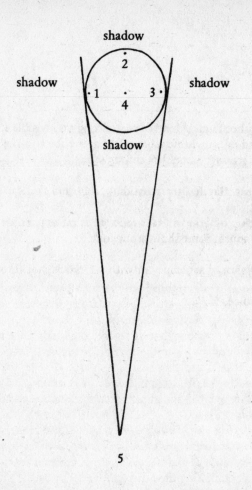

Set: circular, about 5 m. diameter, surrounded by deep shadow.

Lighting: a gradual lightening from dark periphery to maximum
light at centre.

1. West, roads.
2. North, sanctum.
3. East, closet.
4. Standing position.
5. Camera.

1. *Dark. 5 seconds.*
2. *Fade up to* M. *5 seconds.*
3. V: When I thought of her it was always night. I came in—
4. *Dissolve to* S *empty. 5 seconds.* M1 *in hat and greatcoat emerges from west shadow, advances five steps and stands facing east shadow. 2 seconds.*
5. V: No—
6. *Dissolve to* M. *2 seconds.*
7. V: No, that is not right. When she appeared it was always night. I came in—
8. *Dissolve to* S *empty. 5 seconds.* M1 *in hat and greatcoat emerges from west shadow, advances five steps and stands facing east shadow. 5 seconds.*
9. V: Right. Came in, having walked the roads since break of day, brought night home, stood listening [*5 seconds.*], finally went to closet—
10. M1 *advances five steps to disappear in east shadow. 2 seconds.*
11. V: Shed my hat and greatcoat, assumed robe and skull, reappeared—
12. M1 *in robe and skullcap emerges from east shadow, advances five steps and stands facing west shadow. 5 seconds.*
13. V: Reappeared and stood as before, only facing the other way, exhibiting the other outline [*5 seconds.*], finally turned and vanished—
14. M1 *turns right and advances five steps to disappear in north shadow. 5 seconds.*
15. V: Vanished within my little sanctum and crouched, where none could see me, in the dark.
16. *Dissolve to* M. *5 seconds.*
17. V: Let us now make sure we have got it right.
18. *Dissolve to* S *empty. 2 seconds.* M1 *in hat and greatcoat emerges from west shadow, advances five steps and stands facing east shadow. 2 seconds. He advances five steps to*

*disappear in east shadow. 2 seconds. He emerges in robe and
skullcap from east shadow, advances five steps and stands
facing west shadow. 2 seconds. He turns right and advances
five steps to disappear in north shadow. 2 seconds.*

19. V: Right.

20. *Dissolve to* M. *2 seconds.*

21. V: Then crouching there, in my little sanctum, in the dark,
    where none could see me, I began to beg, of her, to appear,
    to me. Such had long been my use and wont. No sound, a
    begging of the mind, to her, to appear, to me. Deep down
    into the dead of night, until I wearied, and ceased. Or of
    course until—

22. *Dissolve to* W. *2 seconds.*

23. *Dissolve to* M. *2 seconds.*

24. V: For had she never once appeared, all that time, would I
    have, could I have, gone on begging, all that time? Not just
    vanished within my little sanctum and busied myself with
    something else, or with nothing, busied myself with
    nothing? Until the time came, with break of day, to issue
    forth again, shed robe and skull, resume my hat and great-
    coat, and issue forth again, to walk the roads.

25. *Dissolve to* S *empty. 2 seconds.* M1 *in robe and skullcap
    emerges from north shadow, advances five steps and stands
    facing camera. 2 seconds. He turns left and advances five
    steps to disappear in east shadow. 2 seconds. He emerges in
    hat and greatcoat from east shadow, advances five steps
    and stands facing west shadow. 2 seconds. He advances five
    steps to disappear in west shadow. 2 seconds.*

26. V: Right.

27. *Dissolve to* M. *5 seconds.*

28. V: Let us now distinguish three cases. One: she appeared
    and—

29. *Dissolve to* W. *2 seconds.*

30. *Dissolve to* M. *2 seconds.*

31. V: In the same breath was gone. *2 seconds.* Two: she
    appeared and—

32. *Dissolve to* W. *5 seconds.*

33. V: Lingered. *5 seconds.* With those unseeing eyes I so begged
    when alive to look at me. *5 seconds.*

34. *Dissolve to* M. *2 seconds.*

35. V: Three: she appeared and—

36. *Dissolve to* W. *5 seconds.*

37. V: After a moment—

38. W*'s lips move, uttering inaudibly:* '. . . clouds . . . but the clouds . . . of the sky . . .', V *murmuring, synchronous with lips:* '. . . but the clouds . . .' *Lips cease. 5 seconds.*

39. V: Right.

40. *Dissolve to* M. *5 seconds.*

41. V: Let us now run through it again.

42. *Dissolve to* S *empty. 2 seconds.* M1 *in hat and greatcoat emerges from west shadow, advances five steps and stands facing east shadow. 2 seconds. He advances five steps to disappear in east shadow. 2 seconds. He emerges in robe and skullcap from east shadow, advances five steps and stands facing west shadow. 2 seconds. He turns right and advances five steps to disappear in north shadow. 2 seconds.*

43. *Dissolve to* M. *5 seconds.*

44. *Dissolve to* W. *2 seconds.*

45. *Dissolve to* M. *2 seconds.*

46. *Dissolve to* W. *5 seconds.*

47. V: Look at me. *5 seconds.*

48. *Dissolve to* M. *5 seconds.*

49. *Dissolve to* W. *2 seconds.* W*'s lips move, uttering inaudibly:* '. . . clouds . . . but the clouds . . . of the sky . . .', V *murmuring, synchronous with lips:* '. . . but the clouds . . .' *Lips cease. 5 seconds.*

50. V: Speak to me. *5 seconds.*

51. *Dissolve to* M. *5 seconds.*

52. V: Right. There was of course a fourth case, or case nought, as I pleased to call it, by far the commonest, in the proportion say of nine hundred and ninety-nine to one, or nine hundred and ninety-eight to two, when I begged in vain, deep down into the dead of night, until I wearied, and ceased, and busied myself with something else, more . . . rewarding, such as . . . such as . . . cube roots, for example, or with nothing, busied myself with nothing, that MINE, until the time came, with break of day, to issue forth again,

void my little sanctum, shed robe and skull, resume my hat
and greatcoat, and issue forth again, to walk the roads.
[*Pause.*] The back roads.

53. *Dissolve to* s *empty. 2 seconds.* M1 *in robe and skullcap
emerges from north shadow, advances five steps and stands
facing camera. 2 seconds. He turns left and advances five
steps to disappear in east shadow. 2 seconds. He emerges in
hat and greatcoat from east shadow, advances five steps
and stands facing west shadow. 2 seconds. He advances five
steps to disappear in west shadow. 2 seconds.*

54. v: Right.

55. *Dissolve to* M. *5 seconds.*

56. *Dissolve to* W. *5 seconds.*

57. v: '... but the clouds of the sky ... when the horizon fades
... or a bird's sleepy cry ... among the deepening shades ...'
5 seconds.

58. *Dissolve to* M. *5 seconds.*

59. *Fade out on* M.

60. *Dark. 5 seconds.*

A Piece of Monologue

Written in English for actor David Warrilow in 1979 and performed by him in New York in 1980. First published by *Kenyon Review* in 1979.

Curtain.
Faint diffuse light.
Speaker stands well off centre downstage audience left.
White hair, white nightgown, white socks.
Two metres to his left, same level, same height, standard lamp,
skull-sized white globe, faintly lit.
Just visible extreme right, same level, white foot of pallet bed.
Ten seconds before speech begins.
Thirty seconds before end of speech lamplight begins to fail.
Lamp out. Silence. SPEAKER, *globe, foot of pallet, barely visible*
in diffuse light.
Ten seconds.
Curtain.

SPEAKER: Birth was the death of him. Again. Words are few.
Dying too. Birth was the death of him. Ghastly grinning
ever since. Up at the lid to come. In cradle and crib. At
suck first fiasco. With the first totters. From mammy to
nanny and back. All the way. Bandied back and forth. So
ghastly grinning on. From funeral to funeral. To now. This
night. Two and a half billion seconds. Again. Two and a
half billion seconds. Hard to believe so few. From funeral
to funeral. Funerals of . . . he all but said of loved ones.
Thirty thousand nights. Hard to believe so few. Born dead
of night. Sun long sunk behind the larches. New needles
turning green. In the room dark gaining. Till faint light
from standard lamp. Wick turned low. And now. This
night. Up at nightfall. Every nightfall. Faint light in room.
Whence unknown. None from window. No. Next to none.
No such thing as none. Gropes to window and stares out.
Stands there staring out. Stock still staring out. Nothing
stirring in that black vast. Gropes back in the end to where
the lamp is standing. Was standing. When last went out.

Loose matches in right-hand pocket. Strikes one on his
buttock the way his father taught him. Takes off milk
white globe and sets it down. Match goes out. Strikes a
second as before. Takes off chimney. Smoke-clouded.
Holds it in left hand. Match goes out. Strikes a third as
before and sets it to wick. Puts back chimney. Match goes
out. Puts back globe. Turns wick low. Backs away to edge
of light and turns to face east. Blank wall. So nightly. Up.
Socks. Nightgown. Window. Lamp. Backs away to edge of
light and stands facing blank wall. Covered with pictures
once. Pictures of . . . he all but said of loved ones. Unframed.
Unglazed. Pinned to wall with drawing-pins. All shapes and
sizes. Down one after another. Gone. Torn to shreds and
scattered. Strewn all over the floor. Not at one sweep. No
sudden fit of . . . no word. Ripped from the wall and torn
to shreds one by one. Over the years. Years of nights.
Nothing on the wall now but the pins. Not all. Some out
with the wrench. Some still pinning a shred. So stands
there facing blank wall. Dying on. No more no less. No.
Less. Less to die. Ever less. Like light at nightfall. Stands
there facing east. Blank pinpocked surface once white in
shadow. Could once name them all. There was father. That
grey void. There mother. That other. There together.
Smiling. Wedding day. There all three. That grey blot.
There alone. He alone. So on. Not now. Forgotten. All
gone so long. Gone. Ripped off and torn to shreds.
Scattered all over the floor. Swept out of the way under
the bed and left. Thousand shreds under the bed with the
dust and spiders. All the . . . he all but said the loved ones.
Stands there facing the wall staring beyond. Nothing there
either. Nothing stirring there either. Nothing stirring anywhere. Nothing to be seen anywhere. Nothing to be heard
anywhere. Room once full of sounds. Faint sounds.
Whence unknown. Fewer and fainter as time wore on.
Nights wore on. None now. No. No such thing as none.
Rain some nights still slant against the panes. Or dropping
gentle on the place beneath. Even now. Lamp smoking
though wick turned low. Strange. Faint smoke issuing
through vent in globe. Low ceiling stained by night after

night of this. Dark shapeless blot on surface elsewhere
white. Once white. Stands facing wall after the various
motions described. That is up at nightfall and into gown
and socks. No. In them already. In them all night. All day.
All day and night. Up at nightfall in gown and socks and
after a moment to get his bearings gropes to window. Faint
light in room. Unutterably faint. Whence unknown. Stands
stock still staring out. Into black vast. Nothing there.
Nothing stirring. That he can see. Hear. Dwells thus as if
unable to move again. Or no will left to move again. Not
enough will left to move again. Turns in the end and
gropes to where he knows the lamp is standing. Thinks he
knows. Was last standing. When last went out. Match one
as described for globe. Two for chimney. Three for wick.
Chimney and globe back on. Turns wick low. Backs away
to edge of light and turns to face wall. East. Still as the
lamp by his side. Gown and socks white to take faint light.
Once white. Hair white to take faint light. Foot of pallet
just visible edge of frame. Once white to take faint light.
Stands there staring beyond. Nothing. Empty dark. Till
first word always the same. Night after night the same.
Birth. Then slow fade up of a faint form. Out of the dark.
A window. Looking west. Sun long sunk behind the
larches. Light dying. Soon none left to die. No. No such
thing as no light. Starless moonless heaven. Dies on to
dawn and never dies. There in the dark that window.
Night slowly falling. Eyes to the small pane gaze at that
first night. Turn from it in the end to face the darkened
room. There in the end slowly a faint hand. Holding aloft
a lighted spill. In the light of spill faintly the hand and
milkwhite globe. Then second hand. In light of spill.
Takes off globe and disappears. Reappears empty. Takes
off chimney. Two hands and chimney in light of spill.
Spill to wick. Chimney back on. Hand with spill disappears.
Second hand disappears. Chimney alone in gloom. Hand
reappears with globe. Globe back on. Turns wick low.
Disappears. Pale globe alone in gloom. Glimmer of brass
bedrail. Fade. Birth the death of him. That nevoid smile.
Thirty thousand nights. Stands at edge of lamplight staring

beyond. Into dark whole again. Window gone. Hands gone. Light gone. Gone. Again and again. Again and again gone. Till dark slowly parts again. Grey light. Rain pelting. Umbrellas round a grave. Seen from above. Streaming black canopies. Black ditch beneath. Rain bubbling in the black mud. Empty for the moment. That place beneath. Which . . . he all but said which loved one? Thirty seconds. To add to the two and a half billion odd. Then fade. Dark whole again. Blest dark. No. No such thing as whole. Stands staring beyond half hearing what he's saying. He? The words falling from his mouth. Making do with his mouth. Lights lamp as described. Backs away to edge of light and and turns to face wall. Stares beyond into dark. Waits for first word always the same. It gathers in his mouth. Parts lips and thrusts tongue forward. Birth. Parts the dark. Slowly the window. That first night. The room. The spill. The hands. The lamp. The gleam of brass. Fade. Gone. Again and again. Again and again gone. Mouth agape. A cry. Stifled by nasal. Dark parts. Grey light. Rain pelting. Streaming umbrellas. Ditch. Bubbling black mud. Coffin out of frame. Whose? Fade. Gone. Move on to other matters. Try to move on. To other matters. How far from wall? Head almost touching. As at window. Eyes glued to pane staring out. Nothing stirring. Black vast. Stands there stock still staring out as if unable to move again. Or gone the will to move again. Gone. Faint cry in his ear. Mouth agape. Closed with hiss of breath. Lips joined. Feel soft touch of lip on lip. Lip lipping lip. Then parted by cry as before. Where is he now? Back at window staring out. Eyes glued to pane. As if looking his last. Turns away at last and gropes through faint unaccountable light to unseen lamp. White gown moving through that gloom. Once white. Lights and moves to face wall as described. Head almost touching. Stands there staring beyond waiting for first word. It gathers in his mouth. Birth. Parts lips and thrusts tongue between them. Tip of tongue. Feel soft touch of tongue on lips. Of lips on tongue. Fade up in outer dark of window. Stare beyond through rift in dark to other dark. Further dark. Sun long sunk behind the larches. Nothing stirring. Nothing faintly stirring. Stock still eyes glued to pane. As if looking his last. At that first night. Of thirty thousand odd. Turn away in the end to darkened room.

Where soon to be. This night to be. Spill. Hands. Lamp. Gleam of brass. Pale globe alone in gloom. Brass bedrail catching light. Thirty seconds. To swell the two and a half billion odd. Fade. Gone. Cry. Snuffed with breath of nostrils. Again and again. Again and again gone. Till whose grave? Which . . . he all but said which loved one's? He? Black ditch in pelting rain. Way out through the grey rift in dark. Seen from on high. Streaming canopies. Bubbling black mud. Coffin on its way. Loved one . . . he all but said loved one on his way. Her way. Thirty seconds. Fade. Gone. Stands there staring beyond. Into dark whole again. No. No such thing as whole. Head almost touching wall. White hair catching light. White gown. White socks. White foot of pallet edge of frame stage left. Once white. Least . . . give and head rests on wall. But no. Stock still head haught staring beyond. Nothing stirring. Faintly stirring. Thirty thousand nights of ghosts beyond. Beyond that black beyond. Ghost light. Ghost nights. Ghost rooms. Ghost graves. Ghost . . . he all but said ghost loved ones. Waiting on the rip word. Stands there staring beyond at that black veil lips quivering to half-heard words. Treating of other matters. Trying to treat of other matters. Till half hears there are no other matters. Never were other matters. Never two matters. Never but the one matter. The dead and gone. The dying and the going. From the word go. The word begone. Such as the light going now. Beginning to go. In the room. Where else? Unnoticed by him staring beyond. The globe alone. Not the other. The unaccountable. From nowhere. On all sides nowhere. Unutterably faint. The globe alone. Alone gone.

Rockaby

Written in English in 1980. First performed in Buffalo, NY, in 1981. First published by Faber and Faber, London, in 1982.

Light:

Subdued on chair. Rest of stage dark.

Subdued spot on face constant throughout, unaffected by successive fades. Either wide enough to include narrow limits of rock or concentrated on face when still or at mid-rock. Then throughout speech face slightly swaying in and out of light.

Opening fade-up: first spot on face alone, long pause, then light on chair.

Final fade-out: first chair, long pause with spot on face alone, head slowly sinks, come to rest, fade out spot.

W:

Prematurely old. Unkempt grey hair. Huge eyes in white expressionless face. White hands holding ends of armrests.

Eyes:

Now closed, now open in unblinking gaze. About equal proportions section 1, increasingly closed 2 and 3, closed for good halfway through 4.

Costume:

Black lacy high-necked evening gown. Long sleeves. Jet sequins to glitter when rocking. Incongruous flimsy head-dress set askew with extravagant trimming to catch light when rocking.

Attitude:

Completely still till fade-out of chair. Then in light of spot head slowly inclined.

Chair:

Pale wood highly polished to gleam when rocking. Footrest. Vertical back. Rounded inward curving arms to suggest embrace.

Rock:
Slight. Slow. Controlled mechanically without assistance from w.

Voice:
Towards end of 4, say from 'saying to herself' on, gradually softer. Lines in italics spoken by w with v. A little softer each time. w's 'more' a little softer each time.

w : *Woman in chair.*
v : *Her recorded voice.*
Fade up on w *in rocking-chair facing front downstage slightly*
off centre audience left.
Long pause.

w : More.
    [*Pause. Rock and voice together.*]
v : till in the end
    the day came
    in the end came
    close of a long day
    when she said
    to herself
    whom else
    time she stopped
    time she stopped
    going to and fro
    all eyes
    all sides
    high and low
    for another
    another like herself
    another creature like herself
    a little like
    going to and fro
    all eyes
    all sides
    high and low
    for another
    till in the end
    close of a long day

to herself
whom else
time she stopped
time she stopped
going to and fro
all eyes
all sides
high and low
for another
another living soul
going to and fro
all eyes like herself
all sides
high and low
for another
another like herself
a little like
going to and fro
till in the end
close of a long day
to herself
whom else
time she stopped
going to and fro
time she stopped
time she stopped
  [*Together: echo of 'time she stopped', coming to rest of
  rock, faint fade of light.
  Long pause.*]
w: More.
  [*Pause. Rock and voice together.*]
v: so in the end
close of a long day
went back in
in the end went back in
saying to herself
whom else

time she stopped
time she stopped
going to and fro
time she went and sat
at her window
quiet at her window
facing other windows
so in the end
close of a long day
in the end went and sat
went back in and sat
at her window
let up the blind and sat
quiet at her window
only window
facing other windows
other only windows
all eyes
all sides
high and low
for another
at her window
another like herself
a little like
another living soul
one other living soul
at her window
gone in like herself
gone back in
in the end
close of a long day
saying to herself
whom else
time she stopped
time she stopped
going to and fro
time she went and sat

at her window
quiet at her window
only window
facing other windows
other only windows
all eyes
all sides
high and low
for another
another like herself
a little like
another living soul
one other living soul
   [*Together: echo of 'living soul', coming to rest of rock,*
   faint fade of light.
   Long pause.]
w: More.
   [*Pause. Rock and voice together.*]
v: till in the end
the day came
in the end came
close of a long day
sitting at her window
quiet at her window
only window
facing other windows
other only windows
all blinds down
never one up
hers alone up
till the day came
in the end came
close of a long day
sitting at her window
quiet at her window
all eyes
all sides

high and low
for a blind up
one blind up
no more
never mind a face
behind the pane
famished eyes
like hers
to see
be seen
no
a blind up
like hers
a little like
one blind up no more
another creature there
somewhere there
behind the pane
another living soul
one other living soul
till the day came
in the end came
close of a long day
when she said
to herself
whom else
time she stopped
time she stopped
sitting at her window
quiet at her window
only window
facing other windows
other only windows
all eyes
all sides
high and low
time she stopped

time she stopped
> [*Together: echo of 'time she stopped', coming to rest of rock, faint fade of light.*
> *Long pause.*]

w: More.
> [*Pause. Rock and voice together.*]

v: so in the end
close of a long day
went down
in the end went down

down the steep stair
let down the blind and down
right down
into the old rocker
mother rocker
where mother rocked
all the years
all in black
best black
sat and rocked
rocked
till her end came
in the end came
off her head they said
gone off her head
but harmless
no harm in her
dead one day
no
night
dead one night
in the rocker
in her best black
head fallen
and the rocker rocking
rocking away
so in the end

close of a long day
went down
in the end went down
down the steep stair
let down the blind and down
right down
into the old rocker
those arms at last
and rocked
rocked
with closed eyes
closing eyes
she so long all eyes
famished eyes
all sides
high and low
to and fro
at her window
to see
be seen
till in the end
close of a long day
to herself
whom else
time she stopped
let down the blind and stopped
time she went down
down the steep stair
time she went right down
was her own other
own other living soul
so in the end
close of a long day
went down
let down the blind and down
right down
into the old rocker

and rocked
rocked
saying to herself
no
done with that
the rocker
those arms at last
saying to the rocker
rock her off
stop her eyes
fuck life
stop her eyes
rock her off
rock her off

[*Together: echo of 'rock her off', coming to rest of rock, slow fade out.*]

Ohio Impromptu

Written in 1981. First performed at Ohio State University in 1981. First published by Faber and Faber, London, in 1982.

L = *Listener.*
R = *Reader.*
As alike in appearance as possible.
Light on table midstage. Rest of stage in darkness.
Plain white deal table say 8' x 4'.
Two plain armless white deal chairs.
L seated at table facing front towards end of long side audience right. Bowed head propped on right hand. Face hidden. Left hand on table. Long black coat. Long white hair.
R seated at table in profile centre of short side audience right. Bowed head propped on right hand. Left hand on table. Book on table before him open at last pages. Long black coat. Long white hair.
Black wide-brimmed hat at centre of table.
Fade up.
Ten seconds.
R turns page.
Pause.

R : [*Reading.*] Little is left to tell. In a last—
    [L *knocks with left hand on table.*]
    Little is left to tell.
    [*Pause. Knock.*]
    In a last attempt to obtain relief he moved from where they had been so long together to a single room on the far bank. From its single window he could see the downstream extremity of the Isle of Swans.
    [*Pause.*]
    Relief he had hoped would flow from unfamiliarity. Unfamiliar room. Unfamiliar scene. Out to where nothing ever shared. Back to where nothing ever shared. From this he had once half hoped some measure of relief might flow.
    [*Pause.*]

Day after day he could be seen slowly pacing the islet.
Hour after hour. In his long black coat no matter what the
weather and old world Latin Quarter hat. At the tip he
would always pause to dwell on the receding stream. How
in joyous eddies its two arms conflowed and flowed united
on. Then turn and his slow steps retrace.
[*Pause.*]
In his dreams—
[*Knock.*]
Then turn and his slow steps retrace.
[*Pause. Knock.*]
In his dreams he had been warned against this change. Seen
the dear face and heard the unspoken words, Stay where
we were so long alone together, my shade will comfort
you.
[*Pause.*]
Could he not—
[*Knock.*]
Seen the dear face and heard the unspoken words, Stay
where we were so long alone together, my shade will
comfort you.
[*Pause. Knock.*]
Could he not now turn back? Acknowledge his error and
return to where they were once so long alone together.
Alone together so much shared. No. What he had done
alone could not be undone. Nothing he had ever done
alone could ever be undone. By him alone.
[*Pause.*]
In this extremity his old terror of night laid hold on him
again. After so long a lapse that as if never been. [*Pause.
Looks closer.*] Yes, after so long a lapse that as if never
been. Now with redoubled force the fearful symptoms
described at length page forty paragraph four. [*Starts to
turn back the pages. Checked by L's left hand. Resumes
relinquished page.*] White nights now again his portion. As
when his heart was young. No sleep no braving sleep till—
[*Turns page.*]—dawn of day.
[*Pause.*]
Little is left to tell. One night—

[*Knock.*]

Little is left to tell.

[*Pause. Knock.*]

One night as he sat trembling head in hands from head to
foot a man appeared to him and said, I have been sent by—
and here he named the dear name—to comfort you. Then
drawing a worn volume from the pocket of his long black
coat he sat and read till dawn. Then disappeared without a
word.

[*Pause.*]

Some time later he appeared again at the same hour with
the same volume and this time without preamble sat and
read it through again the long night through. Then disappeared without a word.

[*Pause.*]

So from time to time unheralded he would appear to read
the sad tale through again and the long night away. Then
disappear without a word.

[*Pause.*]

With never a word exchanged they grew to be as one.

[*Pause.*]

Till the night came at last when having closed the book
and dawn at hand he did not disappear but sat on without
a word.

[*Pause.*]

Finally he said, I have had word from—and here he named
the dear name—that I shall not come again. I saw the dear
face and heard the unspoken words, No need to go to him
again, even were it in your power.

[*Pause.*]

So the sad—

[*Knock.*]

Saw the dear face and heard the unspoken words, No need
to go to him again, even were it in your power.

[*Pause. Knock.*]

So the sad tale a last time told they sat on as though
turned to stone. Through the single window dawn shed no
light. From the street no sound of reawakening. Or was it
that buried in who knows what thoughts they paid no

heed? To light of day. To sound of reawakening. What thoughts who knows. Thoughts, no, not thoughts. Profounds of mind. Buried in who knows what profounds of mind. Of mindlessness. Whither no light can reach. No sound. So sat on as though turned to stone. The sad tale a last time told.

[*Pause.*]

Nothing is left to tell.

[*Pause.* R *makes to close book.*

Knock. Book half closed.]

Nothing is left to tell.

[*Pause.* R *closes book.*

Knock.

Silence. Five seconds.

Simultaneously they lower their right hands to table, raise their heads and look at each other. Unblinking. Expressionless.

Ten seconds.

Fade out.]

Quad

Quad was first transmitted in Germany by Süddeutscher Rund-funk in 1982 under the title *Quadrat 1+2*. It was first trans-mitted by BBC2 on 16 December 1982. First published by Faber and Faber, London, in 1984.

A piece for four players, light and percussion.

The players (1, 2, 3, 4) pace the given area, each following his particular course.

Area: square. Length of side: 6 paces.

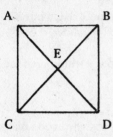

Course 1: AC, CB, BA, AD, DB, BC, CD, DA
Course 2: BA, AD, DB, BC, CD, DA, AC, CB
Course 3: CD, DA, AC, CB, BA, AD, DB, BC
Course 4: DB, BC, CD, DA, AC, CB, BA, AD

1 enters at A, completes his course and is joined by 3. Together they complete their courses and are joined by 4. Together all three complete their courses and are joined by 2. Together all four complete their courses. Exit 1. 2, 3 and 4 continue and complete their courses. Exit 3. 2 and 4 continue and complete their courses. Exit 4. End of 1st series. 2 continues, opening 2nd series, completes his course and is joined by 1. Etc. Unbroken movement.

1st series (as above):   1, 13, 134, 1342, 342, 42
2nd series: 2, 21, 214, 2143, 143, 43
3rd series: 3, 32, 321, 3214, 214, 14
4th series: 4, 43, 432, 4321, 321, 21

Four possible solos all given.
Six possible duos all given (two twice).

Four possible trios all given twice.

Without interruption begin repeat and fade out on 1 pacing alone.

Light (2)
Dim on area from above fading out into dark.
Four sources of differently coloured light clustered together.
Each player has his particular light, to be turned on when he enters, kept on while he paces, turned off when he exits.
Say 1 white, 2 yellow, 3 blue, 4 red. Then
1st series: white, white + blue, white + blue + red, white + blue + red + yellow, blue + red + yellow, red + yellow.
2nd series: yellow, yellow + white, yellow + white + red etc.
All possible light combinations given.

Percussion
Four types of percussion, say drum, gong, triangle, wood block.
Each player has his particular percussion, to sound when he enters, continue while he paces, cease when he exits.
Say 1 drum, 2 gong, 3 triangle, 4 wood block. Then
1st series: drum, drum + triangle, drum + triangle + wood block etc. Same system as for light.
All possible percussion combinations given.
Percussion intermittent in all combinations to allow footsteps alone to be heard at intervals.
Pianissimo throughout.
Percussionists barely visible in shadow on raised podium at back of set.

Footsteps
Each player has his particular sound.

Costumes
Gowns reaching to ground, cowls hiding faces.
Each player has his particular colour corresponding to his light. 1 white, 2 yellow, 3 blue, 4 red.
All possible costume combinations given.

Players
As alike in build as possible. Short and slight for preference.
    Some ballet training desirable. Adolescents a possibility. Sex
indifferent.

Camera
Raised frontal. Fixed. Both players and percussionists in
frame.

Time (3)
On basis of one pace per second and allowing for time lost at
angles and centre approximately 25 minutes.

Problem (4)
Negotiation of E without rupture of rhythm when three or four
players cross paths at this point. Or, if ruptures accepted, how
best exploit?

1. This original scenario (*Quad I*) was followed in the Stuttgart
production by a variation (*Quad II*). (5)
2. Abandoned as impracticable. Constant neutral light throughout.
3. Overestimated. *Quad I*, fast tempo. 15' approx. *Quad II*, slow
tempo, series 1 only, 5' approx.
4. E supposed a danger zone. Hence deviation. Manoeuvre established at outset by first solo at first diagonal (CB). E.g. series 1:

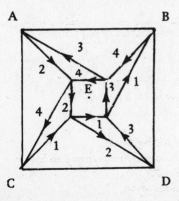

5. No colour, all four in identical white gowns, no percussion, footsteps only sound, slow tempo, series 1 only.

Catastrophe

For Vaclav Havel

Written in French in 1982. First performed at the Avignon
Festival in 1982. First published in English by Faber and Faber,
London, in 1984.

Director (D).
His female assistant (A).
Protagonist (P).
Luke, in charge of the lighting, offstage (L).

Rehearsal. Final touches to the last scene. Bare stage. A and L have just set the lighting. D has just arrived.

D in an armchair downstairs audience left. Fur coat. Fur toque to match. Age and physique unimportant.
A standing beside him. White overall. Bare head. Pencil on ear. Age and physique unimportant.
P midstage standing on a black block 18 inches high. Black wide-brimmed hat. Black dressing-gown to ankles. Barefoot. Head bowed. Hands in pockets. Age and physique unimportant.

D and A contemplate P. Long pause.

A: [*Finally.*] Like the look of him?
D: So so. [*Pause.*] Why the plinth?
A: To let the stalls see the feet.
      [*Pause.*]
D: Why the hat?
A: To help hide the face.
      [*Pause.*]
D: Why the gown?
A: To have him all black.
      [*Pause.*]
D: What has he on underneath? [A *moves towards* P.] Say it.
      [A *halts.*]
A: His night attire.
D: Colour?
A: Ash.

[D *takes out a cigar.*]

D: Light. [A *returns, lights the cigar, stands still.* D *smokes.*]
How's the skull?

A: You've seen it.

D: I forget. [A *moves towards* P.] Say it.
[A *halts.*]

A: Moulting. A few tufts.

D: Colour?

A: Ash.
[*Pause.*]

D: Why hands in pockets?

A: To help have him all black.

D: They mustn't.

A: I make a note. [*She takes out a pad, takes pencil, notes.*]
Hands exposed.
[*She puts back pad and pencil.*]

D: How are they? [A *at a loss. Irritably.*] The hands, how are
the hands?

A: You've seen them.

D: I forget.

A: Crippled. Fibrous degeneration.

D: Clawlike?

A: If you like.

D: Two claws?

A: Unless he clench his fists.

D: He mustn't.

A: I make a note. [*She takes out pad, takes pencil, notes.*]
Hands limp.
[*She puts back pad and pencil.*]

D: Light. [A *returns, relights the cigar, stands still.* D *smokes.*]
Good. Now let's have a look. [A *at a loss. Irritably.*] Get
going. Lose that gown. [*He consults his chronometer.*]
Step on it, I have a caucus.
[A *goes to* P, *takes off the gown.* P *submits, inert.* A *steps
back, the gown over her arm.* P *in old grey pyjamas, head
bowed, fists clenched. Pause.*]

A: Like him better without? [*Pause.*] He's shivering.

D: Not all that. Hat.
[A *advances, takes off hat, steps back, hat in hand. Pause.*]

A: Like that cranium?

D: Needs whitening.

A: I make a note. [*She takes out pad, takes pencil, notes.*]
Whiten cranium.
[*She puts back pad and pencil.*]

D: The hands. [A *at a loss. Irritably.*] The fists. Get going. [A
advances, unclenches fists, steps back.] And whiten.

A: I make a note. [*She takes out pad, takes pencil, notes.*]
Whiten hands.
[*She puts back pad and pencil. They contemplate* P.]

D: [*Finally.*] Something wrong. [*Distraught.*] What is it?

A: [*Timidly.*] What if we were ... were to ... join them?

D: No harm trying. [A *advances, joins the hands, steps back.*]
Higher. [A *advances, raises waist high the joined hands,
steps back.*] A touch more. [A *advances, raises breast-
high the joined hands.*] Stop! [A *steps back.*] Better. It's
coming. Light.
[A *returns, relights cigar, stands still.* D *smokes.*]

A: He's shivering.

D: Bless his heart.
[*Pause.*]

A: [*Timidly.*] What about a little ... a little ... gag?

D: For God's sake! This craze for explicitation! Every i dotted
to death! Little gag! For God's sake!

A: Sure he won't utter?

D: Not a squeak. [*He consults his chronometer.*] Just time. I'll
go and see how it looks from the house.
[*Exit* D, *not to appear again.* A *subsides in the armchair,
springs to her feet no sooner seated, takes out a rag, wipes
vigorously back and seat of chair, discards rag, sits again.
Pause.*]

D: [*Off, plaintive.*] I can't see the toes. [*Irritably.*] I'm sitting
in the front row of the stalls and can't see the toes.

A: [*Rising.*] I make a note. [*She takes out a pad, takes pencil,
notes.*] Raise pedestal.

D: There's a trace of face.

A: I make a note.
[*She takes out pad, takes pencil, makes to note.*]

D: Down the head. [A *at a loss. Irritably.*] Get going. Down his

head. [A *puts back pad and pencil, goes to* P, *bows his
head further, steps back.*] A shade more. [A *advances,
bows the head further.*] Stop! [A *steps back.*] Fine. It's
coming. [*Pause.*] Could do with more nudity.

A: I make a note.

[*She takes out pad, makes to take her pencil.*]

D: Get going! Get going! [A *puts back the pad, goes to* P,
stands irresolute.] Bare the neck. [A *undoes top buttons,
parts the flaps, steps back.*] The legs. The shins. [A *advances, rolls up to below knee one trouser-leg, steps back.*]
The other. [*Same for other leg, steps back.*] Higher. The
knees. [A *advances, rolls up to above knees both trouser-
legs, steps back.*] And whiten.

A: I make a note. [*She takes out pad, takes pencil, notes.*]
Whiten all flesh.

D: It's coming. Is Luke around?

A: [*Calling.*] Luke! [*Pause. Louder.*] Luke!

L: [*Off, distant.*] I hear you. [*Pause. Nearer.*] What's the
trouble now?

A: Luke's around.

D: Blackout stage.

L: What?

[A *transmits in technical terms. Fade-out of general light.
Light on* P *alone.* A *in shadow.*]

D: Just the head.

L: What?

[A *transmits in technical terms. Fade-out of light on* P's
body. Light on head alone. Long pause.]

D: Lovely.

[*Pause.*]

A: [*Timidly.*] What if he were to . . . were to . . . raise his head . . .
an instant . . . show his face . . . just an instant.

D: For God's sake! What next? Raise his head? Where do you
think we are? In Patagonia? Raise his head? For God's
sake! [*Pause.*] Good. There's our catastrophe. In the bag.
Once more and I'm off.

A: [*To* L.] Once more and he's off.

[*Fade-up of light on* P's *body. Pause. Fade-up of general
light.*]

D: Stop! [*Pause.*] Now . . . let 'em have it. [*Fade-out of general light. Pause. Fade-out of light on body. Light on head alone. Long pause.*] Terrific! He'll have them on their feet. I can hear it from here.

[*Pause. Distant storm of applause.* P *raises his head, fixes the audience. The applause falters, dies.*

Long pause.

Fade-out of light on face.]

Nacht und Träume

Nacht und Träume was written for, and produced by, Süddeutscher Rundfunk in 1982. It was first transmitted on 19 May 1983. First published in English by Faber and Faber, London, in 1984.

Elements.
Evening light.
Dreamer (A).
His dreamt self (B).
Dreamt hands R (right) and L (left).
Last 7 bars of Schubert's *Lied*, *Nacht und Träume*.

1. Fade up on a dark empty room lit only by evening light
   from a window set high in back wall.
   Left foreground, faintly lit, a man seated at a table. Right
   profile, head bowed, grey hair, hands resting on table.
   Clearly visible only head and hands and section of table on
   which they rest.
2. Softly hummed, male voice, last 7 bars of Schubert's *Lied*,
   Nacht und Träume.
3. Fade out evening light.
4. Softly sung, with words, last 3 bars of *Lied* beginning
   'Holde Träume . . .'
5. Fade down A as he bows his head further to rest on hands.
   Thus minimally lit he remains just visible throughout
   dream as first viewed.
6. A dreams. Fade up on B on an invisible podium about 4 feet
   above floor level, middle ground, well right of centre. He is
   seated at a table in the same posture as A dreaming, bowed
   head resting on hands, but left profile, faintly lit by kinder
   light than A's.
7. From dark beyond and above B's head L appears and rests
   gently on it.
8. B raises his head, L withdraws and disappears.
9. From same dark R appears with a cup, conveys it gently to
   B's lips. B drinks, R disappears.
10. R reappears with a cloth, wipes gently B's brow, disappears
    with cloth.

11. B raises his head further to gaze up at invisible face.
12. B raises his right hand, still gazing up, and holds it raised palm upward.
13. R reappears and rests gently on B's right hand, B still gazing up.
14. B transfers gaze to joined hands.
15. B raises his left hand and rests it on joined hands.
16. Together hands sink to table and on them B's head.
17. L reappears and rests gently on B's head.
18. Fade out dream.
19. Fade up A and evening light.
20. A raises head to its opening position.
21. *Lied* as before (2).
22. Fade out evening light.
23. Close of *Lied* as before (4).
24. Fade down A as before (5).
25. A dreams. Fade up on B as before (6).
26. Move in slowly to close-up of B, losing A.
27. Dream as before (7–16) in close-up and slower motion.
28. Withdraw slowly to opening viewpoint, recovering A.
29. Fade out dream.
30. Fade out A.

What Where

The première of this play took place at the Harold Clurman
Theatre, New York, on 15 June 1983. First published
by Faber and Faber, London, in 1984.

BAM
BEM
BIM
BOM
VOICE OF BAM (V)

Note

Players as alike as possible.
Same long grey gown.
Same long grey hair.
V in the shape of a small megaphone at head level.

*Playing area (P) rectangle 3m × 2m, dimly lit, surrounded by
shadow, stage right as seen from house. Downstage left, dimly
lit, surrounded by shadow, V.*

General dark.
Light on V.
Pause.

V: We are the last five.
   In the present as were we still.
   It is spring.
   Time passes.
   First without words.
   I switch on.
   [*Light on P.*
   BAM *at 3 head haught,* BOM *at 1 head bowed.*
   Pause.]
   Not good.
   I switch off.
   [*Light off P.*]
   I start again.
   We are the last five.

It is spring.
Time passes.
First without words.
I switch on.
[*Light on* P.
BAM *alone at 3 head haught.*
Pause.]
Good.
I am alone.
It is spring.
Time passes.
First without words.
In the end Bom appears.
Reappears.
[BOM *enters at* N, *halts at 1 head bowed.*
Pause.
BIM *enters at* E, *halts at 2 head haught.*
Pause.
BIM *exits at* E *followed by* BOM.
Pause.
BIM *enters at* E, *halts at 2 head bowed.*
Pause.
BEM *enters at* N, *halts at 1 head haught.*
Pause.
BEM *exits at* N *followed by* BIM.
Pause.
BEM *enters at* N, *halts at 1 head bowed.*
Pause.
BAM *exits at* W *followed by* BEM.
Pause.
BAM *enters at* W, *halts at 3 head bowed.*
Pause.]
Good.
I switch off.
[*Light off* P.]
I start again.
We are the last five.
It is spring.
Time passes.

I switch on.
[*Light on* P.
BAM *alone at 3 head haught.*
Pause.]
Good.
I am alone.
It is spring.
Time passes.
Now with words.
In the end Bom appears.
Reappears.
[BOM *enters at* N, *halts at 1 head bowed.*]

BAM: Well?
BOM: [*Head bowed throughout.*] Nothing.
BAM: He didn't say anything?
BOM: No.
BAM: You gave him the works?
BOM: Yes.
BAM: And he didn't say anything?
BOM: No.
BAM: He wept?
BOM: Yes.
BAM: Screamed?
BOM: Yes.
BAM: Begged for mercy?
BOM: Yes.
BAM: But didn't say anything?
BOM: No.
V: Not good.
    I start again.
BAM: Well?
BOM: Nothing.
BAM: He didn't say it?
V: Good.
BOM: No.
BAM: You gave him the works?
BOM: Yes.
BAM: And he didn't say it?
BOM: No.

BAM: He wept?

BOM: Yes.

BAM: Screamed?

BOM: Yes.

BAM: Begged for mercy?

BOM: Yes.

BAM: But didn't say it?

BOM: No.

BAM: Then why stop?

BOM: He passed out.

BAM: And you didn't revive him?

BOM: I tried.

BAM: Well?

BOM: I couldn't.
      [*Pause.*]

BAM: It's a lie. [*Pause.*] He said it to you. [*Pause.*] Confess he
     said it to you. [*Pause.*] You'll be given the works until
     you confess.

V: Good.
      In the end Bim appears.
      [BIM *enters at* E, *halts at 2 head haught.*]

BAM: [*To* BIM.] Are you free?

BIM: Yes.

BAM: Take him away and give him the works until he confesses.

BIM: What must he confess?

BAM: That he said it to him.

BIM: Is that all?

BAM: Yes.

V: Not good.
      I start again.

BAM: Take him away and give him the works until he confesses.

BIM: What must he confess?

BAM: That he said it to him.

BIM: Is that all?

BAM: And what.

V: Good.

BIM: Is that all?

BAM: Yes.

BIM: Then stop?

BAM: Yes.

BIM: Good. [*To* BOM.] Come.

[BIM *exits at* E *followed by* BOM.]

V: Good.

    I am alone.

    It is summer.

    Time passes.

    In the end Bim appears.

    Reappears.

    [BIM *enters at* E, *halts at 2 head bowed.*]

BAM: Well?

BIM: [*Head bowed throughout.*] Nothing.

BAM: He didn't say it?

BIM: No.

BAM: You gave him the works?

BIM: Yes.

BAM: And he didn't say it?

BIM: No.

V: Not good.

    I start again.

BAM: Well?

BIM: Nothing.

BAM: He didn't say where?

V: Good.

FIM: Where?

V: Ah!

BAM: Where.

BIM: No.

BAM: You gave him the works?

BIM: Yes.

BAM: And he didn't say where?

BIM: No.

BAM: He wept?

BIM: Yes.

BAM: Screamed?

BIM: Yes.

BAM: Begged for mercy?

BIM: Yes.

BAM: But didn't say where?

BIM: No.

BAM: Then why stop?

BIM: He passed out.

BAM: And you didn't revive him?

BIM: I tried.

BAM: Well?

BIM: I couldn't.
[*Pause.*]

BAM: It's a lie. [*Pause.*] He said where to you. [*Pause.*] Confess he said where to you. [*Pause.*] You'll be given the works until you confess.

V: Good.
In the end Bem appears.
[BEM *enters at* N, *halts at 1 head haught.*]

BAM: [*To* BEM.] Are you free?

BEM: Yes.

BAM: Take him away and give him the works until he confesses.

BEM: What must he confess?

BAM: That he said where to him.

BEM: Is that all?

BAM: Yes.

V: Not good.
I start again.

BAM: Take him away and give him the works until he confesses.

BEM: What must he confess?

BAM: That he said where to him.

BEM: Is that all?

BAM: And where.

V: Good.

BEM: Is that all?

BAM: Yes.

BEM: Then stop?

BAM: Yes.

BEM: Good. [*To* BIM.] Come.
[BEM *exits at* N *followed by* BIM.]

V: Good.
I am alone.
It is autumn.
Time passes.

In the end Bem appears.
Reappears.
[BEM *enters at* N, *halts at 1 head bowed.*]

BAM: Well?

BEM: [*Head bowed throughout.*] Nothing.

BAM: He didn't say where?

BEM: No.

V: So on.

BAM: It's a lie. [*Pause.*] He said where to you. [*Pause.*] Confess he said where to you. [*Pause.*] You'll be given the works until you confess.

BEM: What must I confess?

BAM: That he said where to you.

BEM: Is that all?

BAM: And where.

BEM: Is that all?

BAM: Yes.

BEM: Then stop?

BAM: Yes. Come.
[BAM *exits at* W *followed by* BEM.]

V: Good.
It is winter.
Time passes.
In the end I appear.
Reappear.
[BAM *enters at* W, *halts at 3 head bowed.*]

V: Good.
I am alone.
In the present as were I still.
It is winter.
Without journey.
Time passes.
That is all.
Make sense who may.
I switch off.
[*Light off* P.
Pause.
Light off V.]